Adobe

PAGEMAKER 7.0 BASICS, COMPREHENSIVE

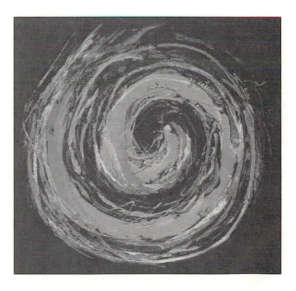

Rick Braveheart

THOMSON

COURSE TECHNOLOGY™

Australia • Canada • Mexico • Singapore • Spain • United Kingdom • United States

THOMSON

™

COURSE TECHNOLOGY

Adobe PageMaker 7.0 BASICS, Comprehensive
by Rick Braveheart

Senior Vice President
Chris Elkhill

Managing Editor
Chris Katsaropoulos

Senior Product Manager
Dave Lafferty

Product Manager
Robert Gaggin

Product Marketing Manager
Kim Ryttel

Associate Product Manager
Jodi Dreissig

Development Editor
Anne Chimenti
Custom Editorial Productions, Inc.

Production Editor
Anne Chimenti
Custom Editorial Productions, Inc.

Compositor
GEX Publishing Services

Get Back to the Basics...
With these *exciting new products*
from South-Western Computer Education!

This new edition from our *BASICS* series provides a step-by-step introduction to the latest version of Adobe's popular desktop publishing software, PageMaker 7.0.

Other books include:

NEW! Internet BASICS by Barksdale, Rutter, & Teeter
35+ hours of instruction for beginning through intermediate features

0-619-05905-2	Textbook, Soft Spiral Bound Cover
0-619-05906-0	Instructor Resource Kit
0-619-05907-9	Review Pack (Data CD)

NEW! Microsoft OfficeXP BASICS by Morrison
35+ hours of instruction for beginning through intermediate features

0-619-05908-7	Textbook, Hard Spiral Bound Cover
0-619-05906-0	Instructor Resource Kit
0-619-05909-5	Activities Workbook
0-619-05907-9	Review Pack (Data CD)

NEW! Microsoft Office 2001Macintosh BASICS by Melton & Walls
35+ hours of instruction for beginning through intermediate features

0-619-05912-5	Textbook, Hard Spiral Bound Cover
0-619-05914-1	Instructor Resource Kit
0-619-05913-3	Workbook
0-619-05915-X	Review Pack (Data CD)

Microsoft Works 2000 BASICS by Pasewark & Pasewark
35+ hours of instruction for beginning through intermediate features

0-538-72340-8	Text, Hard Spiral Bound Cover
0-538-72411-0	Text, Perfect Bound, packaged with Data CD-ROM
0-538-72342-4	Activities Workbook
0-538-72341-6	Electronic Instructor's Manual Package
0-538-72343-2	Testing CD Package

Computer Concepts BASICS by Pusins and Ambrose
35+ hours of instruction for beginning through intermediate features

0-538-69501-3	Text, Hard Spiral Bound
0-538-69502-1	Activities Workbook
0-538-69503-X	Electronic Instructor's Manual Package
0-538-69504-8	Testing CD Package

Join Us On the Internet **http://www.course.com**

How to Use This Book

What makes a good computer instructional text? Sound pedagogy and the most current, complete materials. Not only will you find an inviting layout, but also many features to enhance learning.

Objectives— Objectives are listed at the beginning of each lesson, along with a suggested time for completion of the lesson. This allows you to look ahead to what you will be learning and to pace your work.

Step-by-Step Exercises—Preceded by a short topic discussion, these exercises are the "hands-on practice" part of the lesson. Simply follow the steps, either using a data file or creating a file from scratch. Each lesson is a series of these step-by-step exercises.

Vocabulary—Terms identified in boldface and italic throughout the lesson and summarized at the end.

Enhanced Screen Shots—Screen shots now come to life on the pages with color and depth.

Marginal Boxes— These boxes provide additional information about the topic of the lesson.

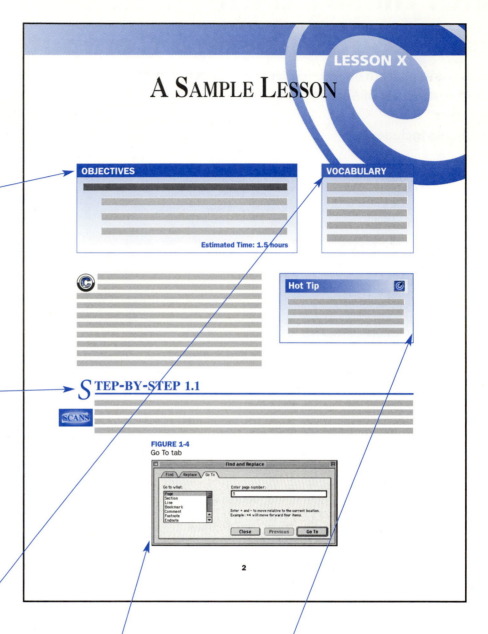

How to Use This Book

Summary—At the end of each lesson, you will find a summary to prepare you to complete the end-of-lesson activities.

Vocabulary Review—Review vocabulary terms presented in the lesson.

Review Questions—Review material at the end of each lesson enables you to prepare for assessment of the content presented.

Lesson Projects—End-of-lesson hands-on application of what has been learned in the lesson allows you to actually apply the techniques covered.

SCANS (Secretary's Commission on Achieving Necessary Skills)—The U.S. Department of Labor has identified the school-to-careers competencies.

Critical Thinking Activities—Each lesson gives you an opportunity to apply creative analysis and use the Help system to solve problems.

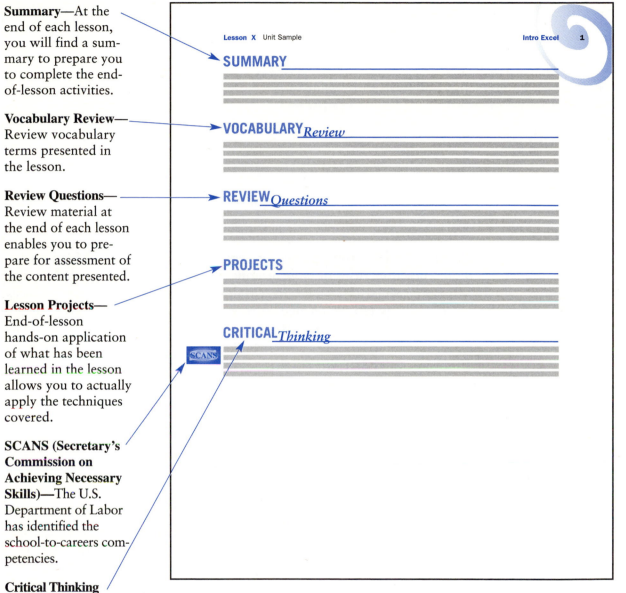

Lesson **X** Unit Sample   **Intro Excel** **1**

SUMMARY

VOCABULARY*Review*

REVIEW*Questions*

PROJECTS

CRITICAL*Thinking*

SCANS

PREFACE

For Tierney Bannon Coad and Barbara Braham

Kwe Kwe

A warm welcome to you, or in my Native American Iroquois language, Kwe Kwe. You are about to begin a journey of learning and discovery. With some study and effort on your part, it can become a journey filled with great satisfaction, creativity, and challenges that will provide you with new tools for presenting your ideas.

Today, desktop publishing is a fast-growing area for personal computer users. Many organizations that once relied on typesetting firms or large printing companies are now producing their own printed materials using regular PC's and PageMaker. Because of its many features, PageMaker can produce almost any type of printed work you can imagine, from books, newspapers, brochures and stationery, to business cards, flyers, catalogs, and magazines. And with the latest version of PageMaker that you are about to learn, you can even create Web pages for the Internet!

Learning desktop publishing now is also a great way to prepare for your future. As desktop publishing continues to grow, there will be an increased demand for people who are skilled with programs such as PageMaker. Taking this course will help to prepare you for this opportunity.

About This Book

This book is divided into 19 lessons, each covering a specific topic or group of related PageMaker commands. In each lesson you will find a list of objectives and new vocabulary terms, followed by a detailed description of specific topics and program commands. Three Unit Reviews are included where you will test your knowledge and practice what you have learned up to that point using real-world desktop-publishing projects.

This book also includes three ways to practice your newly learned skills: 1) Each lesson includes Step-by-Step exercises and Projects. The exercises are found within the lesson and provide a chance to practice a command or a technique that you have just read about; 2) Desktop-publishing projects are found at the end of each lesson and provide you with a hands-on method for practicing the commands and techniques you have learned up to that point: and 3) At the end of each lesson you will also find test questions to help you assess your learning.

To make your learning more realistic, this book uses a real-world case simulation throughout the lessons. You will become an employee of Caribbean Sun Travel Tours, a travel agency located in Key West, Florida. In your position as an employee for this company, you will use the ideas presented in this book to create published documents for this travel agency.

Here is one final suggestion. PageMaker is a great program that's fun to learn and use. But it also contains numerous commands and features. Keep a notebook for this course, or make notes in the margins of this book if it is your own copy. Your notes might include program shortcuts that you discover, summaries of the steps needed to perform certain complex activities, ways to correct mistakes you frequently make, or anything else that will help your learning go faster or reinforce your learning.

Working with the Material

Most lessons in this book cover one major topic, consisting of several related subjects. Although some lessons are completely self-contained, most build on ideas presented in earlier lessons. Therefore, it is recommended that you work with the material from beginning to end. This will prevent confusion whenever there is a reference to an idea discussed in an earlier lesson.

As you begin this course, you may already have some knowledge of PageMaker, or experience with programs having similar functions. As you work through this book and already know the topic covered in a lesson, don't just skip the material. Scan it for ideas that you might not know, or techniques that are unique to PageMaker. And make certain to read any entries titled Hot Tips or Notes. These entries highlight problems or difficulties that often arise, or explain unusual ways to use a command or a feature. Also, be certain to complete all Step-by-Step exercises found within each lesson. Doing so will help reinforce your learning and also help you avoid problems later on, since some Step-by-Step exercises use material created in earlier lessons.

As you continue in this course, take advantage of the index and glossary. The index of this book is designed to help you find a topic or command quickly. It is comprehensive and easy to use, since it often lists the same command or feature under several related topics. Likewise, the detailed glossary is a great reference source for terms or phrases that are presented in the lessons.

This book will help you understand desktop publishing and give you the basic skills needed to use PageMaker. However, mastering this material will also require additional work on your part. Reading the text and completing the exercises and projects will provide you with the basic skills needed to use the various commands and features. But that does not mean you should stop there. Hands-on practice is the best way to deepen your learning. After completing a lesson, work with the commands or features on your own using a project that you create.

Making a Difference

Each of us has the chance to make a difference in this world. Have you thought about how YOU will make a difference? Some people do it through their words, some through their ideas, and some by helping worthy causes. What ever method you choose, remember that PageMaker is an excellent tool for presenting words and ideas and for assisting organizations to help others.

During this course, think about ways you can use what you've learned to make a difference in your daily activities, and if possible, start now. Since hands-on experience is the best way to learn, look for opportunities to start applying your desktop-publishing skills and help others at the same time. One way to do this is to talk with community, school or non-profit groups about volunteering your time to help them design and/or create printed materials. Volunteering in this way gives you valuable experience and benefits others as well.

Acknowledgments

With the completion of this, my 55th and final textbook, there are several people I want to express my appreciation to for all they have done during my writing career. Most importantly, my deepest thanks to Barbara Braham for years of sincere encouragement, honest feedback, and frequent sacrifices. I am also very much indebted to Amy Davis and Ben Willard who introduced me to writing, and to Dave Lafferty who, over the years, has taken frequent risks and worked hard to bring so many of my book ideas to life. And, finally my deep thanks to Bill Adrion, a skillful guide and friend, for pointing out the path and helping me on the journey. Many thanks!

Also, I offer a very special thank you to Tierney Bannon Coad, a young and highly talented writer, for being patient and supportive month after month while I completed this manuscript, reawakening my imagination, bringing smiles to my heart, and reminding me always what true friendship is all about.

For her work on this book, my heartfelt thanks to Anne Chimenti, Development and Production Editor at Custom Editorial Productions, Inc. Her unique talent with words, gift for managing details, gentle art of suggestion-giving and sense of humor have added greatly to this book. Thanks too, Anne, for resolving many problems, rearranging the schedule, and steering me safely through numerous challenges along the way, all with great finesse. You are a treasure. Also, thanks to Tina Edmondson for excellent copyediting and many valuable suggestions, and to Robert Gaggin at Course Technology for overseeing this book and managing all of its details. All of you have added greatly to this book and any mistakes that remain in this book are entirely my own.

Challenge Yourself

Learning and using a new program such as PageMaker can be an exciting adventure. It can also provide you with many rewards in the future. Challenge and enjoy yourself as you work with the ideas presented in this book. Also, don't be afraid to experiment on your own, even if it means making an occasional mistake. Of course, you need to use care when working with a computer, but mistakes happen to everyone and are, in themselves, additional ways to learn. Have fun and enjoy this journey!

Rick Braveheart
Columbus, Ohio

START-UP CHECKLIST

WINDOWS HARDWARE REQUIREMENTS

✓ Any Intel® Pentium® processor
✓ Microsoft® Windows® 98,
  Windows NT® 4.0 with Service Pack 5 or 6,
  Windows 2000, Windows Millennium
  Edition, or Windows XP (recommended
  upgrade procedure)
✓ 32 MB of available RAM (48 MB or more
  recommended)
✓ 175 MB of available hard-disk space for
  installation (200 MB or more recommended)

✓ Video card with 800x600 resolution and
  8-bit/256 colors (24-bit, high-resolution
  display recommended)
✓ CD-ROM drive
✓ For Adobe® PostScript® printers: Adobe
  PostScript Level 2 or later

WINDOWS SOFTWARE REQUIREMENTS

✓ Adobe PageMaker 7.0

What's New

- Create Web pages (HTML files) from a publication
- Create Adobe Acrobat (PDF) files from a publication
- New Template palette containing hundreds of professionally designed publications
- New Picture palette containing hundreds of clip art and image graphics
- More extensive import filters

Before You Start

Instructor Resource Kit CD-ROM

The *Instructor Resource Kit* CD-ROM contains a wealth of instructional material you can use to prepare for teaching this course. The CD-ROM stores the following information:

- The solution files for this course.

- ExamView® tests for each lesson. ExamView is a powerful testing software package that enables instructors to create and administer printed, computer (LAN-based), and Internet exams. ExamView includes hundreds of questions that correspond to the topics covered in this text, enabling learners to generate detailed study guides that include page references for further review. The computer-based and Internet testing components enable learners to take exams at their computers and instructors to save time by automatically grading each exam.

- Electronic *Instructor's Manual* that includes instructor lesson plans, student study guides, SCANS correlation, scheduling suggestions, answers to the lesson and unit review questions, and references to the solutions for Step-by-Step exercises, end-of-lesson activities, and Unit Review projects.

- Copies of the figures that appear in the student text, which can be used to prepare transparencies.

- Additional instructional information about individual learning strategies, portfolios, and career planning, and a sample Internet contract.

- PowerPoint presentations showing PageMaker features for each lesson in the text.

SCANS

The Secretary's Commission on Achieving Necessary Skills (SCANS) from the U.S. Department of Labor was asked to examine the demands of the workplace and whether new learners are capable of meeting those demands. Specifically, the Commission was directed to advise the Secretary on the level of skills required to enter employment.

SCANS workplace competencies and foundation skills have been integrated into *Adobe PageMaker 7.0 BASICS, Comprehensive*. The workplace competencies are identified as 1) ability to use resources, 2) interpersonal skills, 3) ability to work with information, 4) understanding of systems, and 5) knowledge and understanding of technology. The foundation skills are identified as 1) basic communication skills, 2) thinking skills, and 3) personal qualities.

Exercises in which learners must use a number of these SCANS competencies and foundation skills are marked in the text with the SCANS icon.

TABLE OF CONTENTS

Unit 1 PageMaker BASICS

Unit 2 ENHANCING PAGEMAKER DOCUMENTS

Unit 3 ADVANCED FEATURES

PageMaker BASICS

Unit 1

Estimated Time for Unit: 24.5 hrs.

INTRODUCTION TO DESKTOP PUBLISHING

OBJECTIVES

Upon completion of this lesson, you should be able to:

- Define desktop publishing.
- Explain the difference between traditional publishing and desktop publishing.
- Identify the key people involved in producing traditionally typeset documents and describe their responsibilities.
- Compare desktop publishing to traditional publishing techniques.
- Identify some of PageMaker's key features.
- Identify some documents that are frequently desktop published.

Estimated Time: 2.5 hours

VOCABULARY

Boards

Clip art

Copywriter

Desktop publishing

Graphic artist

Graphic designer

Paste-up artist

Plates

Publication

Rules

Typeface

Typeset quality print

Typography

Introducing Desktop Publishing

What do Honda of America, Chevron Oil, West Virginia Telephone Company, Atlantic Monthly, The Ohio State University, and the Swiss Railroad system all have in common? They are only a few of an estimated six million organizations worldwide that use desktop publishing to produce many of their documents.

During the past decade, desktop publishing has become one of the fastest growing areas of personal computer use in businesses. The reason for this growth is due to the many benefits of desktop publishing. Organizations that use desktop publishing often find that they can produce documents faster, maintain greater control over those documents, and produce work at less cost than by using outside typesetting services.

So what is *desktop publishing*? It is using a personal computer and a software program to produce high-quality, printed documents that combine text and graphics. Today, organizations use desktop publishing to produce a wide range of publications such as forms, catalogs, brochures, newsletters, flyers, and much more.

Desktop publishing software, like PageMaker, includes features found in most word processing programs such as the ability to key, edit, save, print, and check the spelling of your work. This software also lets you vary the size and style of your text, position graphics (or electronic pictures)

3

anywhere on a page, and view an entire page of your document on-screen. When printed on a laser or ink jet printer, this software can also produce **typeset quality print** (or near typeset quality), which means the final printed product resembles the quality of output produced with a traditional typesetting machine.

If a company lacks desktop publishing, producing printed documents normally requires the outside services of a typesetting and/or commercial printing company. Although such companies can produce excellent work, certain problems can arise. For example, a company loses some control over the production of its work when it turns to outside sources. In addition, while typesetting or commercial printing companies understand **typography** (using type to produce printed documents) they may not understand a customer's industry or its business. As a result, they can miss an error or omission that would be obvious to a person in the industry or business. Also, because typesetting and printing companies require skilled professionals and expensive equipment, the cost for publishing work commercially can often be beyond the reach of many companies.

Since it was first introduced in 1984 by Paul Brainard, the CEO of Aldus Corporation, desktop publishing has dramatically changed the way organizations produce printed and even electronic documents. Small firms that could rarely afford typesetting in the past now find they can easily create documents that rival the work of large competitors. Similarly, large companies that previously spent huge sums of money on typesetting and printing services now find they can create much of the same work in-house, less expensively.

PageMaker was the first popular desktop publishing program available on the personal computer. Newer versions of the program have evolved over the years and have added even more powerful and highly sophisticated features, while at the same time making the program easier to use. With today's current version of the program, it's possible to create almost any publication that was or could be created using traditional typesetting methods. In fact, many graphic design and typesetting firms are now using desktop publishing to create work for their customers.

Why Use Desktop Publishing?

To understand the advantages of desktop publishing, think about any printed material that you have seen in the last 24 hours, such as a newspaper, flyer, brochure, magazine, or even this textbook. Now imagine that same document keyed with only a basic word processing program or old-fashioned typewriter. Although the word processed or typewritten version would contain the same text, all the words would be of one or just a few different sizes and there would be no pictures or illustrations. How excited would you feel, for example, about reading a 100-page magazine in which all the text was the same size and there were no pictures? To better understand this point, look at the newsletter shown in Figure 1-1. Although the text is easy to read, this newsletter is not very interesting to look at.

Figure 1-2 is the same newsletter as appears in Figure 1-1, but this version was created using the desktop publishing features of PageMaker. While both newsletters contain the same words, the desktop published version looks more interesting and professional.

FIGURE 1-1
A keyed newsletter

```
                         AIRFARE NEWS
                                            Volume 3, Issue 6

     Air Travel Prices Drop

     Lower fuel costs help airlines reduce  long-distance fares to
     many destinations.
     In a recent statement aimed at encouraging more airline
     travel, the top four airline carriers announced a sharp de-
     crease in the price for long-distance air travel. Members of
     the Air Carriers Association indicated that the reason for the
     decrease was the cost of jet fuel. Increased production of
     aviation fuel in the United Stated during the past six months
     has resulted in a large surplus. This excess has caused fuel
     suppliers to lower prices in an effort to stimulate sales.
          "We have waited months for a chance like this to lower
     fares," said Freda Johnston, President of the Association.
     Beginning in April, fares for domestic travel will drop ap-
     proximately 15 percent for trips under 500 miles and 20 per-
     cent for air travel of longer distances. Travelers on flights
     to Europe will realize an even greater savings if they book
     flights within the next three to four weeks. Johnston was fur-
     ther quoted as saying, "There is no way to know how long this
     reduction will remain in effect."
          Regardless of your travel destination, industry experts
     are unanimous in suggesting you purchase your tickets within
     the next 30 days for the best possible savings.

     Watching Out
     by Annie Wong
     Keep a careful eye on your luggage to insure it reaches its
     intended destination. "There's a significant increase today in
     the number or suitcases that are being stolen from baggage
     claim areas," says Jose Ortega, a private security consultant.
     Mr. Ortega said that the number or suitcases stolen has risen
     by 30 percent during the past two years alone.
          One of the reasons for the increase in crime is the de-
     creasing number of airports having secured baggage areas and
     baggage inspectors. To lower costs, airports have eliminated
     most security personnel in the baggage claim areas. This makes
     it easy for anyone, either knowingly or unknowingly, to leave
     with another person's suitcase.
          The cost to the airline industry is staggering. Last
     month alone, there were nearly 1,800 claims for lost luggage
     with a total estimated value of over 5 million dollars.

                             (continued on page 2)
```

FIGURE 1-2
A desktop published newsletter

The newsletter in Figure 1-2 demonstrates several reasons why desktop publishing is becoming so popular. First, because desktop publishing lets you include text in different sizes on the same page, you can identify different types of entries for the reader. Printing the titles of newspaper articles in a large size, for example, makes each article easier to identify. Likewise, using a different *typeface* (printed characters of a certain design) on the same page helps add variety to the document.

Desktop publishing is also popular because it lets you combine graphics and text on the same page. Pictures or illustrations can help improve a document's clarity. One chart or illustration, for example, can often help explain a complicated topic that otherwise might require several paragraphs or pages of text to explain. PageMaker includes various drawing tools that you can use to create simple drawings or illustrations within the program. It also provides a way to electronically add pictures or illustrations to your work that were created with other software programs.

Traditional Publishing Methods

To understand desktop publishing better, let's look at how documents are published tradition-ally. Suppose that the marketing department of a bank wants to create a brochure announcing a new, low-cost checking account service. They might begin by writing the text for the brochure. In the publishing industry, this process is called creating the copy. These same people might also create a hand-drawn sketch to better see how they would like the brochure to look. Because the brochure is about low-cost checking, they might select a picture of cash or coins for the cover and an illus-tration of a person writing a check for the inside of the brochure. Because the bank lacks printing or desktop publishing capabilities, it would normally contract for this service with an outside design or printing company.

Figure 1-3 shows how this brochure would then be produced. First, the overall responsibility for the brochure is assigned to a *graphic designer*. His or her role is to understand what the client wants to accomplish with each printed piece, to design and develop detailed specifications for the work, and then to oversee its development.

FIGURE 1-3
Traditional typesetting project

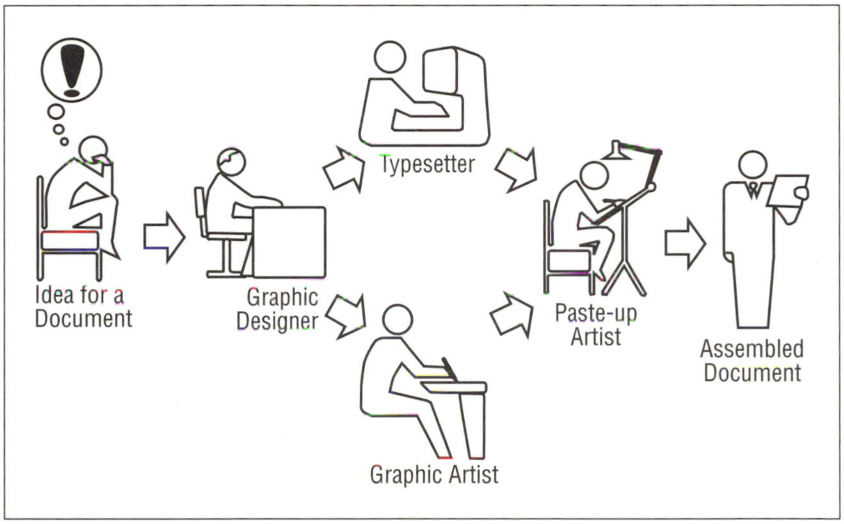

In our banking example, the graphic designer might first meet with the bank's employees to discuss the purpose of this brochure and/or review the copy. The graphic designer would also try to understand any special requirements or thoughts the bank might have about the brochure, such as how quickly it's needed, if they require a certain ink or paper color, how many copies of the brochure will be printed, and so on.

Using this information, the graphic designer then will create detailed specifications for the brochure. In preparing these specifications, the designer will determine where every part of the brochure will appear on each page. The graphic designer also decides other details such as the exact size and style of the type used for the titles and the body of the document, how the text will align, and suggests pho-tographs or illustrations that are needed. Finally, the graphic designer will prepare a hand-drawn sketch (called a rough) showing the exact position of each element.

The graphic designer then assigns various parts of the brochure to other individuals. A *copywriter* writes or refines the copy. A typesetter then transfers the text into a typesetting machine and, by using special commands, selects the correct type size and style for the text. At the same time, a *graphic artist* produces the needed art either by hand or by selecting the art from books of prepared pictures called *clip art*. The graphic artist might also include photographs called stock art. Next, the typeset pages and graphics are given to a *paste-up artist,* who aligns and glues the typeset text and graphics onto special pieces of paper called *boards*. Finally, each board is photographed using a special camera, and the resulting film, called *plates*, is then placed on a printing press to produce the final printed brochure.

Desktop Publishing Methods

Compared to traditional publishing methods, desktop publishing can often simplify and speed up many of the steps involved in producing a published document. Suppose that an employee of the marketing department from the same bank had a personal computer equipped with PageMaker. To create the checking account brochure, the marketing department could assign the development of the brochure to this employee. As with the traditional approach, this person would receive the copy and the hand-drawn sketch showing where each part of the brochure will appear. This person could then begin using PageMaker to create the brochure on-screen. By issuing various commands to the program, he or she would specify the size of the paper on which the brochure will be printed and select the number of pages it will contain. Then, he or she would key the text directly into either PageMaker or into a standard word processing program, such as Word, and then transfer the text into PageMaker. Next, he or she would position the text in the proper place in the on-screen brochure and select the appropriate type sizes and styles. Because of the way PageMaker operates, you can see immediately on-screen how the brochure will look when it's printed.

The person creating the advertising piece also could use the program to add simple graphic elements, such as lines or boxes, to the brochure. Since many people are not graphic artists, the program makes it easy to add graphics from other software programs. For example, you can purchase computer disks containing high-quality photographs or illustrations. In this case, our bank employee might use this type of resource to select several illustrations or photographs for use in the brochure.

> ## Hot Tip
>
> Thinking about a career in the graphic design industry? The American Institute of Graphic Arts, AIGA, is a national association of graphic arts professionals and students. They exchange ideas, set standards for the industry, and share information among members. Their Web site, *www.aiga.org*, is an excellent source of articles and ideas on graphic design.

Because PageMaker always shows on-screen how your work will look when it's printed, PageMaker makes it easy to experiment with different layouts and design ideas. For example, our bank employee could quickly replace one graphic with a different graphic or enlarge the size of the brochure's title. When finished, he or she can produce a printout at the push of a button. If only a small quantity of brochures were needed, the brochures could be printed immediately on the same computer. Otherwise, the printout would be sent to the printing department or a printing company.

Desktop Publishing with PageMaker

A document created with PageMaker is called a *publication*. PageMaker has a full range of word processing, drawing, and publishing features. With these features, you can create publications of almost unlimited length, make changes easily, and print a publication at any time.

As you create or modify a publication, you can use various features to give your work a published look, and in doing so, make it look more interesting and often more readable. Here is a quick look at some of the features you will learn about in this book.

Selecting the Typeface

As you add text to a publication, PageMaker lets you choose from various typefaces or print styles. And, as you often see in professional publications, you can even mix different typefaces on the same page. Although most computers today come with dozens of different typefaces, there are thousands of typefaces available for the personal computer. Typefaces are each identified by a unique name. Here are some.

Arial   *Park Avenue*   Times New Roman   Veranda

Bodoni   `Courier`   Garamond   **Charter BT**

Different typefaces will change the look and feel of a publication. Certain typefaces, for example, look more businesslike or formal, whereas others look more elegant, informal, or lighthearted.

Selecting the Print Size

PageMaker gives you tremendous flexibility in varying the size of your text. As mentioned earlier, using different size type aids the reader and helps a publication look more interesting. Also, the type of publication determines the print size that's used. Printing the body of a publication in one size, subtitles in a larger size, and main titles in an even larger size helps the reader locate various types of entries quickly.

Using the proper typeface and print size also affects how easy or difficult it is to read the text. Printing text in very small sizes or with certain typefaces, for example, can make a publication very difficult to read. Look at the following instances of typeface and size.

Type creates the personality of your document.

Type creates the personality of your document.

Type creates the personality of your document.

Clearly, the first example is easy to read. In the second example, however, the elaborate typeface, while attractive to look at, makes the reading more difficult. And in the third example, the text is too small for easy reading.

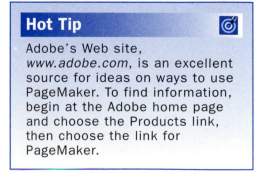

Hot Tip

Adobe's Web site, *www.adobe.com*, is an excellent source for ideas on ways to use PageMaker. To find information, begin at the Adobe home page and choose the Products link, then choose the link for PageMaker.

Drawing Tools

In the graphic arts industry, lines drawn on a page are called *rules*. PageMaker's drawing tools let you draw horizontal or vertical rules anywhere on a page. You can use these rules, for example, between columns of text, to set off an important paragraph, or create a border completely around a page.

PageMaker also contains other drawing tools that create circles, ovals, squares, rectangles, and other shapes. You can use these tools, for example, to create decorative designs, illustrations, or charts. As you create these drawings, you can control their size, shape, and shade or add color to the inside of the art. Each card in Figure 1-4 was created entirely with PageMaker.

FIGURE 1-4
Business cards created using drawing tools

Adding Graphics

One of PageMaker's more exciting features lets you add electronic graphics to your publications. Examples of these graphics include digital stock photography or prepared illustrations called clip art that you can purchase or create using a drawing program like CorelDraw or Adobe

Illustrator. Today there are thousands of such graphic files available that you can add to your publication. Some are provided free with certain programs, whereas others must be purchased at computer stores or through mail order. Figure 1-5 shows several examples.

FIGURE 1-5
Examples of clip art (top) and digital stock photography (bottom)

Bottom images copyright PhotoDisc, Inc.

A Look at Published Documents

PageMaker can produce a wide range of publications. Some of these publications are created for use internally in an organization, such as business forms, directories, status reports, and so on. Other publications are created for use outside of an organization, such as flyers, catalogs, annual reports, brochures, and newsletters. Figures 1-6, 1-7, 1-8, and 1-9 on the following pages illustrate how PageMaker's desktop publishing features can be used to create many different types of publications. These few examples, however, show only a small sample of what is possible with this program.

Proposals and Reports

Business publications, like reports and proposals, compete each day with similar documents for their readers' attention. Business reports usually outline the anticipated or completed tasks and results of a project. Proposals, on the other hand, outline the anticipated tasks and estimated costs to acquire a service or product. In certain industries, like consulting, accounting, or manufacturing, the quality and appearance of these documents are extremely important because they are written for current or future customers. Using desktop publishing to produce proposals and reports can make those publications look more interesting and leave the reader with a positive, lasting impression.

Figure 1-6 shows the first page from a desktop published proposal and a report. Notice how the pages look easy to read and are well organized. Vertical and horizontal rules help separate the different text entries while graphics make the report look less intimidating. Notice also how different size text was used to identify different types of entries in the proposal.

FIGURE 1-6
A desktop published report

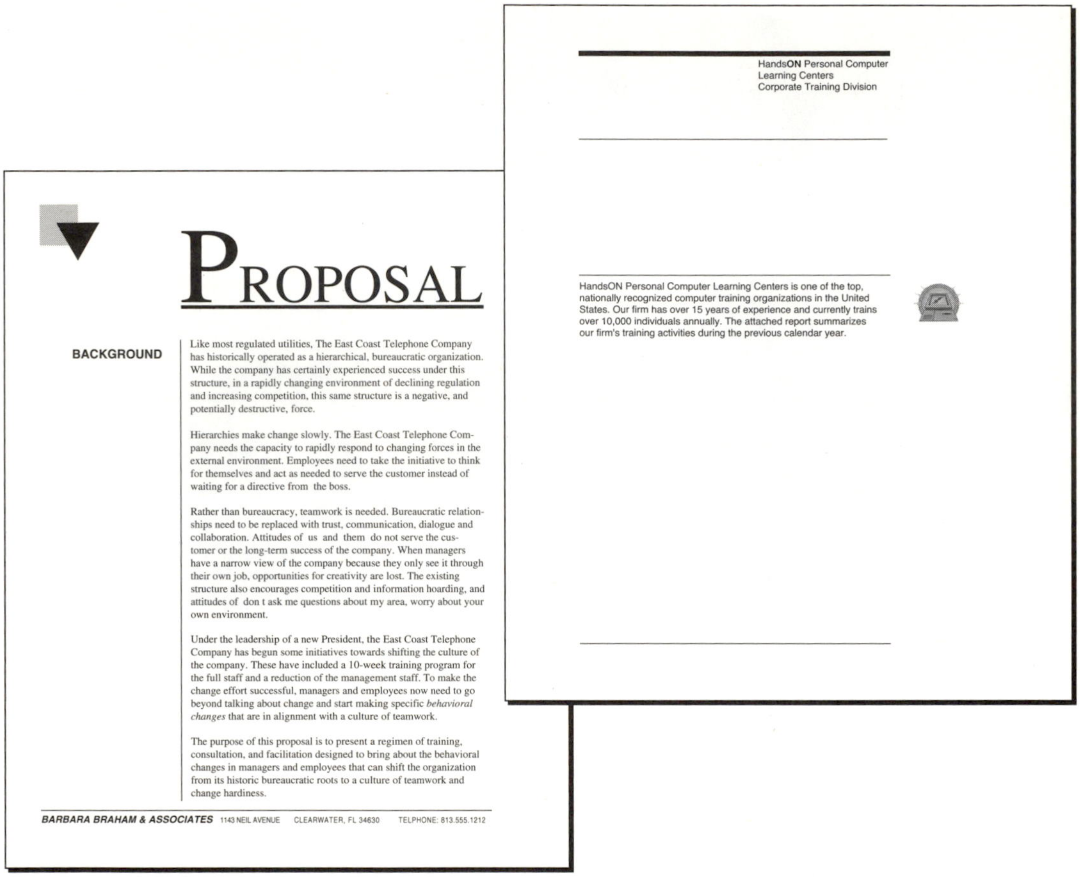
HandsON Personal Computer
Learning Centers
Corporate Training Division

HandsON Personal Computer Learning Centers is one of the top, nationally recognized computer training organizations in the United States. Our firm has over 15 years of experience and currently trains over 10,000 individuals annually. The attached report summarizes our firm's training activities during the previous calendar year.

PROPOSAL

BACKGROUND

Like most regulated utilities, The East Coast Telephone Company has historically operated as a hierarchical, bureaucratic organization. While the company has certainly experienced success under this structure, in a rapidly changing environment of declining regulation and increasing competition, this same structure is a negative, and potentially destructive, force.

Hierarchies make change slowly. The East Coast Telephone Company needs the capacity to rapidly respond to changing forces in the external environment. Employees need to take the initiative to think for themselves and act as needed to serve the customer instead of waiting for a directive from the boss.

Rather than bureaucracy, teamwork is needed. Bureaucratic relationships need to be replaced with trust, communication, dialogue and collaboration. Attitudes of us and them do not serve the customer or the long-term success of the company. When managers have a narrow view of the company because they only see it through their own job, opportunities for creativity are lost. The existing structure also encourages competition and information hoarding, and attitudes of don t ask me questions about my area, worry about your own environment.

Under the leadership of a new President, the East Coast Telephone Company has begun some initiatives towards shifting the culture of the company. These have included a 10-week training program for the full staff and a reduction of the management staff. To make the change effort successful, managers and employees now need to go beyond talking about change and start making specific *behavioral changes* that are in alignment with a culture of teamwork.

The purpose of this proposal is to present a regimen of training, consultation, and facilitation designed to bring about the behavioral changes in managers and employees that can shift the organization from its historic bureaucratic roots to a culture of teamwork and change hardiness.

BARBARA BRAHAM & ASSOCIATES 1143 NEIL AVENUE CLEARWATER, FL 34630 TELPHONE: 813.555.1212

Forms

In the United States, it is estimated that organizations create over 300,000 new forms, such as employment applications or order forms, annually. More importantly, the type of information collected on those forms changes regularly. By using PageMaker, it's easy to create good-looking forms, and to change those forms as the need arises.

The invoice in Figure 1-7 contains fill-in-the-blank areas created using vertical and horizontal rules. Bold and large size text helps identify each element and important areas, such as the space for the customer's name and address, and are set off with rectangles. The total column is created using a lightly shaded rectangle to set it off and add a more colorful appearance.

FIGURE 1-7
A desktop published form

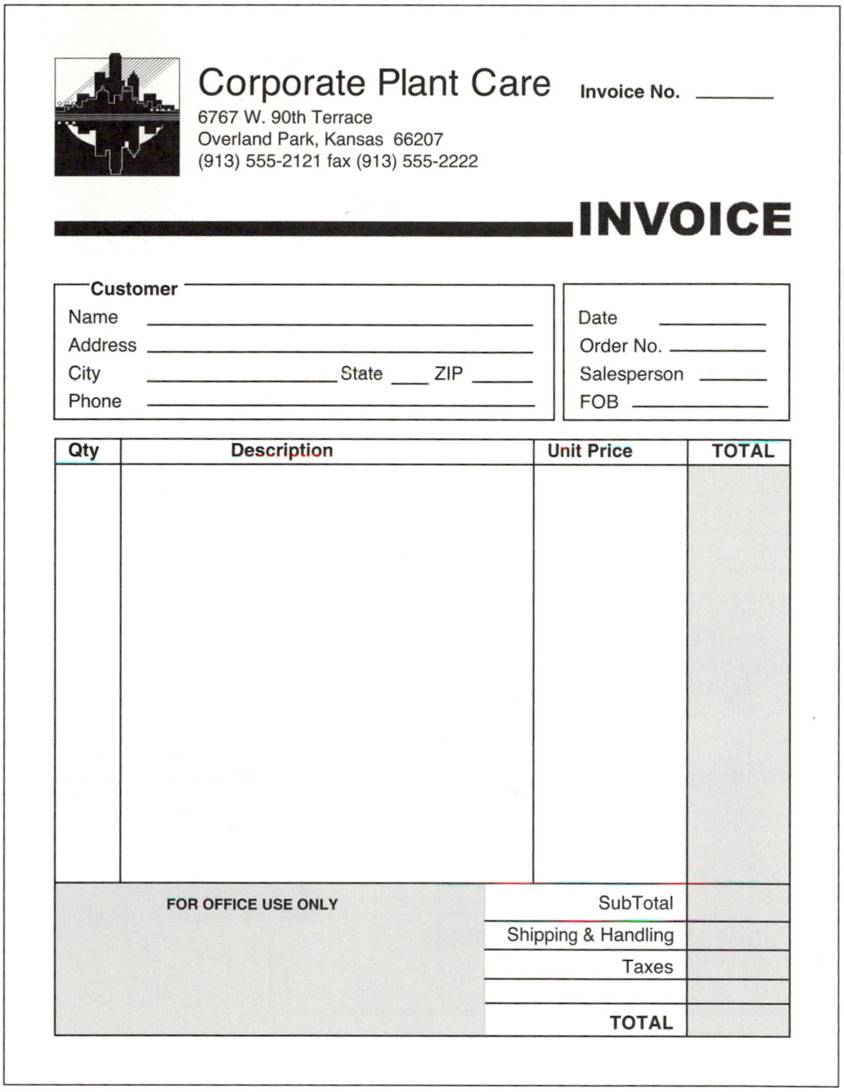
Corporate Plant Care
Invoice No. ______
6767 W. 90th Terrace
Overland Park, Kansas 66207
(913) 555-2121 fax (913) 555-2222

INVOICE

Customer
Name ______
Address ______
City ______ State ___ ZIP ______
Phone ______

Date ______
Order No. ______
Salesperson ______
FOB ______

Qty	Description	Unit Price	TOTAL

FOR OFFICE USE ONLY	SubTotal	
	Shipping & Handling	
	Taxes	
	TOTAL	

Newsletters, Flyers, and Brochures

Currently, the fastest growing use for desktop publishing is in producing newsletters, flyers, and brochures. Such documents are normally used by an organization to share information about a product, event, or service. Because existing or potential customers read these documents, they must look professional and be of the highest quality.

Figure 1-8 is an example of both a flyer and a brochure. In the flyer, narrow columns of type, a graphic, and different type sizes add interest and keep the work lively. In the brochure, a large graphic helps draw the reader into the publication.

FIGURE 1-8
A desktop published flyer and brochure

Photo copyright Tammy Davis

Miscellaneous Publications

Desktop publishing can also be used to produce many other types of publications, such as résumés, letterheads, business cards, fax transmittal forms, and so on. In addition, such publications can be easily modified and reprinted as needed. Figure 1-9 is an example of a fax transmittal form and a letterhead created using PageMaker.

FIGURE 1-9
Other desktop published examples

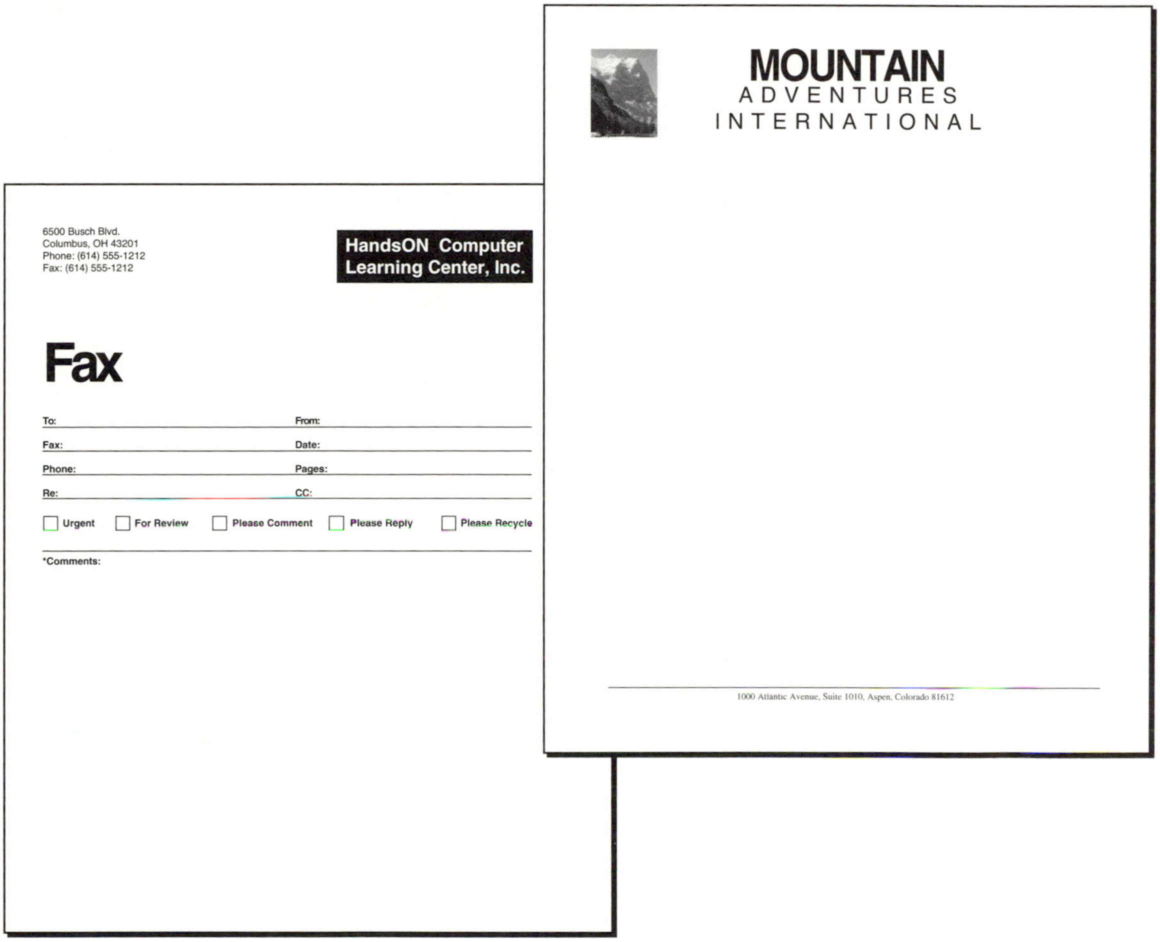
6500 Busch Blvd.
Columbus, OH 43201
Phone: (614) 555-1212
Fax: (614) 555-1212

HandsON Computer Learning Center, Inc.

Fax

To: From:
Fax: Date:
Phone: Pages:
Re: CC:

☐ Urgent ☐ For Review ☐ Please Comment ☐ Please Reply ☐ Please Recycle

*Comments:

MOUNTAIN
ADVENTURES
INTERNATIONAL

1000 Atlantic Avenue, Suite 1010, Aspen, Colorado 81612

SUMMARY

In this lesson you learned how to:

- Define desktop publishing and explain the differences between traditional publishing and desktop publishing.
- Identify the key people involved in producing traditionally typeset documents and describe their responsibilities.
- Compare desktop publishing to traditional publishing techniques.
- Identify some of PageMaker's key features and the concept of a publication.

■ Identify some documents that are frequently desktop published.

■ Enhance a PageMaker publication by changing typeface, type size, and graphics.

VOCABULARY*Review*

Define the following terms:

Boards	Graphic designer	Typeface
Clip art	Paste-up artist	Typeset quality print
Copywriter	Plates	Typography
Desktop publishing	Publication	
Graphic artist	Rules	

REVIEW*Questions*

TRUE/FALSE

Circle T if the statement is true or F if the statement is false.

T   F   **1.** Today there are an estimated 30,000 organizations worldwide that use desktop publishing.

T   F   **2.** Desktop publishing was first introduced in the mid-1950s.

T   F   **3.** The role of a graphic artist is to understand what the client wants to accomplish with each printed piece, to design and develop detailed specifications for the work, and then to oversee its development.

T   F   **4.** The role of a graphic designer is to prepare any illustrations that are needed.

T   F   **5.** Books of prepared illustrations that can be used in a publication are called clip art.

T   F   **6.** With traditional publishing methods, illustrations and typeset text are glued onto pieces of heavy paper called boards.

T   F   **7.** With PageMaker, you always see on-screen how a publication will look when it's printed.

T   F   **8.** With PageMaker, you can use only one typeface or type size on a page.

T   F   **9.** PageMaker provides drawing tools that let you draw horizontal and vertical lines almost anywhere on a page.

T   F   **10.** Because of its publishing orientation, a document created with PageMaker is called a publication.

FILL IN THE BLANK

Complete the following sentences by writing the correct word or words in the blanks provided.

1. _____ is the term used to describe a computer printout that closely resembles the print quality of that produced by a traditional typesetting machine.

2. A desktop publishing program such as PageMaker lets you place both _____ and _____ on the same page in a publication.

3. Typography means using _____ to produce a printed document.

4. In the United States, it is estimated that organizations create over _____ new forms annually.

5. In the graphic arts industry, lines drawn on a page are called _____.

PROJECTS

SCANS **PROJECT 1-1**

Locate and then visit a local organization or business that uses desktop publishing to produce all or some of its publications. During this visit, ask the following questions and record your answers.

1. What type of desktop publishing software and equipment does the organization use?

2. What are the advantages and disadvantages of desktop publishing for this particular business?

3. What types of publications do they currently produce with desktop publishing? If possible, obtain samples of some of those publications to discuss in class.

4. What desktop publishing training is required or provided by the organization?

5. Does the organization have any plans to expand its desktop publishing activities? If so, what are those plans?

SCANS **TEAMWORK PROJECT**

Obtain samples of three different published documents such as a flyer, newsletter, or magazine page. Discuss these documents with your classmates or group. In this discussion:

■ Decide whether or not the document looks interesting. If so, describe why. If it does not look interesting, discuss what you think could be done to improve the appearance.

■ Discuss whether the document is easy or difficult to read, and why.

■ Describe anything that especially caught your attention, such as the use of a particular color, an illustration, or a photo.

SCANS WEB PROJECT

Visit the Adobe Web site at *www.adobe.com*. Take time to look over the Adobe home page and notice how you can navigate to different parts of the site. Then, follow the links to the Products section, and within that, select the PageMaker link. Examine some of the different kinds of information available to you.

CRITICAL*Thinking*

SCANS ACTIVITY 1-1

Suppose you work for a travel agency that specializes in travel tours to the Caribbean. What types of travel agency publications can you create using PageMaker? Make a list of the different publications that you can think of. Then, next to each item in your list, indicate whether that publication would be used internally by employees of the travel agency or externally by customers or potential customers.

GETTING STARTED WITH PAGEMAKER

Introduction

PageMaker is a program that lets you use the computer to create high-quality documents called publications. In this lesson, you will learn how to start the program, identify different parts of PageMaker's screens, and issue basic commands to the program. You will also see how to open a previously created publication, display different parts of this publication, and finally close the publication and quit the program.

19

Starting PageMaker

In order to start and use PageMaker, you need to understand various terms related to the computer mouse, most of which you probably know already. Here is a quick review.

- *Click:* To place the mouse pointer on a specific item on-screen and then press the left mouse button once.

- *Double-click:* To place the mouse pointer on a specific item on-screen and then press the left mouse button twice, rapidly.

- *Press:* To place the mouse pointer at a certain location on-screen and then hold down the left mouse button until the desired task is accomplished.

- *Drag:* To place the mouse pointer at a certain location or on a specific item on-screen. Then, while pressing and holding down the mouse button, move the mouse to a different location and release the mouse button.

PageMaker 7

You can start PageMaker with the mouse by using either the program icon or the Start menu. Starting the program varies somewhat depending upon your computer setup. If the PageMaker icon appears on your desktop, double-click the icon. You can also begin the program by using the Start menu. The PageMaker icon is not present on all computers, but the Start menu gives you a consistent way to begin the program.

STEP-BY-STEP 2.1

1. Click the **Start** button and move the mouse pointer to **Programs**.

2. The list of programs that appears will be similar to that shown in Figure 2-1. Move the mouse pointer to the entry labeled **Adobe** and then to the entry labeled **Adobe PageMaker 7.0**. When a menu listing the PageMaker applications appears (see Figure 2-2), click on **Adobe PageMaker 7.0** to start the program.

STEP-BY-STEP 2.1 Continued

3. After a short pause, an introductory screen appears for brief time while the program loads. The introductory screen then disappears when the program is ready to use. Keep PageMaker open and on your screen for use throughout the rest of this lesson.

FIGURE 2-1
Programs list - Starting PageMaker 7.0

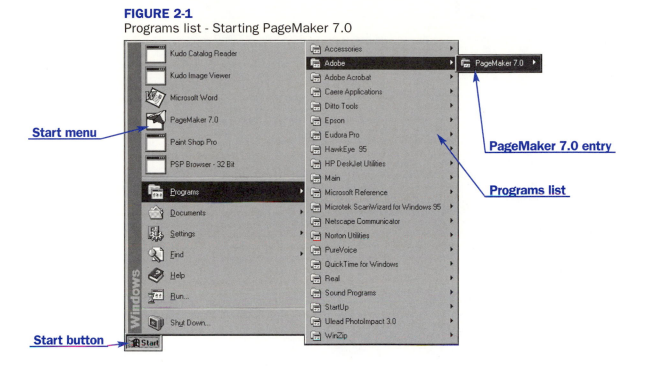

FIGURE 2-2
Application menu - Starting PageMaker 7.0

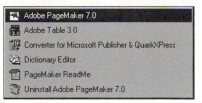

Menus, Toolbars, and Palettes

When PageMaker begins, it displays a work area. Depending upon your computer setup and who used the program last, the work area may look different from computer to computer. Figures 2-3 and 2-4 show two examples of how your work area might look.

FIGURE 2-3
One example of a PageMaker work area

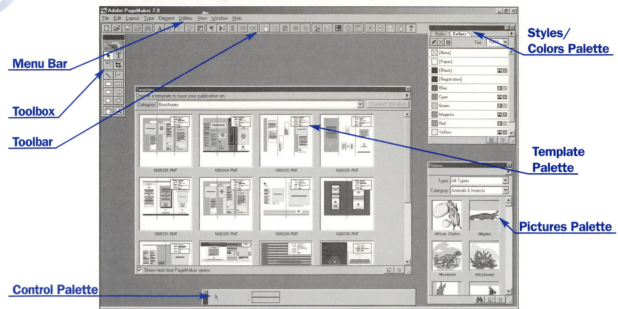

FIGURE 2-4
Another example of a PageMaker work area

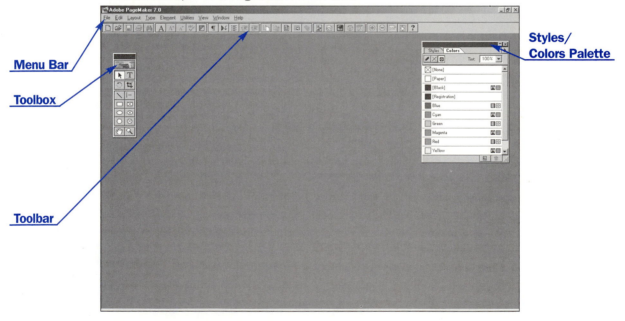

Regardless of your computer setup, the work area always includes a menu bar and a toolbar at the top of the screen. You will use the menu bar and toolbar to issue PageMaker commands or instructions that tell the program to perform some type of action.

> **Hot Tip**
>
> Don't worry if your screens do not look exactly like those shown in this book.

The main portion of the work area can also contain one or more large areas referred to as palettes. A ***palette*** is a group of related tools or features you can use when creating or editing your work. You can display or remove palettes as they are needed.

Using Menus

Choosing an entry from the menu bar displays a pull-down menu like the File pull-down menu shown in Figure 2-5. There are different ways to choose, or select, an entry from a menu bar or from a pull-down menu.

To choose an entry from the menu bar using the mouse, place the mouse pointer on the selection and then click to reveal a pull-down menu. To choose an entry from a pull-down menu using the mouse, move the mouse pointer to the desired entry and then click.

FIGURE 2-5
File pull-down menu

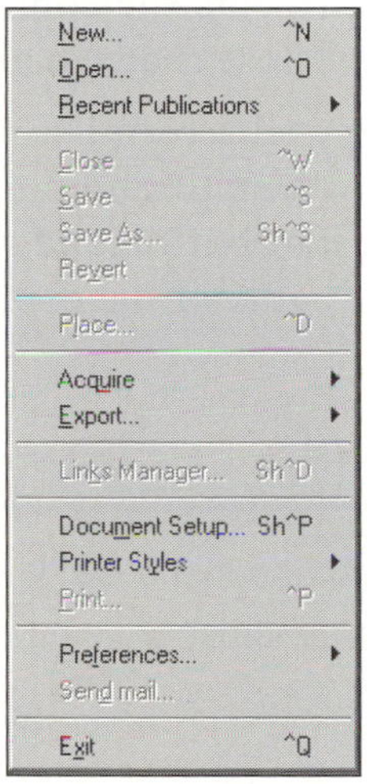

Many entries in the pull-down menus also have shortcut keys—keys that you can press to issue a specific command quickly. Look at Figure 2-5 and find the characters ^N located to the right of the New command. These characters are the shortcut keys for the New command. The symbol ^ is used as an abbreviation for the Ctrl key. The shortcut ^N for example, means that you can hold down the Ctrl key and press N to issue the New command instead of using the pull-down menu.

Some pull-down entries contain a right-pointing arrow (▶) like the Recent Publications entry in Figure 2-5. If you choose this type of entry, an additional menu will appear from which you can choose a different entry.

When a menu entry is gray, like the Save or Print entry in Figure 2-5, it is not available to use or does not apply to anything you are doing at the moment. As you continue to work with the program, different menu items will be available or unavailable at different times.

To remove or cancel an unwanted pull-down menu, click anywhere away from the pull-down menu or press the Esc key.

STEP-BY-STEP 2.2

1. Place the mouse pointer on the word **File** in the menu bar and click.

2. Remove the pull-down menu by clicking anywhere away from the menu bar and from the pull-down menu.

3. Place the mouse pointer on the word **Type** in the menu bar and click.

4. Remove the pull-down menu by clicking anywhere away from the menu bar and pull-down menu. Keep this screen open for the next Step-by-Step.

Using the Toolbar

Besides pull-down menus and shortcuts, you can use the toolbar to issue many commands. In many cases, the toolbar is a faster way to issue commands. The toolbar contains a series of pictures, or buttons, which represent specific PageMaker commands. To issue a command using the toolbar, click on the button that represents the command. As with menu entries, some buttons are available at specific times only. Those that are not available appear in light gray.

The toolbar contains many buttons, and remembering which button issues which command can seem confusing at first. It's easy, however, to find out the command associated with any button. Simply place the mouse pointer on that button and wait. After a second or two, a small box called a *ToolTip* appears containing the name of the command.

STEP-BY-STEP 2.3

1. Locate the toolbar found just beneath the menu bar. Without clicking, place your mouse pointer over the first button on the toolbar. After a moment, the name New will appear, indicating that the button is used to issue the New command.

2. On your own and without clicking, find out the purpose of the other buttons in the toolbar. Keep this screen open for the next Step-by-Step.

Viewing/Hiding Palettes

Depending on your computer setup, one more palette will appear when PageMaker begins. Palettes are helpful for using various advanced features of the program. However, if you are new to PageMaker, palettes can make the program seem confusing. Also, the size of some palettes can hide large portions of the screen, making it difficult to work. To solve this problem, you can hide or display palettes as needed.

You can use the Window menu to hide or display different palettes. To hide the Control palette, for example, choose Hide Control Palette from the Window menu. To display the hidden Control palette, choose Show Control Palette from the Window menu. Table 2-1 lists the different commands for hiding or displaying several of PageMaker's palettes.

TABLE 2-1
PageMaker palettes

PALETTE NAME	TO HIDE THE PALETTE	TO DISPLAY THE PALETTE
Control	Choose Hide Control Palette from the Window menu.	Choose Show Control Palette from the Window menu.
Styles	Choose Hide Styles from the Window menu.	Choose Show Styles from the Window menu.
Colors	Choose Hide Colors from the Window menu.	Choose Show Colors from the Window menu.
Pictures	Choose Plug-in Palettes from the Window menu, then choose Hide Picture Palette.	Choose Plug-in Palettes from the Window menu, then choose Show Picture Palette.
Templates	Choose Plug-in Palettes from the Window menu, then choose Hide Template Palette.	Choose Plug-in Palettes from the Window menu, then choose Show Template Palette.

S TEP-BY-STEP 2.4

1. If the Control palette appears on-screen, hide that palette by choosing **Hide Control Palette** from the **Window** menu.

2. Choose **Show Control Palette** from the **Window** menu to display the Control palette.

3. If the Colors/Styles palette appears on-screen, hide that palette by choosing **Hide Colors** from the **Window** menu.

4. Choose **Show Colors** from the **Window** menu.

5. If the Template palette appears on-screen, hide that palette by choosing **Plug-in Palettes** from the **Window** menu, then choose **Hide Template Palette**.

6. If the Pictures palette appears on-screen, hide that palette by choosing **Plug-in Palettes** from the **Window** menu, and then choose **Hide Picture Palette**. Keep this screen open for the next Step-by-Step.

Understanding Dialog Boxes

As you issue certain commands, PageMaker opens or displays a dialog box. A *dialog box* lets you choose options that control how a command is carried out. Figure 2-6 shows an example of a Save Publication dialog box and the parts of the box.

FIGURE 2-6
Example of a dialog box

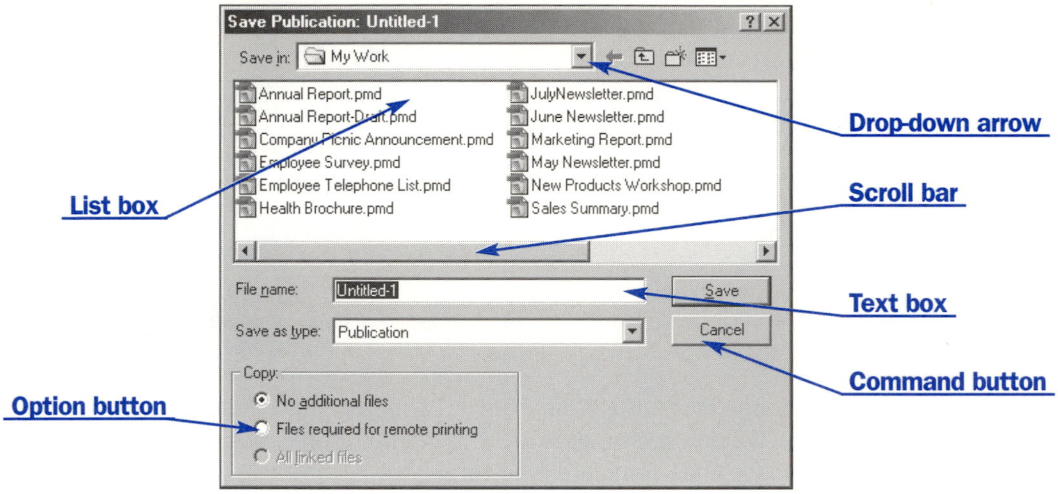

Within a dialog box, you can use the mouse to select options or you can press the Tab key to move between options. Dialog boxes can contain one or more of the following types of items.

■ *Text box:* A **text box** is an area in which you key required information. As you key, a vertical bar (|) called the insertion point indicates where the next character you key will appear.

■ *List box:* A **list box** is a list of choices from which you can select. To make a selection, click on the choice.

■ *Option button:* An option button is a circular-shaped button, sometimes referred to as a radio button, that lets you select only one of a series of options. To select an option button, click on the circle in front of the option. An option button contains a solid dot (•) when it is selected.

■ *Check box:* (Not shown in Figure 2-6.) A check box is a small square (☐) that appears in front of a specific option. To select a check box option, click on the box in front of the option. A check mark (✔) appears inside the box when the option is selected. To deselect that same option, click the box again.

■ *Drop-down list:* Like a list box, a drop-down list shows choices from which you can select. To keep the dialog box less cluttered, the choices do not appear until you click on the drop-down arrow (▼).

■ *Command button:* A **command button** tells the program to accept or forget the selections you have made in a dialog box. Most dialog boxes contain OK and Cancel command buttons that you can use to complete or cancel your request.

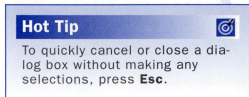

■ *Scroll bar*: A *scroll bar* appears when a list box is too small to display all of its information. Click on an arrow at one end of the scroll bar to view other entries. If you click on the downward pointing arrow, you will see the lower entries. If you click on the upward pointing arrow, you will move back toward the beginning of the list.

> **Hot Tip**
>
> To quickly cancel or close a dialog box without making any selections, press **Esc**.

After selecting the options you want within a dialog box, click OK to accept the selections and close the dialog box. To cancel or close a dialog box without making any selections, click Cancel or press the Esc key.

S TEP-BY-STEP 2.5

1. Choose **Open** from the **File** menu. Briefly examine the dialog box and then click **Cancel** to close the dialog box.

2. Choose **New** from the **File** menu.

3. In the Orientation section of the dialog box, observe the two options Tall and Wide. Tall is currently selected. Select **Wide** by clicking inside the radio button preceding the option. Notice how a dot appears inside the Wide radio button indicating that it is selected.

4. Notice that Double-sided is checked in the Options section. Click once inside that check box to remove the check mark and deselect the option. Also, notice how some other features, like the Facing pages option, are no longer available.

5. Click the **Cancel** button to close this dialog box without saving any of your changes. Keep PageMaker open and on your screen for the next Step-by-Step.

Getting Help with PageMaker

The Help feature in PageMaker contains information on hundreds of the program's topics and features. You can use Help to display information about a command or a feature you have either forgotten or simply want to learn more about. By using Help, you can look up general information, such as a description of a program feature; or specific information, such as how to use a certain command.

> **Important**
>
> In order for the Help feature to work properly, Internet Explorer version 4.0 or later, or Netscape Communicator version 4.0 or later must be installed on your computer.

You can request Help by choosing Help Topics from the Help menu (or by pressing F1) or by clicking the Help button in the toolbar. After a short pause, the Adobe PageMaker Help window appears like the one in Figure 2-7. PageMaker provides three different ways to locate information: Contents, Index, and Search. When you finish using Help, choose Close from the File menu in the Help window to return to your publication.

FIGURE 2-7
The Adobe PageMaker Help window

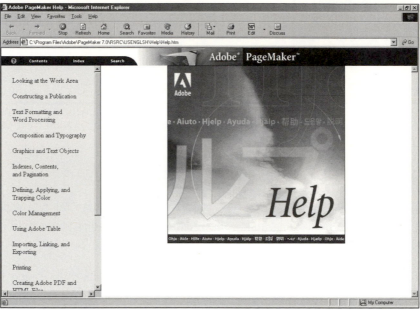

Use Contents Help

If you are looking for general information or guidance on using the program, select the Contents option. Choosing Contents in the Help window displays a list of general topics along the left side of the window, such as topics on constructing a publication (see Figure 2-7). Click on a general topic to view a list of specific Help entries that are available, and then click on an entry that interests you to read more about it.

Use Index Help

If you know the name of the PageMaker feature or command you want information about, select the Index option. Choosing Index in the Help window displays a list of alphabetical letters. Click on the letter that the name of the command or feature begins with, such as *P* for information on *Printing*. A list of all Help entries beginning with that letter appears. Each entry is followed by one or more numbers indicating different information screens related to that command. An entry such as Print command 1, 2 for example, means that there are two different entries related to that topic. Click on a number to read the entry.

Use Search Help

You can also use Help to search for specific information on your own. Choosing Search in the Help window displays a box labeled Find pages containing. Inside that box, key the name of the command or feature you want to know about and then click the Search button. PageMaker displays a list of suggested Help topics. Click on a suggested topic to view a list of specific Help entries that are available, and then click on an entry that interests you to read more about it.

STEP-BY-STEP 2.6

1. Choose **Help Topics** from the **Help** menu.

2. Click **Contents**. Read the first few entries in the list of general topics that appears, such as Looking at the Work Area or Constructing a Publication. Click the entry **Looking at the Work Area**. Notice how a list of specific Help topics appears near the middle of the screen. In that specific list, click on **About the work area** and read the information that appears.

3. Click **Index** and then click **S**. A list of Help topics beginning with the letters appears on the left side of the screen. Locate the entry labeled **Save As command 1**, **2** and click on the **1** to read information about that command. Now, read more information about the **Save As** command by clicking on the **2** that follows the entry. Briefly look over some of the Help information that appears.

4. Practice using the Search option to look up information on naming a publication. Click **Search**. Next, click inside the box labeled Find pages containing and key **naming a publication**. Then click the **Search** button. In the list of entries that appears, click **Naming and saving a publication**. Briefly look over some of the Help information that appears.

5. Cancel the Help feature by choosing **Close** from the **File** menu. Leave PageMaker open and on your screen for the next Step-by-Step.

Opening a Publication

After starting PageMaker, you can choose to create a new publication or work with a publication that has already been created. In this section you'll learn how to open an existing publication so that you can view, edit or print the publication. In the next lesson, you'll learn how to create a new publication.

Like other computer files, PageMaker publications are stored on disk. You can use the Open command to find and open publications on different types of disk drives, such as an internal hard drive or floppy disk drive, a computer network hard drive or even a CD-ROM.

As you may already know, most disks can be divided into folders. Like file folders, these disk folders help you keep groups of related files together. For example, you might use one folder to hold all the files needed for creating a newsletter publication.

To open an existing publication, choose Open from the File menu, or click the Open button on the toolbar. Either method displays the Open Publication dialog box (see Figure 2-8) in which you can open a publication stored on any disk drive or in any folder connected to your computer.

FIGURE 2-8
Open Publication dialog box

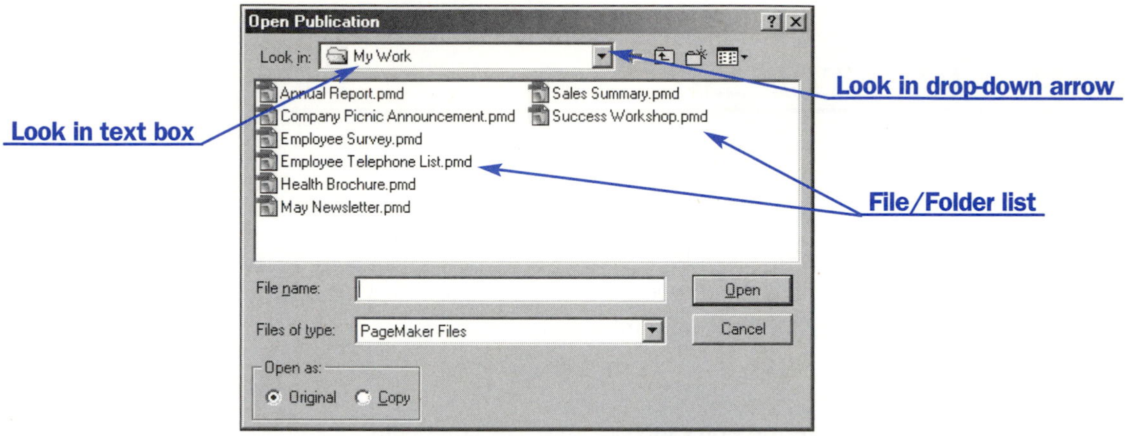

Files stored on a disk are identified by a filename, which is a name assigned to that file by the person who created it. Whenever PageMaker saves a publication on a disk, it adds the three character file extension pmd to the end of the filename. That file extension indicates to the computer that the file was created and will be used by PageMaker.

When first opening a publication, you need to identify the disk drive and folder (if appropriate) in which it is stored. The Open Publication dialog box lists publications stored in the disk or folder shown in the Look in text box. Names of any publications stored there appear in the File/Folder List. If the publication you want to work with appears, click on its name and then click the Open button. Otherwise, use the Look in drop-down arrow to display a list of all available disks. Choose the disk containing the file you want to open. Then, if the work is stored in a folder, double-click on the name of that folder in the File/Folder list.

> **Hot Tip**
>
> All PageMaker publication file-names include the file extension *pmd*, such as *Grades.pmd*. Every publication used in these lessons has this file extension, so it will not be used in this book. Therefore, when you are instructed to open the publication named *Grades*, you will open the publication with the filename *Grades.pmd*.

The Publication Window

After you start PageMaker and open a publication, the *publication window* like the one in Figure 2-9, appears. Depending on your computer setup, your publication window may vary slightly from that shown in the figure. You use the publication window to create and edit or modify your work.

FIGURE 2-9
A publication window

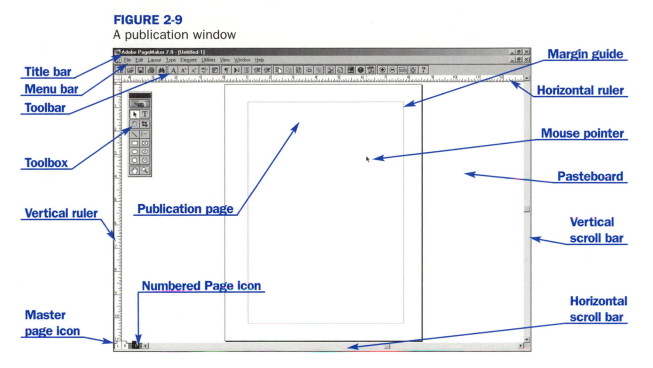

A publication window is made up of the following parts:

- *Horizontal and vertical rulers*: Located along the left (vertical) and top (horizontal) edge of the window, they help measure and position text and graphics. Rulers can be hidden or displayed as needed.

- *Horizontal and vertical scroll bars*: The light gray areas found along the bottom (horizontal) and right (vertical) edges of the publication window. Click the arrows found at each end of these scroll bars to move different parts of the current page or pasteboard into view.

- *Margin guides*: Dotted or thin lines that indicate the top, bottom, left, and right margins on a page. Like a word processing program, these *margin guides* help control where text normally appears on a page and create white space between the body of the publication and the edges of the page.

- *Master page icon(s)*: Master pages are special publication pages that can contain text or graphics that you want to appear on every page in the publication. A *master page icon* indicates an L for a left-hand page and an R for a right-hand page. To include a title such as *Vacation Report* at the top of every page in a report, you would key that title at the top of a master page. Those words would then appear on every page in the report.

- *Menu bar*: Provides access to the commands used to control the program.

■ *Numbered page icon(s)*: Numbered symbols located in the lower-left corner of the publication window that identify each page in a publication. A **numbered page icon** shows up as page number 1 or 2, for example. The page you are currently working on is highlighted. To view a different page in the publication, click on the icon that represents that page.

■ *Pasteboard*: The area outside the edges of the page. Use the **pasteboard** to temporarily store text or graphics that you will later position on a certain page in the publication. When printing a publication, anything located on the pasteboard does not print.

■ *Publication page*: The area in which all the text and graphics for a particular page will appear is called a **publication page**. A solid line represents the electronic edge of the publication page area.

■ *Title bar*: The **title bar** contains the name of your publication, such as *My Work.pmd*. If you have not yet saved the publication, the name *Untitled-1* will appear.

■ *Toolbar*: Located under the menu bar, the **toolbar** displays buttons you can click to access commands.

■ *Toolbox*: A collection of PageMaker tools you can use when creating a publication. Each picture or icon in the **toolbox** represents a different tool, such as a text tool, or a tool for drawing lines.

S TEP-BY-STEP 2.7

1. Open the **Cayman** file from the data files that accompany this book.

    a. Choose **Open** from the **File** menu.

    b. From the data files that accompany this book, use the Look in drop-down list to locate the disk and folder in which the publication named Cayman is stored. Your instructor will provide complete details on where the data files are stored.

2. Carefully examine the publication window. Notice that this publication contains four pages as indicated by the four numbered page icons. Also notice how the first numbered page icon is highlighted, indicating that you are viewing the first page in the publication.

3. Click the numbered page icon labeled **2**. Next, click the numbered page icon labeled **4** to view the last page.

4. Click the **R** master page icon. Practice moving the publication window to the right. Click twice on the left arrow (◀) located at the left edge of the horizontal scroll bar.

5. Click twice on the right arrow (▶) located at the right edge of the horizontal scroll bar. Notice that the publication window moves to the left.

6. Click once on the up arrow (▲) located at the top of the vertical scroll bar to move the page downward.

7. Click once on the down arrow (▼) located at the bottom of the vertical scroll bar to move the page upward. Keep this publication on-screen for use in the next Step-by-Step.

Closing a Publication

Closing a publication removes it from the screen so that you can create or edit other publications, or quit the PageMaker program. You normally close a publication when you are finished working with it. If you try to close a publication that was not previously stored on disk, or try to close an edited publication, PageMaker asks if you want to save your work on disk.

To close a publication, choose Close from the File menu. If you previously saved your publication, PageMaker clears the screen. If you have not previously saved your work or if you made changes that have not been saved, PageMaker asks if you want to save those changes. Choose Yes to save the changes or No if you do not want to save those changes.

S TEP-BY-STEP 2.8

1. Choose **Close** from the **File** menu.

2. If a message asking if you want to save your changes appears, choose **No**. Notice how PageMaker clears the publication window. Keep PageMaker open for use in the next Step-by-Step.

Exiting or Quitting PageMaker

Like other computer applications, when you are finished using the program, you need to exit or quit PageMaker. To quit PageMaker, choose Exit from the File menu, or click the Close box located in the upper-right corner of the window. If you have already saved and closed your publication, the program will end when you choose to quit. If you have created or changed a publication but have not yet saved it to a disk, a message appears asking if you want to save your work before closing. Choose Yes to save your work or choose No to quit PageMaker without saving your work. You can also choose Cancel to cancel the request.

S TEP-BY-STEP 2.9

1. Choose **Exit** from the **File** menu.

2. If a message appears asking if you want to save your untitled work before closing, choose **No**. Shut down the computer if you are finished for the day.

SUMMARY

In this lesson you learned how to:

■ Identify the parts of the publication window.

■ Work with the toolbar, menu bar and pull-down menus.

■ Use shortcut keys, dialog boxes, and the Help feature.

■ Hide or display various palettes.

- Open and close a publication.
- Exit PageMaker.

VOCABULARY *Review*

Define the following terms:		
Command button	Numbered page icon	Scroll bar
Control Palette	Option button	Text box
Dialog box	Palette	Title bar
List box	Pasteboard	Toolbox
Margin guide	Publication page	ToolTip
Master page icon	Publication window	

REVIEW *Questions*

MATCHING

Match the lettered items in Figure 2-10 with the numbered items listed below.

FIGURE 2-10
PageMaker Window

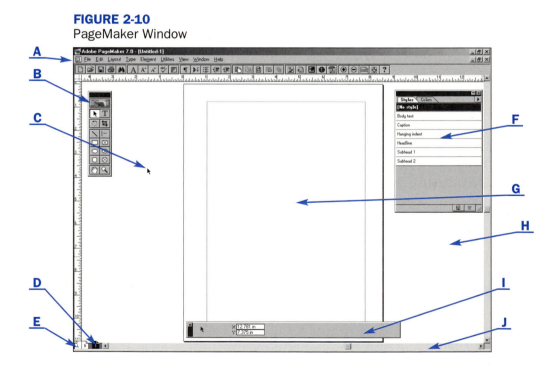

_____ **1.** Master page icons

_____ **2.** Styles/Colors palette

_____ **3.** Mouse pointer

_____ **4.** Control palette

_____ **5.** Numbered page icons

_____ **6.** Publication page

_____ **7.** Horizontal scroll bar

_____ **8.** Toolbox

_____ **9.** Menu bar

_____ **10.** Pasteboard

TRUE/FALSE

Circle T if the statement is true or F if the statement is false.

T   F   **1.** A text box is an area in which you key required information.

T   F   **2.** A scroll bar lets you move different parts of the current page or pasteboard into view.

T   F   **3.** Click means to press the left mouse button twice.

T   F   **4.** The small circle that appears before certain dialog box options is called a check box.

T   F   **5.** A list box in a dialog box shows choices from which you can select options.

WRITTEN QUESTIONS

Write a brief answer to the following questions.

1.   What is the purpose of the pasteboard?

2.   What is the purpose of the horizontal and vertical rulers?

3.   What does opening a publication mean?

4.   What type of entries would you place on a master page?

5.   Once you select a particular command, how do you choose options to control how the command is carried out?

PROJECTS

PROJECT 2-1

Open the **Cayman** publication from the data files and then answer the following questions.

1.   Examine the horizontal and vertical rulers. What is the approximate size of this publication? If the rulers do not appear on your screen, choose **Show Rulers** from the **View** menu.

2.   What is the approximate width of the margins around this page? (a) one-half inch (b) one inch (c) one and one-half inches (d) two inches.

3.   How many numbered pages are there in this publication?

4.   What does the pasteboard in this publication contain? (a) a picture (b) text (c) text and a picture (d) nothing.

5.   Use the numbered page icons to view the third page in this publication. What type of entry, if any, is contained on this page? (a) a picture (b) text (c) text and a picture (d) nothing.

6.   Keep this publication open and on-screen for use in the next project.

PROJECT 2-2

With the Cayman publication still on-screen, point to each button on the toolbar one at a time. For each button, wait for its ToolTip to appear before moving on to the next button. Although you may not understand all the descriptions just yet, this technique will be valuable as you begin learning more features of the program.

Close the Cayman publication without saving it. If a message appears asking if you want to save your changes before closing, choose **No**.

WEB PROJECT

Visit the Adobe Web site at *www.adobe.com* and find out what types of support services they offer for PageMaker. Which of those support services provide helpful information on better ways to use the program? Which of the support services let you read about the experiences of other PageMaker users?

TEAMWORK PROJECT

Discuss with your instructor and classmates different methods for naming files that are stored on disk, such as using short filenames like *Letter1* or more descriptive filenames such as *May Vacation Report*.

CRITICAL *Thinking*

ACTIVITY 2-1

Use the Help feature to find information about PageMaker's work area. Then, use the Help feature to find information about the Colors and Styles palettes.

CREATING A PUBLICATION

OBJECTIVES

Upon completion of this lesson, you should be able to:

- Start a new publication.

- Insert and remove pages from a publication.

- Change the on-screen viewing size.

- Explain and use different tools in the toolbox.

- Use the Pointer tool to change or remove a graphic.

- Define an insertion point and use the Text tool for keying text.

- Use the Zoom and the Hand tools to examine a specific area of a page.

- Save a publication to a disk.

Estimated Time: 3.5 hours

VOCABULARY

Default

Double-sided

Facing pages

Hand tool

I-beam

Orientation

Pointer tool

Sizing handles

Story

Text block

Word wrap

Introduction

In this lesson, you will learn the basics about how to use PageMaker to create a new publication. First, you will practice specifying the size and type of the publication that you want. Then, you will be introduced to the various ways to view your work on screen, how to use PageMaker's tools to key text and perform simple drawing tasks, and how to save your newly created publication to a disk.

Starting a New Publication

P ageMaker enables you to create a new, blank publication while working on an existing one, or you can create a new publication after closing an old one. To create a new publication, click the New button on the toolbar, or choose New from the File menu to display the Document Setup dialog box shown in Figure 3-1.

FIGURE 3-1
Document Setup dialog box

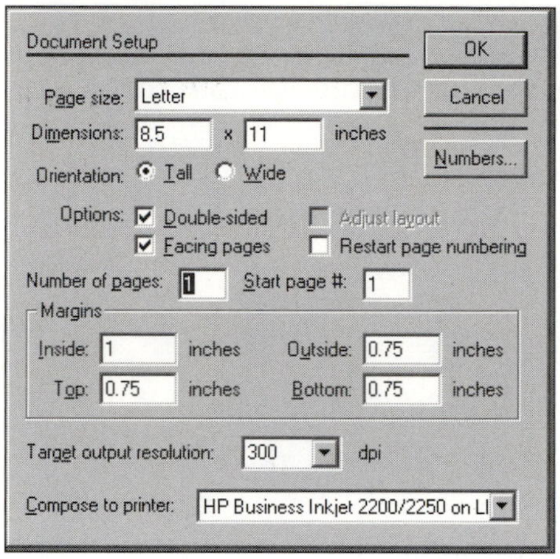

Use the Document Setup dialog box to specify various publication settings, such as the paper size, number of pages in the publication, and margin settings. Although you can change these settings after creating the publication, it's generally easier to decide on the settings beforehand because then you can see how the finished work will look as you create it.

When the dialog box first appears, PageMaker automatically sets each option to its default setting. A *default* is a standard setting that is automatically selected each time you start a new publication. For example, PageMaker assumes that you want to create a publication on letter size paper (8.5 by 11 inches). Default settings make your task of creating a publication easier because you need to change only those few settings (if any) that are different for the publication you are currently creating.

Some of the more important dialog box options include:

■ *Page size and dimensions*: These two options let you specify the size of the final printed publication. For page size, a word is used to identify different paper sizes that are available, such as letter or legal size. When you select a page size, PageMaker inserts the dimensions for that selection in the Dimensions text boxes. In Figure 3-1, notice how the dimensions of the Page size named Letter are 8.5 by 11 inches. If you are creating an unusual sized publication, such as a business card, you can also key the exact dimensions of that publication, such as 2 by 3.5 inches, in the Dimensions text boxes.

It's important to understand that the Page size and Dimensions entries represent the final size of the publication; not necessarily the size of the paper on which that publication will be printed. For example, if you were creating a business card, the dimensions might be 2 by

3.5 inches even though you might print it on an 8.5 by 11 inch piece of paper. You can use this feature to create oversized publications, such as posters, that when printed would span many letter size pages. When printing, PageMaker can adjust the printout to fit whatever paper is loaded in your printer. With small or short publications, like a single business card, the program prints your work centered on the paper. For oversized publications, it prints the work across as many pieces of paper as needed.

- *Orientation*: The **orientation** option determines whether you want your work to print upright across the tallest portion of the paper (called Tall or Portrait) or sideways along the widest portion of the paper (called Wide or Landscape). This book, for example, is printed using Portrait (Tall) orientation.

- *Double-sided*: The **double-sided** option indicates whether the final publication will have printed text on both sides of a page, like this book. When a publication is double-sided, PageMaker creates two master pages; one each for an odd- and even-numbered page. On the other hand, if a publication is single-sided where printed text will appear on only one side of the paper, PageMaker creates only one master page.

- *Facing pages*: For double-sided publications, select **facing pages** when one page will appear opposite the next page. For example, page 4 faces page 5 in this book, whereas in a single-sided business report, the pages do not usually face each other.

- *Margins*: Margins help control how close text and other elements, such as graphics, come to the edge of a page. Margin guides in the publication window show the current margin settings. In the Document Setup dialog box, the margin entries Inside, Outside, Top, and Bottom appear as the standard selections for double-sided publications, while the margin entries Left, Right, Top, and Bottom appear for single-sided publications.

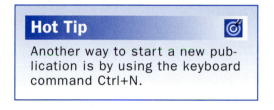

Hot Tip

Another way to start a new publication is by using the keyboard command Ctrl+N.

STEP-BY-STEP 3.1

1. Choose **New** from the **File** menu.

2. Specify that you want to create a letter size (8.5 by 11 inches) publication by keeping the Page size and Dimensions settings unchanged. Observe how the Margins section of the dialog box includes four settings labeled Inside, Top, Outside, and Bottom. These are the standard margin settings for a double-sided publication.

3. Change to a single-sided publication by deselecting the **Double-sided** option. The check mark will disappear from inside this check box. Notice how the Margins section of the dialog box now contains the four margin settings called Left, Top, Right, and Bottom.

4. Double-click in the left margin box. Change the left margin to **0.5** inches.

5. Following instructions similar to step 4, change the right, top, and bottom margin settings each to **0.5** inch and then click **OK**. Keep the new publication window open for use in the next Step-by-Step.

Inserting Pages

You can add pages at anytime while working on a publication. Adding pages is rarely a problem since any publication can contain up to 999 pages. You can choose to insert the new page or pages either before or after the current page that you are working on in the publication.

S TEP-BY-STEP 3.2

1. Choose **Insert Pages** from the **Layout** menu to display an Insert Pages dialog box like the one shown in Figure 3-2.

FIGURE 3-2
Insert Pages dialog box

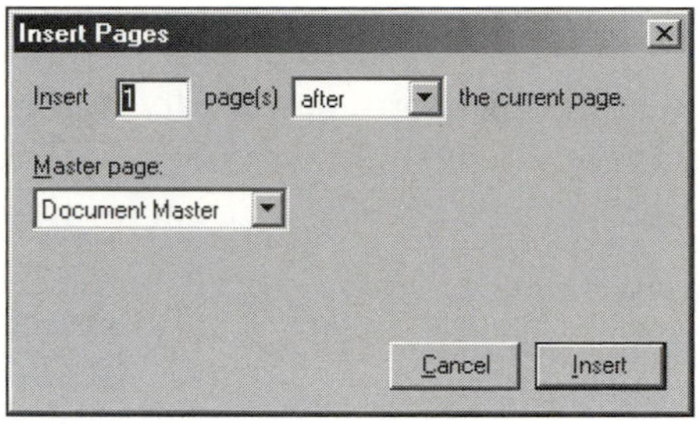

2. Notice how the default number 1 is highlighted in the Insert text box on your screen. This indicates that PageMaker is automatically ready to insert one page into the publication. Key **2** in the **Insert** text box. Make sure that **after** is selected in the current page text box.

3. Click the **Insert** button. Notice how the numbered page icons now indicate that you are looking at the second of a three page publication. Keep this publication open for use in the next Step-by-Step.

Removing Pages

As you work, you can remove pages from the publication. The Remove Pages command on the Layout menu lets you remove one page or a series of pages from the publication. Use extreme caution when removing pages, however, because you could lose work on any page that you remove by mistake.

> **Important**
>
> Use care when removing pages from a publication. Unlike many popular programs, PageMaker offers only a limited Undo command to bring back pages that you removed accidentally.

S TEP-BY-STEP 3.3

1. Choose **Remove Pages** from the **Layout** menu to display a dialog box similar to the one shown in Figure 3-3.

FIGURE 3-3
Remove Pages dialog box

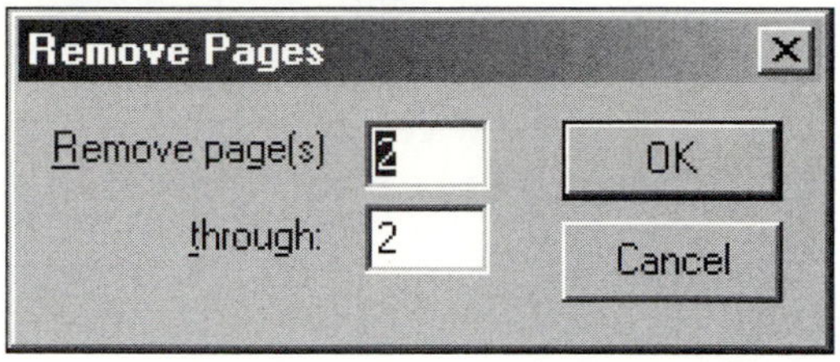

2. Key **3** in the **Remove page(s)** text box and key **3** in the **through** text box.

3. Complete the command by clicking **OK**. When a warning message appears indicating that you are about to remove the pages and their contents, click **OK**. Notice that the numbered page icons now indicate that two pages remain in the publication. Keep this publication open for use in the next Step-by-Step.

Changing the Viewing Size

When you begin a new publication, the publication window normally shows both the publication page and a portion of the pasteboard. This view is called Fit in Window or also the Actual Size. With a publication designed for printing on letter size paper, this viewing size is roughly the same as looking at an 8.5 by 11 inch piece of paper from a distance of about 10 feet. Although the Fit in Window size lets you see the overall page, anything on the page, such as text, is usually too small to read.

Besides the Fit in Window size, PageMaker offers many other sizes for viewing your work. For example, you can view your work on the screen using the Actual Size view (roughly the size it will appear when printed), or at 25%, 50%, 75%, 200%, and 400% of its actual size. You can change the viewing size by using either the menu bar or the mouse.

Change Viewing Size with the Menu Bar

You can use the View pull-down menu shown in Figure 3-4 to select from a wide range of viewing sizes. For example, you can choose Actual Size (or Fit in Window) from the View menu. You can also use the View menu to select from a number of viewing sizes. To do so, choose Zoom To from the View menu and then pick a different viewing size ranging from 25% to 400% from the submenu that appears. Choosing

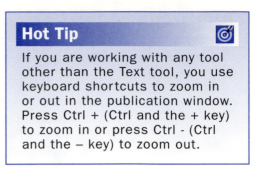

Hot Tip

If you are working with any tool other than the Text tool, you use keyboard shortcuts to zoom in or out in the publication window. Press Ctrl + (Ctrl and the + key) to zoom in or press Ctrl - (Ctrl and the – key) to zoom out.

200%, for example, displays your work at twice its actual size. You can create or edit work in any viewing size, although some entries might be difficult to see in certain viewing sizes.

FIGURE 3-4
View pull-down and Zoom To submenu

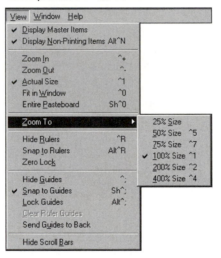

STEP-BY-STEP 3.4

1. Notice how the publication window shows the entire publication page and a portion of the pasteboard. This is the Fit in Window viewing size. Choose **Zoom To** from the **View** menu and then choose **25% Size** from the submenu. Now you are viewing the publication at 25% of its actual size.

2. Choose **Zoom To** from the **View** menu and then choose **50% Size** from the submenu.

3. Choose **Zoom To** from the **View** menu and then choose **100% Size** from the submenu.

4. Choose **Fit in Window** from the **View** menu. Keep this publication open for use in the next Step-by-Step.

Change Viewing Size with the Mouse

Besides choosing from the menus, you can also change viewing sizes by using the right mouse button. This method is usually faster than choosing from the menu bar. When you right-click within an area of the publication page or pasteboard, the Zoom menu shown in Figure 3-5 appears from which you can select a different viewing size, such as 75% Size or Fit in Window.

FIGURE 3-5
Zoom menu

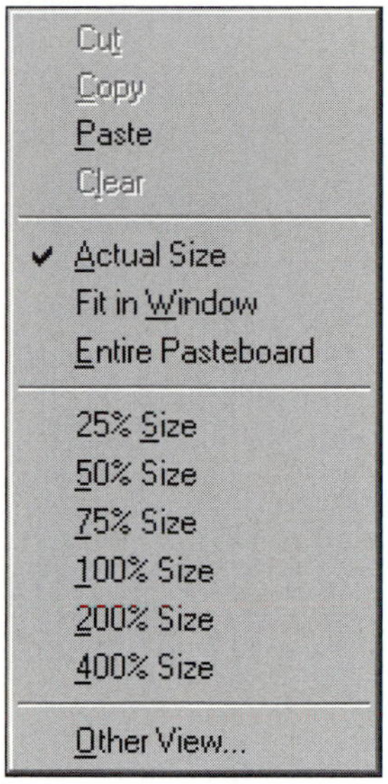

Cut
Copy
Paste
Clear
✔ Actual Size
Fit in Window
Entire Pasteboard
25% Size
50% Size
75% Size
100% Size
200% Size
400% Size
Other View...

Use the keyboard with the right-click feature to create a keyboard shortcut for changing the viewing size. To switch between the Actual Size and the Fit in Window size, hold down the Ctrl and Alt keys and click the right mouse button.

S TEP-BY-STEP 3.5

1. Notice how the publication window currently appears in the Fit in Window viewing size. Place the mouse pointer anywhere within the publication page or pasteboard and then right-click. When the menu appears, click **25% Size**.

2. Place the mouse pointer anywhere within the publication page or pasteboard and right-click. When the menu appears, click **100% Size**.

3. Now use the right mouse button to change to the **Fit in Window** size.

4. Position the mouse pointer on the screen and in the area where the top and the left margin guides intersect. Next, hold down the **Ctrl** and **Alt** keys and then click the right mouse button once.

5. Position the mouse pointer anywhere in the publication page or pasteboard. Next, hold down the **Ctrl** and **Alt** keys and then click the right mouse button once. Release all keys that you are holding down.

6. Practice using the mouse to enlarge the area of the publication page near the top and right margin guides. Then, change back to the Fit in Window size. Keep this publication open for use in the next Step-by-Step.

Working with the Toolbox

The toolbox shown in Figure 3-6 contains various tools that you can select to access different PageMaker features. For example, one of these tools lets you key text, another tool lets you draw a straight line, and a different tool allows you to move different parts of the page into view.

FIGURE 3-6
PageMaker toolbox

Just as palettes can be hidden or displayed as needed (see Lesson 2), you can also hide or display the toolbox. Hiding the toolbox is helpful for making more space available on the screen to view the publication or the pasteboard. To hide the toolbox, choose Hide Tools from the Window menu. To display a hidden toolbox, choose Show Tools from the Window menu.

To use a tool from the toolbox, first click that tool. As you click, the mouse pointer changes shape to remind you

Hot Tip

When using any tool except the Text tool, you can hide all of the currently displayed palettes and the toolbox by pressing the Tab key. Press Tab again to display them.

which tool you have selected and helps you use the tool more effectively. Table 3-1 identifies all of the tools in the toolbox, the shape of the mouse pointer, and the purpose of each tool.

TABLE 3-1
Toolbox tools and pointers

TOOL	POINTER	TOOL NAME	PURPOSE
▶	▶	Pointer	Moves, resizes, or removes text or graphics.
T	I	Text	Inserts or edits text.
↻	+	Rotate	Rotates text or graphics.
⬚	⬚	Cropping	Removes unwanted portions of a graphic.
╲	+	Line	Draws a straight line in any direction.
|–	+	Constrained-line	Draws a vertical, horizontal, or 45 degree line.
▢	+	Rectangle	Draws rectangles and squares.
◯	+	Ellipse	Draws circles and ovals.
⬡	+	Polygon	Draws polygon (six-sided) shapes.
🔍	🔍	Zoom	Enlarges or reduces an area of a page.
✋	✋	Hand	Moves a different part of a page into view.
*Other tools in the toolbox that are not covered in this course include:			
⊠	+	Framed Rectangle	Draws framed rectangles and squares.
⊗	+	Framed Ellipse	Draws framed circles or ovals.
⊘	+	Framed Polygon	Draws framed polygon shapes.

Using the Drawing Tools

As shown in Table 3-1, the toolbox includes various tools for drawing different types of objects on a page. For example, you can use the ellipse tool for drawing ovals or circles, the rectangle tool for drawing rectangles or squares, and the line tool for drawing straight lines. To draw an object, first click the appropriate tool in the toolbox. The mouse pointer will change from an arrow into a cross hair (+). Now, place the mouse pointer (the cross hair) where you want the drawing to begin. Then, hold down the mouse button and drag or move the cross hair to create the object.

Suppose you want to create a straight horizontal line running across the page from the left to the right margin guide. First, click on the constrained-line tool in the toolbox and then place the cross hair where you want the line to begin (in this example, along the left margin guide). Next, press and hold down the left mouse button and drag the cross hair to where you want the line to end (in this example, near the right margin guide). Finally, release the mouse button. To finish drawing the object, click a different tool in the toolbox, such as the pointer tool, or begin drawing another object.

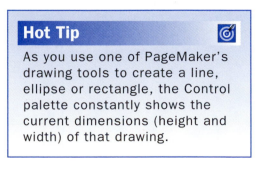

Hot Tip

As you use one of PageMaker's drawing tools to create a line, ellipse or rectangle, the Control palette constantly shows the current dimensions (height and width) of that drawing.

STEP-BY-STEP 3.6

1. Practice drawing a straight line. Don't worry too much about how the line looks. In a moment you'll learn how to change or erase a line. Click the **Constrained-line** tool in the toolbox. Move the mouse pointer onto the page and place the cross hair roughly two-thirds of the way down the page and on the left margin guide. Then, press and hold down the left mouse button, drag the cross hair straight across the page to the right margin guide and then release the mouse button. When you release the mouse, small squares will appear at both ends of the line. These squares will disappear as you begin step 2, and are explained later in this lesson.

2. Click the **Rectangle** tool in the toolbox. Place the cross hair near the intersection of the top and left margin guides in the upper-left area of the page. Next, press and hold down the left mouse button. Now, without releasing the mouse button, drag the cross hair downward and to the right at roughly a 45 degree angle. Observe how a rectangle starts to appear as you move the cross hair. When the rectangle is roughly one-quarter the size of the page, release the mouse button.

3. Click the **Ellipse** tool in the toolbox. Place the cross hair near the intersection of the top and right margin guides. Then press and hold down the left mouse button, and slowly drag the cross hair downward and to the left at roughly a 45 degree angle until the oval fills approximately one-quarter of the page. Finally, release the mouse button.

4. Click the **Pointer** tool in the toolbox to complete the oval and remove the handles that surround it. Keep this publication open for use in the next Step-by-Step.

Using the Pointer Tool with Graphics

Y ou can use the *Pointer tool* to move, resize, or remove a graphic. To use this feature, first click it in the toolbox. Next, select the graphic object that you want to change by clicking anywhere along the edge of the object. As illustrated in Figure 3-7 and introduced in Step-by-Step 3.6, when you select an object, small squares called *sizing handles* (or handles) appear around the object. If you select a line, for example, handles appear at the beginning and end of the line. For all other objects, such as a rectangle or an oval, eight handles appear around the edges of the object. (*NOTE: These are similar to the handles that appear immediately after you draw an object.*)

FIGURE 3-7
A selected line (top) and rectangle (bottom)

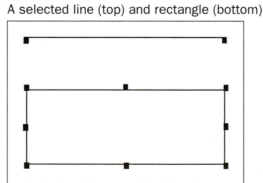

Resize a Graphic

To change the size of a selected graphic, place the mouse pointer on a handle and then drag the handle in the direction you want the size to change. By dragging the center handle at the top or bottom, you can change the height. By dragging the center handle on one of the sides, you can change the width. Or, if you drag a corner handle, you can change both the height and width. When you finish dragging a handle, release the mouse button and then click once anywhere away from the graphic object to deselect it and to hide its handles.

S TEP-BY-STEP 3.7

1. Click the **Pointer** tool in the toolbox.

2. Click anywhere along the edge of the oval. Eight handles will appear around the oval when it is selected.

3. Place the mouse pointer on the upper-left corner handle. Press and hold down the mouse button. A two-headed arrow will appear if the mouse pointer is positioned properly.

4. While still holding down the mouse button, drag the mouse pointer downward and to the right on roughly a 45-degree angle. When the oval is approximately one-half of its original size, release the mouse button.

5. Click in any blank area of the page to deselect the oval. Keep this publication on-screen for use in the next Step-by-Step exercise.

Move or Erase a Graphic

To move a selected graphic somewhere else on the page, place the mouse pointer anywhere along the edge of the graphic. Do not place the pointer on a handle. Then, drag the graphic object to its new location on the page. Finally, click once anywhere away from the graphic object to deselect it and to remove its handles. To remove a selected graphic object from a page, press the Delete key.

S TEP-BY-STEP 3.8

1. While still using the Pointer tool, click once anywhere along the edge of the rectangle.

2. Place the mouse pointer along the edge of the rectangle but away from any handles. Then press, and while holding down the mouse button, drag the rectangle to any other location on the page. Finally, release the mouse button.

3. Deselect the rectangle by clicking in any blank area of the page.

4. Using instructions you already know, select the oval. Press the **Delete** key. Finally, close this publication without saving it.

Using the Text Tool

The Text tool is used for keying or editing short text entries in a publication. PageMaker offers another feature called the story editor for working with long text entries. We will cover this topic in a later lesson.

To key or edit text, click the Text tool. The mouse pointer will change into a large capital letter I called the *I-beam*. Place the I-beam on the page where you want the text to appear (or within the text you want to edit), and then click. A thin blinking vertical bar (I) called the insertion point will appear and indicates where PageMaker is ready to insert your typing. Now, key as you normally would. If you make a mistake, you can erase a character easily by pressing the Backspace (or Delete) key to erase the character to the left (or right) of the insertion point.

Any text on a publication page appears within a rectangular-shaped area called a *text block*. A page can contain one or more text blocks. While using the text tool, you create a text block whenever you click in a blank area on a page (or pasteboard) and then begin keying. All the text blocks that make up a separate unit in a publication, such as a single article in a newspaper publication, are called a *story*. A story can consist of one or more text blocks.

While keying text, it's easy to insert and delete text and to move the insertion point for making corrections.

Keying Text

As you key in PageMaker, the text appears on-screen and the insertion point moves to the right and is always in front of the text you are currently keying. Most basic techniques used for keying or editing in PageMaker are similar to those used in a word processing program. To key an uppercase letter or special character, for example, hold down the Shift key and then key the character. Press the Space bar to insert space between words, or press the Tab key to indent a line, such as at the beginning of a paragraph. To insert a missing character, or to add additional text to information you've already keyed, simply position the insertion point where you want to insert the text and begin keying.

If a word overlaps the right margin or right edge of the text block, PageMaker moves the insertion point to the next line as you key. This feature is called *word wrap*, and it eliminates the need to press Enter at the end of each line. Normally, you press Enter only to end a paragraph or occasionally to insert a blank line.

Moving Text

While working with the text tool, remember that the I-beam (mouse pointer) looks like the capital letter I and the insertion point looks like a vertical bar. Figure 3-8 shows the I-beam positioned between the words *Here are* and the insertion point positioned just after the word *facts*.

FIGURE 3-8
The I-beam and insertion point

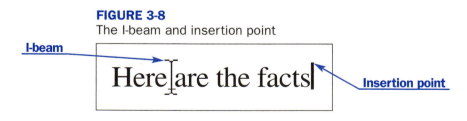

You can move the insertion point in a text block by using either the mouse or the keyboard. To use the mouse, place the mouse pointer where you want the insertion point located and then click. To move the insertion point using the keyboard, press the ↑ or ↓ key to move up or down one line, or press the ← or → key to move left or right one character at a time. When moving the insertion point, it's important to note that it will only move in the area of the text block that already contains text.

STEP-BY-STEP 3.9

1. Choose **New** from the **File** menu.

2. In the Document Setup dialog box, specify a single-sided publication by deselecting the **Double-sided** option. Then, using instructions you already know, change both the left and right margins to **2** inches. Finally, click **OK**.

3. Enlarge the area around the top and left margin guides to the actual viewing size.

4. Click the **Text** tool in the toolbox. Place the I-beam slightly below the top margin guide and just | T | to the right of the left margin guide (see Figure 3-9 for the correct position) and then click.

FIGURE 3-9
Correct position of I-beam before clicking

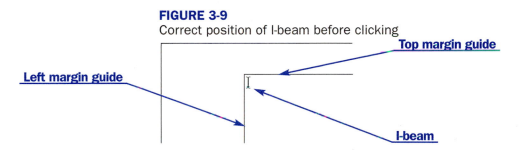

5. Key **NOTICE TO ALL EMPLOYEES** and then press **Enter** twice.

6. Key the following paragraph exactly as it is, including the errors within the first four words. Press **Enter** only when you've finished keying the entire paragraph.

There wil be aa meeting for all hourly employees at 10:30 AM on Wednesday, May 19th. The purpose of this meeting will be to discuss the new vacation policy that takes effect in June. Please plan to attend this meeting.

STEP-BY-STEP 3.9 Continued

7. Now correct the errors. Using the arrow keys on the keyboard, position the insertion point just to the right of the letter **I** in **wil**. Now, change **wil** to **will** by keying **I**. Next press the → key until the insertion point is located between the letters **aa**, and press **Delete**. Finally, move the insertion point just to the left of the first **e** in the word **employees**, key **hourly**, and press the **spacebar** once. Keep this publication open for use in the next Step-by-Step.

Moving the Insertion Point

While working with the text tool, you can move the insertion point using keyboard commands. These keyboard commands are often faster than using the mouse if your hands are already on the keyboard. Table 3-2 lists the different keyboard commands for moving the insertion point both short and long distances.

TABLE 3-2
Moving the insertion point with keyboard commands

TO MOVE THE INSERTION POINT:	PRESS THIS/THESE:
Left or right one character	← or →
Left one word	Ctrl + ←
Right one word	Ctrl + →
Up or down one line	↑ or ↓
To the beginning of the line	Home
To the end of the line	End
To the beginning of current/previous paragraph	Ctrl + ↑
To the beginning of the next paragraph	Ctrl + ↓
To the beginning of previous sentence	Ctrl + Home
To the beginning of next sentence	Ctrl + End

STEP-BY-STEP 3.10

1. Press the down arrow until the insertion point is at the beginning of the first paragraph that begins with the words *There will be.*

2. Move the insertion point right three words by pressing **Ctrl+→** three times.

3. Move the insertion point left three characters by pressing ← three times.

STEP-BY-STEP 3.10 Continued

4. Move the insertion point to the end of the paragraph by pressing **Ctrl+↓**.

5. Move the insertion point to the beginning of the text block by pressing **Ctrl+↑** twice. Keep this publication open for use in the next Step-by-Step.

Selecting Text with the Mouse

Selecting text means to identify certain text that you want to change, such as several words or sentences. You can select text using either the mouse or the keyboard. As shown in Figure 3-10, selected text appears highlighted on the screen, and any commands that you issue apply only to the highlighted text.

FIGURE 3-10
Selected text highlighted

While using the Text tool, place the mouse pointer just to the left of the first character you want to select. Next press, and while holding down the left mouse button, move the pointer past the last character you want to select, and then release the mouse button. If you select the wrong text, just start again. To deselect text and remove the highlighting, press any arrow key or click anywhere on the page.

To select a word or paragraph, double- or triple-click anywhere on that word or in the paragraph. To select all the text in the text block, choose Select All from the Edit menu. Selecting text is a valuable editing tool. For example, if you want to delete a paragraph, triple-click in the paragraph to select the entire paragraph and then press Delete. You can replace selected text with different text by simply keying the new text. For example, if you select a sentence and then begin keying, the new text will replace the old sentence.

STEP-BY-STEP 3.11

1. Select the words **will be** by first placing the mouse pointer just to the left of the letter **w** in the word **will**. While holding down the mouse button, drag the mouse pointer to the right just past the **e** in the word **be**. Finally, release the mouse button.

2. Click anywhere in the text to deselect it.

STEP-BY-STEP 3.11 Continued

3. Select the word **meeting** by double-clicking anywhere on the word.

4. Deselect the text.

5. Select and replace the word **Wednesday** with the word **Tuesday**.

6. Practice selecting an entire paragraph by triple-clicking anywhere in the paragraph. Now deselect the text by clicking anywhere in the text. Keep this publication on-screen for use in the next Step-by-Step exercise.

Selecting Text with the Keyboard

While using the Text tool, you can use the keyboard commands listed in Table 3-3 to select text. If your hands are already on the keyboard, these commands are usually faster because they eliminate moving your hands from the keyboard to the mouse and then back again.

TABLE 3-3
Selecting text with keyboard commands

TO SELECT THIS:	PRESS THIS/THESE
The character to the left	Shift + ←
The character to the right	Shift + →
To the start of the word	Ctr + Shift + ←
To the end of the word	Ctrl + Shift + →
To start of the paragraph	Ctrl + Shift + ↑
To end of the paragraph	Ctrl + Shift + ↓
To the start of the text	Ctrl + Shift + Page Up
To the end of the text	Ctrl + Shift + Page Down

You can use these commands repeatedly to select additional text, such as two words or several paragraphs in a row. To deselect text, if needed, press any arrow key on the keyboard or click anywhere in the text.

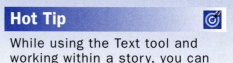

Hot Tip

While using the Text tool and working within a story, you can select all of the text by pressing Ctrl+A.

STEP-BY-STEP 3.12

1. Using the keyboard, move the insertion point just to the left of the letter **w** in the word **will**. Next, hold down the **Ctrl** and **Shift** keys and then press →. Finally, release all the keys.

2. Deselect the text by pressing any of the four arrow keys.

3. In the first sentence, select and replace the word **employees** with the word **staff**. Using the keyboard, move the insertion point to the left of the first **e** in **employees**. Next, press **Ctrl+Shift+→**. Then release all the keys. Finally, key **staff** and then press the **spacebar**. Keep this publication open for use in the next Step-by-Step.

Using the Zoom Tool

Another easy way to change the viewing size (and also control what part of the page you bring into view) is to use the Zoom tool in the toolbox. The zoom tool lets you quickly enlarge (or reduce) the area of the page or pasteboard that you see on the screen.

To magnify or enlarge an area, click the Zoom tool. (Refer to Table 3-1 if you need to remind yourself what this tool looks like.) The mouse pointer will change to a magnifying glass-shaped zoom pointer that contains a plus sign. Next, position the pointer over the area of the page that you want to enlarge and then click. If you click repeatedly, the area around the pointer becomes even larger with each click. When you have reached the maximum viewing size, the plus sign disappears from inside the pointer.

You can also use the zoom pointer to see more of the page or pasteboard. While using the Zoom tool, press and hold down the Ctrl key. A minus sign will appear inside the zoom pointer. Now, while continuing to hold down the Ctrl key, click to expand your view of the page or pasteboard. If you click repeatedly, the viewing area will continue to expand with each click. To turn off the Zoom tool, select any other tool from the toolbox, such as the Pointer tool.

STEP-BY-STEP 3.13

1. Click the **Zoom** tool in the toolbox.

2. Place the zoom pointer over any text in the on-screen publication.

3. Magnify (enlarge) the area around the text by clicking the mouse button. Magnify the area even further by clicking again.

4. Place the zoom pointer anywhere in the text. Hold down the **Ctrl** key then click the mouse button twice to view more of the page. Then release the **Ctrl** key.

5. Keep this publication open for use in the next Step-by-Step.

Using the Hand Tool

One of the easiest ways to move a different part of a page into view is by using the Hand tool. The Hand tool is also known as the grabber hand. With the *Hand tool* you can electronically grab hold of a page or pasteboard and then move it on-screen in any direction.

To use this feature, click on the hand tool in the toolbox to reveal the hand pointer. Next, position the hand pointer anywhere on the on-screen page. Placing the pointer in the center of the screen often works best. Then press, and while holding down the mouse button, drag the pointer. As you do, PageMaker will move the page electronically in the same direction. When you finish, release the mouse button. To turn off the hand tool, select any other tool from the toolbox, such as the pointer tool.

S TEP-BY-STEP 3.14

1. Click the **Hand** tool in the toolbox.

2. Place the hand pointer that appears in the center of the screen.

3. Press, and while holding down the mouse button, drag the hand pointer upward and to the left about 1 inch. Then release the mouse button. Notice how the page has moved on the screen.

4. Place the hand pointer in the center of the screen.

5. Press, and while holding down the mouse button, drag the hand pointer downward and to the right several inches. Then, release the mouse button.

6. Click the **Pointer** tool in the toolbox to turn off the hand tool. Keep this publication open for use in the next Step-by-Step.

Saving a Publication

While you create or edit a publication, your work is stored in the computer's memory. If you turn the computer off or if the power fails, your work could be lost. Saving your work on a computer disk keeps it safe and available for future use.

To save a new publication, click the Save button on the toolbar or choose Save from the File menu to display the Save Publication dialog box shown in Figure 3-11.

FIGURE 3-11
The Save Publication dialog box

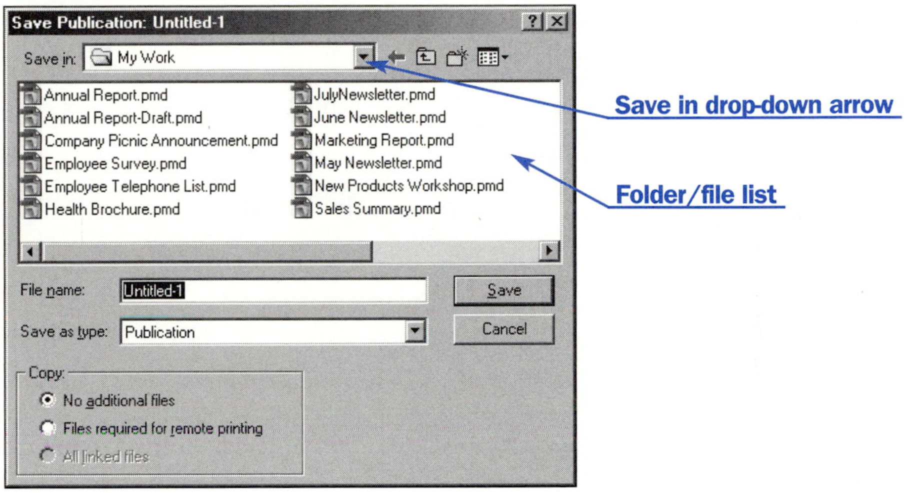

Use the File name text box to key a name for the new publication. A filename should be descriptive enough, such as Spring Newsletter or Annual Report, so that you can use the filename to easily identify the publication later on. When saving a new publication, PageMaker suggests a filename such as Untitled-1. To change that suggested name, simply key a different filename. Filenames can contain letters, numbers, spaces, and most special characters except for the * ? / \ " < > | ; : symbols.

After keying the filename, use the Save in as type down arrow and/or Folder/File list to select the disk drive and/or the folder where you want the publication saved.

As you continue working with a publication that you have already saved on disk, it's a good idea to save the publication regularly. A good rule of thumb is to save your work every 10 to 20 minutes. This way if there is a computer problem or power loss, you will lose only a few minutes of work. In the next lesson you will learn about the Save as command for saving publications more efficiently.

STEP-BY-STEP 3.15

1. Choose **Save** from the **File** menu.

2. Key **Employee Notice** in the File name text box.

STEP-BY-STEP 3.15 Continued

3. Choose the disk drive and folder in which you want to save the file. (Your instructor will provide further information on where the files from this course are to be stored.) Click **Save**.

4. Close the publication.

SUMMARY

In this lesson you learned how to:

- Begin a new publication using the Document Setup dialog box.

- Define publication setup terms such as orientation, single- and double-sided.

- Change the viewing size of the publication window.

- Use the Text, Pointer, Zoom, and other basic drawing tools in the toolbox.

- Insert and remove pages in a publication.

- Key and edit text and describe basic PageMaker text terms, such as text block, story, word wrap, and I-beam.

- Explain various mouse commands such as dragging and right-clicking.

- Save a publication to a disk.

VOCABULARY *Review*

Define the following terms:		
Default	I-beam	Story
Double-sided	Orientation	Text block
Facing pages	Pointer tool	Word wrap
Hand tool	Sizing handles	

REVIEW *Questions*

MATCHING

Match the lettered items in Figure 3-12 to the numbered statements listed below.

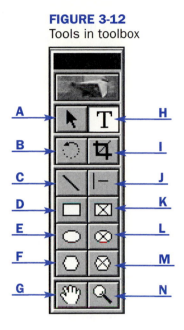

FIGURE 3-12
Tools in toolbox

___ 1. This tool is used for keying text.

___ 2. This tool is used for drawing constrained-lines.

___ 3. This tool is used for drawing an oval or circle.

___ 4. This tool is used to move a different part of a page into view.

___ 5. This tool is used when moving or resizing a graphic.

TRUE/FALSE

Circle T if the statement is true or F if the statement is false.

T   F   **1.** Two sizing handles appear around a circle when it is selected.

T   F   **2.** The term drag means to move something on-screen.

T   F   **3.** You can insert only one page at a time in a publication.

T   F   **4.** While using the text tool, a thin, blinking vertical bar (|) called the insertion point indicates where PageMaker will insert your text.

T   F   **5.** If you select text and then key, the new text you key appears in the place of the selected text.

FILL IN THE BLANK

Complete the following sentences by writing the correct word or words in the blanks provided.

1. The Document Setup dialog box option that lets you choose either Tall or Wide for your publication is called _____.

2. The term _____ is a standard setting that is automatically selected each time you start a new publication.

3. The term _____ means to identify a graphic or text that you want to change.

4. To remove a graphic from a publication, select the graphic and then press _____.

5. When you begin a new publication, PageMaker displays the full page of the publication and a portion of the pasteboard. This is called the _____ Size.

PROJECTS

SCANS **PROJECT 3-1**

You have been hired as a consultant with Caribbean Sun Travel Tours. In this project you are to create a 2-by-3.5-inch business card. When finished, your on-screen publication should look similar to the sample shown in Figure 3-13.

FIGURE 3-13
Caribbean Sun Travel Tours business card

Rick Braveheart

CARIBBEAN SUN TRAVEL TOURS

6600 Duval Street
Key West, FL 32358
(303) 555-1234

1.   Start a new PageMaker publication. When the Document Setup dialog box appears:
     A. Select **Wide** orientation.
     B. Specify a **3.5** inch width and a **2** inch height.
     C. Make this a **single-sided** publication.
     D. Change the top, bottom, left, and right margin settings each to **0.25** inches.
     E. Click **OK**.

2.   Now begin keying the text entries for the publication.
     A. Click the **Text** tool in the toolbox. Then, place the I-beam slightly below the top margin
         guide and just to the right of the left margin guide, and click.
     B. Change the view to **Actual Size**.
     C. Key your first and last name, and then press **Enter** twice.
     D. In all uppercase characters, key **CARIBBEAN SUN TRAVEL TOURS** and then press
         Enter twice.
     E. Key **6600 Duval Street** and press **Enter**.
     F. Key **Key West, FL 32358** and press **Enter**.
     G. Key (303) 555-1234.

3.   Using the **Constrained-line** tool in the toolbox, draw a thin line beneath the words
     CARIBBEAN SUN TRAVEL TOURS. Before you begin, examine the location and length
     of the line in Figure 3-13 so you know how long to draw your line.

4.   Using the **Rectangle** tool in the toolbox, draw a thin rectangle down the right side of the
     business card similar to the one shown in Figure 3-13.

5.   Save the publication with the name **Business Card** to the folder or disk indicated by your
     instructor. Then, close the publication.

PROJECT 3-2

1.   Open the PageMaker publication named **Business Card**.

2.   Use the **View** menu to view the publication at **25% Size**. Now view the publication at
     100% Size and then at **200% Size**.

3.   Use the Zoom tool to enlarge the page further. Click the **Zoom** tool in the toolbox, then
     place the zoom pointer near the word **Caribbean** and click.

4.   Use the **Hand** tool to practice moving the page left and right about 1 inch on the screen.

5.   Change to the **Actual Size** view by right-clicking with the mouse.

6.   Change to the **Entire Pasteboard** view by right-clicking with the mouse.

7.   Place the mouse pointer somewhere near the center of the business card publication on your screen. While holding down the **Ctrl** key, click the right mouse button to change to the **Actual View** size.

8.   Choose **Close** from the **File** menu, and then click **No** when asked if you want to save the publication before closing.

PROJECT 3-3

In this project you will create a 5-by-7-inch notice announcing an upcoming event at Caribbean Sun Travel Tours. When you finish, your publication should look similar to the sample solution shown in Figure 3-14.

FIGURE 3-14
Vision Testing publication

NATIONAL VISION WEEK

Free Exams October 15-21

Have your eyes examined free of charge at Caribbean Sun Travel Tours office during National Vision Testing Week. Eye doctors will be available daily between 1PM and 5PM. just stop in for your free exam or telephone us for an appointment.

To schedule an appointment or request more information, call julie at (303) 555-1200

Caribbean Sun Travel Tours
6600 Duval Street
Key West, FL 32358

1.   Start a new PageMaker publication. When the Document Setup dialog box appears:
   A.   Select **Tall** orientation.
   B.   Specify a 5 inch width and a 7 inch height.
   C.   Make this a single-sided publication by deselecting the **Double-sided** check box.
   D.   Change the top, bottom, left, and right margin settings each to **1** inch.
   E.   Click **OK**.

2.   Click the **Text** tool in the toolbox. Then, place the I-beam slightly below the top margin guide and just to the right of the left margin guide, and click. Next, key **NATIONAL VISION WEEK** and press **Enter** twice. Finally, key **Free Exams October 15-21**.

3. Press **Enter** twice and then key the following paragraph:

   Have your eyes examined free of charge at Caribbean Sun Travel Tours office during National Vision Testing Week. Eye doctors will be available daily between 1PM and 5PM. Just stop in for your free exam or telephone us for an appointment.

4. Press **Enter** twice and key the following sentence:

   To schedule an appointment or request more information, call Julie at (303) 555-1200.

5. Press **Enter** four times. Next, key the following three lines, pressing **Enter** at the end of each line:

   Caribbean Sun Travel Tours
   6600 Duval Street
   Key West, FL 32358

6. Click the **Rectangle** tool in the toolbox. Draw a rectangle within the margin area of the page. Create the rectangle so it is about 0.5 to 1 inch away from each of the margin guides. Before you begin, examine the location and size of the rectangle in the sample solution shown in Figure 3-14.

7. Save the publication with the name **Vision Testing** to the disk drive and folder or disk indicated by your instructor. Close the publication.

 TEAMWORK PROJECT

As you work with most publications, you frequently need to change the viewing size to see more or less of the on-screen page in the publication window. Discuss with your instructor and your classmates the different ways for changing the viewing size. Then, think about and discuss some of the different situations in which one method would be better or easier to use than other methods.

CRITICAL*Thinking*

ACTIVITY 3-1

Examine a monthly issue of a national magazine. Now imagine that you are creating the publication in PageMaker. See if you can identify two or three places in that magazine where you would use PageMaker's drawing tools, such as the constrained-line or rectangle tool. Write a 50-word summary describing where and how the drawing tools would liven up the magazine.

WORKING EFFECTIVELY

Introduction

If you will be using PageMaker often, knowing how to use it effectively will increase your satisfaction with the program and help you produce publications more easily. In this lesson, you will learn how to undo commands that you issued accidentally and also create different versions of a publication. You will also see how to display and work with an on-screen ruler, how to use ruler guides to help align your work, and how to print all or part of a publication.

Undoing and Redoing an Action

As you edit a publication, PageMaker remembers most of the actions you perform and lets you undo or reverse many of those actions, such as adding or deleting text. For example, if you accidentally delete a paragraph, you can restore it. Besides undoing editing actions, you can also undo the effect caused by many (but not all) of the commands covered in later lessons, such as moving text.

To undo the last action you performed, click on Edit in the menu bar and then choose Undo. A word will follow the Undo command, which identifies the type of action that will be undone. You will notice that the word that appears after Undo changes with different types of actions that you have performed. For example, if you delete a paragraph, Undo Edit will appear as the first choice in the Edit pull-down menu. In this case, choosing that entry will restore and highlight the last deleted paragraph. To complete the Undo action, press any arrow key on the keyboard or click once anywhere in the publication to remove the highlighting.

Unlike some popular programs, PageMaker's Undo command will undo only the last action you performed. You need to issue the Undo command before performing any other action because Undo reverses only your most recent action. For example, if you delete a paragraph and then move the insertion point or click elsewhere in the publication, you will no longer be able to restore the deleted paragraph.

You can also use a Redo command to reverse the effect of an Undo command. For example, if you delete a sentence and then use Undo to restore the sentence, you can use the Redo command to remove it again. To reverse the effect of your last Undo command, click Edit on the menu bar, then click Redo. As with Undo, the word that appears after Redo identifies the type of action that you will do over.

STEP-BY-STEP 4.1

1. Open the publication named **Cayman** from the data files and make sure that page 1 of the publication is on-screen.

2. Enlarge the area around the subtitle **Do they really** to the Actual Size.

3. Click the **Text** tool in the toolbox.

4. Select the word **they** in the subtitle by double-clicking anywhere on that word.

5. Key **the Cayman's** and then press the spacebar once to replace the selected word.

6. Undo your recent editing change by choosing **Undo Edit** from the **Edit** menu.

7. Notice how the original word *they* reappears and is highlighted. Click once anywhere in the publication to remove the highlighting.

8. Select the words **We think so** in the subtitle and then press **Delete** to erase the words.

9. Click once anywhere else in the publication to simulate performing another action within the publication. Then, click **Edit** on the menu bar. Notice how the Undo Edit command is no longer available to restore the words you just deleted. Keep this publication on-screen for use in the next Step-by-Step.

Reverting to a Previously Saved Publication

Besides undoing your last action, PageMaker lets you restore your publication to the way it was before you began your current editing session. For example, suppose you open an existing publication and make various editing changes to it. To abandon or delete the changes you just made and change the publication back to the way it was previously, choose Revert from the File menu. An alert box like the one shown in Figure 4-1 appears. An *alert box* is a small dialog box containing a brief question and two or three buttons containing possible responses. Click OK to remove all of your current editing changes or click Cancel to cancel the command.

FIGURE 4-1
Revert alert box

You can also restore a publication to the last time it was mini-saved. As you work, PageMaker automatically saves your work each time you insert or remove pages, click on a page number icon, change the document setup, or print. This process is called *mini-save*. To restore the publication to its last mini-saved version, hold down the Shift key and then choose Revert from the File menu. An alert box containing the message Revert to last mini-save? appears. Click OK to revert to the last mini-saved version or click Cancel to cancel the command.

STEP-BY-STEP 4.2

1. Choose **Revert** from the **File** menu.

2. When the alert box containing the message **Revert to last-saved version?** appears, choose **OK** and then observe how the prior version of the publication reappears. Keep this publication open for use in the next Step-by-Step.

Using the Save As Command

Although it is extremely important to save your work regularly, the Save command can cause your publication to consume large amounts of space on disk. This is because PageMaker saves not only the publication but also all the mini-save information about each action that you perform (for use by the Undo and Revert commands). For example, if you replace a paragraph with a different paragraph, the program remembers both the old and new paragraphs. Even if you open a publication and replace all of its text with a single word, the size of the publication on disk would be even larger than when you first opened the publication.

Instead of always using the Save command to save your editing changes, you can use the Save As command to save your work on disk. Save As allows your work to be saved in the smallest size possible, thus reducing the amount of space it requires on disk. Each time you issue the Save As command, PageMaker stores only the current on-screen version of your publication and not the mini-save information. Although you can no longer use the Revert command to restore the publication to a previous version, the Save As command can reduce the size of the publication on disk by as much as 60 percent.

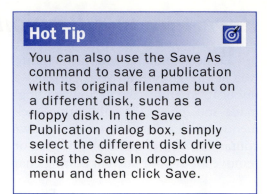

Hot Tip

You can also use the Save As command to save a publication with its original filename but on a different disk, such as a floppy disk. In the Save Publication dialog box, simply select the different disk drive using the Save In drop-down menu and then click Save.

You can also use the Save As command to save a copy of the on-screen publication with a different filename. This feature keeps the original publication on disk, while also creating another version of it with a different publication name. You can then open and edit either version. Using the Save As command to create a copy of a publication is very useful for trying out different design or layout ideas, without affecting the original publication.

To issue the Save As command, choose Save As from the File menu. A dialog box similar to the one used when saving a publication appears. If you are simply using the Save As command to reduce the size of the publication, click Save. If you are using the Save As command to create a copy of the publication, key a different publication name in the File name text box and then click Save. Next, an alert box like the one in Figure 4-2 appears. Click Yes to save the publication and remove all mini-save information, or click No to cancel the request.

FIGURE 4-2
Save Publication alert box

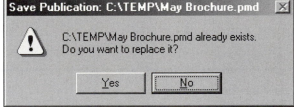

STEP-BY-STEP 4.3

1. Save the Cayman publication in the smallest size possible. Start by choosing **Save As** from the **File** menu.

2. When the Save dialog box appears, click **Save**.

3. When the Save Publication alert box appears, click **Yes**. Keep this publication open for use in the next Step-by-Step.

Printing a Publication

At any time, you can print all or part of the on-screen publication. Click the Print button on the toolbar, or choose Print from the File menu to reveal a Print Document dialog box like the one in Figure 4-3. Next, choose from any print options needed, and then click Print to start the printing. The various print options are discussed below.

FIGURE 4-3
Print Document dialog box

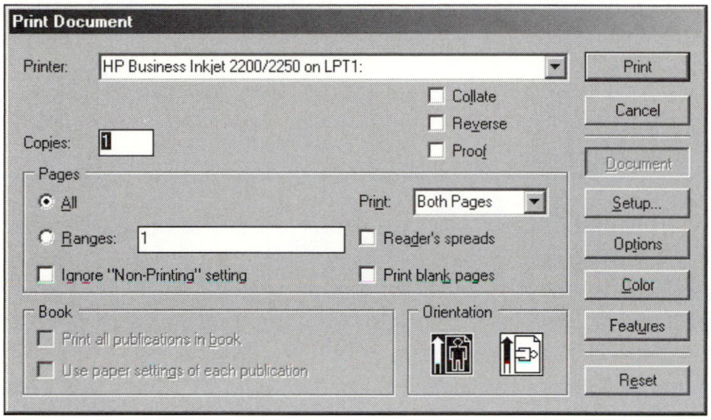

Select a Different Printer

The Printer text box shows the name of the printer to which PageMaker is ready to print your work. This option is available because some computers today are connected to several printers, such as a desktop printer connected directly to the computer and another connected to a network. Another reason is that certain publications are created on one computer but printed at a different location, such as at a local print shop or a commercial printing company. Each time you get ready to print, you will need to make sure the printer that is currently selected is the printer to which you want to print your work.

Specify the Pages to Print

The Pages section of the dialog box lets you specify those pages of the publication you want to print. To print the entire publication, make certain the All option (the default) is selected. To print only certain pages, such as pages 3 through 6, double-click inside the Ranges text box and key the page number to print. You can designate a range of pages, or specify individual pages you want to print. Use a hyphen to separate a range of pages, such as 3-7. Use a comma to separate individual pages, such as 2,6,8. You can also combine these methods. For example, keying 2,4-6 would print pages 2, 4, 5, and 6.

> **Hot Tip**
>
> Save a tree! An estimated 120 million trees are cut down annually to produce paper that is used in computer printers. Save these valuable resources (and your own time) by previewing and editing your work on the screen instead of printing draft copies.

Print Options

You can select from other print options, such as printing multiple copies, collating pages, and reversing the printing order. To print more than one copy of each page, key the number of copies needed in the Copies text box. If you are printing several copies of a multi-page publication, and want each copy printed in page number order, select Collate. For example, if you print two copies of a three-page publication using the Collate option, PageMaker will print pages 1, 2, and 3 for the first copy, and then pages 1, 2, and 3 for the second copy.

You can use the Reverse option to change the order in which pages are printed. Normally, the program prints the pages in numerical order, such as pages 1, 2, and 3. Select Reverse if you want the pages printed in the opposite order, such as pages 3, 2, and 1.

STEP-BY-STEP 4.4

1. Choose **Print** from the **File** menu.

2. If the printer you want to use does not appear in the Printer text box, select the correct printer from the Printer drop-down list. (Ask your instructor for more information if necessary.)

3. Double-click inside the **Ranges** text box and key **1** to print the first page only.

4. Click **Print** to print the page. Keep this publication open for use in the next Step-by-Step.

Working with Rulers

PageMaker's on-screen rulers are valuable tools that can save time and also make your work easier. As shown in Figure 4-4, PageMaker can display both a vertical and a horizontal ruler in the publication window. If the rulers aren't visible, choose Show Rulers from the View menu. To hide the rulers, choose Hide Rulers from the View menu. These rulers make it easy to position text or graphics or to measure the location of something on a page.

FIGURE 4-4
Horizontal and vertical rulers

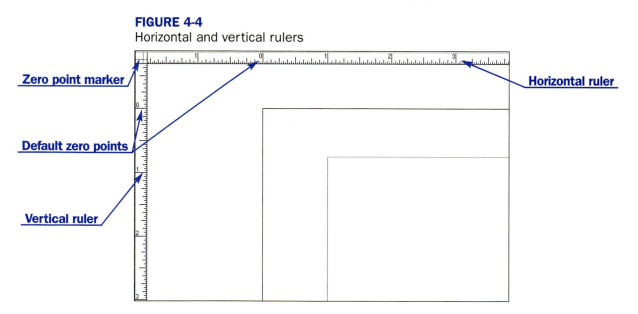

The *zero point* is the position on a ruler where the measurements begin. On a single-sided publication, the zero point will appear at the point where the top and left edges of the on-screen page intersect. Figure 4-4 shows the zero point on a single-sided publication. For a double-sided publication, the zero point will fall between the left- and right-hand pages.

> **Hot Tip**
>
> You can also use a keyboard command to hide or display the rulers. Press *Ctrl+R* (hold down the Ctrl key and press R) to hide the rulers; press *Ctrl+R* again to display the rulers.

To offer you even more flexibility, you can move the zero point. For example, you can move the zero point to the intersection of the top and left margin guides as shown in Figure 4-5. You can then use the rulers to measure distances from those margin guides instead of from the edge of the page. By moving the zero point you can use the rulers to measure size, such as the width of a column of text or the size of a graphic.

FIGURE 4-5
Zero points aligned with margin guides

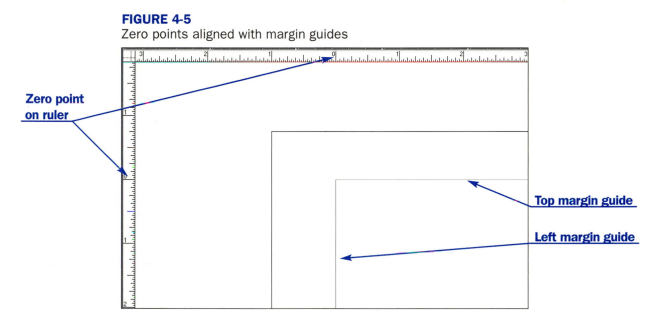

Zero point on ruler

Top margin guide

Left margin guide

To move the zero point, place the mouse pointer inside the zero point marker. This marker is the small box located at the intersection of both rulers (refer to Figure 4-4). Next, drag the pointer to the place where you want the zero point located, such as at the intersection of the top and left margin guides.

To protect against moving the zero point by accident, you can lock it. To lock the zero point, choose Zero Lock from the View menu. A checkmark will appear in front of that option when the zero point is locked. You can perform the same instruction again to unlock the zero point.

STEP-BY-STEP 4.5

1. If the rulers are not displayed on the screen, display them by choosing **Show Rulers** from the **View** menu.

2. Observe how the zero point on the horizontal and vertical rulers falls at the intersection of the top and left edges of the page. Place the mouse pointer inside the zero point marker. (If necessary, refer to Figure 4-4 for its location.)

3. While holding down the mouse button, drag the pointer to the intersection of the top and left margin guides. Then release the mouse button. (*NOTE: If the zero point does not move, choose **Zero Lock** from the **View** menu. Then perform step 3 again.*)

4. Observe how the zero point on each ruler is now aligned with the top and left margin guides. Keep this publication open for use in the next Step-by-Step.

Working with Ruler Guides

R*uler guides* are lightly shaded horizontal or vertical lines that you can place anywhere in a publication page. Because you can add as many as 120 ruler guides to a publication, these guides make it easy to position or align text or graphics on any or on all pages in a publication. Ruler guides, like margin guides, do not print when you print a publication. Ruler guides only appear on-screen within the publication page, and not in the pasteboard.

To create a ruler guide on just one page, turn first to that page in the publication. Next, click on the Pointer tool in the toolbox. Then, place the mouse pointer inside the horizontal (or vertical) ruler, and press and hold down the mouse button until a two-headed pointer appears. Now, drag the pointer to the place on the page where you want the ruler guide located. As you drag the pointer, a ruler guide like the one in Figure 4-6 appears on-screen. When it is positioned correctly, release the mouse button. To create additional rulers, simply repeat the process.

You can also create one ruler guide that appears on all pages throughout a publication. To do this, first turn to the master page. Then apply the same steps as outlined above for creating a ruler guide on just one page. After a ruler guide is created on a master page, it appears in the same position on each numbered page throughout the publication

To remove any ruler guide, first click on the Pointer tool. Then, drag the guide back into the ruler.

FIGURE 4-6
Positioning a horizontal ruler guide

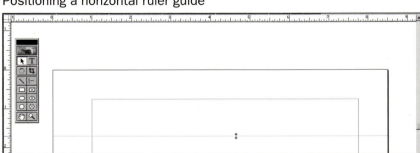

S TEP-BY-STEP 4.6

1. Turn to page 3 of the on-screen publication. Make certain that the zero point is positioned at the intersection of the top and left margin guides.

2. Click the **Pointer** tool in the toolbox.

3. Place the mouse pointer in the middle of the horizontal ruler, centered between the left and right edge of that ruler, and also centered between the top and bottom edge of the ruler.

4. Press and hold down the mouse button until a two-headed pointer appears. While holding down the mouse button, drag the pointer downward. Notice how the ruler guide appears as a thin line on the screen. When the ruler guide is positioned **3** inches from the top margin guide (use the vertical ruler to check the distance), release the mouse button.

5. Add another horizontal ruler guide and position it **5** inches from the top margin guide.

6. Place the mouse pointer in the middle of the vertical ruler, centered between the left and right edge of that ruler and also centered between the top and bottom edge of the ruler.

7. Press and hold down the mouse button and drag the two-headed pointer to the right. As you do, notice how a vertical ruler guide appears on the screen. When the ruler guide is positioned **2** inches from the left margin guide (use the horizontal ruler to check the distance), release the mouse button.

8. Add another vertical ruler guide and position it **4** inches from the left margin guide.

STEP-BY-STEP 4.6 Continued

9. When finished, your screen will look similar to the one in Figure 4-7. Keep this publication open for use in the next Step-by-Step.

FIGURE 4-7
Position of ruler guides after completing step 9

Hiding Guides and Using Snap To Guides

As mentioned earlier, you can add many ruler and margin guides to a page. However, the ruler and margin guides can sometimes make it difficult to see your work. To overcome this problem, you can hide or display these guides. To hide them, choose Hide Guides from the View menu. PageMaker will then hide all the ruler and margin guides leaving the contents of the page clearly

Hot Tip

You can create as many as 120 ruler guides in a single publication. Each ruler guide added to a numbered page counts as one toward the 120. Ruler guides added to master pages however, count as one on every page on which they appear. For example, if you add a ruler guide to the master page in a five page publication, that one guide will count as five toward the 120 limit.

visible. Figure 4-8 shows an example of a page before and after hiding the guides. To display hidden guides, choose Show Guides from the View menu.

FIGURE 4-8
A publication window before (top) and after (bottom) hiding the guides

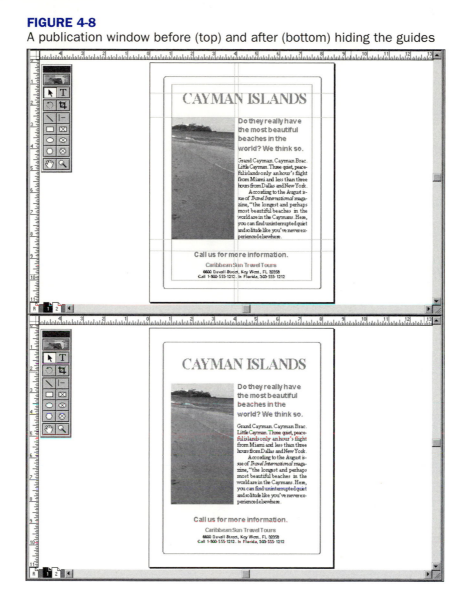

Using ruler guides to align your work is even easier if you choose Snap to Guides from the View menu. When this option is selected, anything you move close to a ruler guide, such as text or a graphic, will move or jump onto the ruler guide. You can always move the text or graphic away from the ruler guide, if needed.

STEP-BY-STEP 4.7

1. Click the **Rectangle** tool in the toolbox.

2. Notice how the two horizontal and two vertical ruler guides on-screen create a 2 inch square area near the center of the page. Place the mouse pointer (a cross hair) at one of the corners of this square area. Then, while holding down the mouse button, drag the cross hair to the opposite corner of the square area. Finally, release the mouse button. (*NOTE: Don't worry if you do not see the square immediately on the screen. The lines are partially hidden by the ruler guides.*)

3. Choose **Hide Guides** from the **View** menu. Notice how the square that was previously hidden by the ruler guides is now clearly visible.

4. Choose **Show Guides** from the **View** menu. Close this publication without saving it.

SUMMARY

In this lesson you learned how to:

■ Use the Undo and Redo commands to reverse editing actions.

■ Use the Revert command to restore an earlier version of a publication.

■ Use the Save As command to save a different version of the publication.

■ Print all or only certain pages within a publication.

■ Display and hide both the Ruler and ruler guides and change the zero point on a ruler.

VOCABULARY *Review*

Define the following terms.

Alert box	Ruler guides	Zero point
Mini-save		

REVIEW *Questions*

TRUE/FALSE

Circle T if the statement is true or F if the statement is false.

T   F   1. To undo or reverse your last editing action, choose the first entry in the Edit menu that begins with the word Undo.

T F   **2.** You can undo or reverse any of your last five actions.

T F   **3.** An alert box is a small dialog box containing a brief question and two or three buttons containing possible responses to that question.

T F   **4.** If you open a publication, delete all of its entries, and then save the publication using the Save command, the size of the publication would be even larger than when you first opened the publication.

T F   **5.** You can use the Save As command to save your work on disk in the smallest size possible.

T F   **6.** When printing multiple copies of a three-page publication, you can select Collate to print each copy in page number order; for example page 1, 2, and 3 for copy one, page 1, 2, and 3 for copy two, and so on.

T F   **7.** By default, the zero point on both the horizontal and vertical ruler falls at the intersection of the top and left margin guide for a single-sided publication.

T F   **8.** The small box located at the intersection of the horizontal and vertical ruler is called the zero point marker.

T F   **9.** To add a horizontal ruler guide to a page, place the mouse pointer in the horizontal ruler, hold down the mouse button, and then drag the pointer to the right.

T F **10.** To remove a ruler guide permanently from a page, click on the ruler guide and then press Delete.

FILL IN THE BLANK

Complete the following sentences by writing the correct word or words in the blanks provided.

1. You can choose Revert from the _____ menu to restore your publication to the way it was before you began your current editing session.

2. As you work on a publication, PageMaker automatically performs a(n) _____ - _____ each time you insert or remove pages, click on a page number icon, change the document setup, or print.

3. You can save a PageMaker publication on disk in the smallest size possible by using the _____ command.

4. When printing, you can use the Range text box to specify which pages to print. To print only page 2 and pages 4 through 6, you would key the entry _____ in the Range text box.

5. You can add as many as _____ ruler guides to a publication.

PROJECTS

PROJECT 4-1

1. Open the publication named **Employee Notice** from the data files.

2. Click the **Text** tool, and then click an insertion point roughly **1** inch below the last line of text and just to the right of the left margin guide.

3. Enlarge the area around the insertion point to **Actual Size**, if necessary.

4. Key **Effective date:** and then press the **spacebar**. Next, key today's date.

5. Insert one new page after the current page.

6. Use the **Rectangle** tool to draw a small rectangle anywhere on the new page of the publication.

7. Use the **Revert** command to go to the last mini-save version on the publication.

8. Use the **Revert** command to restore the publication to the way it was before you began this editing session.

9. Close the publication without saving your work. (*NOTE: If an alert box appears asking if you want to save your work before closing, choose No.*)

PROJECT 4-2

1. Begin a new publication.

2. When the Document Setup dialog box appears, specify that you want a five page, double-sided publication. Click **OK**.

3. Turn to the master pages by clicking on either the **L** or **R** master page icon.

4. If the rulers are not already on-screen, display or show the rulers.

5. Because this publication has left and right facing pages, notice how the zero point in the horizontal ruler falls at the intersection of those two pages. Add a horizontal ruler guide **3** inches from the top edge of the page.

6. Add another horizontal ruler guide and position it **8** inches from the top edge of the page.

7. Observe how ruler guides that are added to master pages appear on all numbered pages by turning first to page one and then to page two, and finally to page three. Close this publication without saving it.

PROJECT 4-3

1. Open the publication named **Employee Notice** from the data files.

2. Use the **Save As** command to create a copy of this publication and save that copy with the filename **New Notice**.

3. **Print** all of the pages in the on-screen publication.

4. Use the **Save** command to save the on-screen publication. *NOTE: In this exercise, the Save command will appear only if you print the publication.*

5. Close the publication.

PROJECT 4-4

1. Open the publication named **Business Card** from the data files.

2. Print this one page publication.

3. Use the **Save As** command to save the on-screen publication in the smallest size possible and without changing its filename.

4. Close the on-screen publication.

SCANS   **TEAMWORK PROJECT**

Discuss with your instructor and classmates the characteristics of the Undo and Redo commands in popular software programs such as Microsoft Word, WordPerfect, Excel or others with which you may be familiar. Now, compare those characteristics to the more limited Undo and Redo commands of PageMaker. Discuss what procedures you think would help make up for the limited capabilities of those two commands in PageMaker.

CRITICAL *Thinking*

SCANS **ACTIVITY 4-1**

As mentioned earlier in this lesson, an estimated 120 million trees are cut down annually to produce the paper that is used in personal computer printers. While trees are a renewable resource, their logging and manufacturing process can create pollution. Likewise, the seedlings that are replanted when trees are harvested convert only small amounts of carbon dioxide into oxygen and do little to prevent soil erosion. Using the Web or other resources, find out what you can do to conserve and recycle paper used for personal computers. Write a one page report summarizing your findings.

IMPORTING AND POSITIONING TEXT

Introduction

In this lesson, you will learn different ways to insert text that was created in a different program, such as a word processing program, into a publication. You will also learn more about how the text in a publication is divided into text blocks and how you can control the size and position of these text blocks. This lesson also explains how to format text into columns and ways to position entries on master pages.

Importing Text into a Publication

There are three ways you can add text to an on-screen publication. The first method is to key text directly into the on-screen publication page. Although this method is adequate for short text entries or editing corrections, it is slow and somewhat awkward to use. The second method is to use PageMaker's built-in story editor. The *story editor* is a basic word-processing program that includes a spell-checking feature and a variety of other timesaving techniques. The story editor is covered in depth in Lesson 6. The third method of adding text to a publication is to key the text first using a word processing program, and then import that word processing file into your

PageMaker publication. To *import* means to copy information created in one program into a different program. Once you create a file in a word-processing program, for example, it is easy to import that file into a PageMaker publication. Most word-processing programs such as Microsoft Word or Corel WordPerfect offer more powerful commands and features than PageMaker for keying and editing lengthy text entries. Therefore, importing is commonly used with medium to lengthy publications.

To import a file that was created with a word processing program, click the Place button on the toolbar or choose Place from the File menu. This command displays the Place dialog box shown in Figure 5-1. Click the name of the word processing file to import. Use the Look in drop-down list if needed to select the correct disk/folder.

FIGURE 5-1
The Place dialog box

Place		? X
Look in:	🗀 My Work	◁ 🖆 🖆 ⊞▾

📄 Accounting Summary.doc
📄 Advertising on the Internet.doc
📄 Annual Report.pmd
📄 Annual Report-Draft.pmd
📄 Business coaching report.doc
📄 Instruction manual.doc
📄 Company Picnic Announcement.pmd
📄 Employee Survey.pmd
📄 Employee Telephone List.pmd
📄 Executive Coaching.doc
📄 Health Brochure.pmd
📄 How_to_booklet.doc

File name:	Instruction manual.doc	Open
Files of type:	Importable Files	Cancel

Kind: Microsoft Word Document   CMS source...
Size: 25K   Last modified: 12/15/1999 3:19 PM   Place URL...

Place
⦿ As new story
○ Replacing entire story
○ Inserting text

Options
☐ Show filter preferences   ☑ Convert quotes
☑ Retain format   ☐ Read tags
☑ Retain cropping Data

The Options section of the dialog box contains features that let you control how PageMaker reads the word processing file. By default, the Retain format and Convert quotes options are selected. When the Retain format option is selected, PageMaker will read both the text and any formatting applied to the text. For example, if the first line of each paragraph is indented in the

word processing file, the text would also appear indented when imported into the publication. By deselecting the Retain format option, the program will read only the text and ignore any formatting. When the Convert quotes option is selected, PageMaker will convert any quotation marks created using the inch character (") in the word processing file into professional open (") and close (") quotation marks when the file is imported into the publication.

When you are ready to begin importing, click Open. After reading the word processing file, PageMaker displays a Text Placement icon (also called a loaded text icon) like the one shown in Figure 5-2. Position this icon where you want the text to start appearing in the publication, and then click the mouse button. If you place the icon just to the right of the left margin guide and then click, text will flow between the left and right margin guides on the page.

FIGURE 5-2
Text Placement icon

STEP-BY-STEP 5.1

1. Begin a new PageMaker publication. When the Document Setup dialog box appears, specify a **single-sided** publication and change the total number of pages to **4**. Finally, click **OK**.

2. Click the **Place** button on the toolbar or choose **Place** from the **File** menu.

3. From the data files that accompany this lesson, select the file named **Services.rtf** and then click **Open**. After a brief pause, the Text Placement icon will appear.

4. As illustrated in Figure 5-3, position this icon slightly below the top margin guide and just to the right of the left margin guide, and then click. Keep this publication on-screen for use in the next Step-by-Step.

FIGURE 5-3
Correct position of Text Placement icon

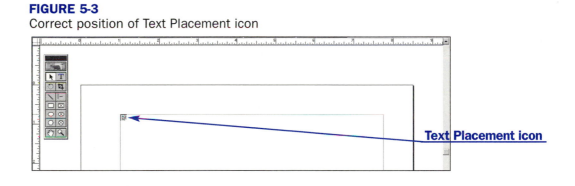

Text Placement icon

Controlling Text Blocks

As you learned in Lesson 3, all the text in any story appears within one or more text blocks. To see a text block, click on any text while using the Pointer tool. PageMaker will then display windowshades that identify the top, bottom, and width of the block. A *windowshade* is a thin line with a loop in the center. The small squares that appear at each end of a windowshade are called handles. Handles indicate the left and right edge of the text block. Figure 5-4 shows both windowshades and handles.

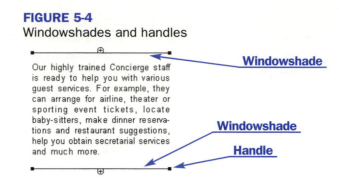

FIGURE 5-4
Windowshades and handles

Like a shade on a window that can be raised or lowered, PageMaker's windowshades let you shorten or lengthen a text block or change its width. As shown in Figure 5-5, the loops in the center of the windowshade indicate how much of the story appears within the text block. An empty loop in the top (or bottom) windowshade indicates the start (or end) of a story.

FIGURE 5-5
Empty windowshade loops indicate the start (top)
and/or end (bottom) of a text block

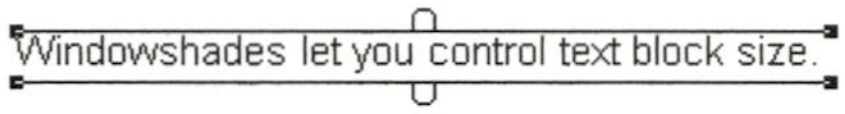

Windowshades let you control text block size.

A plus sign (+) in the top loop of a windowshade (see Figure 5-6) indicates that the text in this block is a continuation of text from a previous text block. A plus sign (+) in the bottom windowshade indicates that the text in this text block is continued in another text block. Text block that contain plus signs are called ***threaded*** text blocks, because all the characters are connected as if with a single piece of thread. If text is added or removed from a threaded text block the text in all subsequent text blocks adjusts automatically.

FIGURE 5-6
A plus sign in a windowshade loop indicates a threaded text block

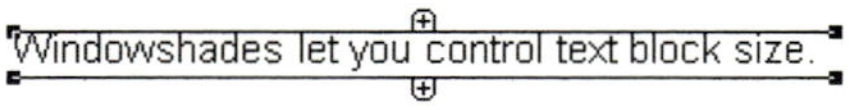

Windowshades let you control text block size.

A downward pointing arrow (▼) in the bottom windowshade (see Figure 5-7) indicates that there is more text in a story, but that text has not yet been placed into the publication. If you click on the downward pointing arrow, PageMaker will display the Text Placement icon. Position the icon where you want the next text block to appear and then click to place the remaining text.

FIGURE 5-7
A downward arrow indicates more text to be placed

Windowshades let you control text block size.

STEP-BY-STEP 5.2

1. Notice the windowshades that appear at the top and bottom of the text you just placed in Step-by-Step 5.1. (If the windowshades no longer appear, click the **Pointer** tool and then click anywhere in the text to display the windowshades.) The ▼ symbol in the bottom windowshade indicates that the story contains additional text that has not yet been placed.

2. Click on the ▼ symbol in the bottom windowshade to display the Text Placement icon.

3. Turn to page two by clicking the Numbered Page icon labeled **2**.

4. Position the Text Placement icon slightly below the top margin guide and just to the right of the left margin guide, and then click.

5. When the text block appears, observe how the loop in the bottom windowshade is empty, indicating that there is no more text in the story to place. Keep this publication on-screen for use in the next Step-by-Step.

Modifying a Text Block

After you create a text block, you can modify it in many ways. For example, you can move it to a different location on the page, increase its width, or reduce its length. To modify a text block, select it by clicking the Pointer tool and then clicking anywhere within that block to display the windowshades. If you need to deselect a text block while still using the Pointer tool, click anywhere outside the text block. (*NOTE: You can only select a text block while using the Pointer tool, not the Text tool. The Text tool is only used to key or edit text within a text block.*)

To move a selected text block, place the mouse pointer in the center of the block. Then, while holding down the mouse button, drag the block to a new location. If you drag the text block immediately after clicking, a rectangle will appear outlining the size of the text block. To watch the actual text move (instead of an outlined rectangle), press and hold down the mouse button, then pause for a second or two before dragging the text.

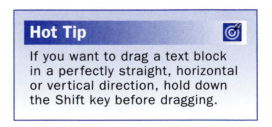

Hot Tip

If you want to drag a text block in a perfectly straight, horizontal or vertical direction, hold down the Shift key before dragging.

To change the length of a text block (that is, to make it shorter or longer), place the mouse pointer over the loop in the bottom windowshade and then press and hold down the mouse button. If positioned properly, a double-headed arrow will appear like the one shown in Figure 5-8. Now, drag the handle upward (to shorten) or downward (to lengthen) the text block.

FIGURE 5-8
Changing the length of a text block

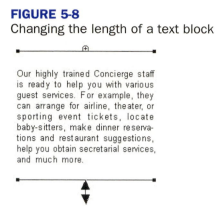

When changing the length of a text block it is very important to press and hold down the mouse button instead of clicking on the windowshade loop. If you click by mistake on a loop that contains a plus sign, for example, the Text Placement icon will appear indicating that PageMaker is ready to place all remaining text in the story. If this occurs, cancel the command by clicking once on the Pointer tool and then start again.

To change the width or length of a text block, place the mouse pointer over the handle on the left or right edge of either windowshade. Then, press and hold down the mouse button. If the mouse pointer is positioned properly, a two-headed arrow and an outline indicating the size of the text block will appear like the one shown in Figure 5-9. Now drag the handle left or right to change the width, and then release the mouse button. Dragging a handle at the right side of the windowshade farther to the right, for example, increases the width of the text block.

FIGURE 5-9
Changing the width or length of a text block

S TEP-BY-STEP 5.3

1. Turn to the first page in the publication.

2. Click the **Pointer** tool. Then, click anywhere in the text to select the text block. (*NOTE: If window-shades do not appear at the top and bottom of the text, perform this step again.*)

3. Carefully place the mouse pointer inside the loop in the bottom windowshade. This loop currently displays a plus sign. Now, press and hold down the mouse button. (*NOTE: If a double-headed arrow does not appear, release the mouse button and start this step again.*) Then, while continuing to hold down the mouse button, drag the pointer upward until it is positioned roughly in the center of the page. Then release the mouse button. Notice how the text block is now shorter.

4. If the text block is not already selected, select the text block. Now, carefully place the mouse pointer over the left handle (■) of the bottom windowshade, then press and hold down the mouse button. (*NOTE: If a two-headed arrow does not appear, release the mouse button and start this step again.*) While continuing to hold down the mouse button, drag the pointer straight to the right about one-third of the way across the page. Then release the mouse button. Notice how the text block is now narrower.

5. If the text block is not still selected, select it.

6. Read this instruction completely before beginning. Place the mouse pointer in the center of the selected text block, between the top and bottom windowshades. Then, press and, while continuing to hold down the mouse button, immediately drag the text block to the left so that it aligns on the left margin guide. Notice how only an outline of the text block appears. Release the mouse button to position the text block in the new location.

7. If the text block is still not selected, select the text block.

8. Read this instruction completely before beginning. Place the mouse pointer in the center of the selected text block between the top and bottom windowshades. Then, press and, while continuing to hold down the mouse button, pause for two to three seconds. While still holding down the mouse button, drag the text block until it is roughly centered on the page from top to bottom and from left to right. Notice this time how the actual text instead of only its outline appears. Finally, release the mouse button. Keep this publication on-screen for use in the next Step-by-Step.

Dividing and Joining Text Blocks

As shown in Figure 5-10, you can divide one text block into two or more smaller text blocks. You might do this, for example, to position each block at different places on a page. You can also join together several smaller text blocks that are threaded together into a single, large text block.

FIGURE 5-10
A large text block divided into smaller text blocks

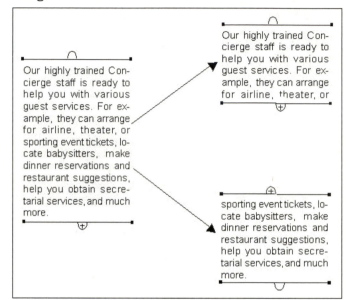

To divide a text block, select the block as described earlier. Next, place the mouse pointer over the loop in the bottom windowshade. Then, drag the loop upward until only as much of the text that you want to appear in the first text block remains. When you release the mouse button, a plus sign (+) will appear in the bottom loop. Click on the plus sign. When the Text Placement icon appears, position the symbol where you want the second text block to appear, and click.

To join two smaller text blocks which are threaded together, while using the Pointer tool click anywhere in one of the text blocks. Then place the mouse pointer inside the plus (+) sign that appears in the top or bottom loop and drag the loop either upward (for the top loop) or downward (for the bottom loop).

> **Hot Tip**   ◎
>
> To delete all the text blocks on a page, click the **Pointer** tool, then choose **Select All** from the **Edit** menu or press **Ctrl+A**. Then, press **Delete**.

STEP-BY-STEP 5.4

1. Turn to the second page in the publication.

2. Select the text block.

STEP-BY-STEP 5.4 Continued

3. Carefully place the mouse pointer inside the loop of the bottom windowshade. Then, press and while continuing to hold down the mouse button, drag the pointer upward until it is positioned roughly in the center of the page. Then release the mouse button. Notice how the text block is now shorter.

4. Click the ▼ symbol in the bottom windowshade to display the Text Placement icon.

5. Carefully position the Text Placement icon roughly one inch below the on-screen text block and just to the right of the left margin guide, and then click.

6. In the new text block you just created, observe the plus sign in the loop of the top windowshade. This plus sign indicates that the text in this block is threaded to the text in the previous text block. Keep this publication on-screen for use in the next Step-by-Step.

Using a Bounding Box

Normally when you key or place text onto a page, the text flows between the left and right margin guides (or column guides, which will be discussed later in this lesson). Sometimes, however, you might want to fit the text into a larger or smaller area. For example, you might want to key an informative note in a small, two-inch square area of a page, or you might want to key a title that extends beyond the normal margin guides.

To key or place text within a specific area, use a ***bounding box*** to identify and control the size of the text block in which you want the text to fit. You can create a bounding box when you place text, or before you begin keying text. To create a bounding box while placing text, position the Text Placement icon where you want the upper-left corner of the bounding box located. Now, instead of clicking, press and hold down the mouse button, and drag it over the area in which you want the text to appear. This procedure is also called ***drag placing***. As you drag the icon, a rectangle indicating the size of the bounding box appears, like the one in Figure 5-11. When you release the mouse button, the text you are placing will appear within the bounding box, like the text shown in Figure 5-12.

FIGURE 5-11
Drag Text Placement icon to create a bounding box

FIGURE 5-12
Text you key or place remains inside the box

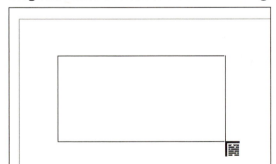

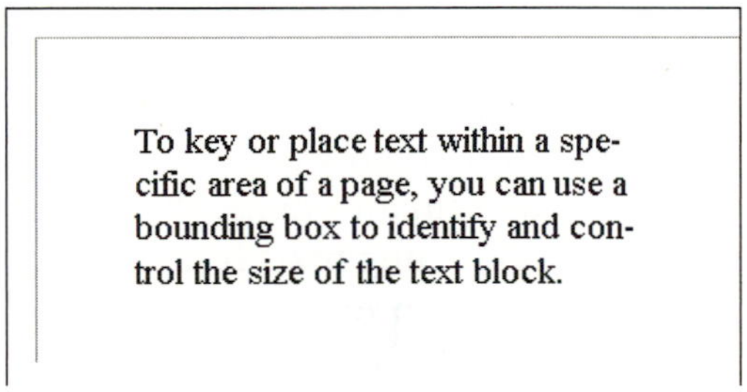

To key or place text within a specific area of a page, you can use a
bounding box to identify and control the size of the text block.

To create a bounding box in which you will key text, click the Text tool. Then place the I-beam where you want the upper-left corner of the bounding box located, and while holding down the mouse button, drag over the area in which you want the text to appear. As you drag the I-beam, a rectangle will appear to show you the size of the bounding box. After you release the mouse button, begin keying the text. As you key, the text will automatically fit within the size of the bounding box.

You might be wondering what happens if you place or key more text than would normally fit within the size of the bounding box that you defined. If such a situation occurs, PageMaker simply continues to enlarge the depth of the bounding box automatically to fit the additional text.

STEP-BY-STEP 5.5

1. Click the **Text** tool to remove any windowshades from the text block you were working on in the last Step-by-Step.

2. Turn to the first page in the publication.

3. Place the I-beam in the center of the page (from left to right) and roughly one inch below the last text block.

4. Read this instruction completely before beginning. Press and hold down the mouse button. Now, drag the I-beam downward and to the right to create a bounding box. Drag the box until it is roughly one-inch square. Then release the mouse button and key your first and last name several times. As you key, notice how the text wraps within the area of the bounding box.

5. Close this publication without saving it.

Controlling Text Flow

When placing a text file into a publication, PageMaker offers three options that control how the text flows onto the page. These options are manual, semi-autoflow, and autoflow. Each is described below.

■ *Manual text flow*: This is PageMaker's default setting. Position the Text Placement icon where you want the text to start appearing, then click. The text then flows downward until it reaches the bottom of the page. If there is more text to place (indicated by a ▼ symbol in the bottom windowshade), you must click on the ▼ symbol and then continue placing the text. If more pages are needed to hold the additional text, you need to manually insert those new pages into the publication before you can place the remaining text.

■ *Semi-autoflow* (also called semiautomatic): After you position the Text Placement icon and click, text flows downward until it reaches the bottom of the page. If there is more text to place, the program automatically displays the Text Placement icon so you can continue placing the remaining text. If more pages are needed to hold the additional text, you still need to manually insert those new pages into the publication before you can place that remaining text. The advantage of this method is that you do not need to click on the ▼ symbol in the windowshade to continue placing additional text.

■ *Autoflow* (also called automatic): After you position the Text Placement icon and click, text flows downward on the page. However, unlike the other two text flow options, when the text reaches the bottom of the page, it then automatically continues flowing down the next page in the publication. This is called *autoflow*. Also, PageMaker automatically inserts into the publication as many pages as are needed to hold all the text that is being placed.

To place text using manual text flow, place the text as instructed earlier in this lesson. For the semi-autoflow option, press and continue to hold down the Shift key as you position each Text Placement icon that appears.

If you want to place a file using autoflow, you must first choose Autoflow from the Layout menu. A check mark appears in front of the Autoflow entry in the pull-down menu when the feature is selected. Next, click the Place button on the toolbar or choose Place from the File menu, and then select the file to place as you normally would. Position the Text Placement icon where you want the text to appear, and then click. The text will automatically flow from one page to the next.

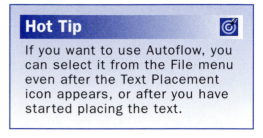

Hot Tip

If you want to use Autoflow, you can select it from the File menu even after the Text Placement icon appears, or after you have started placing the text.

Depending on the type of text flow you want to use, one of three different Text Placement icons will appear, as shown in Figure 5-13. These icons indicate whether the manual text flow, semi-autoflow, or autoflow is in effect.

FIGURE 5-13
The manual, semi-autoflow, and autoflow icons

STEP-BY-STEP 5.6

1. Begin a new publication.

2. When the Document Setup dialog box appears, specify a **single-sided** publication and then click **OK.**

3. Read this step completely before beginning. Choose **Autoflow** from the **Layout** menu. (*NOTE: If a check mark already appears in front of the Autoflow option do not perform this step.*)

4. Click the **Place** button on the toolbar or choose **Place** from the **File** menu. Then, from the data files that accompany this lesson, select the file named **Services.rtf** and click **Open.**

5. When the Autoflow icon appears, position that icon slightly below the top margin guide and just to the right of the left margin guide, and then click. Observe how PageMaker automatically flows text down the first page, inserts a second page to the publication, and then continues flowing the remaining text onto that second page.

6. Close this publication without saving it.

Working with Columns

By default, the pages in all standard PageMaker publications contain one column that fits between the top, bottom, left, and right margin guides. It's easy, however, to create pages with up to 20 columns per page. You simply indicate how many columns are needed and how much space you want between those columns and PageMaker does the rest. After adding columns to a page, you can immediately begin keying or placing text into those columns. You can also create columns of equal width or have columns of different widths on the same page.

Adding Columns to a Publication

You first need to decide on which page or pages you want columns. To create columns on a specific page, turn to that page in the publication. To create columns on all pages in the publication, turn to the master pages.

Choose Column Guides from the Layout menu to display the Column Guides dialog box shown in Figure 5-14. In the Number of columns text box, key the number of columns needed. In the Space between columns text box, key the amount of space you want inserted between each column. Space between columns is called the *gutter*. The gutter keeps the text in one column separated from the text in an adjacent column. By default, PageMaker automatically places 0.167 inches of space between each column. When finished making the dialog box entries, click OK.

FIGURE 5-14
Column Guides dialog box

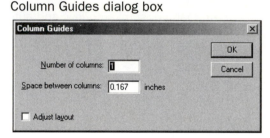

When the publication window reappears, column guides like those shown in Figure 5-15 appear and identify the columns. Column guides indicate the boundary or edge of each column. Like margin guides on a page, column guides control how text will fit within a column.

FIGURE 5-15
Column guides control text flow within each column

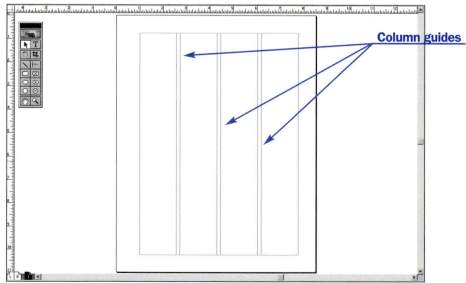

STEP-BY-STEP 5.7

1. Begin a new publication. When the Document Setup dialog box appears, specify a **single-sided** publication and change the total number of pages to **4**. Then, click **OK**.

2. Make sure you are on page 1 of the publication. Choose **Column Guides** from the **Layout** menu. Next, key **4** in the Number of columns text box (leave the gutter at its default setting), and then click **OK**.

3. Turn to the second page of the publication.

4. Add three columns to this page and leave the gutter between columns at its default setting.

5. Turn to the third page of the publication.

6. Add two columns to this page and leave the gutter between columns at its default setting. Keep this publication on-screen for use in the next Step-by-Step.

Creating Columns of Different Widths

When you first add columns to a publication, PageMaker divides the distance between the left and right margin guides by the number of columns requested (less the gutter) to determine how wide to make each column. As a result, each column is the same width. At times, however, you may want columns of different widths, such as one wide and one narrow column.

You can change the width of columns after adding them to a page. To change a column's width, carefully place the mouse pointer on the left or right column guide of the column you want to change. Then, press and hold down the mouse button. If the mouse pointer is positioned correctly, a double-headed arrow will appear. Now drag the column guide left or right. As you do so, the column width will change. When the column is the width you desire, release the mouse button.

Because it's so easy to change the width of a column, PageMaker lets you lock the column guides so that you don't change them by accident. To lock column guides, select Lock Guides from the View menu. A check mark appears in front of Lock Guides in the pull-down menu if this option is selected. To unlock the column guides so you can change the widths again, simply deselect Lock Guides from the View menu.

STEP-BY-STEP 5.8

1. Make certain that page three of the publication is still on-screen.

2. Place the mouse pointer over one of the column guides that appears near the center of the page and then hold down the mouse button. (*NOTE: If a double-headed arrow does not appear, release the mouse button and try again.*)

3. While still holding down the mouse button, drag the column guide to the left roughly one inch and then release the mouse button. (*NOTE: If the column guide does not move, unlock the column guides by performing Step 5 below. Then, begin Step 3 again.*)

STEP-BY-STEP 5.8 Continued

4. Choose **Lock Guides** from the **View** menu. Now, try to change the width of the column by dragging the same column guide. Notice that when the column guides are locked, you cannot move the column guides.

5. Deselect **Lock Guides** to unlock the column guides. Keep this publication on-screen for use in the next Step-by-Step.

If you create columns of different widths and then change your mind, it's easy to make all the columns equal width again. To do so, choose Column Guides from the Layout menu. The word Custom will appear in the Number of columns text box. In that text box, key the number of columns desired, and then click OK. PageMaker will then reset the columns to equal width.

STEP-BY-STEP 5.9

1. Make certain that page three of the publication is still on-screen. Notice how this page contains columns of different widths.

2. Choose **Column Guides** from the **Layout** menu. Then, key **2** in the Number of columns text box and click **OK**. Observe how both of the columns are again of equal width. Keep this publication on-screen for use in the next Step-by-Step.

Positioning Entries on Master Pages

As you learned in Lesson 2, anything you place on a master page, such as text or a graphic, will appear on all numbered pages in a publication. Such elements are referred to as *repeating elements* because they appear or are repeated on each publication page. The most frequently used repeating elements include headers, footers, and page numbers.

Adding Headers and Footers

As shown in Figure 5-16, *headers* and *footers* are entries that appear in the top margin (header) or bottom margin (footer) of the pages in a publication. These entries are often used to display identifying information about the publication, such as its title or publication date. Because of the type of information usually contained in headers and footers, you will most likely want to add them to the master page, so that information will appear on each page of the publication. Any header or footer can contain one or more lines of text and can also contain graphics, such as a rule or line created with the Constrained-line tool.

FIGURE 5-16
Headers and footers in a publication

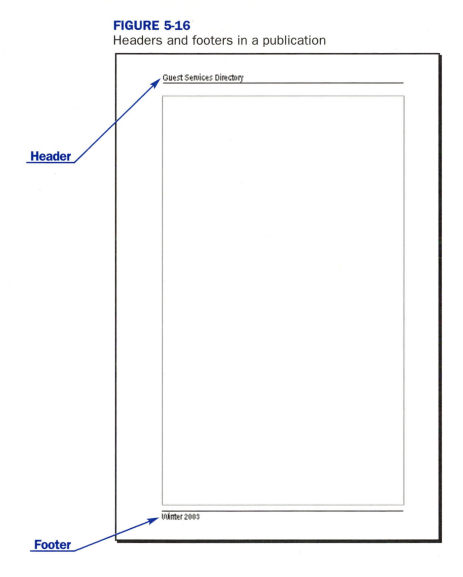

There are two ways you can add a header or footer to your master page. Using the Text tool, you can key a header or footer directly on a master page. You can also key the header or footer in the pasteboard and then drag that text into the correct position on the master page. Because many computer printers cannot print close to the edge of a page, use care to keep the header and footer away from this unprintable area (usually between 0.25 and 0.35 inches from the edge of the page). If you are working with a publication that has both a left- and right-hand master page (a publication with facing pages), you will need to create the header and footer on both master pages.

Adding a Page Number

In many publications, you will often want page numbers to appear on the printed pages. You can do so by adding a page number marker to the header or footer. A *page number marker* is a symbol that indicates where the page number will appear. While creating the header or footer with the Text tool, position the insertion point where you want the page number to appear. Then press Ctrl+Alt+P. If you are working with a publication that has facing pages, you will need to perform this operation twice in the appropriate header or footer of both the left and the right master page.

Because master pages do not print as part of the publication, page number markers on a master page are indicated with the characters LM (for left master) and RM (for right master). However, the page numbers will appear correctly on each numbered page in the publication.

STEP-BY-STEP 5.10

1. Turn to the master page (a right-hand master since this is a single-sided publication) in the publication.

2. Enlarge the area near the top and left edge of the page to **Actual Size**.

3. Click the **Text** tool.

4. Place the I-beam in any area of the pasteboard located just above the top edge of the page and then click.

5. Key **Sales Report for** and press **Enter**. Then, key **Second Quarter** but do not press Enter.

6. Click the **Pointer** tool so you can drag this text into the header. Drag the two lines of text so that both lines are centered between the top edge of the page and the top margin guide, and also so that the text aligns even with the left margin. Figure 5-17 shows the correct position.

FIGURE 5-17
Correct positioning for header

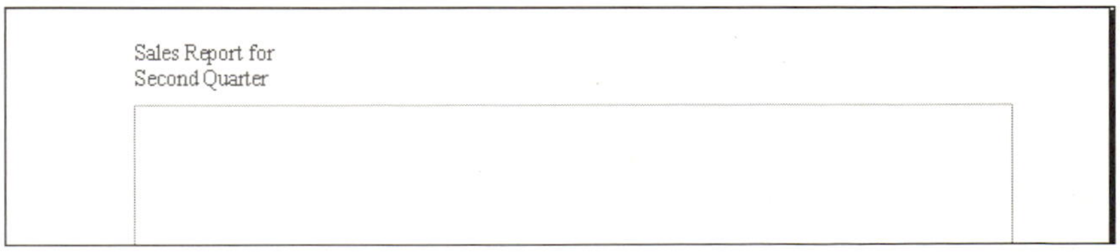

Sales Report for
Second Quarter

7. Next, reposition the master page on-screen so that you are viewing the area around the bottom and left margin guides of the page. If you are not already, view the page in Actual Size.

STEP-BY-STEP 5.10 Continued

8. Click the **Text** tool and place the I-beam directly below the left margin guide and in the space between the bottom margin guide and the bottom edge of the page. Then click to position the insertion point for keying a footer.

9. Key **Page** and then press the **spacebar** once.

10. Insert the page number marker by pressing **Ctrl+Alt+P**. The letters RM will appear. (*NOTE: If needed, use the Pointer tool to drag the footer into the correct position.*)

11. Turn to page two in the publication and examine the header and footer. Then, enlarge the area around the footer, if needed, to observe how the correct page number appears. Close this publication without saving it.

SUMMARY

In this lesson you learned how to:

- Use text blocks to control how and where text from a story appears in a publication.

- Key text for use in other programs, such as a word processing program, and then import it into a PageMaker publication using the Place command.

- Use the Place command to import text

- Choose from three text flow options: manual, autoflow, and semi-autoflow.

- Use the Column Guides command to create up to 20 columns on a page. Columns can be of equal or differing widths.

- Create headers and footers to identify information at the top or bottom of each page in a publication, such as a report title or page number.

- Use bounding boxes to control the size of text you will key or place.

VOCABULARY *Review*

Define the following terms:

Autoflow	Gutter	Repeating elements
Bounding box	Headers	Story editor
Drag placing	Import	Threaded
Footers	Page number marker	Windowshade

REVIEW *Questions*

TRUE/FALSE

Circle T if the statement is true or F if the statement is false.

T F **1.** You can add a maximum of 30 columns to a page.

T F **2.** All text in a story is stored in one or more text blocks.

T F **3.** Windowshades appear only when a text block is selected.

T F **4.** An empty loop in a top windowshade indicates the start of a story.

T F **5.** A downward pointing arrow ▼ in a bottom windowshade indicates the end of the story.

T F **6.** To select a text block, click the Text tool and then click anywhere in the text.

T F **7.** To drag a text block and see the actual text instead of just an outline, press and hold down the mouse button for several seconds before dragging the text block.

T F **8.** You can drag a handle in a selected text block to change the width of the text block.

T F **9.** It is not possible to divide one text block into several smaller text blocks.

T F **10.** Use a bounding box to identify and control the size of a text block in which you want to place or key text.

T F **11.** With semi-autoflow, text flows to the bottom of a page and then automatically begins flowing down the next page.

T F **12.** To select autoflow, choose Autoflow from the File menu.

T F **13.** After adding columns to a page, you can change the width of those columns.

T F **14.** If you create columns on the master pages, those columns will appear on all pages in the publication.

T F **15.** A bounding box identifies the number of pages in a publication that you wish to print.

FILL IN THE BLANK

Complete the following sentences by writing the correct word or words in the blanks provided.

1. You can use a(n) _____ _____ to control the size of a new text block in which you want to key text.

2. A small square that appears at each end of a windowshade is called a(n) _____.

3. To import a text file into a PageMaker publication, issue the _____ command.

4. Clicking on the handle at the right side of a windowshade and dragging it farther to the right would _____ the width of the text block.

5. The space between two columns is referred to as the _____.

PROJECTS

PROJECT 5-1A

1. Start a new, single-sided publication containing two pages. Make the right and bottom margins each **1** inch, and change the top margin setting to **2.5** inches. Keep the left margin setting at **1** inch.

2. Turn to the master page and change the number of columns on each page in the publication from 1 to 3. Leave the gutter space at its default setting.

3. While remaining on the master page, use the **Text** tool to create a footer for this publication. The text in this footer should align evenly with the left margin guide, and appear centered in the space between the bottom margin guide and the bottom edge of the page. When creating the footer, key the word **Page** followed by a space and then insert the page number marker. When finished, your footer should look similar to the one in Figure 5-18. If not, drag the footer into the correct position.

4. Turn to page one in the publication. Keep this publication on-screen for use in Project 5-1B.

FIGURE 5-18
Sample on-screen solution for the publication created in project 5-1A

Page RM

PROJECT 5-1B

1. Make certain that Autoflow is not turned on.

2. Use the **Place** command to import the file named **Sales1.rtf** into the left-hand column on the first page of the publication that you created in Project 5-1A. Position the Text Placement icon in the left-hand column slightly below the top margin guide and just to the right of the left column guide and click. (*NOTE: The imported text will fill only a portion of the column.*)

3. Turn on Autoflow so that PageMaker will automatically insert as many pages as needed to hold any future text that you place.

4. Use the **Place** command to import the file named **Sales2.rtf** into the middle column of the on-screen page. Position the Text Placement icon in the middle column slightly below the top margin guide and just to the right of its left column guide before clicking. (*NOTE: The imported text will automatically flow onto page two of the publication.*)

5. Turn back to page one in the publication.

6. Use the **Pointer** tool to drag the text block in the left-hand column downward so that it is centered vertically from top to bottom in that column.

7. Keep this publication on-screen for use in Project 5-1C.

PROJECT 5-1C

1. Make certain that you are still on page one of the publication from Project 5-1B.

2. Create a bounding box with the **Text** tool and key a title that will appear on the first page of this publication. Start the bounding box (see Figure 5-19) roughly 1 inch from the top and 1 inch from the left edge of the page. Then, drag downward to the right until the I-beam is positioned just above the top and right-most margin guides. Inside the bounding box, key **Caribbean Sun Travel Tours** and press **Enter** twice. Then in all upper-case characters, key **SALES DEPARTMENT ANNUAL REPORT.**

FIGURE 5-19
Sample of bounding box needed in step 2 of Project 5-1C

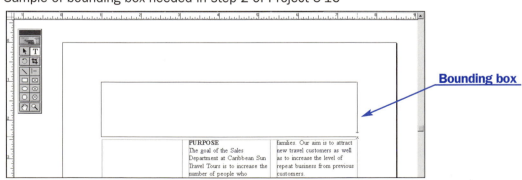

3. If needed, use the **Pointer** tool to move (drag) the text you just keyed in step 2 so that it is centered vertically between the top edge of the page and the top margin guides.

4. Turn to page two in the publication.

5. Create a bounding box at the top of the second page. Inside that bounding box, key **Sales Report** and press **Enter,** then key (**continued**). If needed, drag the bounding box so that it appears centered vertically between the top edge of the page and the top margin guides.

6. When finished, your completed publication should look similar to the sample solution in Figure 5-20. Make any corrections needed. (*NOTE: Your solution will vary somewhat based on the default font setting used by your version of PageMaker.*)

7. Save the publication with the name **Sales Report 3 Columns**. Print and then close the publication.

FIGURE 5-20
Sample solution to the Sales Report 3 Columns publication

Caribbean Sun Travel Tours

SALES DEPARTMENT ANNUAL REPORT

SUMMARY
This document describes the Sales Department activities at Surfside Resort. It highlights the purpose, organization and major activities conducted by the department. This report was prepared at the request of BJ Properties Limited.

PURPOSE
The goal of the Sales Department at Caribbean Sun Travel Tours is to increase the number of people who purchase services from our firm. Our goals are to increase both the number of corporate and individual customers.

ORGANIZATION
The Sales Department at Caribbean Sun Travel Tours was established in 1972. Prior to that time, the General Manager conducted all sales activity. Today, the Sales Department reports to the Assistant General Manager. The staff includes a Manager, Sales Associate, Administrative Assistant and two part-time Sales Associates.
    The Department has two primary areas of activity: individual sales and corporate sales. Within these areas we focus on selling specific services such as corporate awards, corporate travel programs, individual sales, and so on.

INDIVIDUAL SALES
This type of sales is directed toward individuals and families. Our aim is to attract new

travel customers as well as to increase the level of repeat business from previous customers.
    The Sales Department conducts its individual sales activity through speeches, advertising and by direct mail. Last year, for example, our staff spoke to 137 groups and organizations, and mailed over 500,000 direct mail brochures.
    Our staff also prepares national magazine and newspaper advertisements and monitors the response to those advertisements. Currently, 58% of our new customers have heard about Caribbean Sun Travel Tours through magazine and newspaper advertisements. During the past year our staff also prepared six magazine articles about our Caribbean Winter tours.
    The overall activities of our Department have produced a sales increase during the past year of over 120 percent.

CORPORATE SALES
Our sales department also places great emphasis on corporate sales. We work with profes-

Page 1

Sales Report
(continued)

sional organizations, corporations, and associations on arranging travel for their employees and members.
    Corporate sales are an especially important source of income since much of the travel booked is at non-discounted rates. During the past year, for example, of the 12,550 airline seats booked for this group of customers, over 11,000 seats were at non-discounted rates. Last year, corporate sales accounted for nearly 38% of all income for the property.
    Because of the importance placed on corporate sales, we employ one full-time Sales Associate who specializes in this group. This Sales Associate has twenty years experience working with corporations and previously served as President of the National Business Travel Planners Association.
    Our Department is especially proud of a recent corporate sales achievement. In April, we booked the largest corporate travel event in our history; the American Speakers Conference to be held July 19-23. This contract resulted in the sale of 5,200

airline seats and 14,275 nights of hotel room accommodations.

OTHER SERVICES
In addition to its sales efforts, the Sales Department works with national business and travel groups to rate our services. During the past year, we have had much success in this arena. Caribbean Sun Travel Tours was recently awarded a Best Buy rating from *Traveling On* magazine, and rated a 10 by the Business Travelers Association.

FUTURE PLANS
Although we have accomplished much during the past year, our goal is to achieve even more during the coming year. First, we plan to initiate an International Sales program by September 1st. Many international groups hold their meetings in the Caribbean, and Florida is one of the most sought after locations for these meetings.
    Our international program will include hiring a full-time Sales Associate to administer the program, produce specialized brochures and attend conferences held

by international meeting planners.
    Second, we plan to increase the sales volume for both individual and corporate sales during the next year. We will do this through an aggressive media advertising campaign in national and local business magazines. Our plan is to increase sales volume by an average of 29%.

Page 2

PROJECT 5-2

1. Start a new, single-sided publication containing two pages. Change the left, right, and bottom margins each to **1.5** inches, and change the top margin to **3** inches.

2. Turn to the master page and change the number of columns on each page from one to two. In the Space between columns text box, key **0.3**.

3. While still on the master page, add a horizontal ruler guide 1 inch from the top edge of the page and add a second horizontal ruler guide 2 inches from the top edge of the page.

4. While still on the master page, create a header by clicking the **Text** tool and then clicking an insertion point in the pasteboard and above the top edge of the page. Next, key **Caribbean Sun Travel Tours** and press **Enter** twice. Then, in all uppercase characters, key **SALES DEPARTMENT ANNUAL REPORT**. Finally, drag the header onto the master page so that the first line falls just below the top horizontal ruler guide and the text aligns evenly with the left margin guide.

5. Turn to page one in the publication.

6. Use the **Place** command to import the file named **Sales1.rtf** into the publication. When the Text Placement icon appears, position the icon in the left column slightly below the top column guide and just to the right of the left column guide and click.

7. Using the **Pointer** tool, drag the text block that you just created in Step 6 upward so that the title (**SUMMARY**) falls just below the second horizontal ruler guide. Then, change the width of the text block so that it extends all the way to the right margin guide on the page. (*NOTE: To do this easily, drag the right handle of the bottom windowshade to the intersection of the top and right margin guides.*)

8. Turn on Autoflow. Use the **Place** command to import the file named **Sales2.rtf** into the publication. When the Autoflow icon appears, position the icon in the left column slightly below the top column guide and just to the right of the left column guide and click. When finished, your completed publication should look similar to the sample solution in Figure 5-21. Make any corrections needed. (*NOTE: Your solution will vary somewhat based on the default font setting used by your version of PageMaker.*)

9. Save the publication with the name **Sales Report 2 Columns**. Print the publication and then close the publication.

FIGURE 5-21
Sample solution to the Sales Report 2 Columns publication

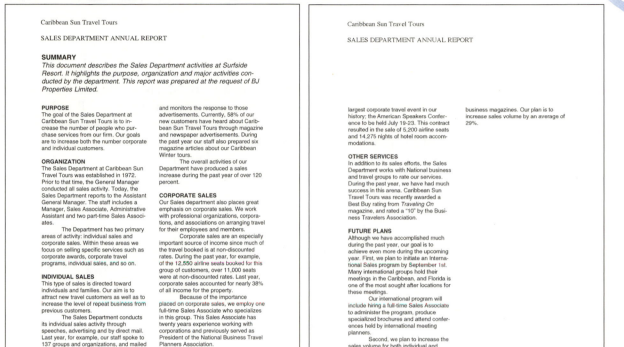

TEAMWORK PROJECT

As a group, study a lengthy publication such as a national magazine or local newspaper and find stories that are presented on more than one column or on additional pages. Now, imagine that you are creating that same publication in PageMaker and that all of the text for each story has been keyed into separate files using a word processing program. Discuss in your group which of the text flow options you could use (manual, semi-autoflow, and autoflow) to place text into the publication, and how you would go about placing that text.

Extra Challenge

Complete the Critical Thinking activity. Then, bring the documents you gathered to your next class. In small groups, present and discuss the different types of publications that you found. Also, discuss how you might lay out those publications in PageMaker using the columns feature.

SCANS **CRITICAL** *Thinking*

ACTIVITY 5-1

During the next few days, gather a collection of printed documents that are two or more pages long and that contain two or more columns on a page. These documents might include such things as flyers, brochures, magazines, catalogs, and newspapers. Then, examine the documents closely and think about how you might lay out the same documents using PageMaker's columns feature. How many columns would each publication require? Would those columns be of equal or different widths? If the publication has facing pages, would the column widths be the same or different on the left and right master page? Write a brief report describing your findings and attach to that report a copy of the document (flyer, brochure, magazine, etc.) upon which your report is based.

USING THE STORY EDITOR

OBJECTIVES

Upon completion of this lesson, you should be able to:

■ Explain the major features of the story editor.

■ Switch between the layout view and the story editor, and explain the differences between the two views.

■ Use the Find and Change commands to locate and change text.

■ Use the Copy, Cut, and Paste commands to move and copy text.

■ Use the Place command to import a text file directly into the story editor.

■ Use the Spell command to check a story for errors.

■ Identify the different types of hidden characters that can appear in the story editor, and explain how to display and hide those characters.

Estimated Time: 3 hours

VOCABULARY

Layout view

Story editor

Introduction

PageMaker contains a built-in word processing feature called the story editor. In this lesson, you'll learn how to use the story editor to key and edit text, locate and replace text, and perform spell checking. You'll also see how to copy or move text from one place to another.

Understanding the Story Editor

Although you can use the Text tool to key and edit all text for a publication, it is a slow and often awkward way to work, especially with lengthy text. PageMaker's *story editor* is a powerful word processing feature that lets you key and edit text quickly. With the story editor, you have access to many of the same features found in popular word processing programs, such as the ability to search and replace text, and check for spelling errors.

There are several ways you can use the story editor. First, you can use it to edit text that you have already keyed or placed into a publication. Second, you can import lengthy text files directly into the story editor. You may also use it to key lengthy text entries directly into a publication.

Characteristics of the Story Editor

Up to this point, you have been working in PageMaker's layout view. The *layout view* allows you to see the publication page with its text and graphics, much like it will appear when printed (see Figure 6-1). The layout view does not, however, have features that are normally found in a word processing program that make it easier to work with lengthy text. To access these features, you need to switch from the layout view to the story editor view.

FIGURE 6-1
Example of the layout view

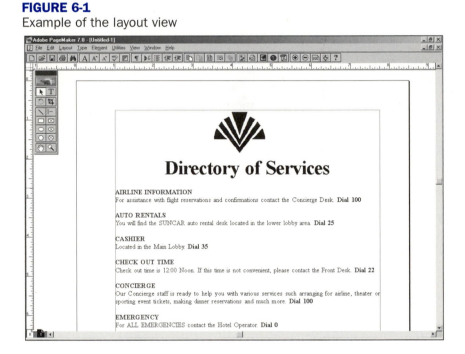

In addition to the layout view, you can also view the publication and key or edit text using the story editor view. A story editor window appears when you switch to the story editor (see Figure 6-2). While in the story editor window, you can key, edit, or format text. You cannot, however, access any of the toolbox tools, such as the Rectangle tool. Because they are unavailable, the toolbox buttons will appear dimmed while you work in the story editor window. Also, although you can change type specifications while working in the story editor window, all text will only appear in one size and typeface until you change back to the layout view.

FIGURE 6-2
Text in the story editor window

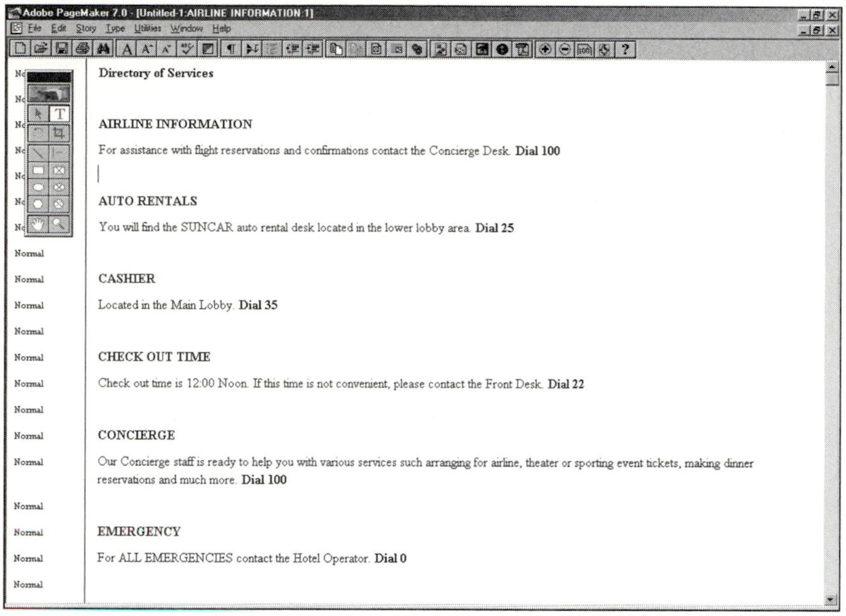

Switching to the Story Editor Window

While working in layout view, you can use the story editor to edit text within an existing story or you can key new text into the publication. To edit text within an existing story, click the Text tool. Then, click anywhere in the text you want to edit. Finally, choose Edit Story from the Edit menu. After a short pause, the text from that story appears in the story editor window. When you finish keying or editing the text in the story editor, choose Edit Layout from the Edit menu to return to the layout view.

To key new text into a publication using the story editor, make certain the insertion point is not located within any text in the publication. An easy way to do this is to click the Pointer tool. Then, choose Edit Story from the Edit menu. When the story editor window appears, you can begin keying text. When you finish keying, choose Edit Layout from the Edit menu to return to the layout view. PageMaker then displays the normal Text Placement icon. Position the icon where you want the new story to appear, and then click to transfer the text from the story editor into the publication.

STEP-BY-STEP 6.1

1. From the data files that are provided with this book, open the publication named **Services**.

2. Place the on-screen story from this publication into the story editor by clicking the **Text** tool and then clicking anywhere in the body of the text.

3. Choose **Edit Story** from the **Edit** menu. Remain in the story editor window for the next Step-by-Step.

Working in the Story Editor Window

When the story editor window appears (as shown earlier in Figure 6-2), it contains an insertion point, and, if you are editing an existing story, it contains the text from that story. The end of the story is indicated by a vertical bar (|). You can immediately begin keying or editing as you normally would. To key new text, simply begin keying. To edit text in an existing story, place the insertion point where you want to begin editing (by using the arrow keys or the mouse), and then make the editing changes needed. As you work with text in the story editor, you can use nearly all of the features described in previous lessons to move the insertion point, key, or make editing changes.

STEP-BY-STEP 6.2

1. Press the **Page Down** key slowly several times to examine all the text in the story. Then, press the **Page Up** key until you reach the beginning of the story.

2. In the title of the story, select the word **AIRLINE** by double-clicking the word—it will appear highlighted. Next, key **TRANSPORTATION** and then press the **spacebar** once.

3. In the first line of the story, select the word **flight**. Next, key **airline and train** and then press the **spacebar** once. Remain in the story editor window for the next Step-by-Step.

Finding Text

The story editor contains a Find feature that lets you locate a word or phrase anywhere within the current story, or even within any story in the publication. In a long story, for example, you can use the Find feature to locate a certain word or phrase anywhere in that story without having to read the entire text word for word.

To search for a word or phrase in the story editor window, place the insertion point where you want the search to begin. Next, choose Find from the Utilities menu to display the Find dialog box shown in Figure 6-3. In the Find what text box, key the characters, words, or phrase that you want to locate. You can include characters, numbers, punctuation marks, and even spaces.

FIGURE 6-3
The Find dialog box

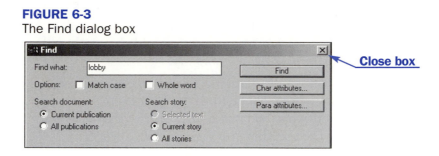

Close box

There are two options in the Find dialog box you may find useful: Match case and Whole word. When you enter words or phrases that you want to find, PageMaker, by default, does not match any upper- or lowercase letters. For example, if you key *an* in the Find what text box, PageMaker will search for *an, An,* and *AN.* If you need to match upper- and lowercase letters exactly, select the Match case option.

The Find feature, also by default, searches for matching characters, not words. If you key *the* in the Find what box, besides finding the word *the,* PageMaker might also find these three characters within other words, such as *there* and *these.* To locate entire words instead of matching characters, select the Whole word option.

When using the Find feature, PageMaker will search only the story that you are currently working with in the story editor. If you want to search all the stories in the current publication, select the All stories option.

When you are finished selecting the options in the Find dialog box, click Find. If PageMaker finds a matching entry, it highlights the entry in the story editor window and the Find dialog box remains on the screen. To search for the next occurrence of the same entry, click Find next. When you are finished using the Find feature, click the Close box (X) in the top right-hand corner of the Find dialog box.

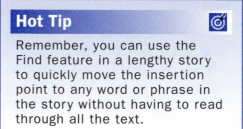

Hot Tip

Remember, you can use the Find feature in a lengthy story to quickly move the insertion point to any word or phrase in the story without having to read through all the text.

STEP-BY-STEP 6.3

1. Position the insertion point at the beginning of the story and then choose **Find** from the **Utilities** menu. The Find dialog box appears.

2. In the Find what text box, key **lobby**.

3. Select the **Whole word** option. Click **Find**. Notice how the first occurrence of the word *lobby* appears highlighted in the story editor window and the Find dialog box remains on-screen.

4. Search for the next occurrence of lobby by clicking **Find next**.

5. Click the **Close** box in the Find dialog box (if needed, see Figure 6-3 for its location). Remain in the story editor window for the next Step-by-Step.

Changing Text

The story editor also contains a Change feature that lets you find text and replace it with other text. In some popular word processing programs, this is referred to as the search and replace feature. You can use the Change feature to replace one word with a different word. For example, you can change *you'll* to the words *you will*. You can also change phrases or abbreviations using the Change feature. For example, you could change an abbreviation such as *IAC* with a company name such as *Import Auto Company*.

To begin changing text, first place the insertion point in the story where you want the changes to begin. Next, choose Change from the Utilities menu to display the dialog box shown in Figure 6-4. In the Find what text box, key the text that you want to locate or find. In the Change to text box, key the text that you want to substitute.

FIGURE 6-4
The Change dialog box

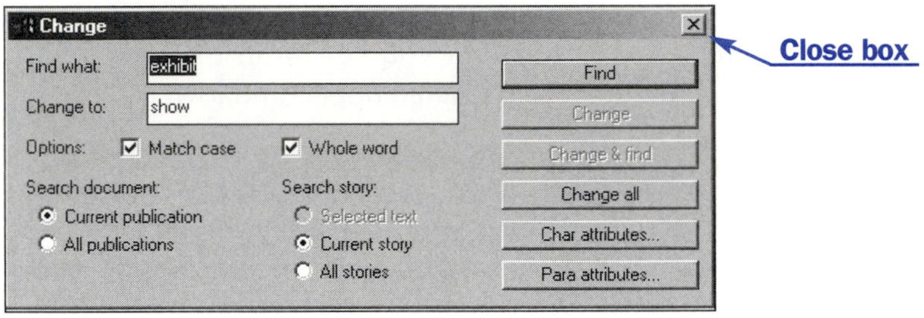

Close box

To have PageMaker find only entries in upper- or lowercase, select Match case. To find matching words (not matching characters), select the Whole word option. To have the changes made in all stories of the current publication, select the All stories option.

When you are finished selecting the options in the Change dialog box, click Find. If PageMaker locates the entry, it highlights that entry in the story editor and keeps the Change dialog box on-screen. Click Change & find to change the highlighted entry and locate the next occurrence, or click Find next to skip the highlighted entry and locate the next occurrence. To replace all occurrences of the entry automatically, click Change all. When finished using the Change feature, click the Close box in the top right corner of the Change dialog box.

S TEP-BY-STEP 6.4

1. Position the insertion point at the beginning of the story and then choose **Change** from the **Utilities** menu. (The last word you searched for may appear in the text box.)

2. In the Find what text box, key **Dial**, making certain to capitalize the first letter of the word.

3. Click inside the Change to text box and then key **Touch**, making certain to capitalize the first letter of the word.

4. Select the options **Match case** and **Whole word**, and then click **Find**.

5. Click **Change & find** to change the first occurrence of the word Dial.

STEP-BY-STEP 6.4 Continued

6. Click **Change & find** to replace the next occurrence of the word Dial.

7. Click **Change all** to replace all remaining occurrences of Dial throughout the story.

8. Click the **Close** box in the Change dialog box. (If needed, see Figure 6-4 for its location.)

9. Press the **Page Up** key and notice how all occurrences of the word Dial have been replaced with the word Touch. Remain in the story editor window for the next Step-by-Step.

Copying and Moving Text

At times, you may want to move text from one place to another in the same story, or you may want to use the same text in several different places. PageMaker's Copy, Cut, and Paste features let you perform these actions. When you copy text, it appears twice—in its old and new locations. When you move text, the text is deleted from its original location and moved elsewhere.

Copying Text

To copy text, first select the text to copy and then choose Copy from the Edit menu. This command copies the selected text into the computer's memory. Next, place the insertion point where you want the copied text to appear and choose Paste from the Edit menu. A copy of the text now appears in the new location. Remember that the text also appears in its previous location as well.

Cutting and Pasting Text

To move text from one location to another, first select the text you want to move and then choose Cut from the Edit menu. This command deletes the text from its current location and stores it in the computer's memory. Next, place the insertion point where you want the text to appear and choose Paste from the Edit menu. The text now appears in its new location.

STEP-BY-STEP 6.5

1. Move the insertion point to the last line of text in the story. Then, select the entire last line of text beginning with the words **The pool is located** by triple-clicking anywhere in that line of text.

2. Choose **Copy** from the **Edit** menu.

3. Locate the line of text just below the HEALTH CLUB entry that begins "The Health Club has." Next, using the mouse, select the words **Touch 125** at the end of that line and then choose **Paste** from the **Edit** menu. Notice how the line of text you copied now appears in the new location.

4. Place the mouse pointer just to the left of the **C** in **CASHIER** and select the word **CASHIER** as well as the next two lines immediately below the entry (the line of text that reads "Located in ..." and the blank line beneath that). Then, select this text by dragging the mouse pointer downward.

STEP-BY-STEP 6.5 Continued

5. Choose **Cut** from the **Edit** menu and observe how the text is deleted from its previous location.

6. Move the insertion point downward until it is positioned just to the left of the **P** in **POOL**.

7. Choose **Paste** from the **Edit** menu and press the **spacebar** once. Notice how the text you cut now appears in this new location.

8. Choose **Edit Layout** from the **Edit** menu to close the story editor and transfer your editing changes into the publication.

9. Using the **Save As** command, save this publication with the new name **Services Revised**. Then, close the publication but leave PageMaker open for the next Step-by-Step.

Placing a Text File into the Story Editor

In Lesson 5, you learned how to place a text file created in a different program (such as a word processing program) directly on a publication page. However, you can also place a text file right into the story editor. Doing so lets you examine the text, check for spelling errors, or perform other editing activities before you position the work in the publication.

While using the story editor, choose Place from the File menu. A dialog box similar to the Open dialog box appears. Here, select the file you want to import and then click Open.

STEP-BY-STEP 6.6

1. Start a new, single-sided publication containing only one page. Keep the margins at their default settings.

2. Choose **Edit Story** from the **Edit** menu to open the story editor.

3. Choose **Place** from the **File** menu. Then, from the data files that are provided with this book, select the file named **Policy.rtf.** Finally, click **Open**. (*NOTE: This story intentionally contains several spelling errors—do not correct them. You'll learn how to check for and correct spelling errors in the next section.* Leave the publication open for the next Step-by-Step.)

Check for Spelling Errors

The story editor contains a Spelling feature that lets you check for possible spelling errors. It can also identify other potential problems such as irregular capitalization *(tHe)* or words mistakenly keyed twice *(to to)*.

While using the story editor, position the insertion point where you want the spell checking to begin. Then, click the Spelling button or choose Spelling from the Utilities menu. Doing so displays the dialog box shown in Figure 6-5.

FIGURE 6-5
The Spelling dialog box

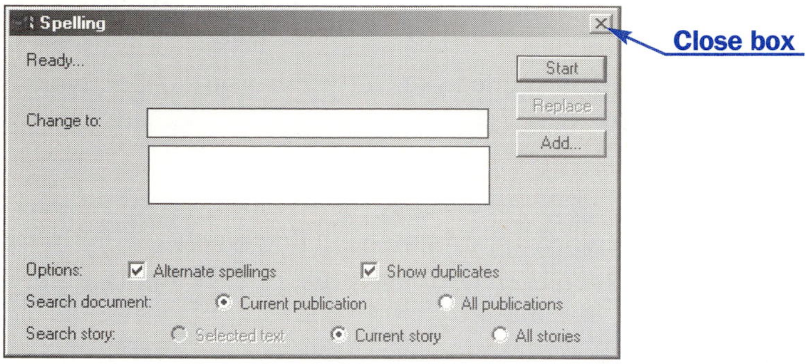

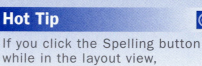

Before you begin spell checking, select the options that you want to use. To have PageMaker suggest correct spellings for misspelled words, make certain the Alternate spellings option is selected. To have the program identify duplicate words, such as *to to*, make certain the Show duplicates option is selected.

Next, indicate what text you want to spell check. Normally, PageMaker will spell check only the current story you are working with in the story editor. If you want it to check all stories in the current publication, select the All stories option. When you are finished selecting the options in the Spelling dialog box, click Start to begin the spell check.

> **Hot Tip**
>
> If you click the Spelling button while in the layout view, PageMaker transfers the current story into the story editor and then starts the spell checking feature.

Spelling Errors

Spell checking works by examining each word in the story against the built-in dictionary. If a word in the story is not in PageMaker's dictionary, it highlights the word in the story editor and suggests possible corrections. These corrections appear in a Change to list box like the one shown in Figure 6-6. To choose a suggested word, click on the word and then click Replace. If the highlighted word is incorrect but the correct word is not listed, key the correction in the Change to text box, and then click Replace.

FIGURE 6-6
Suggested spelling changes appear in the Change to list box

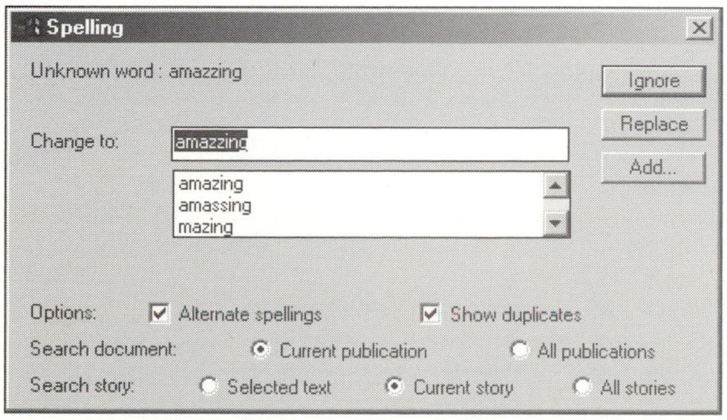

Add a Word

The built-in dictionary may not always contain certain words that you use in a publication, such as proper names or certain technical terms. If a word like this appears when spell checking, Pagemaker will highlight the word. To add the highlighted word to the dictionary so that it will not appear as an error in the future, choose Add and then click OK.

Ignore

If the highlighted word is spelled correctly but you do not want it added to the dictionary, click Ignore to skip the word.

Duplicate Words

The message Duplicate word appears in the dialog box if a word appears twice in succession such as *the the*. Click Ignore to keep both double words, or click Replace to remove the second word.

Irregular Capitalization

If the spell check finds irregular capitalization, such as *tHe*, the message Possible capitalization error appears in the dialog box. Click Ignore to keep the irregular capitalization, or click Replace to correct the capitalization.

Quit the Spelling Feature

When all words have been checked, a message indicating that the spell checking is complete appears in the dialog box. To finish spell checking, click the Close box in the top right corner of the Spelling dialog box.

> **Hot Tip**
>
> The Spelling feature cannot identify the improper use of words such as "I went two the story" instead of "I went to the store." Therefore, always proofread your work. Also, before adding a word to the spelling dictionary, make certain the word is spelled correctly. Otherwise, spell check will assume the word is correct from that point on.

STEP-BY-STEP 6.7

1. Make certain the insertion point is located at the beginning of the story. The first paragraph in this story intentionally contains several spelling errors. A copy of the text from this story appears in Figure 6-7. Choose **Spelling** from the **Utilities** menu.

FIGURE 6-7
A story containing various spelling errors

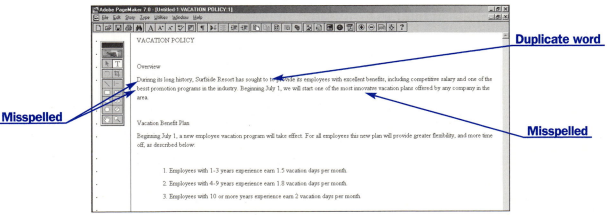

STEP-BY-STEP 6.7 Continued

2. When the Spelling dialog box appears, make certain that both the Alternate spellings and Show duplicates options are selected, then click **Start**.

3. The word *Durinng* will appear as an error. Correct the spelling by clicking the word **During** in the Change to list box. Then click **Replace**.

4. The word *Surfside* will appear as an error, but in this instance, it is the correct name of a company. Click **Ignore** to skip this word.

5. Next, the spell check finds the duplicate words *to to*. Click **Replace** to delete the second word.

6. The word *besst* will appear as an error. Correct the spelling by clicking **best** in the Change to list box, and then click **Replace**.

7. Next, spell check highlights the word *innovatve*. Following instructions similar to those in step 6, use the **Replace** option to correct the word with **innovative**.

8. When a message appears indicating that the spelling check is complete, click the **Close** box in the Spelling dialog box (if needed, see Figure 6-5 for its location). If any text remains highlighted after spell checking is finished, click once anywhere in the story to remove the highlighted text. Keep the publication open for the next Step-by-Step.

View/Hide Hidden Characters

All text in a publication contains hidden characters. These characters show where certain keys were pressed, such as the spacebar, the Enter key, and the Tab key. To keep the publication easy to read on the screen, these characters are always hidden in the layout view, but they can be displayed in the story editor window. Seeing the location of these characters can prove helpful when you're trying to edit a story or resolve certain problems. For example, suppose you accidentally keyed two spaces between two words. This extra space might be difficult to see in the publication window, but could be easily identified by displaying the hidden characters in the story editor.

To view hidden characters in the story editor window, choose Display ¶ from the Story menu. Follow the same instructions to hide those characters, if needed. Any previously hidden characters will now appear as special symbols in the story. These symbols are:

Key Pressed	Symbol
Spacebar	•
Enter (or Return)	¶
Tab	→

You can key or edit text with the hidden characters displayed. Once you select the hidden characters feature, all hidden characters will continue to appear in the story editor window until you turn this feature off. Hidden characters, however, never appear in the layout view.

STEP-BY-STEP 6.8

1. Choose **Display ¶** from the **Story** menu to reveal the hidden characters. Examine the text and notice how the symbols • and ¶ appear throughout the entire story indicating where the spacebar and Enter key were pressed. Notice also at the end of the story where the → symbol appears indicating where the Tab key was pressed.

2. Choose **Display ¶** from the **Story** menu to hide the hidden characters.

3. Choose **Edit Layout** from the **Edit** menu to place the text from this story into the publication window. When the Text Placement icon appears, position the icon slightly below the top margin guide and just to the right of the left margin guide, and then click.

4. Save this publication with the name **Vacation Policy** and then close the publication.

SUMMARY

In this lesson you learned how to:

- Use the story editor to key, edit, and place text.

- Display or hide hidden characters in the story editor window.

- Use the Find feature to locate a word or phrase anywhere within a story.

- Use the Change feature to replace one word or phrase with a different word or phrase, anywhere within a story.

- Use the Copy, Cut, and Paste features to copy or move text.

- Identify misspelled words, duplicated words, and irregular capitalization.

VOCABULARY *Review*

Define the following terms:

Layout view   Story editor

REVIEW *Questions*

TRUE/FALSE

Circle T if the statement is true or F if the statement is false.

T   F   **1.** Choose Story Editor from the File menu to activate the story editor.

T   F   **2.** You cannot use the story editor to create a new story for a publication.

T   F   **3.** When using the Find feature in the story editor, PageMaker matches upper- and lowercase letters by default.

T   F   **4.** By using the Find feature option, you can locate a word or phrase not only in the current story, but within all stories in the publication.

T   F   **5.** Choose Modify from the Edit menu to find a word or phrase in the story editor and replace it with a different word or phrase.

T   F   **6.** Choose Spell from the Utilities menu to activate the spelling check.

T   F   **7.** You can add a word or phrase into PageMaker's spelling dictionary.

T   F   **8.** The spelling check cannot identify irregular capitalization, such as *tHe*.

T   F   **9.** After turning on the hidden characters feature, any previously hidden characters are visible in both the story editor window as well as the publication window.

T   F   **10.** The Spelling feature can identify the improper use of words such as "I went two the store."

FILL IN THE BLANK

Complete the following sentences by writing the correct word or words in the blanks provided.

1. When using the Find feature, select the _____ _____ option to locate entire words instead of matching characters found within words

2. To spell check the story that appears in the story editor window, choose Spelling from the _____ menu.

3. Choose _____ from the File menu to import a text file into the story editor that was created using a different program, such as a word processing program.

4. When hidden characters are displayed, the symbol ¶ is used to represent the _____ key.

5. When using the Change feature to replace all occurrences of one word with another in all stories throughout the entire publication, you need to select the _____ option.

MULTIPLE CHOICE

Select the best response for the following sentences.

1. To place a text file into the story editor:
   A. Choose Import from the File menu.
   B. Choose Import from the Story menu.
   C. Choose Place from the File menu.
   D. Choose Place from the Story menu.
   E. None of the above.

2. To switch from the story editor to the layout view, choose:
   A. Edit Layout from the Edit menu.
   B. Layout Window from the Edit menu.
   C. Edit Layout from the File menu.
   D. Layout Window from the File menu.
   E. None of the above.

3. When using the Find feature, you need to do the following to make certain that PageMaker exactly matches the text with upper- and lowercase letters:
   A. Select the Upper/Lower case option.
   B. Select the Case option.
   C. Select the Exact match option.
   D. Select the Match case option.
   E. None of the above.

4. When viewing hidden characters, special symbols are used to show the location in the text where certain keys were pressed. Which of the following statements is true?
   A. The symbol [represents the Tab key.
   B. The symbol • represents the spacebar.
   C. The symbol ~ represents the Enter key.
   D. The symbol → represents the start of the story.
   E. All of the above are true.

5. Which of the following statements is true about the story editor?
   A. Keying text in the story editor is generally faster than keying text in layout view.
   B. The story editor shows only the text from the current story.
   C. The story editor window does not show exactly how the text will look when positioned in the layout view.
   D. You can use the story editor to create a new story or edit an existing story.
   E. All of the above are true.

PROJECTS

SCANS **PROJECT 6-1**

1. Start a new, single-sided publication containing only one page. Change the left and right margin settings each to **1.5** inches. Keep the other margins at their default settings.

2. Open the story editor window.

3. Choose **Place** from the **File** menu. Then, from the data files that are provided with this book, select the file named **PM-Test.rtf**. Examine the text that appears in the story editor. To save time when keying the original document, the letter T was substituted for the word True, the letter F was substituted for the word False, and the characters PM were substituted for the word PageMaker.

4. Use the **Change** feature with both the **Match case** and the **Whole word** options to replace the letter T with the word **True** throughout the story.

5. Use the **Change** feature with both the **Match case** and **Whole word** options to replace the letter F with the word **False** throughout the story.

6. Use the **Change** feature with both the **Match case** and **Whole word** options to replace the characters **PM** with the word **PageMaker** throughout the story.

7. In the current story, two spaces were accidentally inserted between two words in each of the first two test questions. Display the hidden characters in the story and then locate and remove one of the spaces from each occurrence.

8. This story contains three spelling errors. Use the Spelling feature to identify and correct these errors.

9. Choose **Edit Layout** from the **Edit** menu. When the Text Placement icon appears, position the icon slightly below the top margin guide and just to the right of the left margin guide, and then click.

10. Save the publication with the name **Questionnaire** and then close the publication.

SCANS **TEAMWORK PROJECT**

As you know, the text for a publication can be keyed directly into PageMaker, or created in another program and then imported into a publication. In small groups, review the types of publications in the list that follows. Then, discuss which of those publications you might key directly into PageMaker, and which you might create first in a word processing program and then import into a publication. Explain your decisions.

Business card

One-page flyer

Magazine

Wedding invitation

Small brochure

School newsletter

Résumé

Travel brochure

Textbook, such as this one

CRITICAL *Thinking*

SCANS **ACTIVITY 6-1**

In this lesson, you learned that you could use the Change command to save time when keying the same phrase repeatedly in a lengthy document. Think of three to five different situations in which this feature would be helpful and what Change options you might use in each situation. Then, discuss those situations and how you would use the Change options with your classmates.

UNDERSTANDING TYPOGRAPHY

OBJECTIVES

Upon completion of this lesson, you should be able to:

- Define basic typographic terms.
- Identify the parts of a character.
- Explain how the size of characters are measured.
- Explain and identify different categories of typefaces.
- Explain and identify proportional and monospaced typefaces.
- Identify the names of some popular typefaces.

Estimated Time: 2 hours

VOCABULARY

Ascender

Baseline

Body text

Character

Descender

Display text

Monospaced typeface

Pitch

Points

Proportional typeface

Sans serif

Script

Serif

Typeface

Typography

X-height

Introduction

Typography is the foundation of desktop publishing. Understanding and applying typographic techniques helps set published documents apart from their word-processed counterparts. In this lesson, you will be introduced to basic typographic terms and techniques. In the next lesson, you will learn how to apply these principles to your desktop publishing projects using PageMaker.

Why Learn About Typography?

As mentioned in Lesson 1, *typography* means using type to produce printed documents. In this lesson, you will be introduced to the important typographic terms for identifying and working with type. The lesson also describes general guidelines on how to match type to a specific publication and how to identify type that you see in other printed documents. The intent of this lesson is not necessarily to provide you with firm rules to follow, but instead to give you general guidelines that can help you produce professional-looking publications.

Typography is the key ingredient in desktop publishing. With PageMaker, a computer, and a laser or ink jet printer, anyone can create publications that look as if they were typeset. But, creating high-quality, desktop published documents requires more than just keying the text or drawing a few lines on a page. Applying typographic techniques to your desktop publishing projects is essential if you want to produce publications that look professional and are easy to read. You also need to know how to select appropriate typefaces and sizes for the different parts of a document. Without understanding even these basic concepts, you are likely to create published documents that are good-looking disasters.

Examine the three entries in Figure 7-1. Although all three examples contain the same text, the first one looks boring and uninteresting. The second example shows how good typographic techniques can help make an entry look more interesting and inviting to read. The different typefaces (one for the title and another for the body) give the entry a more published appearance. The third example shows how publishing disasters can occur if basic typographic techniques are not followed. In the third entry, the typeface is elegant but inappropriate. Also, poor spacing between lines of text make the entry very hard to read.

FIGURE 7-1
Comparing keyed and typographic entries

A keyed entry	**Understanding Typography** The term <u>typography</u> means using type or type-like qualities when creating a document or publication. Most often this means using text in different sizes or styles, as in a newspaper or magazine. With a program like PageMaker, almost anyone can produce publictions that look as if they were typeset.
An entry using good typographic techniques	**Understanding Typography** The term *typography* means using type or type-like qualities when creating a document or publication. Most often this means using text in different sizes or styles, as in a newspaper or magazine. With a program like PageMaker, almost anyone can produce publications that look as if they were typeset.
An entry using poor typographic techniques	*Understanding Typography* *The term typography means using type or type-like qualities when creating a document or publication. Most often this means using text in different sizes or styles, as in a newspaper or magazine. With a program like PageMaker, almost anyone can produce publications that look as if they were typeset.*

Understanding a Typeface

Remember being introduced to typefaces in Lesson 1? To a reader, the most visible part of a publication is the typeface in which the text appears. A *typeface* is a family or a collection of alphanumeric characters in which all the characters have a similar, related design. Today there are thousands of typefaces, and each typeface has a unique, identifying name. Some typefaces bear the name of their designer, such as Zapf Chancery, designed by Hermann Zapf. Others resemble the location where they were designed, such as Helvetica, which was designed in Switzerland. Several typefaces are named for an unusual identifying feature, such as Light Italic or Condensed.

Hot Tip

You can add an almost unlimited number of typefaces to a personal computer. Choosing the correct typeface to use when you have access to hundreds can become confusing. While you are new to desktop publishing, limit yourself to working with just a few of the basic typefaces mentioned in this lesson. They are easy to read and usually provide good-looking results.

Differences between typefaces are sometimes glaring, and at other times are less obvious. Certain typefaces were designed for good readability, others for fitting lengthy text in a small space, and still others for special purposes such as attracting attention or simulating the look of handwriting. While most computers today include dozens of typefaces, you can add any number of additional typefaces to your computer.

The names of some popular typefaces include Arial, Garamond, Helvetica, Times, Times New Roman, Univers and Veranda. Examples of these typefaces appear in Figure 7-2. Today, many newspapers, business publications, and newsletters are printed with these or similar typefaces.

FIGURE 7-2
Examples of some popular typefaces

Arial
ABCDEFGHIJKLMNOPQRSTUVWXYZ1234567890
abcdefghijklmnopqrstuvwxyz!@#$%^&*()
Here is a sentence that appears in Arial.

Garamond
ABCDEFGHIJKLMNOPQRSTUVWXYZ1234567890
abcdefghijklmnopqrstuvwxyz!@#$%^&*()
Here is a sentence that appears in Garamond.

Helvetica
ABCDEFGHIJKLMNOPQRSTUVWXYZ1234567890
abcdefghijklmnopqrstuvwxyz!@#$%^&*()
Here is a sentence that appears in Helvetica.

Times
ABCDEFGHIJKLMNOPQRSTUVWXYZ1234567890
abcdefghijklmnopqrstuvwxyz!@#$%^&*()
Here is a sentence that appears in Times.

Times New Roman
ABCDEFGHIJKLMNOPQRSTUVWXYZ1234567890
abcdefghijklmnopqrstuvwxyz!@#$%^&*()
Here is a sentence that appears in Times New Roman.

Univers
ABCDEFGHIJKLMNOPQRSTUVWXYZ1234567890
abcdefghijklmnopqrstuvwxyz!@#$%^&*()
Here is a sentence that appears in Univers.

Veranda
ABCDEFGHIJKLMNOPQRSTUVWXYZ1234567890
abcdefghijklmnopqrstuvwxyz!@#$%^&*()
Here is a sentence that appears in Veranda.

The best typeface to use for a specific publication depends on the message you want to convey, the audience, and the organization for which it is being created. Some typefaces are strong and dramatic, others are traditional or sophisticated, and still others are more casual. Traditional typefaces, like Times or Helvetica, have been used for decades and are considered more conservative and easy to read. More modern typefaces, with names such as Avant Garde and Futura, have a more up-to-date look. But, this more modern look can sometimes be inappropriate if used in publications designed for more traditional organizations. You will learn more about selecting appropriate typefaces later in this lesson.

Parts of a Typeface

The most basic element in typography is a *character* such as the letter A or the number 4. Each character in a typeface is unique, and the parts of any character are identified using certain terms. These terms are shown in Figure 7-3 and are described below.

FIGURE 7-3
Elements of a typeface

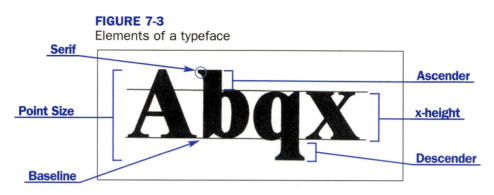

All of the characters in a typeface run along a *baseline*, which is an imaginary horizontal line used for positioning each character and determining the spacing between each line of text. The bottom of all uppercase characters and the base of all lowercase characters fall on this baseline. The *x-height* is the height of the lowercase letter x. The body of lowercase characters in a typeface are designed to be no taller than this x-height. Because some typefaces have a higher x-height than other typefaces, their characters tend to look larger than characters in typefaces with lower x-heights.

An *ascender* is the part of certain lowercase letters that extends above the x-height. Ascenders appear in the letters b, d, f, h, k, and l. A *descender* is the part of certain lowercase letters that falls below the baseline. Descenders appear in the letters g, j, p, and q. Both ascenders and descenders help give a typeface its unique, distinctive look.

Measuring Type

When you use a word processor, characters are often measured by their *pitch,* which means the number of characters per inch. In typography, characters are measured by their height using a measurement system called *points*. There are 72 points to an inch. Here are examples of text in different point sizes:

8-point 10-point 18-point 24-point 36-point

When measuring type, the point size is the distance from the top of all ascenders to the bottom of all descenders, plus a small amount of additional space above and below to keep one line of text separated from the next.

Choosing the appropriate point size to use for text entries in a publication is very important, because the size affects how easy or difficult the text is to read and how the publication looks overall. Over the years, certain standards have evolved that suggest the best point sizes to use for certain types of entries. Body text is normally in the 9- to 13-point size range. *Body text* refers to the text used in the body or major portion of a publication The text used for headings and subheadings is called *display text* and is always larger than body text. Subheadings normally appear in a 14- to 18-point size while head-ings usually appear in a 24-point size or larger. Studies have shown that lengthy body text entries are easiest to read in a 10- to 12-point size. Certain kinds of publica-tions, however, like newspapers, magazines, or tele-phone directories, often print text in smaller point sizes, like 9-points or less, in an effort to fit more text onto each page. Text in such small point sizes can be somewhat more difficult to read.

Typeface Categories

Typefaces can be grouped into three categories—serif, sans serif, and script. A *serif* typeface has small lines or strokes that appear at the ends of characters. Here are some examples of serif typefaces:

Bodoni   **Cheltenham**   Garamond
Goudy   Perpetua   Times New Roman

Several studies on readability have shown that text in serif typefaces is generally easier to read when used in 9- to 12-point sizes than sans serif text. The serifs give each character a more distinctive shape, which helps your eye identify each word faster. Serifs also help your eye move easily across each line of text. This is why you usually find serif typefaces used in lengthy publi-cations, such as newspapers, books, and magazines.

Sans serif is French for *without serif*. Because sans serif typefaces lack the extra lines or strokes found in serif typefaces, they can often look similar to the untrained eye. Here are exam-ples of sans serif typefaces:

Arial   Avant Garde   Futura
Helvetica   Univers   Veranda

Typefaces without serifs are especially easy to read when used in large point sizes such as 18-points and above. Most newspapers and many magazines use sans serif typefaces for the titles of articles or stories. Sans serif typefaces are also easy to read when used in small sizes like 6- or 8-points. The text in many telephone books and government forms, for example, appears in an 8-point, sans serif typeface.

Script typefaces resemble handwriting or calligraphy. These typefaces were originally designed to lend an elegant look to publications such as announcements or invitations. Many of the newer script typefaces look less formal than their earlier counterparts and are sometimes used to add a more personal look to a publication, or to attract attention. Here are some examples of script typefaces:

Brush Script   *Caflisch Script*   *Commercial Script*
English   *Shelley Volante*   *Vladimir Script*

Because of their elegant or unusual character design, text printed in a script typeface can take longer to read. As a result, you need to be extremely careful where you use script typefaces. They should be used only in publications with limited amounts of text.

The Effect of X-Height

As mentioned earlier, two typefaces having a different x-height can cause the characters in one typeface to look larger than the characters in the other typeface. In the example below, the word PageMaker appears in both the Avant Garde and the Times New Roman typeface. Both examples appear in a 36-point size.

PageMaker
PageMaker

As you can see, the characters in the first entry look taller because Avant Garde has a taller x-height than the second entry in the Times typeface. Because they are larger, characters in typefaces with taller x-heights tend to attract the reader's eye. Thus they are best used for display text like titles and subheads.

Characters in typefaces with taller x-heights are also generally wider than characters in typefaces with shorter x-heights. Text printed in a typeface with a taller x-height requires more horizontal space on a page than the same text printed in a typeface having a lower x-height. The examples in Figure 7-4 show the same Abraham Lincoln quote printed in the same point size, but using three typefaces each having a different x-height. Notice the differences.

FIGURE 7-4
Examples of typefaces with different x-heights

Times	"The best thing about the future is that it only comes one day at a time."
Avant Garde	"The best thing about the future is that it only comes one day at a time."
Bookman	"The best thing about the future is that it only comes one day at a time."

As you can see, different x-heights produce text of widely varying lengths. In the examples shown in Figure 7-4, the same quote requires only two lines in the Times typeface, but three lines in the Avant Garde and Bookman typefaces.

Understanding how x-height affects the width of characters is important when you're selecting typefaces for a publication. For example, if you need to fit a great deal of text onto only a few pages, you could select a typeface with a lower x-height.

Letterspacing

Another characteristic of a typeface is the amount of space each character uses. On many standard word processors or even old fashioned typewriters, every character uses the same amount of space. Thin characters, like the capital letter I, use the same amount of space as wider characters, like the capital letter X. A *monospaced typeface* is when all the characters in a typeface use the same amount of space. Courier, for example, is a monospaced typeface.

Typefaces in which different characters use different amounts of space are known as *proportional*. The capital letter X uses much more space than a thin character like the capital letter I in a proportional typeface. Because typeface characters have different widths, the text tends to look more interesting than monospaced text. Also, because some characters in a proportional typeface are less wide than other characters, you can fit more text onto a page by using a proportional typeface. In Figure 7-5, the first entry appears in a monospaced typeface and requires four lines, but the second entry shown in a proportional typeface and requires only two and one-half lines. Do you think the proportional typeface looks more interesting?

FIGURE 7-5
Text in monospaced (top) and proportional (bottom) typeface

```
Serifs are the thin lines or strokes
that can appear at the beginning and
end of characters. Typefaces that lack
serifs are called sans serif.
```

Serifs are the thin lines or strokes that can appear at the beginning and end of characters. Typefaces that lack serifs are called sans serif.

At this point, you might be asking yourself—*When would I use a monospaced typeface?* Although they are sometimes seen in published documents, such as word processing and computer programming books, monospaced typefaces do have other important uses, especially in publications containing numbers. Because monospaced numbers have the same width, it is often easier for your eye to scan up and down through columns of numbers.

Recognizing a Typeface

Although it requires some practice, you can often recognize some typefaces by looking closely at their key characters. Type designers create these characters to give each typeface its own unique identity. These key characters include the letters G, M, T, Q, g, m, t, q, the question mark (?), and the numeral 1. Figure 7-6 lists examples of key characters in different typefaces.

If you look closely at the key characters in Figure 7-6, you will notice the same character looks significantly different in different typefaces. Usually the letters Q and g are the most unique and identifying characters of a typeface. If you watch for these key characters in the publications you see daily, you can often identify the typeface that was used.

FIGURE 7-6
Key characters help identify a typeface

Arial	Q	M	g	1
Avant Garde	Q	M	g	1
Bodoni	Q	M	g	1
Bookman	Q	M	g	1
Century Schoolbook	Q	M	g	1
Futura	Q	M	g	1
Garamond	Q	M	g	1

Typefaces Can Affect the Reader's Response

As you have seen in this lesson, all typefaces have unique characteristics. Because of the shape of their characters or their popular use in certain types of documents, typefaces can sometimes evoke a certain feeling in the reader. Some typefaces can make a publication feel more formal, businesslike, lighthearted, or important. The entries in Figure 7-7 show examples of how different typefaces can give a very different feeling to entries.

FIGURE 7-7
Different typefaces convey different feelings

TYPEFACE	AN EXAMPLE
Times	A Proposal for Stress Management Training
Century Schoolbook	The dog ran after the cat
Arial	SCHOOLS CLOSE FOR TWO WEEKS!
Avant Garde	OUR COMPUTERS ARE DEPENDABLE
Zapf Chancery	You are cordially invited to attend our grand opening.

Almost since the time the printing press was first developed, serif typefaces have been used in printed documents. The Times typeface was originally designed in the 1930s to produce attractive looking printed documents such as newspapers and magazines that were easy to read, especially in small point sizes. Modified versions of that typeface such as Times Roman and Times New Roman were later created in the 1970s to produce easy to read text on personal computer printers. Because these typefaces are still widely used today, they give text a professional and familiar feeling. Century Schoolbook, another serif typeface, was designed with a tall x-height for exceptional readability. Created in the 1920s, this typeface was widely used for years in elementary school textbooks such as the *Dick and Jane* series.

Because of the uniform, geometric shape of their characters, sans serif typefaces like Arial or Veranda have a clean look that conveys a feeling of importance. Today, such typefaces are widely used for display text in headlines or titles. Another sans serif typeface, Avant Garde, was designed with wide, geometric characters to convey a modern, crisp feeling.

Script typefaces like Zapf Chancery are elegant and give text a more formal, almost handwritten look. But as mentioned earlier, text in script typefaces generally takes longer to read because of the elaborate nature of their characters.

SUMMARY

In this lesson you learned how to:

- Explain how typography means using type to produce printed documents.
- Identify the three categories of typefaces including serif, sans serif and script.
- Explain how characters in a typeface are measured by their point size.
- Define the parts of a character including the baseline, ascender, descender and x-height.
- Explain letterspacing and describe both monospaced or proportional letterspacing.
- Identify key characters and describe how they can often be used to help identify a specific typeface.

VOCABULARY *Review*

Define the following terms:

Ascender	Monospaced typeface	Script
Baseline	Pitch	Serif
Body text	Points	Typeface
Character	Proportional typeface	Typography
Descender	Sans serif	X-height
Display text		

REVIEW *Questions*

TRUE/FALSE

Circle T if the statement is true or F if the statement is false.

T   F   **1.** Typography means using type to produce printed documents.

T   F   **2.** Sans serif is French for without serif.

T   F   **3.** All the characters in a typeface run along the baseline.

T   F   **4.** There are 72 points to an inch.

T   F   **5.** For body text, studies have shown that lengthy text entries are easiest to read in a 10- to 12-point size.

T   F   **6.** Typefaces with a taller x-height generally use less space on each line than those with a lower x-height.

T   F   **7.** In a proportional typeface, every character uses the same amount of space.

T   F   **8.** You can often identify a typeface by examining its key characters P or F.

T   F   **9.** Script typefaces, like Zapf Chancery, contain elegant characters that give a publication a more formal, almost handwritten look.

T   F **10.** Times is an example of a serif typeface.

FILL IN THE BLANK

Complete the following sentences by writing the correct word or words in the blanks provided.

1. Typefaces can be grouped into three categories: serif, sans serif and _____.

2. In a _____ typeface, every character uses the same amount of space.

3. All characters in a typeface run along an imaginary horizontal line called the _____.

4. The thin lines or strokes that appear at the end of certain typeface characters are called _____.

5. The part of a lowercase letter that extends above the x-height is called a(n) _____.

MATCHING

Write the letter of the item in Figure 7-8 that identifies the typeface elements listed below.

FIGURE 7-8

___ **1.** X-height

___ **2.** Ascender

___ **3.** Baseline

___ **4.** Descender

___ **5.** The serif portion of a character

PROJECTS

PROJECT 7-1

To help you understand typefaces better, six sample entries which use different typefaces appear in the table below (Figure 7-9). By examining the key characters, determine which typeface was used for each entry. Mark your answer in the space on the right. Use the information in the Recognizing a Typeface section presented earlier in this lesson to help you make your selection.

FIGURE 7-9
Identify these typefaces

SAMPLE ENTRY	TYPEFACE USED
QUICK! YOU BETTER FINISH THAT LETTER.	
QUICK! YOU BETTER FINISH THAT LETTER.	
QUICK! YOU BETTER FINISH THAT LETTER.	
QUICK! YOU BETTER FINISH THAT LETTER.	
QUICK! YOU BETTER FINISH THAT LETTER.	

SCANS PROJECT 7-2

Carefully examine the newspaper advertisement shown in Figure 7-10. Then, using the charts and examples from this lesson, determine the typographic settings for various entries in the advertisement. Complete the questions that follow Figure 7-10.

FIGURE 7-10
Newspaper advertisement

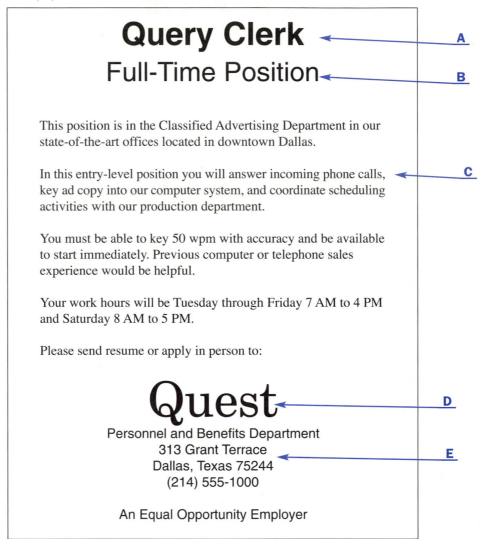

1. What typeface was used for the main heading (A)?

2. What is the approximate point size of the subtitle (B)?

3. What is the approximate point size of the body text (C)?

4. What typeface was used for the company name (D)?

5. What is the approximate point size of the department name and address (E)?

PROJECT 7-3

Four sample entries are shown below in Figure 7-11. Each entry is printed using a different typeface. Match the most appropriate typeface in Figure 7-11 to the numbered statements listed below.

FIGURE 7-11
Select the appropriate typeface

ENTRY NUMBER	SAMPLE ENTRY
A.	Each typeface has a distinctive appearance.
B.	*Each typeface has a distinctive appearance.*
C.	Each typeface has a distinctive appearance.
D.	Each typeface has a distinctive appearance.

____ **1.** A wedding announcement.

____ **2.** A publication to which you want to give a basic, word-processed appearance.

____ **3.** Body text used in a newspaper or business report.

____ **4.** Text that will appear in a 6- or 8-point size.

SCANS   🌐 **WEB ACTIVITY**

Typefaces are sold online through a number of different Web sites. Several of the leading typeface publishers and distributors include Agfa Monotype Corporation at *http://www.fonts.com*; International Typeface Corporation at *http://www.itcfonts.com*; and Adobe Type Library at *http://www.adobe.com/type/main.html*. Each of these Web sites lets you see all of the typefaces that they offer. Visit one or more of these sites and check out some of the different typefaces. If the Web site you visit provides a listing of the most popular typefaces they sell, examine some of them to see what is currently popular. Finally, pick one typeface and determine how much it would cost to purchase it for use in your publications. Write a brief report that describes your actions and findings.

SCANS   🤝 **TEAMWORK PROJECT**

1. In a group, collect one of each of the following publications:
   A. The front page from a national newspaper, such as *USA Today* or the *New York Times*.
   B. A page that contains articles from a national magazine, such as *Time* or *Newsweek*
   C. One page from a national newspaper or magazine that contains a full-page advertisement.

2. Next, closely examine each of the publications and answer the following questions:
   A. What typeface(s) and point size(s) were used?
   B. Does the page contain serif, sans serif, or a combination of serif and sans serif typefaces?
   C. Why do you think the particular type specifications were used for each specific page?

SCANS **CRITICAL***Thinking*

In this lesson, you learned that all monospaced typeface characters have the same width. During the next week, look closely at the documents you encounter on a daily basis, such as flyers you see at school, catalogs or junk mail you receive at home. See if you can locate an example in which a monospaced typeface was used.

CHANGING TYPE SPECIFICATIONS

Introduction

As you create or edit text in a publication, you can apply various type specifications. In this lesson, you will learn how to select from different typefaces, point sizes, type styles, and type cases.

Understanding Type Specifications

All text in a PageMaker publication appears with certain type specifications. *Type specifications* consist of a typeface, point size, and type style. In the last lesson, you learned that a typeface includes all characters of a certain design. In PageMaker, a typeface is referred to as a *font,* such as the Arial or the Times New Roman font. You learned in Lesson 7 that point size refers to the height of a character. Type styles, such as bold or italics, are different ways of adding emphasis to text.

Selecting the Font

The text in any publication can use many fonts. Unless you specifically select a font for the text, PageMaker automatically chooses the standard, default font which is Times New Roman, Times Roman, or Times. You can choose a font while editing existing text or while keying new text entries. To change the font that is used for existing text, first select the text that you want to change with the Text tool. If you are changing the font for new text, first position the insertion point where you want the new font to begin. Then, whether you are changing the font for new or existing text, choose Font from the Type menu to display submenus like the ones shown in Figure 8-1. This list shows the names of all fonts available in your computer, in alphabetical order. If your computer has more fonts available than PageMaker can display in a single submenu, the word More appears at the top of that list. Choose More to display additional font lists (see Figure 8-1). A check mark appears in front of the font that is currently selected. To choose a different font, click it in the submenu.

FIGURE 8-1
Single (left) and multiple (right) submenus

More		More		More		More	
Abadi MT Condensed		Abadi MT Condensed		Banjoman Open Bold		CG Times	
Abadi MT Condensed Extra Bold		Abadi MT Condensed Extra Bold		Baskerville Old Face		Charter Bd BT	
Abadi MT Condensed Light		Abadi MT Condensed Light		Bauhaus 93		Charter BT	
Adolescence		Adolescence		Beesknees ITC		Cheltenhm BdCn BT	
AGaramond		AGaramond		Bell MT		Cheltenhm BdHd BT	
Albertus Extra Bold		Albertus Extra Bold		BellGothic Blk BT		Cheltenhm BdItHd BT	
Albertus Medium		Albertus Medium		BellGothic BT		Cheltenhm BT	
Algerian		Algerian		Bermuda Solid		Cheltenhm XBdCn BT	
AlicoScriptSSK		AlicoScriptSSK		Bernard MT Condensed		ChelthmITC Bk BT	
Almanac MT		Almanac MT		BernhardMod BT		Chiller	
American Uncial		American Uncial		Bickley Script		Clarendon Condensed	
AmeriGarmnd BT		AmeriGarmnd BT		BinnerD		Colonna MT	
Amherst		Amherst		Blackadder ITC		Comic Sans MS	
Andale Mono IPA		Andale Mono IPA		BlackAdderll		CommercialScript BT	
Andy		Andy		Bodoni Bd BT		CommonBullets	
Animals 1		Animals 1		Bodoni Bk BT		Compacta Bd BT	
Annifont		Annifont		Bon Apetit MT		Compacta Blk BT	
Antique Olive		Antique Olive		Book Antiqua		Conga	
Architecture		Architecture		Bookman Old Style		Cooper Black	
Arial		Arial		Bradley Hand ITC		Copperplate Gothic Bold	
Arial Black		Arial Black		Braggadocio		Copperplate Gothic Light	
Arial Condensed Bold		Arial Condensed Bold		Britannic Bold		CopprplGoth Bd BT	
Arial Narrow		Arial Narrow		Broadway		Courier New	
Arial Narrow Special G1		Arial Narrow Special G1		Brush Script		CourierPS	
Arial Narrow Special G2		Arial Narrow Special G2		Brush Script MT		Creepy	
Arial Rounded MT Bold		Arial Rounded MT Bold		Californian FB		Curlz MT	
Arial Special G1		Arial Special G1		Calisto MT		Desdemona	
Arial Special G2		Arial Special G2		Calligraph421 BT		Directions MT	
Ashford		Ashford		Caslon Bd BT		DomCasual BT	
Ashley		Ashley		CaslonOldFace BT		Dutch801 Rm BT	
augie		augie		CaslonOldFace Hv BT		Edda	
Augsburger Initials		Augsburger Initials		Castellar		Edwardian Script ITC	
Avant Guard		Avant Guard		CentSchbook BT		Elephant	
AvantGarde Bk BT		AvantGarde Bk BT		Century Gothic		EnglischeSchT	
AvantGarde Md BT		AvantGarde Md BT		Century Schoolbook		EnglischeSchTDemBol	
Bandy		Bandy		CG Omega		English157 BT	

S TEP-BY-STEP 8.1

1. Start a new publication. When the Document Setup dialog box appears, keep the default settings by clicking **OK**.

2. Click the **Text** tool. Then, click an insertion point slightly below the top margin guide and just to the right of the left margin guide.

3. Enlarge the area around the insertion point to **Actual Size**.

4. Key **This is the default font** and then press **Enter**.

5. Choose **Font** from the **Type** menu. Then, choose **Arial**, **Helvetica**, or **Univers**.

Hot Tip 🎯

If your computer has many fonts, you can often find yourself with numerous font submenus displayed. Some of those submenus may even hide other lists, making it difficult to select a needed font. To remove these submenus one at a time, simply press the **Esc** key.

STEP-BY-STEP 8.1 Continued

6. Key **This text appears in the font named** followed by a single space. Then, key the name of the font that you selected in step 5 and press **Enter**.

7. Repeat step 6, but this time choose **Times New Roman**, **Times**, or **Times Roman** from the font submenu.

8. Key **This text appears in the font named** followed by a single space. Then key the name of the font that you selected in step 7, and press **Enter**. Keep this publication on-screen for use in the next Step-by-Step.

Selecting the Point Size

As you learned in the previous lesson, different point sizes are best used in certain kinds of entries, such as 9 to 13 points for body text, and 14 to 18 points for subtitles. Although you can specify almost any point size for text, such as 15.5 points, certain point sizes are used more frequently than others in published documents. In PageMaker, a fast way to select a point size is by choosing it from a list of frequently used sizes.

To change the point size, select the text that you want to change or place the insertion point where you want the new point size to begin. Then choose Size from the Type menu to display a font size submenu like the one in Figure 8-2. This list contains a selection of standard, frequently used point sizes. A check mark appears in front of the currently selected point size. Click a different size in the submenu to select it.

> ### Hot Tip
>
> You can also use keyboard shortcuts to select the next greater or smaller standard point size. After selecting the text or positioning the insertion point, press **Ctrl+Alt+>** for the next larger standard size, or press **Ctrl+Alt+<** for the next smaller standard size.

FIGURE 8-2
Font size submenu

STEP-BY-STEP 8.2

1. With the insertion point now located at the beginning of a new line, choose **Size** from the **Type** menu and then choose **8**. Next, key **This text is 8 points** and press **Enter**.

2. Choose **Size** from the **Type** menu and then choose **18**. Next, key **This text is 18 points** and press **Enter**.

3. Choose **Size** from the **Type** menu and then choose **36**. Next, key **This text is 36 points** and press **Enter**. Keep this publication on-screen for use in the next Step-by-Step.

In addition to selecting from a submenu of frequently used point sizes, there are other ways to specify any point size between 4 and 650 points. To select from the menu, choose Size from the Type menu, and then choose Other from the submenu. Then, in the text box labeled Points, key a new point size, such as 13 or 22, and then click OK. If needed, you can specify the new size in one-tenth point increments, such as 10.2 or 12.5.

You can also change point size by using toolbar buttons. Click the Increase Font Size or Decrease Font Size buttons (see Figure 8-3) to increase or decrease the size by one-tenth of a point each time you click.

FIGURE 8-3
Increase and decrease font size

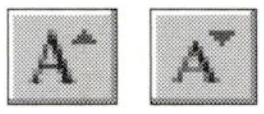

STEP-BY-STEP 8.3

1. With the insertion point now located at the beginning of a new line, choose **Size** from the **Type** menu and then choose **Other**. When the Other Point Size dialog box appears, key **16** and then click **OK**.

2. Key **This text is 16 points** and press **Enter**.

3. Choose **Select all** from the **Edit** menu.

4. Choose **Size** from the **Type** menu and then choose **12**.

5. Remove the highlighting by clicking anywhere within the story. Keep this publication on-screen for use in the next Step-by-Step.

Selecting a Type Style

Type style is a technique that lets you vary the emphasis given to certain characters. Regular characters that have no emphasis, like those in this paragraph, appear using the Normal type style. Examples of type styles that have added emphasis include bold, italics, underlined, and strikethru.

To choose a type style, select the text that you want to change, or place the insertion point where you want the new type style to begin. Then, choose Type Style from the Type menu to display a submenu of different styles like the one shown in Figure 8-4. A check mark appears in front of the current style. Simply choose the style desired from the submenu. Some of the most frequently used styles are described in the following paragraphs.

FIGURE 8-4
Type style submenu

✔ Normal	Sh^Sp
Bold	Sh^B
Italic	Sh^I
Underline	Sh^U
Strikethru	Sh^/
Reverse	Sh^V

Normal

Normal is the default type style. If you open a new PageMaker publication, click the Text tool, and then begin keying, the text appears in the Normal type style. Such text contains standard, upright characters that are not bold, underlined, italic, or set off in any other way. Normal is also used to remove a different type style from text, such as bold or italic.

Bold

Bold is text that appears darker then normal, **like these four words**. Bold is often used in display text to make certain entries easy to identify, such as titles and headings. Bold can also be used in the body of a publication for much the same reason. In many computer books, bold is used to identify certain keys to press, such as press the **Enter** key. Because it is darker than the surrounding text, however, you should avoid using bold for too many sentences or paragraphs. Doing so can make the bold text more difficult to read and make the page look unbalanced.

Underline

Underlined text contains a thin line drawn underneath each character, <u>like these four words</u>. In the past, underlining was normally used to indicate book titles or quotations, or add emphasis to newly introduced terms. In published work today, however, italic is almost always used in place of underlining. Underlining is almost never seen in published documents today because the underline falls within the white space that helps to visually separate two lines of text. Keeping this space free is important because it helps the reader's eye move more easily across each line of text.

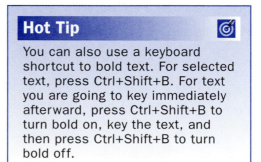

Hot Tip

You can also use a keyboard shortcut to bold text. For selected text, press Ctrl+Shift+B. For text you are going to key immediately afterward, press Ctrl+Shift+B to turn bold on, key the text, and then press Ctrl+Shift+B to turn bold off.

Italic

In published documents, italic is preferred over underline. Italic characters slant to the right *like these four words*. Because italic characters have the same height, shape, and space as other characters in the same font, they are a professional yet quiet way to emphasize text. Entries that normally appear in italic include book titles, newly introduced terms, and quotations.

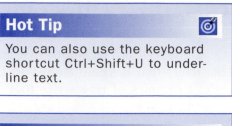

Hot Tip

You can also use the keyboard shortcut Ctrl+Shift+U to underline text.

Strikethru

Strikethru places a thin horizontal line (—) through the text, ~~like these four words~~. Strikethru is often used in legal documents to identify entries in a contract that both parties agree to remove from that contract.

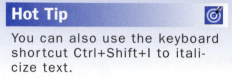

Hot Tip

You can also use the keyboard shortcut Ctrl+Shift+I to italicize text.

Reverse

The reverse type style changes the color of each character to white. When placed against a dark background, the results look like this example: ▮This is reverse text.▮ PageMaker does not create this dark background, however. Instead, you normally position such text over a graphic that already contains a dark background, such as a rectangle containing a dark, solid color.

STEP-BY-STEP 8.4

1. Move the insertion point to the end of the story and press **Enter** to insert a blank line.

2. Select **Type Style** from the **Type** menu and then choose **Bold**. Next, key **This text is bold** and press **Enter**.

3. Turn off bold by selecting **Type Style** from the **Type** menu and then choose **Normal**.

4. Select **Type Style** from the **Type** menu and then choose **Italic**. Next, key **This text is italic** and press **Enter**.

5. Turn off italic by selecting **Type Style** from the **Type** menu and then choose **Normal**.

6. Key **This text is bold and italic** and then press **Enter**.

7. Select the text that you just keyed in step 6. Then, apply bold and italic to the selected text. First select **Type Style** from the **Type** menu and choose **Bold**. Then, with the same text still selected, choose **Type Style** from the **Type** menu and choose **Italic**.

8. Select the entire line of text that reads ***This text is bold and italic*** if it is not already selected.

9. Remove all type styles from the selected text by choosing **Type Style** from the **Type** menu and then select **Normal**. Keep this publication on-screen for use in the next Step-by-Step.

Using the Character Specifications Dialog Box

Although you can use the Font, Size, and Type Style submenus to change type settings, this method can be time consuming if you want to make several changes all at once. For example, if you're keying a heading, you may want to choose a different font (such as Arial), point size (such as 24 points), and type style (such as bold). Instead of returning to the menu three different times, you can use the Character Specifications dialog box to make all of these changes at the same time.

To make several changes at the same time, select the text that you want to change, or place the insertion point where you want the new changes to begin. Then click the Character Specification button on the Toolbar, or choose Character from the Type menu. Doing so displays the Character Specifications dialog box shown in Figure 8-5.

FIGURE 8-5
Character Specifications dialog box

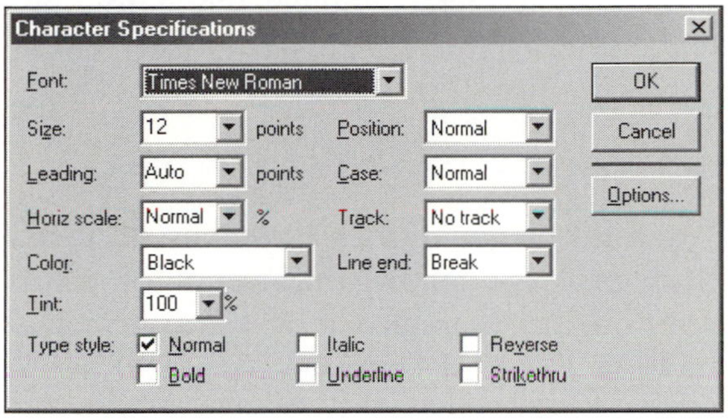

To change the font or point size, click the Font or Size drop-down arrow and then click the selection you want from the list that appears. You can also specify the point size by keying the size in the Size text box. Additionally, you can use the Type style check boxes to select one or more type styles, such as bold and/or italic.

S TEP-BY-STEP 8.5

1. Using the mouse, select the entire line of text that reads **This is the default font**.

2. Click the **Character Specification** button on the Toolbar or choose **Character** from the **Type** menu.

3. Double-click inside the Size text box (to select the current entry) and then key **15**. Next, select **Bold** and **Italic** from the Type style options.

4. Click **OK** to close the dialog box. Remove the highlighting by clicking anywhere within the story. Keep this publication on-screen for use in the next Step-by-Step.

> **Hot Tip**
>
> If your computer has many fonts, it can often take a long time to scroll through the font drop-down list in the Character Specifications dialog box. A faster way to reach the font you want is to click once on the Font drop-down arrow and then key the first character of the font, such as H for Helvetica. PageMaker will display an alphabetical list of all fonts that begin with that character.

Changing Type Case and Position

In PageMaker, there are three character case options—normal, all caps, or small caps—from which to choose in the Character Specifications dialog box. You can determine where text falls on the line, referred to as text position. One way to select the case type or position is from the Character Specifications dialog box. Another way is to use the Control palette, which will be explained later in this lesson.

Type Case

All caps is a publishing term for when text appears in all uppercase characters. Displaying text in uppercase is sometimes used to highlight important information that you want the reader to notice. There are times, however, when text needs to appear in all uppercase, but using too much uppercase text would be distracting. An alternative is to use small caps. When text appears in small caps, uppercase characters (characters you key while holding down the Shift key) appear as they normally would, while other characters appear in lowercase and in a smaller point size. Here is an example:

THIS IS HOW TEXT LOOKS IN SMALL CAPS

Small caps is normally used for personal titles as well as standard and organizational abbreviations. Personal titles include professional, organizational, or scholarly awards such as Bonnie Brown, DDS, or Hannah Dennison, MD. Standard abbreviations include entries that indicate time, like 9:30 AM; frequency, such as 15TH; or centuries, like 600 BC. Examples of organizational abbreviations include NASA, IRS, or NAACP. Small caps is especially useful in documents that contain many standard abbreviations and where keying those abbreviations in all uppercase would distract or confuse the reader.

To change the type case, select the text that you want to change or place the insertion point where you want the uppercase text to appear. Then, choose All caps or Small caps from the Case submenu in the Character Specifications dialog box.

Subscript and Superscript

You can change the vertical position of text by choosing either the subscript or superscript position. Superscript raises a character slightly above other characters on the line, whereas subscript lowers a character somewhat. Subscript is normally used in formulas such as H_2O or CO_2 whereas superscript is used in reference numbers, such as National Study on Quarks[2] or for registered trademarks, such as Fussyfibers.™

To use superscript or subscript, select the text that you want to change or place the insertion point where you want the superscript or subscript to begin. Then, choose Superscript or Subscript from the Position submenu in the Character Specifications dialog box.

PageMaker reduces the point size of superscript text by roughly 60% and raises the text about one-half line above the surrounding characters. It also reduces the point size of any subscript text by about 60% and lowers the text about one-half line below the surrounding characters. You will practice working with the type case and position options in the next Step-by-Step.

Using the Control Palette to Change Type Specifications

A quick way to change type specifications is by using the Control palette. The Control palette, like the one shown in Figure 8-6, contains text boxes and buttons for changing nearly any type specification. Because of its small size, you can keep the Control palette on the screen as you work, or hide it as needed.

FIGURE 8-6
PageMaker Control palette

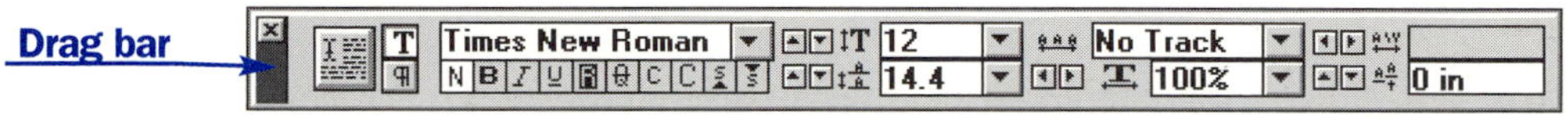

Drag bar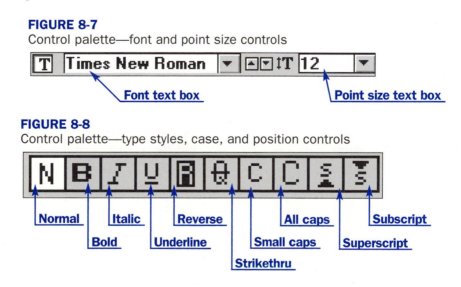

The Control palette is ***context-sensitive,*** which means that the tools appearing inside the palette change based on the type of tool you are currently using from the toolbox. For example, if you are using the Text tool, the Control palette will contain tools for changing text settings, such as the font or point size. If you are using a drawing tool, the Control palette will contain different tools related to drawing lines, rectangles, or ellipses.

To display the Control palette, choose Show Control Palette from the Window menu. To hide the Control palette, choose Hide Control Palette. To move the Control palette to a different location on the screen, place the mouse pointer on the drag bar, shown in Figure 8-6, and then drag the Control palette to where you want it.

When you are working with the Text tool, the Control palette displays information about the current type specifications in the font and point size text boxes shown in Figure 8-7. These boxes are useful because they identify the current font and point size. To make a different selection, click on the drop-down arrows to the right of either text box and choose the font or size you want, or key the new setting in the appropriate text box. You can also use the buttons found at the bottom of the Control palette to select the type style, case, and position. Figure 8-8 identifies each of these buttons. Simply click on a button to select its feature. The button appears lighter than the surrounding buttons when selected.

FIGURE 8-7
Control palette—font and point size controls

Font text box   **Point size text box**

FIGURE 8-8
Control palette—type styles, case, and position controls

Normal   **Italic**   **Reverse**   **All caps**   **Subscript**
Bold   **Underline**   **Small caps**   **Superscript**
Strikethru

STEP-BY-STEP 8.6

1. Choose **Show Control Palette** from the **Window** menu if the Control palette is not visible on the screen.

2. Move the insertion point to the end of the last line of text and press **Enter**.

3. Key the following sentence exactly as it is printed below and press **Enter** at the end.

   Ann Lewis, md and Steven Mayes, dds will discuss the CO2 project at the June meeting.

4. In the line of text you keyed in step 3, select the characters **md**. Then, click on the **Small Caps** button in the **Control palette**.

5. In the line of text you keyed in Step 3, select the characters **dds**. Then, click on the **Small Caps** button in the Control palette.

6. Select the entire line of text that you keyed in step 3 and choose **14** from the font drop-down list in the Control palette.

7. Select **2** in **CO2** and then click the **Subscript** button in the Control palette.

8. Click on any text in the story to remove any highlighting. Keep this publication on-screen for use in the next Step-by-Step.

Changing the Default Type Specifications

When you start a new publication, PageMaker automatically selects the default type specifications for you. The default specifications are usually Times New Roman (or similar) font in a 12-point size with the Normal type style. Thus, if you begin a new publication and then start keying using the Text tool, the text will appear using the default type specifications. PageMaker also uses the default type specifications every time you begin a new story within a publication.

You can change the default type specifications for any publication at any time. Once you change the default type specifications, any new text that you key or place into the publication will automatically appear using those specifications.

To change the default type specifications, click any tool in the toolbox *except* the Text tool. Then, select the new default type specifications using either the pull-down menus or the Character Specifications dialog box. For example, you can use the Character Specifications dialog box to select both the Arial font and the 13-point font size. Now, whenever you use the Text tool to begin a new story, the text will appear using the new default settings.

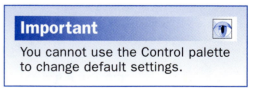

Important

You cannot use the Control palette to change default settings.

S TEP-BY-STEP 8.7

1. Using the Hand tool, drag or move the current page upward so that only the last two or three lines of text appear near the top of the screen.

2. Begin a new story within the publication by first clicking the **Text** tool. Then place the I-beam just to the right of the left margin guide and roughly 1 inch below the last line of text. Click the mouse button.

3. Key **This text appears using the current default type specifications** and then press **Enter**.

4. Change the default type specifications by first clicking the **Pointer** tool. Then, choose **Size** from the **Type** menu, and finally choose **18** from the **Font** submenu.

5. Begin another new story within the publication by clicking the **Text** tool. Place the insertion point just to the right of the left margin guide and roughly one inch below the last line of text that you keyed in step 3.

6. Key **This text appears using the new default type specifications**.

7. Repeat instructions in steps 5 and 6 to create another new story roughly 1 inch below the last line of text that you keyed in step 6. Notice how this new text also appears in an 18-point size. Close this publication without saving it.

SUMMARY

In this lesson you learned how to:

■ Determine how specific type specifications including typeface, point size, and style (such as bold or italic), affect a publication's appearance.

■ Change the type specifications for existing text or text you will key immediately afterward.

■ Use the Type menu to select a different typeface, point size, or font style.

■ Use the Character Specifications dialog box to change many type specifications at the same time.

■ Use the Control palette as a way to change any type specification.

■ Change the default type specifications for a particular publication by first selecting any tool from the toolbox except the Text tool, and then selecting the new specifications.

VOCABULARY *Review*

Define the following terms:		
Context-sensitive	Font	Type specifications

REVIEW *Questions*

TRUE/FALSE

Circle T if the statement is true or F if the statement is false.

T   F   **1.** Bold and italic are examples of type styles.

T   F   **2.** Underlining is a popular way to set off text in published documents.

T   F   **3.** Italic text slants to the left.

T   F   **4.** Reverse type style automatically creates a dark background against any text you key.

T   F   **5.** You cannot use more than one type style with the same text.

T   F   **6.** Subscript text appears about one-half line above the other text.

T   F   **7.** With PageMaker, it is possible to specify point sizes in one-tenth point increments, such as 10.5 points.

T   F   **8.** To display or hide the Control palette, choose Control from the Palette menu.

T   F   **9.** To change the default type specifications, click the Text tool and then select the new default type settings.

T   F   **10.** Small caps is normally used for personal titles as well as standard and organizational abbreviations.

FILL IN THE BLANK

Complete the following sentences by writing the correct word or words in the blanks provided.

1. To select a different point size, you choose Size from the _____ menu.

2. With PageMaker, you can specify a point size between 4 and _____ points.

3. A type style that places a thin horizontal line through the text is called _____.

4. You can change several type settings at one time, such as the font, point size, and type style by using the _____ dialog box.

5. Text that appears in all uppercase characters is referred to as _____ caps.

MULTIPLE CHOICE

Select the best response for the following questions.

1. Which of the following statements is true about the Control palette?
    A. You can use the Control palette to select the font.
    B. You can use the Control palette to select the point size.
    C. You can use the Control palette to select the type style.
    D. You can use the Control palette to select the type position.
    E. All of the above.

2. Which is not an example of a type style?
    A. Bold
    B. Italic
    C. Reverse
    D. Normal
    E. Small caps

3. Which entry does not appear in the Size submenu?
    A. 8
    B. 18
    C. 24
    D. 72
    E. 120

4. In which instance would italic not be appropriate?
    A. For a book title.
    B. To identify an entry in a legal contract that both parties agree to remove from the contract.
    C. To set off a newly introduced term, such as megabyte.
    D. To identify a quotation.

5. Which of the following statements is true?
    A. Body text frequently appears in 10- or 12-point size.
    B. Subtitles frequently appear in 16- or 18-point size.
    C. Titles frequently appear in 24-, 36-, or 48-point size.
    D. All of the above.

PROJECTS

 PROJECT 8-1

In this project, you will use various type specifications to create a letterhead for Caribbean SunTravel Tours similar to the one shown in Figure 8-9. Review the figure before you begin so you know how the publication should look.

FIGURE 8-9
Caribbean Sun letterhead publication

Caribbean Sun
Travel Tours
6600 Duvall Street
Key West, Florida 32358
Telephone: (303) 555-1234

ASSOCIATES
Juan Gomez
Sofia Chang
Rosa Smith
Cynthia Black
Barbara Braham

1. Start a new publication. When the Document Setup dialog box appears, specify a **single-sided** publication with a top margin setting of **0.5** inches and all other margin settings of **0.75** inches.

2. Click the **Text** tool. Place the I-beam slightly below the top margin guide and just to the right of the left margin guide, and then click.

3. Enlarge the area around the insertion point to the **Actual Size**.

4. Using the Control palette, select the **Arial, Helvetica** or **Univers** font and the **24**-point font size. Then, key **Caribbean Sun** and press **Enter**. Next, key **Travel Tours** and press **Enter** again.

5. Using the Size submenu of the Control palette, change to a **10**-point font size.

6. Key the following text. Press **Enter** once at the end of the first and second lines, and three times at the end of the last line.
   6600 Duval Street
   Key West, Florida 32358
   Telephone: (303) 555-1234

7. Using the Control palette, change to an **8**-point font size and select the bold type style. Then, key **ASSOCIATES** and press **Enter**.

8. Using the Control palette, turn off the bold type style.

9. Key the following text, pressing **Enter** at the end of each line.
   Juan Gomez
   Sofia Chang
   Rosa Smith
   Cynthia Black
   Barbara Braham

10. Using the Constrained-line tool, draw a straight line just above the street address and extending from the left to the right margin guide.

11. Print the publication and then compare your printout to Figure 8-9. Make any corrections necessary. Save the publication with the name **Letterhead**, print, and then close the publication.

SCANS PROJECT 8-2

You are to create a help wanted advertisement for the local newspaper. The text for this advertisement is shown in Figure 8-10 and a sample solution appears in Figure 8-11. Review Figure 8-11 before you begin to see what the publication will look like when you are finished. Your ad may vary slightly based on the type specifications you select.

1. Start a new publication. When the Document Setup dialog box appears, make this a **single-sided** publication with a **0.25**-inch margin on all four sides. Change the size of the publication to **3** inches by **7** inches. Choose **Tall** orientation.

2. Using a sans serif typeface such as Arial, Helvetica, or Univers, apply the bold style and a 20- to 24-point size for the title TRAVEL ASSOCIATE WANTED! and also to the company name Caribbean Sun Travel Tours at the bottom of the advertisement. Use a serif typeface, such as Times New Roman or Times and in an 11- or 12-point size for all other text. Because the text must fit within the margin guides, you may need to experiment with different point sizes for both the title and the body text.

FIGURE 8-10
Help wanted ad

```
TRAVEL
ASSOCIATE
WANTED!

Join our rapidly growing travel firm--one
of the largest in the industry. We offer a
wide range of challenging opportunities
for the experienced travel agent. Current
assignments are available in our Key West
office.

At Caribbean Sun Travel Tours we offer: a
four-day work week, profit sharing and
stock purchase, incentives and free trips,
educational reimbursement and three weeks
vacation.

Besides a competitive compensation
package, we offer a stimulating
professional environment and the
opportunity to achieve your expectations.
For prompt consideration, call or send
your resume to:

6600 Duval Street
Key West, FL 32358
Telephone: (305) 555-1234

Caribbean Sun

Travel Tours
```

3. When finished, save the publication as **Travel Ad**. Print and close the publication.

FIGURE 8-11
Finished ad

```
TRAVEL
ASSOCIATE
WANTED!

Join our rapidly growing travel
firm--one of the largest in the industry.
We offer a wide range of challenging
opportunities for the experienced travel
agent. Current assignments are available
in our Key West office.

At Caribbean Sun Travel Tours we
offer: a four-day work week, profit
sharing and stock purchase, incentives
and free trips, educational reimburse-
ment and three weeks vacation.

Besides a competitive compensation
package, we offer a stimulating profes-
sional environment and the opportunity
to achieve your expectations. For
prompt consideration, call or send your
resume to:

5600 Duval Street
Key West, FL 32358
Telephone: (305) 555-1234

Caribbean Sun
Travel Tours
```

SCANS   ## TEAMWORK PROJECT

Choose a partner. In this project, one of you will be the designer and the other will act as the desktop publisher. The designer is to create specifications for letterhead that will be used by your school's publicity department. At a minimum, the letterhead should include the school's name, street address, and telephone number, and your own name (the designer's name). The letterhead can also include boxes or circles using the drawing tools discussed in Lesson 3. The specifications should identify what font and point size you want for each entry and rough, hand-drawn sketches of where you would like each entry to appear on the page. Then, it is the responsibility of the desktop publisher to create the letterhead using PageMaker. When finished, switch roles and perform the same tasks again.

CRITICAL*Thinking*

SCANS   ## ACTIVITY 8-1

You have learned that there are many ways to issue the same command in PageMaker. For example, to issue the Save command, you can click the Save button, choose Save from the File menu, or press Ctrl+S on the keyboard. Reflect on the different kinds of commands that you issue when creating a publication. Also, think about those times when both hands are positioned on the keyboard and other times when one hand is positioned on the mouse. In certain situations, one method for issuing a command can be better or easier than the other two methods. For each method, list two to three different situations where one method would be easier than other methods and briefly explain why.

PageMaker BASICS

COMMAND SUMMARY

FEATURE	MENU COMMAND	KEYSTROKE	TOOLBAR BUTTON	LESSON
Control Palette, show	Window, Show Control Palette	Ctrl+'		2, 8
Control Palette, hide	Window, Hide Control Palette	Ctrl+'		2
Styles Palette, hide	Window, Hide Styles	Ctrl+B		2
Styles Palette, show	Window, Show Styles	Ctrl+B		2
Colors Palette, hide	Window, Hide Colors	Ctrl+J		2
Colors Palette, show	Window, Show Colors	Ctrl+J		2
Pictures Palette, hide	Window, Plug-in Palettes, Hide Picture Palette			2
Pictures Palette, show	Window, Plug-in Palettes, Show Picture Palette			2
Help, request	Help, Help Topics	F1	🔲	2
Open publication	File, Open	Ctrl+O	🔲	2
Close publication	File, Close	Ctrl+W		2
Exit PageMaker	File, Exit	Ctrl+Q		2
New publication	File, New	Ctrl+N	🔲	3
Insert pages	Layout, Insert Pages		🔲	3
Remove pages	Layout, Remove Pages		🔲	3
View size, actual	View, Actual Size	Ctrl+1	🔲	3
View size, 25-400%	View, Zoom To			3
Toolbox, hide	Window, Hide Tools			3
Toolbox, show	Window, Show Tools			3
Save publication	File, Save	Ctrl+S		3, 8
Undo last action	Edit, Undo	Ctrl+Z		4
Revert to previous save	File, Revert (while holding down Shift)			4
Save file as	File, Save As	Ctrl+Shift+S		4, 8
Print publication	File, Print	Ctrl+P	🔲	4
Rulers, show	View, Show Rulers	Ctrl+R		4
Rulers, hide	View, Hide Rulers	Ctrl+R		4
Zero point, lock	View, Zero Lock			5
Guides, hide	View, Hide Guides	Ctrl+;		5

FEATURE	MENU COMMAND	KEYSTROKE	TOOLBAR BUTTON	LESSON
Guides, show	View, Show Guides	Ctrl+;		5
Import text file	File, Place	Ctrl+D	🖼	5
Columns, add	Layout, Column Guides			5
Story Editor	Edit, Edit Story	Ctrl+E		6
Story Editor-find text	Utilities, Find	Ctrl+F	🔍	6
Story Editor, change text	Utilities, Change	Ctrl+H		6
Story Editor, spell check	Utilities, Spelling	Ctrl+L	✓	6
Story Editor, hidden characters view/hide	Story, Display ¶			6
Font, select	Type, Font			8
Point size, select	Type, Size			8
Type style, select	Type, Type Style			8
Character specifications	Type, Character	Ctrl+T	A	8
Case, select	Type, Character, All caps/Small caps (case)			8
Subscript, select	Type, Character, Subscript			8
Superscript, select	Type, Character, Superscript			8
Bold, select	Type, Type Style, Bold	Ctrl+Shift+B		8
Italic, select	Type, Type Style, Italic	Ctrl+Shift+I		8
Underline, select	Type, Type Style, Underline	Ctrl+Shift+U		8
Normal type style	Type, Type Style, Normal	Ctrl+Shift+ Spacebar		8
Strikethru, select	Type, Type Style, Strikethru	Ctrl+Shift+/		8
Reverse, select	Type, Type Style, Reverse	Ctrl+Shift+V		8
Point size, increase		Ctrl+Alt+>	A˄	8
Point size, decrease		Ctrl+Alt+<	A˅	8

FEATURE			TOOLBOX BUTTON	LESSON
Pointer tool			▶	3
Text tool			T	3
Rotate tool			↻	3
Cropping tool			◫	3
Line tool			╲	3
Constrained-line tool			⊢	3
Rectangle tool			▭	3

Ellipse tool	◯	3
Polygon tool	⬡	3
Zoom tool	🔍	3
Hand tool	✋	3

REVIEW *Questions*

TRUE/FALSE

Circle T if the statement is true or F if the statement is false.

T   F   **1.** A script typeface is usually an excellent choice for lengthy documents, such as magazines or newspapers.

T   F   **2.** Crop art are prepared electronic illustrations that you can add to a PageMaker publication.

T   F   **3.** To remove or cancel a pull-down or submenu, you can press the Esc key.

T   F   **4.** When working with a dialog box, a large circle appears inside a checkbox whenever the option is selected.

T   F   **5.** The Document Setup option that determines whether the final publication will have text printed on both sides of each page, like in this book, is called the two-sided option.

T   F   **6.** The Hand tool is used to move a different part of a page or the Pasteboard into view on the screen.

T   F   **7.** When using the Text tool, you can select all the characters in a sentence by double-clicking anywhere within the sentence.

T   F   **8.** Unlike some popular programs, PageMaker's Undo command will undo only the last action you performed.

T   F   **9.** When placing text into a publication using the Autoflow option, PageMaker automatically adds as many pages to the publication as needed to hold the text that is being placed.

T   F   **10.** Entries such as headers or footers are normally created on the master page.

T   F   **11.** PageMaker does not include a method to check for spelling errors.

T   F   **12.** The body of all lowercase characters in a certain typeface is designed to be no taller than the x-height.

T   F   **13.** An ascender is the part of certain lowercase letters that falls below the baseline.

T   F   **14.** In PageMaker, you can specify a point size as large as 999 points.

T   F   **15.** Sans serif typefaces are designed to resemble handwriting or calligraphy.

FILL IN THE BLANK

Complete the following sentences by writing the correct word or words in the blanks provided.

1. Another name for a font in PageMaker is a(n) _____.

2. In PageMaker, a group of related tools or features that appears on-screen and that you can use when creating or editing your work is called a(n) _____.

3. Keys that you press on the keyboard to issue specific PageMaker commands are called _____ keys.

4. All PageMaker 7.0 publications that are stored on disk have _____ as their three-character file extension.

5. A PageMaker publication can contain as many as _____ pages.

6. The tool used to draw a straight vertical, horizontal, or 45-degree line is called the _____ - _____ tool.

7. If you select a graphic object, such as a rectangle, small squares called _____ appear around that object.

8. You can use PageMaker's _____ command to save a publication in the smallest size possible.

9. When PageMaker's rulers are displayed, the position where their measurements begin is called the _____ _____.

10. If you click on a text block while using the Pointer tool, the thin lines which appear at the top and bottom of that text block are called _____.

11. In a publication, you can have as many as _____ columns on a page.

12. All of the characters in a typeface run along an imaginary horizontal line referred to as the _____.

13. Typefaces in which different characters use different amounts of space are known as _____.

14. A technique that lets you vary the emphasis given to certain characters, such as bolding or underlining those characters, is called Type _____.

15. A publishing term for text that appears in all uppercase characters is _____ _____.

SIMULATION

INTRODUCTION

In this on-the-job simulation, you will practice many of the commands and features that you have learned in this unit, and use PageMaker to create a business plan publication for Caribbean Sun Travel Tours. That publication will be submitted to a local bank as part of an application for a business loan.

The purpose of this simulation is to help you practice your new skills. As you know now, the fonts that you have available will vary based on the computer you're using. If your computer does not have a particular font called for in this simulation, select a similar font. Because of the difference between computers, your final work might not look exactly the same as the examples in this simulation, but it should look similar.

Before beginning, review the entire assignment. Look at all the sample pages and study their contents. As you start to create the publication, work smart by saving your work regularly (every 10 to 20 minutes).

BACKGROUND

During the past three years, Caribbean Sun Travel Tours' business has grown rapidly, and this growth has created several problems. For example, people wanting to book a reservation often receive a busy signal when they telephone the company's office. To solve this problem, the telephone company (Florida Southern Telephone) has suggested adding five new telephone lines. Unfortunately, Caribbean Sun Travel Tours will need to replace their existing telephone equipment to handle these new lines. Also, the company's business with customers in Europe and South America has grown rapidly. In the past, the company has accepted collect telephone calls from these customers, but this practice is becoming very costly. Caribbean Sun Travel Tours would like to add several international toll-free telephone lines to save money and also to encourage additional business. Finally, if the needed telephone lines and equipment are added, the company will need more people to handle the anticipated calls. As a result, the company also wants to hire three new travel associates.

The bank loan proposal described on the following pages was written by the president and vice president of Caribbean Sun Travel Tours. The loan will be used to pay for the new services, equipment, and employees, and will be repaid to the bank over a five year period. Your job is to create this desktop published proposal.

GENERAL INSTRUCTIONS

The entire proposal will be five pages long and produced on regular letter size paper (8.5 by 11 inches). As you work on this project, remember it is an important document for the company. Take your time and work carefully.

Notice that samples of each completed page of the proposal appear at the end of this simulation. Refer to these pages if you have any questions about the layout or content.

ADDITIONAL COMMENTS/TIPS

How you create this proposal is up to you. For example, you can key the text for each page into the story editor, spell check your work, and then place the text onto the appropriate page in the publication. Or, you can key the text directly onto the page and then use the story editor to spell check your work. As with all publications, it is extremely important that you proof your work carefully. Good luck and enjoy the challenge!

THUMBNAILS

To give you a general idea of how the final project will look, Figure UR-1 shows thumbnails (a small representation of how each page will appear) of the entire proposal. Don't worry about reading the words in these thumbnails. A full page figure from which you will be keying appears later.

FIGURE UR-1
Thumbnails for the Business Expansion Report

PAGE ONE   PAGE TWO   PAGE THREE

PAGE FOUR   PAGE FIVE

Publication Setup

As you begin your new publication and the Document Setup dialog box appears, make this a five page, single-sided publication. Set the margins as follows:

Left	3 inches
Right	1 inch
Top	2 inches
Bottom	1 inch

Make certain the horizontal and vertical rulers are displayed on the screen. You will need these rulers for positioning certain entries.

Individual Page Requirements

Notice that all titles and subtitles in this publication appear in bold, in a large point size, and with a different font than the body text in the proposal. Begin the title on each page, such as *A Proposal for Business Expansion* on page one, slightly below the top margin guide and just to the right of the left margin guide. Make certain that each title appears in a sans serif font such as Arial, Helvetica, or Univers. Make certain that all subtitles, like the word *Contents* on page one, also use a sans serif font.

Body Text

All text other than titles and subtitles should appear in a serif typeface, such as Times New Roman or Times, and in an 11.5-point font size.

DESCRIPTION—MASTER PAGE

The master page contains the entries that will appear on all pages in this proposal. As Figure UR-2 illustrates, these entries include a two-line header containing the company name, a thin line drawn beneath the company name, and the page number marker.

Specifications

1. In the pasteboard or in a blank area of the page, key **Caribbean Sun,** press **Enter** then key **Travel Tours.** Next, position a horizontal ruler guide 1.25 inches from the top edge of the page, and position a vertical ruler guide 1 inch from the left edge of the page. Now drag the two-line title so that it begins at the intersection of the horizontal and vertical ruler guides.

2. Using the Constrained-line tool, draw a thin horizontal line as shown in Figure UR-2, beginning slightly below the T in the word Travel and ending 1 inch from the right edge of the page (even with the right margin).

3. Add a page number marker as shown in Figure UR-2 to the lower-right corner of the master page. Position this page number marker roughly 0.75 inches from the bottom edge and 1 inch from the right edge of the page (even with the right margin).

FIGURE UR-2
Master page

Caribbean
Travel Tours

RM

Description—Page 1

The first page contains a title, table of contents, and summary for the report, as shown in Figure UR-3.

Specifications

1. Key the two-line title from Figure UR-3 in a sans serif typeface, in bold, and in a 30-point size.

2. Key the word **Contents** shown in Figure UR-3 in a sans serif typeface, in bold, and in an 18-point size.

3. Key the six lines of text from Figure UR-3 in a serif typeface and in an 11.5-point size. For each of these entries, key the text for the first column, press the **Tab** key three times, and then key the entry for the second column. For example, in the first line you would key **Section,** press the **Tab** key three times, and then key **Page**. Also, make certain that the column headings appears in bold.

4. Key the word **Summary**, as shown in Figure UR-3, in a sans serif typeface, in bold, and in an 18-point size. Key all other remaining text on the page in a serif typeface and in an 11.5-point size.

5. After completing page 1, save the publication with the name **Loan Proposal**.

FIGURE UR-3
Page 1 (shown reduced 30%)

Caribbean Sun
Travel Tours

A Proposal for Business Expansion

Contents

Section	Page
Summary	1
Our Strategy	2
Business by Country	3
Travel Activity	4
Loan Request	5

Summary

Because of its rapid growth during the past three years, Caribbean Sun Travel Tours seeks to improve its office services. These expansion activities include the hiring of new employees and adding of additional telephone service.

The reason we seek these additional services is our current growth in sales of over 150 percent annually. Unfortunately, because of our limited staff and telephone equipment, this sales growth has created several operational problems. Currently, for example, it takes us an average of 4 minutes to answer customer calls. The addition of staff and new telephone equipment would eliminate many of our current problems.

We hope the Board of Directors of your bank will approve our request for a 5-year $650,000 loan.

1

Description—Page 2

The second page of this report describes the reasons Caribbean Sun Travel Tours requires a business loan.

Specifications

1. Key the two-line title as shown in Figure UR-4 in a sans serif typeface, in bold, and in a 24-point size.

2. Key all remaining text as it appears in the actual size example shown in Figure UR-4 in a serif typeface and in an 11.5-point size. In the third paragraph of this page, make certain the characters *am* in the time entry (*10-11:30* AM) appear in small caps.

3. Remember to save your work every 10-20 minutes.

Caribbean Sun
Travel Tours

Our
Strategy

At Caribbean Sun Travel Tours, we foresee the next decade as one of tremendous growth and exciting opportunities for the prepared travel agency. We believe that our organization is in a unique position to become one of the most successful leaders in this industry.

There are two important factors which we believe will ensure this success. First, sufficient travel associates to guarantee prompt handling of customer requests are needed. Second, sufficient telephone lines and equipment to receive and serve customers promptly are needed.

Currently, our Key West corporate office uses 15 telephone lines to serve 15 travel associates and 5 management staff. During the past year, a study was done by Florida Southern Telephone that revealed 35 percent of the people who called between 10–11:30 AM received a "busy" signal. Florida Southern Telephone recommended we add 5 new lines. Unfortunately, since our current equipment cannot handle additional lines, a new telephone system is needed.

Also, during the past year, our business from outside the Key West area has grown significantly. The fastest growth areas are from customers in Europe and South America. Last year we began accepting collect calls from such customers. We now spend an average of $19,400 per month on long-distance charges. Three toll-free lines, one each in the US, Europe, and South America, would cut this charge by roughly 25 percent.

2

Description—Page 3

The third page of this report contains descriptive text and a listing of Caribbean Sun Travel Tours' income by country.

Specifications

1. Key the two-line title shown in Figure UR-5 in a sans serif typeface, in bold, and in a 24-point size.

2. Key the remaining text as it appears in the actual size example shown in Figure UR-5 in a serif typeface and in an 11.5-point size. In the first paragraph, make certain the newspaper name *International Herald* appears in italic.

3. When keying the six lines that show sales income by country, key the text for the first column, press the **Tab** key two to three times, as needed, and then key the second column entry.

Caribbean Sun
Travel Tours

Business by Country

During the past year, our business has seen tremendous growth of over 200 percent in the United States alone. During this same time we have also seen a tremendous growth in sales income from customers in Europe and South America. This is the result of advertisements we have run in the *International Herald* and international airline magazines.

The following chart shows our total travel income by country during the past twelve months.

Country	Sales Income
England	2,450,000
Netherlands	1,850,000
Costa Rica	4,500,200
Japan	1,780,400
USA	4,900,000

Currently, reservations booked from customers in Europe and South America produce little profit since we incur the collect long-distance charges. This would change dramatically, however, with the acquisition of the proposed toll-free lines.

3

Description—Page 4

The fourth page of this report identifies the type of business activity in which Caribbean Sun Travel Tours is currently involved.

Specifications

1. Key the two-line title shown in Figure UR-6 in a sans serif typeface, in bold, and in a 24-point size.

2. Key all remaining text as it appears in the actual size example shown in Figure UR-6 in a serif typeface and in an 11.5-point size. Press the **Tab** key once before keying each of the five indented lines.

FIGURE UR-6
Page 4 (shown reduced 30%)

Caribbean Sun
Travel Tours

Travel Activity

Our primary business involves travel planning and reservation services. Arranging employee travel for corporations makes up nearly 55 percent of our activities. The other 45 percent comes from the following sources:

Private cruise-line tours

US rail tours

US bus lines tours

Honeymoon planning

Corporate awards travel program

In addition, last year we expanded our services to include a corporate awards travel program. In this program, organizations award travel prizes to employees for outstanding service or sales. While this program currently produces less than $60,000 profit annually, it is expected to grow to well over $450,000 in profit within the next two years.

4

Description—Page 5

The fifth and last page of this report summarizes the information in the loan request.

Specifications

1. Key the two-line title as shown in Figure UR-7 in a sans serif typeface, in bold, and in a 24-point size.

2. Key all remaining text as it appears in the actual size example shown in Figure UR-7 in a serif typeface and in an 11.5-point size.

3. Save your work and print the publication.

FIGURE UR-7
Page 5 (shown reduced 30%)

Caribbean Sun
Travel Tours

Loan
Request

Because of the problems and opportunities outlined in this report, we would like to request a five-year loan totaling $650,000. These funds will be used to purchase an expanded telephone system, lease three toll-free telephone lines, and help offset the cost of additional staff.

Because we are one of your bank's customers, you are perhaps aware that we currently do have sufficient funds to cover these expenses. While we could incur the cost of these items now, the large expenditure would place a significant drain on our resources and leave us with no emergency funds.

We have been a long-term customer in good standing with your bank for several years and have a history of paying off our previous short-term loans early. We hope you will look favorably upon this request.

5

DESIGN A COVER PAGE

When you finish creating the proposal, design and print a cover page (as a separate publication) to accompany this report. At a minimum, make certain this page includes a title for the report, the name of the bank to which it is being submitted (Florida Bank of Key West), Caribbean Sun Travel Tours' name and address, and the current date. The title should appear in bold and with a serif font. Also, make certain that the text on this title page appears using two different font sizes of your choice. Finally, save this publication as **Loan Cover** and print it before closing the PageMaker program.

PORTFOLIO *Checklist*

Include the following PageMaker publication files from this Unit Review in your student portfolio:

Loan Proposal

Loan Cover

ENHANCING PAGEMAKER DOCUMENTS

Unit 2

Estimated Time for Unit: 26.5 hrs.

WORKING WITH TABS AND INDENTS

OBJECTIVES

Upon completion of this lesson, you should be able to:

- Explain tabs and the various types of tab alignment.

- Set, change, and remove tab settings.

- Describe tab leaders and how to set tabs that have leaders.

- Identify the various types of paragraph indenting techniques.

- Indent paragraphs using the various types of indenting techniques.

Estimated Time: 3.5 hours

VOCABULARY

Bullet

Center-aligned

Decimal-aligned

Hanging indent

Leaders

Left-aligned

Right-aligned

Introduction

Tabs are important desktop publishing tools for aligning text entries in a publication. Indents let you set off text in unusual ways. This lesson explains the different types of tab alignments, as well as how to add, change, and remove tab settings and align text using those settings. You will also learn different types of indenting and how to indent paragraphs in a publication.

Understanding Tabs

Tabs are an important part of desktop publishing. You often use tabs to align columnar types of entries or to indent the first line of a paragraph.

Using tabs correctly is especially important in desktop published documents because most fonts used in PageMaker publications today are proportional fonts. As discussed earlier in this book, with proportional fonts, different characters have different widths. The number 1 or the letter I for example, is much thinner than the number 9 or the letter M. Because of these differences, it is difficult to accurately align columns of words or numbers without using tabs. Using the Space bar to align such columns, for example, usually creates entries that do not align properly, like the example shown below

EMPLOYEE NAME	DEPARTMENT	EXTENSION
H. Drew	Sales	3345
M. Moranda	Marketing	4120
G. Jackson	Operations	9910

It's important to indent paragraphs and align columnar entries using Tab settings and the Tab key, especially when using proportional fonts. Doing so produces entries that align correctly, as demonstrated below.

EMPLOYEE NAME	DEPARTMENT	EXTENSION
H. Drew	Sales	3345
M. Moranda	Marketing	4120
G. Jackson	Operations	9910

Types of Tab Alignment

PageMaker offers four types of tab settings, each of which aligns an entry in a different way. These settings include *left-aligned* where the entry begins at the tab setting; *right-aligned* where the entry ends at the tab setting; *center-aligned* where the entry is centered on a tab setting; and *decimal-aligned* where numbers align on the decimal point. Figure 9-1 shows examples of entries aligned using these various tab alignment settings. Arrows indicate the position of the tab setting that was used to align each entry.

FIGURE 9-1
The different types of tab alignment

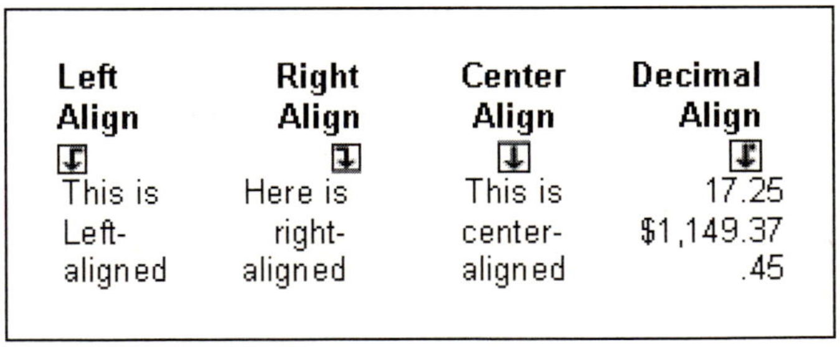

Left Align	Right Align	Center Align	Decimal Align
This is Left-aligned	Here is right-aligned	This is center-aligned	17.25 $1,149.37 .45

When you begin a new publication, PageMaker automatically creates left-aligned tab settings every 0.5 inches. To align text on a tab setting, press the Tab key until the insertion point is at the desired tab setting and then key the text. For example, pressing the Tab key twice would move the insertion point to the left 1 inch, by default.

While left-, right-, and center-aligned tabs are fairly easy to understand, decimal tabs need a little explanation. As illustrated in Figure 9-1, numbers that are aligned on a decimal tab setting will always line up on their decimal points, even if some of the numbers contain commas and/or a dollar sign. Numbers aligned on a decimal tab can also contain any number of digits to the right of the decimal point, or even no decimal point at all. When a number does not contain a decimal point, PageMaker assumes the decimal point will appear after the last numeral in the number.

Setting Tabs

Remember that whenever you start a new document, PageMaker automatically creates left-aligned tab settings every 0.5 inches by default. Whenever you need to align text using a tab setting other than the default settings, you will want to remove all the default tab settings and create just those tab settings you need.

To set or change a tab setting, you can use the Text tool and place the insertion point at the beginning of the line where you want the new tab setting to take effect. You can also select the existing text that you want to change. Then, click the Indents/Tabs button or choose Indents/Tabs from the Type menu to reveal the dialog box and ruler shown in Figure 9-2 will display.

FIGURE 9-2
Indents/Tabs dialog box and ruler

PageMaker uses five different symbols (also called markers) to represent different types of tab settings. These symbols or markers (see Figure 9-3) appear just above the ruler and show the location of the current tab settings. The zero position of the ruler corresponds to the left edge of the text block in which the insertion point is located.

FIGURE 9-3
Tab ruler symbols

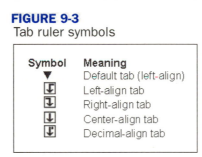

Symbol	Meaning
▼	Default tab (left-align)
⬇	Left-align tab
⬇	Right-align tab
⬇	Center-align tab
⬇	Decimal-align tab

The ▼ symbol, for example, identifies the location of a default tab setting. If you look back at Figure 9-2, you'll see that it has default tab settings positioned every one-half inch. Besides identifying the location of tab settings, you can use the Indents/Tabs ruler to add, change, or remove tab settings. The methods for doing so are discussed below.

To Add a Tab Setting

To add a tab setting to the ruler, place the mouse pointer on the ruler where you want the tab setting located, and then click. Next, choose the type of tab alignment needed (left, right, and so on) by clicking on the appropriate tab alignment button found at the left edge of the dialog box. When you add a new tab setting, PageMaker removes any default tab settings to the left of the new setting.

Here's an example. To add a center-aligned tab setting at the 3.5 inch position, place the mouse pointer on the ruler at the 3.5 inch position, and then click the mouse button. Next, click the Center align tab button. A center-align tab symbol (↓) will appear at the 3.5 inch position, and all default tab settings to the left of this position will disappear.

Removing Tabs

The procedure for removing a tab setting depends upon whether you want to remove default tab settings, or want to remove a tab you have set yourself. To remove default tab settings, simply add a tab setting to the right of where you want all default tabs removed. As discussed in the example above, setting a tab at the 3.5 inch position removes all default tabs to the left of that position.

To remove a tab setting that you have added yourself, drag the tab symbol that you want to remove downward and completely below the ruler. For example, to remove a center-aligned tab setting from the 3.5 inch position, place the mouse pointer on the tab symbol that would appear just above the ruler at the 3.5 inch position. Then, press and while holding down the mouse button, drag that tab symbol straight down below the ruler and then release the mouse button. *NOTE: If you do not drag the symbol completely below the ruler, the setting will not be removed.*

S TEP-BY-STEP 9.1

1. Begin a new publication. When the Document Setup dialog box appears, specify a **single-sided** publication and then click **OK**.

2. Click the **Text** tool, and then click an insertion point slightly below the top margin guide and just to the right of the left margin guide.

3. Enlarge the area around the insertion point to the **Actual Size**.

4. Click the **Indents/Tabs** button or choose **Indents/Tabs** from the **Type** menu. Notice how default tab symbols (▼) appear every 0.5 inches across the ruler.

5. Place the mouse pointer at the 3 inch position in the ruler and then click. Next, click the **Center align** button located at the left side of the Indents/Tabs dialog box. Observe how the new center-align tab setting appears at the 3 inch position and also how PageMaker removes all default tab settings to the left of that position.

6. Place the mouse pointer at the 4 inch position in the ruler and then click. Click the **Right align** button. Observe how the new tab setting appears at the 4 inch position and also how Page-Maker removes the default tab setting from the 3.5 inch position.

7. Following instructions similar to steps 5 and 6 above, add a left-aligned tab setting at the 5 inch position. (If you cannot see the 5 inch position on the ruler, click several times on the right arrow that's located at the right edge of the ruler.)

8. Place the mouse pointer on the tab symbol that's located just above the ruler at the 4 inch position. Now, press and while holding down the mouse button, drag the tab symbol downward below the ruler and then release the mouse. Notice how the tab setting disappears. Keep the Indents/Tabs dialog box on screen for use in the next Step-by-Step.

Moving a Tab Setting

To change the position of a tab setting, simply drag the tab symbol to a different location on the ruler. For example, to move a left-aligned tab setting from the 3.5 to the 4 inch position, you would place the mouse pointer on the tab symbol located at the 3.5 inch position. Then, drag the symbol to the 4 inch position.

When you move a tab setting, PageMaker makes it easy to position the tab accurately. While you are dragging a tab symbol, the current position of that symbol, such as 2.25 (inches) appears in the Position text box. As you continue to drag the tab symbol, the message in the Position text box constantly changes to tell you where the tab setting is currently located.

It's also easy to change a tab setting from one type of alignment to another. To do so, click the tab symbol that you want to change. Then, click the button corresponding to the new tab alignment that you want. For example, to change a tab setting that is already located at the 2 inch position from a left to a center-aligned tab setting, you would click on the tab symbol that is located at the 2 inch position. Then, you would click on the Center align button.

STEP-BY-STEP 9.2

1. Make certain the Indents/Tabs dialog box from Step-by-Step 9.1 is still on-screen. Place the mouse pointer on the **Left align** tab symbol located just above the 5 inch position on the ruler. Then, press and hold down the mouse button. Observe how the current position of that tab setting (5) appears in the Position text box. While holding down the mouse button, slowly drag the tab symbol left to the 4.25 inch position. When the Position text box indicates the correct position, release the mouse button.

2. Using instructions similar to step 1, move the center-aligned tab setting from the 3 inch to the 2 inch position.

3. Change the tab setting at the 4.25 inch position to Center align by first clicking the **Left align** tab symbol located at the 4.25 inch position above the ruler. Then, click the **Center align** button. Keep the Indents/Tabs dialog box on-screen for use in the next Step-by-Step.

Completing the Indents/Tab Ruler

When you have finished adding, changing, or removing tab settings, click OK to place those settings into effect and remove the Indents/Tabs dialog box from the screen. If you want to cancel or forget any changes you have made, click Cancel. To restore PageMaker's default tab settings, click Reset.

STEP-BY-STEP 9.3

1. Make certain the Indents/Tabs dialog box from Step-by-Step 9.2 is still on-screen. Then, click **OK** to close the Indents/Tabs dialog box.

2. Press **Tab** and then key **This text**.

3. Press **Tab** and key **This text**. Then, press **Enter**.

STEP-BY-STEP 9.3 Continued

4. Press **Tab,** and then key **aligns on tabs**.

5. Press **Tab**, key **aligns on tabs** and then press **Enter**. Keep this publication on-screen for use in the next Step-by-Step.

Setting Tabs More Easily

Adding or changing tab settings is often easier if you position the Indents/Tabs ruler so that the ruler's zero position falls on the left edge of the text block in which you want the text to align. Positioning the ruler in this way before setting tabs makes it easier to determine where you want the tab settings located in the on-screen publication.

Look at the Indents/Tabs ruler shown in Figure 9-4. Notice how the zero position of the ruler (the beginning of the ruler) falls on the left margin guide. Notice also how the tab symbols appear directly above the aligned text. To reposition the ruler, place the mouse pointer on the title bar located at the top of the Indents/Tabs dialog box. Then, drag the dialog box until the zero position is located on the left margin guide or left edge of the text block. You can also click on the left or right arrow at the beginning or end of the ruler to move the ruler within the dialog box. If you use this technique while changing the tab settings for selected text, you can see the effect of the change immediately by clicking the Apply button. PageMaker will then align the selected text using the new tab settings, and will also keep the dialog box on-screen.

FIGURE 9-4
Indents/Tabs ruler aligned at the left margin guide

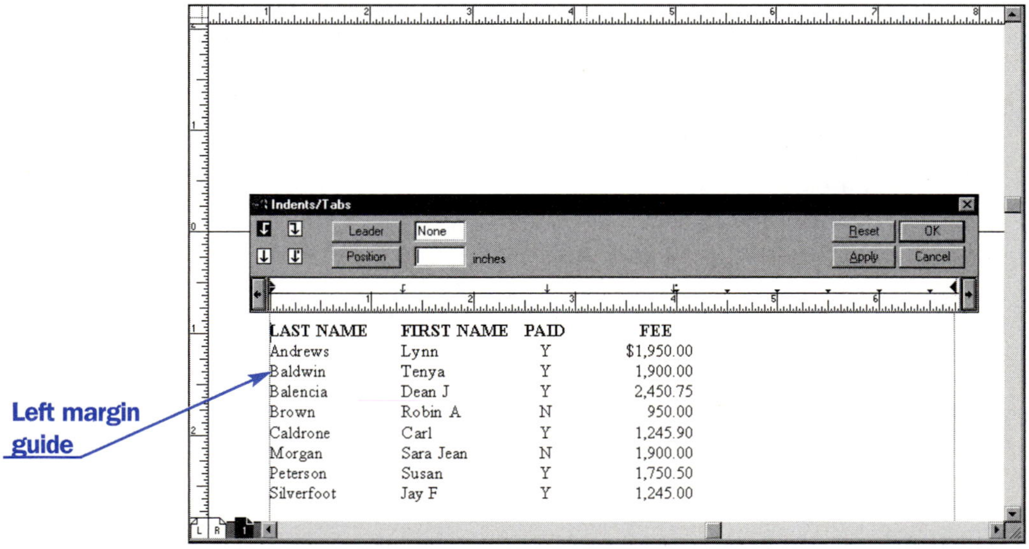

Left margin guide

STEP-BY-STEP 9.4

1. Make certain the insertion point is still located anywhere within the text from Step-by-Step 9.3. Then, select all the text by choosing **Select All** from the **Edit** menu.

2. Click the **Indents/Tabs** button or choose **Indents/Tabs** from the **Type** menu.

STEP-BY-STEP 9.4 Continued

3. If the zero position of the Indents/Tabs ruler already falls on the left margin guide, go on to step 4. Otherwise, place the mouse pointer in the title bar of the Indents/Tabs dialog box. Then, drag the dialog box until the ruler is positioned just above the text and the zero position of the ruler falls along the left margin guide.

4. With all the text still selected, and using instructions you already know, move the tab setting from the 4.25 inch position to the 3.75 inch position. Then, click **Apply** to apply the new tab change. Notice how the right column of text in the publication adjusts. Finally, click **OK** to close the Indents/Tab dialog box.

5. Click once anywhere in the publication window to deselect the text. Keep this publication on the screen for use in the next Step-by-Step.

Tab Leaders

Leaders (rhymes with readers) are a series of dots (.......), dashes (- - - -), or lines (_____) that appear before entries aligned on tab settings. Leaders make it easier to match entries that extend across a page. Dot leaders (shown in Figure 9-5) and dash leaders are commonly used in tables of contents, restaurant menus, and telephone directories.

FIGURE 9-5
Text aligned on dot leader tabs

MENU

SEAFOOD

Broiled Salmon	12.95
Shrimp Scampi	13.50
Lobster Tails	18.95
Baked Lemon Trout	7.95
Lobster Newburg	9.95
Boiled Crab Legs	14.50

DESSERT

Ice Cream	2.25
Chocolate Fudge Cake	2.95
Fruit Salad	3.75

EMPLOYEES

Name	Phone
Adams, Mary	247
Baker, Boda	319
Candy, Jeanna	100
Clemens, Gary	419
Dena, Dedra	112
Edmonds, Eugene	319
Ezuri, Yenda	410
Fujimura, Susan	222
Jenkins, Ulanda	612
Kline, Bob	250
Lemki, Jenna	114
Meyers, Dora	214

Line leaders are often used for creating forms or other documents in which a written response is required, like this:

_____ Age: 18–21 years   _____ Age: 46–64 years

_____ Age: 22–45 years   _____ Age: 65 or over

While adding or changing tab settings, you can request that the tab setting contain a leader. Use the Leader button in the Indents/Tabs dialog box to display the drop-down list shown in Figure 9-6. Inside the list, choose one of the leader selections. Choose .... for a dot leader, - - - - for a dash leader, or _____ for a line leader.

Hot Tip

When setting a tab leader, besides the standard dot, dash, and underline character, you can specify any other character as the leader such as ~ or @. Simply key the character(s) you want to use in the Leader text box.

FIGURE 9-6
The Leader drop-down list

STEP-BY-STEP 9.5

1. Start a new story. While using the **Text** tool, place the I-beam roughly 1 inch below the last line of text and just to the right of the left margin guide, and then click the mouse button.

2. Click the **Indents/Tabs** button or choose **Indents/Tabs** from the **Type** menu.

3. Place the mouse pointer at the 3 inch position on the ruler and click. Next, click the **Right align** button and then click on the **Leader** button. Finally, choose the dot leader entry **....** from the Leader drop-down list. This entry appears just below the word None in the list.

4. Click **OK** to close the Indents/Tabs dialog box.

5. Key **EMPLOYEE TELEPHONE LIST**, and then press **Enter**.

6. Key **Mary Smith**, and then press the **Tab** key.

7. Key **299-1234**, and then press **Enter**. Notice how a series of dots appears between the person's name and the phone number.

8. Key **Louis Ruez**, and then press the **Tab** key. Next, key **281-0487** and press **Enter**.

9. Close this publication without saving it.

Indenting Entries

Indenting is normally used to adjust the left and right edges of paragraphs. Indenting helps set off one paragraph from another or draw attention to a particular entry. As shown in Figure 9-7, there are various types of indents you can create including the paragraph indent (or first line) left indent, full indent, and hanging indent. Each type of indent is described further below.

FIGURE 9-7
Different types of indent techniques

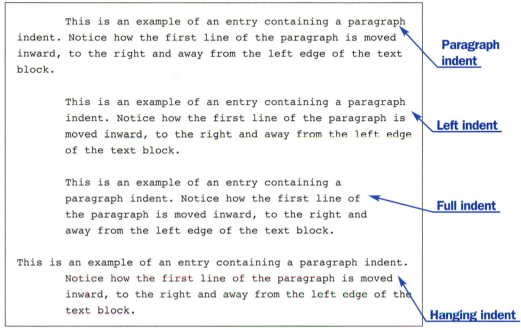

Paragraph/First Line Indent

People often indent the first line of a paragraph by pressing the Tab key. This method, however, is often tedious and time-consuming in a large publication. Instead, by specifying a paragraph indent or a first line indent, PageMaker will automatically indent the first line of any paragraph to the right any distance you specify. All remaining lines in the paragraph will continue to fall along the left edge of the text block.

To create paragraph indents while using the Text tool, place the insertion point where you want the new indent to take effect, or select the text you want to change. Next, choose Indents/Tabs from the Type menu to display the Indents/Tabs ruler. As shown in Figure 9-8, the ruler contains a first line indent symbol as well as left and right margin symbols.

FIGURE 9-8
Example of a first line indent

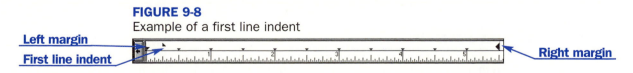

To indent the first line of each paragraph, drag the First line indent symbol to the place above the ruler where you want the first line of each paragraph to begin. For example, in Figure 9-8 the First line indent symbol appears at the 0.25-inch position. With this setting, the first line of a paragraph would automatically be indented one-quarter inch.

S TEP-BY-STEP 9.6

1. Begin a new publication. When the Document Setup dialog box appears, specify a **single-sided** publication with **2** inch margins on the left and right. Keep the top and bottom margins at their default setting. Click **OK**.

2. Click the **Text** tool, and then click an insertion point slightly below the top margin guide and just to the right of the left margin guide.

3. Enlarge the area around the insertion point to the **Actual Size**.

4. Click the **Indents/Tabs** button or choose **Indents/Tabs** from the **Type** menu. Notice how the first line indent symbol (▲) appears at the far left edge of the ruler.

5. Carefully place the mouse pointer on the **First line** indent symbol and drag the symbol to the 0.25 inch position. When finished, your ruler will look similar to the one in Figure 9-8. *NOTE: If you accidentally move the Left margin symbol, drag the symbol back to the zero position on the ruler.*

6. Click **OK** to close the Indents/Tab dialog box. Notice how the insertion point moves inward, away from the left margin guide. Now, key the following and when finished press **Enter** twice.

   This is an example of a first line indent. Notice how the first line begins farther to the right than the remaining lines of text and without the need to press the Tab key.

7. Keep this publication on-screen for use in the next Step-by-Step.

Left Indent

A left indent automatically moves all lines of text in a paragraph to the right. Left indents are normally used to set off one or more paragraphs from the other paragraphs in a publication.

To create a left indent, drag the Left margin symbol to the place above the ruler where you want each line of text (except the first) in the paragraph to begin. As you drag the Left margin symbol, the First line indent symbol will move along with it. Now drag the First line symbol back to the place on the ruler where you want the first line of each paragraph to begin. For example, in Figure 9-9 the Left and First line indent symbols are positioned at the 0.5 inch position, so each line of text including the first will be indented on the left at one-half inch.

FIGURE 9-9
Example of a left indent

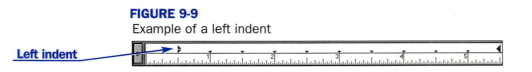

Left indent

S TEP-BY-STEP 9.7

1. Make certain that the insertion point is at the beginning of a new line. Click the **Indents/Tabs** button or choose **Indents/Tabs** from the **Type** menu.

STEP-BY-STEP 9.7 Continued

2. Notice how the Left margin symbol (▶) appears at the far left edge of the ruler. Now, carefully place the mouse pointer on the **Left margin** symbol, and drag the symbol to the 0.5-inch (one-half inch) position. As you do so, the First line indent symbol will move to the right as well. Then, drag the **First line** indent symbol to the left so that it is positioned directly over the Left margin symbol. When finished, your ruler will look like the one in Figure 9-9.

3. Click **OK** to close the Indents/Tabs dialog box. Then, key the following text and when finished press **Enter** twice.

> **This is an example of a left paragraph indent. Notice how the beginning of each line in the paragraph is moved away from the left edge of the text block.**

4. Keep this publication on-screen for use in the next Step-by-Step.

Full Indent

In a full indent, each line of text in a paragraph moves inward on both the left and the right. Full indents are often used for keying quotations or legal citations.

To create a full indent, drag the Left (and Right) margin symbols to the place above the ruler where you want each line of text to begin (and end). For example, in Figure 9-10 each line of text will begin at the 0.5 inch position and end at the 3.5 inch position.

FIGURE 9-10
Example of a full indent

First line indent
Left margin
symbol

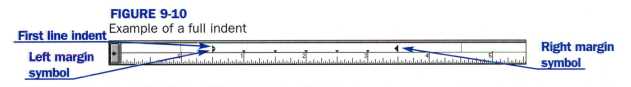

Right margin
symbol

STEP-BY-STEP 9.8

1. Make certain that the insertion point is at the beginning of a new line. Click the **Indents/Tabs** button or choose **Indents/Tabs** from the **Type** menu. Then, specify a full indent that begins at the 0.5 inch position and ends at the 3.5 inch position.

2. Observe how the Right margin symbol (◀) currently appears at the 4.5 inch position in the on-screen ruler. (If you cannot see the 4.5 inch position on the ruler, click several times on the right arrow that's located at the right edge of the ruler.)

3. Drag the **Right margin** symbol to the 3.5 inch position above the ruler. When finished, your ruler will look like the one in Figure 9-10.

4. Click **OK** to close the Indents/Tabs dialog box. Then, key the following text and when finished press **Enter** twice.

> **This is an example of a full paragraph indent. Notice how the beginning and end of each line moves inward on the left and on the right.**

5. Keep this publication on-screen for use in the next Step-by-Step.

Hanging Indent

A *hanging indent* places the first line of text in a paragraph farther to the left than all other lines of text in the paragraph. This indent technique is also called an outdent.

To create a hanging indent, drag the Left margin symbol to the place on the ruler where you want each line of text (with the exception of the first line) to begin. Then drag the First line indent symbol left to the place on the ruler where you want the first line of the paragraph to begin. For example, in Figure 9-11, the settings show that the first line of text appears one-half inch to the left of all remaining lines in the paragraph.

FIGURE 9-11
Example of a hanging indent

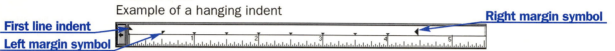

First line indent
Left margin symbol
Right margin symbol

STEP-BY-STEP 9.9

1. Make certain that the insertion point is at the beginning of a new line. Click the **Indents/Tabs** button or choose **Indents/Tabs** from the **Type** menu.

2. Specify a hanging indent of one-half inch and carefully drag the **First line** indent symbol to the left until it touches the zero position on the ruler. *NOTE: If you accidentally move the Left margin symbol, drag that symbol back to the 0.5-inch position on the ruler.*

3. Drag the **Right margin** symbol to the 4.5 inch position in the on-screen ruler. When finished, your ruler will look like the one in Figure 9-11.

4. Click **OK** to close the Indents/Tabs dialog box. Then, key the following text. When finished press **Enter** twice. Keep this publication on-screen for use in the next Step-by-Step.

This is an example of a hanging paragraph indent. Notice how the first line of the paragraph moves to the left away from the remaining lines of text.

Creating Bulleted Entries Manually

As shown in Figure 9-12, a ***bullet*** is a special character (such as •) used to set off one item from another.

FIGURE 9-12
Examples of bulleted entries

• Here is an example of a bullet entry. Notice how the first line of the entry begins with a special bullet character.

• Here is another bullet entry. Bullets can help visually set off entries in a list.

You can create bullet entries by using a hanging indent and one tab setting. To do so, drag the Left margin symbol in the Indents/Tabs dialog box where you want each line of text to begin, with the exception of the bulleted character. Then drag the First line indent symbol to the place on the ruler that you want the bullet character to appear. Finally, set a left-aligned tab directly above the left margin symbol on the ruler.

For example, by using the settings shown in Figure 9-13, the bulleted character appears at the zero position while all text in the paragraph begins at the 0.5 inch position. To key a bullet entry while using those settings and the Text tool, first key the bullet character (•) by pressing Alt+8, then press Tab, and finally key the text. *NOTE: When pressing Alt+8 to create the bullet character, use the number keys along the top row of the keyboard, not the keys on the numeric keypad.*

FIGURE 9-13
Example of a setting used for a bullet entry

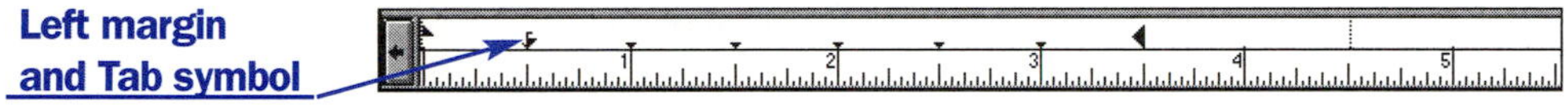

Left margin and Tab symbol

STEP-BY-STEP 9.10

1. Make certain that the insertion point is at the beginning of a new line. Because you have already specified a hanging indent, you need only set one left-aligned tab setting at the 0.5-inch position to key bullet entries. Begin by clicking the **Indents/Tabs** button or by choosing **Indents/Tabs** from the **Type** menu.

2. Position the mouse at the 0.5 inch position on the ruler and then click. Next, click the **Left align** symbol and click **OK** to close the dialog box.

3. Press **Alt+8** (do not use the numeric keypad) to create a bullet character. Then, press **Tab**, key the following text. When finished press **Enter** twice.

    This is an example of a bulleted entry. It is often used to set off individual entries in a list.

4. Keep this publication on-screen for use in the next Step-by-Step.

Creating Bulleted Entries Automatically

PageMaker includes a Bullets and Numbering feature that you can use to add bullets to existing entries. You can also use this feature to select from many different bullet characters such as diamonds, squares and checkmarks.

To create bullet entries while using the Text tool, select the entries or paragraphs that you want to bullet. Next, click the Bullets and Numbering button, or choose Plug-ins from the Utilities menu and then choose Bullets and numbering from the submenu that appears. Either method displays the dialog box shown in Figure 9-14.

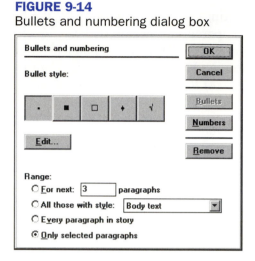

To create a bulleted entry, click one of the bullet characters that appears in the dialog box and then click OK. Although PageMaker adds a bullet and a tab before each selected entry, you can also use the Indents/Tabs dialog box to change how the bulleted entries align.

To remove a bullet from one or more existing entries, select those entries and click the Bullets and Numbering button. Next, click Remove and then click OK. When an alert box containing the message Remove bullets or numbers from the start of each paragraph appears, click OK to complete the operation.

STEP-BY-STEP 9.11

1. Make certain that the insertion point is at the beginning of a new line. Key the following three lines of text and press **Enter** once at the end of each line.

   Bullets help to set off entries.

   You can use different characters for bullets.

   The Bullets and Numbering button is easy to use.

2. Select the three lines of text that you just keyed and click the **Bullets and Numbering** button on the toolbar. Click any of the five bullet characters that appear near the top of the Bullets and Numbering dialog box and then click **OK**.

3. Save this publication under the name **Indents and Bullets** and then close the publication.

> **Hot Tip**
>
> If you want to change the bullet character in existing entries, remember to use the Remove option first. If you forget and simply try to select a different bullet character, PageMaker will keep the old bullet character, but also add the new one to each entry.

SUMMARY

In this lesson you learned how to:

■ Describe the different types of tab alignments.

■ Set, change, and remove tab settings using different types of tab alignments.

■ Describe, set, change or remove tab leaders.

■ Describe various types of paragraph indenting techniques.

■ Use different PageMaker techniques for indenting paragraphs.

VOCABULARY *Review*

Define the following terms:

Bullet	Hanging indent	Left-aligned
Center-aligned	Leaders	Right-aligned
Decimal-aligned		

REVIEW *Questions*

TRUE/FALSE

Circle T if the statement is true or F if the statement is false.

T   F   1. Whenever you set a tab, PageMaker removes any default tab settings to the left of the new tab.

T   F   2. When you begin a new publication, PageMaker normally sets default tabs every three-quarter (0.75) inches.

T   F   3. Numbers aligned using a decimal tab will always line up on their decimal points, even if some of the numbers contain commas and/or a dollar sign.

T   F   4. In the Indents/Tabs ruler, the zero position of the ruler represents the left edge of the paper.

T   F   5. To change an existing tab setting on the Indents/Tabs ruler, you can drag the tab symbol to a different location in the ruler.

T   F   6. A paragraph indent automatically moves each line of a paragraph inward and away from the left and right edge of the text block.

T   F   7. To remove a tab setting on the Indents/Tabs ruler, click on the tab setting and then choose Cut from the Edit menu.

T   F   8. With a hanging indent, the first line of text extends to the left of the remaining lines of text in the paragraph.

T   F   9. Dots that precede tabbed text are called period leaders.

T   F   10. On the Indents/Tabs ruler, you can only add a total of two tab settings.

FILL IN THE BLANK

Complete the following sentences by writing the correct word or words in the blanks provided.

1. When using a(n) _____ font, each character in the font has the same width.

2. In the Indents/Tabs ruler, the symbol ⬛ is used when setting a(n) _____-aligned tab.

3. The indent method where each line of the paragraph, including the first, moves inward away from the left and right edges of the text block is called a(n) _____.

4. In the Indents/Tabs ruler, the symbol ▼ is used to identify a(n) _____ tab setting.

5. _____ are a series of dots (........), dashes (- - - -), or lines (_____) that appear before entries aligned on tab settings.

PROJECTS

SCANS PROJECT 9-1

In this project, you will use various types of tab alignments to create, print, and save the four-column publication shown in Figure 9-15. Take a moment to examine the figure now.

FIGURE 9-15
Sample solution of the Cruises publication in Project 9-1

	UPCOMING CARIBBEAN CRUSES		
DEPARTS	**DURATION**	**PORTS OF CALL**	**AMOUNT**
Jan 2	14-days	8	$ 1,950
Jan 17	7-days	4	1,700
Jan 23	5-days	3	1,150
Feb 2	14-days	5	1,950
Feb 9	21-days	12	2,375
Feb 26	7-days	4	1,650
March 7	5-days	3	975
March 9	3-days	2	675

1. Begin a new publication. When the Document Setup dialog box appears, specify a **single-sided** publication and then click **OK**.

2. Click the **Text** tool, and then click an insertion point slightly below the top margin guide and just to the right of the left margin guide.

3. Enlarge the area around the insertion point to the **Actual Size**.

4. Turn on the bold type style. Then, by using the default tab settings, press the **Tab** key enough times to move the insertion point inward 2 inches. Finally, key **UPCOMING CARIBBEAN CRUISES** in all uppercase letters and press **Enter** twice.

5. Create a left-aligned tab setting at the 2 inch position, a center-aligned tab setting at the 4 inch position, and a decimal-aligned tab setting at the 6 inch position. Then, do the following:

   Key **DEPARTS** and press **Tab**.
   Key **DURATION** and press **Tab**.
   Key **PORTS OF CALL** and press **Tab**.
   Key **AMOUNT** and then press **Enter**.

6. Turn off the bold type style.

7. Key each of the eight lines of entries shown in Figure 9-15. As you key each line, press **Tab** after keying the date, duration, and ports of call entries, then press **Enter** after keying the amount. When finished, your publication should look similar to Figure 9-15. Make any corrections necessary.

8. Print the publication. Then, save the publication under the name **Cruises** and, finally, close the publication.

PROJECT 9-2

In this project, you will create the report shown in Figure 9-16. This report contains a listing of cruise ship names and their destinations. Take a moment to examine the figure now.

FIGURE 9-16
Sample solution of Ships publication in Project 9-2

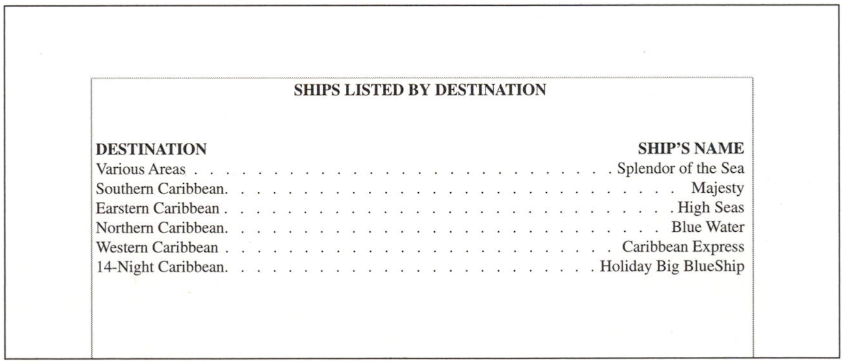

```
                    SHIPS LISTED BY DESTINATION


DESTINATION                                               SHIP'S NAME
Various Areas . . . . . . . . . . . . . . . . . . . . . . Splendor of the Sea
Southern Caribbean. . . . . . . . . . . . . . . . . . . . . . . Majesty
Earstern Caribbean . . . . . . . . . . . . . . . . . . . . . . High Seas
Northern Caribbean. . . . . . . . . . . . . . . . . . . . . . Blue Water
Western Caribbean . . . . . . . . . . . . . . . . . . . Caribbean Express
14-Night Caribbean. . . . . . . . . . . . . . . . . . Holiday Big BlueShip
```

1. Begin a new publication. When the Document Setup dialog box appears, specify a **single-sided** publication and then click **OK**.

2. Click the **Text** tool, and then click an insertion point slightly below the top margin guide and just to the right of the left margin guide.

3. Enlarge the area around the insertion point to the **Actual Size**.

4. Turn on bold, key the title **SHIPS LISTED BY DESTINATION**, and then press **Enter** three times.

5. Using the Indents/Tabs dialog box, create one right-aligned tab setting at the 6.5 inch position. When finished, key **DESTINATION** and press **Tab**, then key **SHIP'S NAME** and press **Enter**. Finally, turn off bold.

6. Using the Indents/Tabs dialog box, remove the existing tab setting at the 6.5 inch position. Then, set a right-aligned tab with a dot leader at the 6.5 inch position. Now, key the remaining 6 lines of text shown in Figure 9-16. To create the first line, for example, key **Various Areas** and press **Tab**, then key **Spendor of the Sea** and press **Enter**.

7. Print the publication. Then, save the publication under the name **Ships**, and close the publication.

PROJECT 9-3

In this project, you will use one tab setting containing a line leader to create the questionnaire shown in Figure 9-17. Take a moment to examine the figure now.

FIGURE 9-17
Sample solution of Questions publication in Project 9-3

QUESTIONNAIRE

Please help us evaluate our travel planning services by answering the following questions.

1. On what day did you visit our offices? _____

2. How long did you wait to talk to a travel agent? _____

3. Do you feel your travel questions were answered? _____

4. How would you rate your travel agent? _____

5. Would you recommend us to a friend? _____

1. Begin a new publication. When the Document Setup dialog box appears, specify a **single-sided** publication and then click **OK**.

2. Click the **Text** tool, and then click an insertion point slightly below the top margin guide and just to the right of the left margin guide.

3. Enlarge the area around the insertion point to the **Actual Size**.

4. Turn on the bold type style. Then, by using the default tab settings, press the **Tab** key enough times to move the insertion point inward 2.5 inches. Finally, key **QUESTIONNAIRE** and then press **Enter** three times.

5. Turn off the bold type style.

6. Key the following sentence and then press **Enter** three times.

    Please help us evaluate our travel planning services by answering the following questions.

7. Create a right-aligned tab setting containing a line leader at the 6.5 inch position. Then, key the five questions shown in Figure 9-17. After keying the text for a particular question, press the **Tab** key (to create the line leader), and then press **Enter** twice to end the line and insert a blank line.

8. When finished, print the publication. Then, save the publication under the name **Questions** and close the publication.

SCANS   **TEAMWORK PROJECT**

Form a team consisting of five to ten students, and appoint a team leader. Then, during the next week, have each team member collect as many examples as possible of publications in which text is aligned in columns and also publications that use leaders. Next, have each team member present to the group all the publication examples they found and explain how those examples might be created in PageMaker. Finally, as a team, vote on the three most interesting publications presented by your group and then have the team leader present and explain those publications to the class.

CRITICAL *Thinking Activity*

SCANS   **ACTIVITY 9-1**

In this lesson, you learned about different types of paragraph indenting such as a left indent, full indent, and hanging indent. During the next week, look closely at the documents you encounter on a daily basis, such as flyers, catalogs, and directories. Challenge yourself to see how many different examples you can locate of various types of paragraph indenting and think about how you might create those same types of indents in a PageMaker publication.

Throughout the history of publishing, various rules and standards have evolved to help ensure that published documents are easy to read and good looking. Many of these rules and standards are different from those used with basic word-processed documents. In fact, if you do not follow some of these rules and standards, you will often produce poor quality results.

In the following sections, you will learn different rules and techniques to help improve the appearance and readability of your publications. Although each rule or technique usually produces only subtle changes, many readers will quickly notice when they are or are not used. Also, because many of these techniques are extremely different from basic word processing techniques that you may already know and use, study them carefully. If you have learned and followed other rules in the past, it may take some time to adjust to these new techniques.

Ending a Sentence

Many people who use basic word processing equipment or even older typewriters often end a sentence with two spaces. They do so because they feel that the extra space helps to visually separate one sentence from the next. Another reason is because many of those devices use monospaced fonts that do not adjust for the different widths of characters. As a result, ending a sentence with two spaces on such devices makes the end of a sentence easier to see, as in this example:

```
This paragraph appears in a monospaced font. Here, each sentence ends with
    a period followed by two spaces. These spaces help to visually separate
    one sentence from the next.
```

Published documents, on the other hand, are created with proportional fonts as you learned in Lesson 7 and printed using high quality printers. Because the fonts and printers adjust automatically for the different widths of each character, only one space is used at the end of a sentence, always! Separating sentences with two spaces often looks too wide and clumsy in published documents. For example, study the space between sentences in the following two entries:

Johannes Gutenberg was born in 1499. Many consider him to be the inventor of the printing press. Gutenberg did, in fact, help develop several printing press designs. His real contribution, however, was moveable type.

Johannes Gutenberg was born in 1499. Many consider him to be the inventor of the printing press. Gutenberg did, in fact, help develop several printing press designs. His real contribution, however, was moveable type.

Both paragraphs contain the same text. However, in the first paragraph, two spaces were used at the end of each sentence. In the second paragraph, only one space separates each sentence. If you look closely, you'll see that two spaces can create a large gap in the even flow of characters on the line. In all desktop published work, always use one space to end a sentence.

Leading

Leading (rhymes with wedding) is the white space that automatically appears between two lines of text in a publication. Without leading, the bottom of the characters on one line would touch the top of the characters on the next line. By default, PageMaker automatically inserts a certain amount of leading between lines to keep the text readable. You can vary the leading, however. You may need to do so to improve the readability of certain text or to adjust the amount of space that text uses on a page.

Understanding Leading

PageMaker normally creates leading by adding space to the top and bottom of each character. It is in this leading space, which is added to the bottom of a character on one line and the top of a character on the next line, that creates the space between the two lines. As shown in Figure 10-3, whenever you select text with the Text tool, the leading space appears at the top and bottom of each character. Also, although leading is the space that appears between two lines of text, it is not the same as line spacing, like double or triple spacing. Line spacing inserts full lines of blank text, whereas leading creates only the space that separates two lines of text.

FIGURE 10-3
Leading is visible when you select text

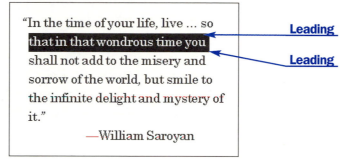

Like font size, leading is measured in points. By default, PageMaker automatically creates leading that is twenty percent larger than the point size being used for the text. For example, if you are using a 10-point font size, the automatic leading is 12 points; with a 12-point font size, the automatic leading is 14.4 points. And, whenever the automatic leading does not produce acceptable results, you can manually specify the leading in a different point size. When a publication is being produced by a graphic design or printing company, the type specifications for that publication normally include both the point and the leading size. A type specification written as 13/15 (referred to as 13 on 15) means a 13-point font size with 15 points of leading.

Leading is also an important tool for adjusting how much text fits on a page. Newspapers and magazines sometimes adjust the leading so that text completely fills a column or a page. For example, in a magazine, sometimes a story ends one line from the bottom of the page (called running short). To make the story fill up the blank line, several words can be added to the story to fill the space. Or, the leading for the entire story could be increased slightly, causing the text to fill the additional space.

Figure 10-4 shows how the same paragraph looks in a 12-point font size, but with different leading values. The example on the left has 16-point leading, the center entry has 14.4-point leading, and the entry on the right has 12-point leading.

FIGURE 10-4
12-point text with different leading values

16 POINTS LEADING	14.4 POINTS LEADING	12 POINTS LEADING
Leading is the space that appears between two lines of text. By default, PageMaker automatically creates leading that is 20 percent larger than the font size. For example, if the font size is 10 points, the leading would automatically be 12 points.	Leading is the space that appears between two lines of text. By default, PageMaker automatically creates leading that is 20 percent larger than the font size. For example, if the font size is 10 points, the leading would automatically be 12 points.	Leading is the space that appears between two lines of text. By default, PageMaker automatically creates leading that is 20 percent larger than the font size. For example, if the font size is 10 points, the leading would automatically be 12 points.

Leading has much to do with how easy or difficult text is to read. Usually, publications containing narrow columns of text, such as newsletters or magazines, look best and are easier to read when the leading is somewhat reduced. Publications containing very long lines of text, on the other hand, look best when the leading is somewhat increased. You need to be careful not to adjust the leading too much. Too little leading makes the text hard to read, whereas too much leading can make it look unprofessional.

Changing Leading

To specify a new leading value, select all the text in the paragraph(s) that you want to change, or place the insertion point where you want the new leading to begin. Next, choose Leading from the Type menu to reveal a submenu like the one shown in Figure 10-5. This submenu includes a variety of different leading values. A check mark appears in front of the current leading value. Simply choose a different value from the submenu to select it.

FIGURE 10-5
Leading submenu

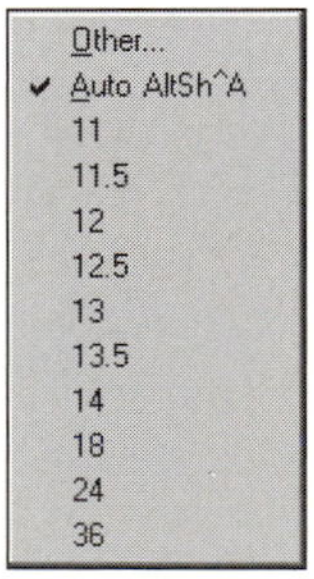

```
Other...
✔ Auto AltSh^A
  11
  11.5
  12
  12.5
  13
  13.5
  14
  18
  24
  36
```

Besides choosing one of the suggested leading values, you can also specify any other leading value between 0 and 1300 points. To do so, choose Other in the Leading submenu to reveal the Other Leading dialog box shown in Figure 10-6. Here, key the new leading size (in points) and then choose OK. *NOTE: The new leading value, if needed, can also be specified in one-tenth point increments, such as 12.2 points.*

FIGURE 10-6
Other Leading dialog box

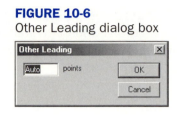

You can also change the leading by using the Control palette. Key the new leading value in the Leading text box shown in Figure 10-7, and then press Enter. Or, you can use the drop-down arrow to the right of the Leading text box to display the list of suggested leading values. You can then select a new leading value from that list.

FIGURE 10-7
Control palette leading features

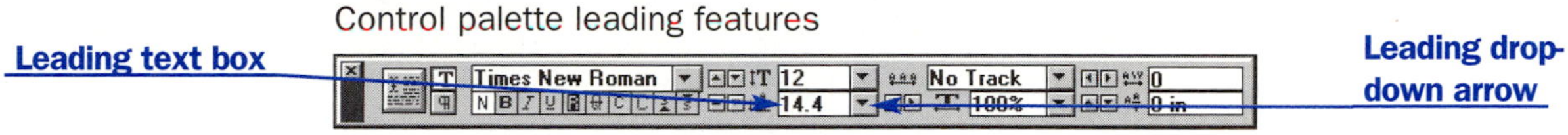

Leading text box   **Leading drop-down arrow**

Determining the best leading is often a trial and error process. Automatic leading usually produces good results for many types of standard publications. In other publications, such as those containing columns or those with unusual publication sizes like brochures or newspapers, adjusting the leading by one or two points is often needed to produce good looking results. Look closely at the leading used in magazines, books, and newspapers to better understand this idea.

STEP-BY-STEP 10.2

1. Turn to page two of the on-screen publication and then enlarge the area around the text on that page to **Actual Size**. This page contains three identical text entries in a 12-point font size with automatic leading (14.4 points).

2. Change the leading for all the text in the second column by first clicking the **Text** tool, then clicking an insertion point anywhere in the second column of text and finally choosing **Select All** from the **Edit** menu. Next, choose **Leading** from the **Type** menu, and then choose **13** from the Leading submenu. Finally, click anywhere in the publication window to deselect the text.

3. Following instructions similar to those in step 2 above, reduce the leading of all the text in the third column to **11** points.

4. If needed, use the **Hand** tool from the toolbox to move the page upward somewhat so that you can see the last line of text in each column. First, notice how changes in the leading alters the amount of space the text requires within each column. Second, notice how using too little space in the last column can make the text more difficult to read. Keep this publication on-screen for use in the next Step-by-Step.

Automatic Paragraph Spacing and Indenting

In many basic word-processed documents, paragraphs are separated with a blank line (by pressing Enter or Return twice) and/or the first line is indented roughly one-half inch. In published work, less space is used to separate paragraphs or to indent the first line of a paragraph.

With PageMaker, you can use the Paragraph Specifications feature to automatically create a certain amount of space between paragraphs and/or to indent each paragraph. This is a great timesaving feature because it eliminates the need to either press Enter twice to end each paragraph or press the Tab key to indent each paragraph.

To use this feature, select the paragraph(s) that you want to change, or place the insertion point where you want the new paragraph spacing or indenting to begin. Then, click the Paragraph Specs button or choose Paragraph from the Type menu to display a dialog box like the one in Figure 10-8.

FIGURE 10-8
Paragraph Specifications dialog box

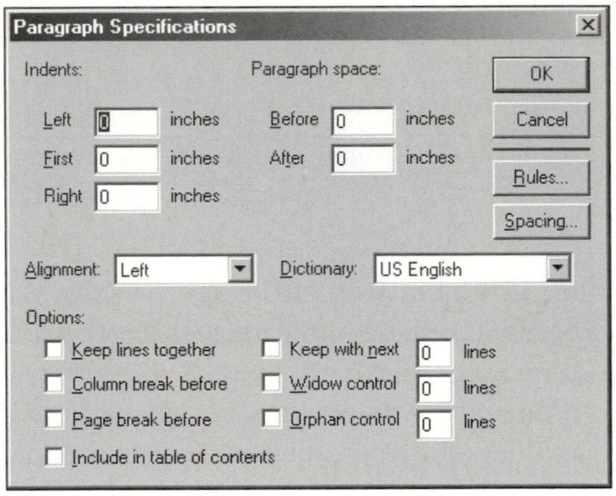

To automatically indent the first line of each paragraph, key the distance for the indent in the text box labeled First. For example, to have all paragraphs indented one-quarter inch you would key 0.25 in the First text box. To automatically separate each paragraph from the previous (and/or next) paragraph with a certain amount of space, key the distance (in fractions of an inch) in the Before (and/or After) text box. For example, to have one-tenth inch of space inserted after each paragraph, you would key 0.1 in the After text box. When finished, click OK to close the dialog box.

The proper paragraph spacing to use varies by font size, the leading size, and personal preference. In typography, a good rule of thumb is to separate paragraphs with a distance equal to between one-half and one full line of space. For example, if you are working with text in a 12-point font size, you would use between 6 and 12 points of space between paragraphs. Examples of text using no space, one-half, and one full line of space appear in Figure 10-9.

FIGURE 10-9
The same paragraphs with different paragraph spacing

NO PARAGRAPH SPACING	ONE-HALF LINE SPACING	ONE FULL LINE SPACING
Johannes Gutenberg was born in 1499 in Germany. While many consider him the inventor of the printing press, printing devices existed long before that time. Gutenberg's major contribution to typography was his invention of moveable type. This allowed books to be typeset quickly. Also, type used for one book could be used in another. For centuries, Gutenberg's idea of moveable type was in use worldwide. Then, beginning in 1964, typesetting was computerized.	Johannes Gutenberg was born in 1499 in Germany. While many consider him the inventor of the printing press, printing devices existed long before that time. Gutenberg's major contribution to typography was his invention of moveable type. This allowed books to be typeset quickly. Also, type used for one book could be used in another. For centuries, Gutenberg's idea of moveable type was in use worldwide. Then, beginning in 1964, typesetting was computerized.	Johannes Gutenberg was born in 1499 in Germany. While many consider him the inventor of the printing press, printing devices existed long before that time. Gutenberg's major contribution to typography was his invention of moveable type. This allowed books to be typeset quickly. Also, type used for one book could be used in another. For centuries, Gutenberg's idea of moveable type was in use worldwide. Then, beginning in 1964, typesetting was computerized.

Besides specifying paragraph spacing in inches or fractions of an inch, PageMaker lets you indicate paragraph spacing in point sizes. For a full line of space, key 0p followed by the point size in the After text box; and for one-half line of space, key 0p followed by a number equal to one-half the point size. For example, suppose you're working in a 12-point font size and want to insert one-half line of space after each paragraph. Because one-half line of space is 6 points, you would key 0p6 in the After text box.

STEP-BY-STEP 10.3

1. Turn to page three in the on-screen publication and then enlarge the area around the text on that page to **Actual Size**. This page contains three identical text entries in a 12-point font size with automatic leading (14.4 points).

2. For all paragraphs in the first column, specify a one-quarter-inch first line indent by clicking the **Text** tool, then clicking an insertion point anywhere in the first column of text and finally choosing **Select All** from the **Edit** menu. Then, click the **Paragraph Specs** button or choose **Paragraph** from the **Type** menu. When the Paragraph Specifications dialog box appears, double-click inside the text box labeled **First,** key **.25** in the text box and then click **OK**.

3. Click anywhere in the publication to deselect the text. Notice how the first line in each paragraph is now indented one-quarter inch.

4. In the second column, place three-quarters of a line of space between all paragraphs by clicking the **Text** tool, then clicking an insertion point anywhere in the second column of text, and finally choosing **Select All** from the **Edit** menu. Then, click the **Paragraph Specs** button or choose **Paragraph** from the **Type** menu. When the Paragraph Specifications dialog box appears, double-click inside the **After** text box, key **0p9** and then click **OK**.

5. Click anywhere in the publication to deselect the text. Notice how a small amount of space now appears between each paragraph. Keep this publication on-screen for use in the next Step-by-Step.

Kerning

PageMaker automatically adds a small amount of space between each character to separate it from the next character. With certain pairs of characters, like the characters WA or AV, however, the space between those characters can sometimes look too wide compared to other characters. This space is especially noticeable with large size fonts of 18 points and above.

Understanding Kerning

Kerning (rhymes with learning) is a technique for adjusting the space between characters. While kerning is normally used to make small changes in the distance between two characters, these changes are often very obvious. The examples in Figure 10-10 illustrate the effect of kerning.

FIGURE 10-10
Unkerned (top) and kerned (bottom) text
(arrows indicate excess character spacing)

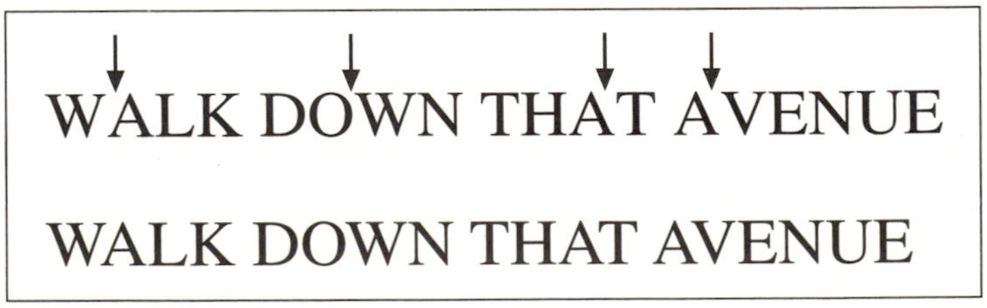

If you look closely, you'll notice that in the first line of text in Figure 10-10, there appears to be extra space between the characters WA, OW, AT, and AV. In the second line, however, the space between each character appears to be more consistent because kerning was used to reduce the space between these same characters.

There are many character combinations that can produce spacing problems. PageMaker knows many such combinations and will, whenever possible, automatically kern the space accordingly. Because the space that appears between characters depends on many conditions, however, automatic kerning does not always produce pleasing results. Here are some examples of the most popular character combinations that can cause spacing problems:

AO	Ao	AT	At	AV	Av	AE	Aw	aw	AY	Ay	ay
FA	Fa	fa	LA	LC	LO	Lo	LW	LY	Ly	my	NO
No	OW	ow	OY	oy	WA	Wa	wa	We	we	WO	
Wo	wo	YA	Ya	ya	YO	Yo	yo				

Because kerning is only noticeable in large point sizes (usually 18 points and above) and when certain conditions are met, it is needed only occasionally. To see if kerning is needed, print the publication and carefully examine any text in larger point sizes for possible character spacing problems. Then, kern only when needed. By the way, you often need to print the publication first because the character spacing can vary somewhat between the screen and the printout.

How to Kern Characters Manually

You can use manual kerning to adjust the space between two characters. Manual kerning lets you increase or decrease the space in small amounts until the space looks correct to your eye.

To manually kern the space between characters, place the insertion point between the characters you want to kern. Then, use the Control palette or the keyboard to adjust the space. To use the Control palette, click on the Kern Down (or Kern Up) button shown in Figure 10-11 to move the characters closer together (or farther apart) by one one-hundredth of an *em space* (the width of the letter m in the current font). Each time you click a kerning button, the space between the characters changes immediately on-screen. To adjust the space in larger increments, hold down the Shift key as you click the kerning button to adjust the space by one-tenth of an em space. You can also specify the amount of kerning needed by keying the value (in fractions of an em space) in the kerning text box in the Control palette.

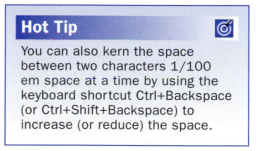

Hot Tip

You can also kern the space between two characters 1/100 em space at a time by using the keyboard shortcut Ctrl+Backspace (or Ctrl+Shift+Backspace) to increase (or reduce) the space.

FIGURE 10-11
Control palette kerning features

You can also use the keyboard to kern space between characters. To decrease (or increase) the space by 1/100 of an em space, hold down the Alt key and then press the ← (or →) key. To decrease (or increase) the space by 1/25 of an em space, hold down the Ctrl and Alt keys and then press the ← (or →) key.

STEP-BY-STEP 10.4

1. Turn to page four in the on-screen publication and then enlarge the area around the first line of text to **Actual Size**. Notice how, when compared to the other characters, there appears to be extra space between the characters W and A in the word WATCH.

2. Using the **Text** tool on the Control palette, click an insertion point between the characters **WA** in the word **WATCH**. Then, reduce the space between those characters by 8/100s of an em space by slowly clicking the **Kern Down** button eight times on the **Control palette**. Notice how the characters move closer together each time you click.

3. Using instructions similar to step 2, reduce the space between the characters **WA** in the word **WAVE** by 8/100s of an em space.

4. Using the **Text** tool, click an insertion point between the characters **A** and **T** in the word **WATCH**. Then, increase the space between those characters by 2/100s of an em space by slowly clicking twice on the **Kern Up** button in the **Control palette**. Notice how the characters move farther apart each time you click. Keep this publication on-screen for use in the next Step-by-Step.

Tracking

Whereas kerning adjusts the space between two characters, *tracking* uniformly adjusts the space between all the characters and the words within selected text. If a story is running too long or short in a publication, for example, you can use tracking on one or more paragraphs to help squeeze or expand the text into the available space on the page. Because some fonts place too much space between characters in larger point sizes (that is, 18 points and above) you can also use tracking to tighten up the spacing.

PageMaker offers six tracking options. Figure 10-12 shows how the same paragraph appears using each of the different options. Even with this short paragraph, you can see how these six tracking options can vary the total length of the paragraph from between eight to ten lines.

FIGURE 10-12
A paragraph using different tracking levels

No Tracking	Loose Tracking	Very Loose Tracking
Johannes Gutenberg was born in 1499 in Germany. While many consider him the inventor of the printing press, printing devices existed long before that time. His major contribution to typography was his invention of moveable type. This allowed books to be typeset quickly.	Johannes Gutenberg was born in 1499 in Germany. While many consider him the inventor of the printing press, printing devices existed long before that time. His major contribution to typography was his invention of moveable type. This allowed books to be typeset quickly.	Johannes Gutenberg was born in 1499 in Germany. While many consider him the inventor of the printing press, printing devices existed long before that time. His major contribution to typography was his invention of moveable type. This allowed books to be typeset quickly.
Normal Tracking	**Tight Tracking**	**Very Tight Tracking**
Johannes Gutenberg was born in 1499 in Germany. While many consider him the inventor of the printing press, printing devices existed long before that time. His major contribution to typography was his invention of moveable type. This allowed books to be typeset quickly.	Johannes Gutenberg was born in 1499 in Germany. While many consider him the inventor of the printing press, printing devices existed long before that time. His major contribution to typography was his invention of moveable type. This allowed books to be typeset quickly.	Johannes Gutenberg was born in 1499 in Germany. While many consider him the inventor of the printing press, printing devices existed long before that time. His major contribution to typography was his invention of moveable type. This allowed books to be typeset quickly.

To adjust tracking, select the text in which you want the tracking adjusted. Then use the menus or the Control palette to adjust the tracking. To use the menus, choose Expert Tracking from the Type menu and then choose a tracking option from the submenu that appears (see Figure 10-13). By default, PageMaker uses no tracking. To decrease the tracking slightly, choose Normal, or choose Tight or Very Tight for even less tracking. To increase the tracking, choose Loose or Very Loose.

FIGURE 10-13
Tracking submenu

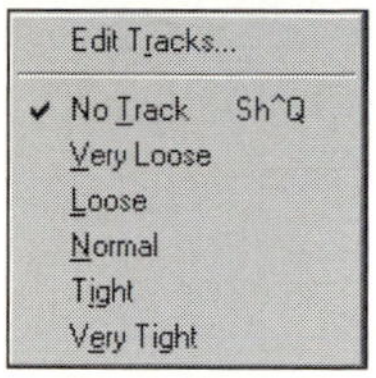

To adjust tracking using the Control palette, first select the text you want adjusted. Then, use the Tracking drop-down arrow shown in Figure 10-14 to display a submenu of tracking options. You can then select an option from this list.

FIGURE 10-14
Control palette tracking options

Tracking drop-down list

Tracking drop-down arrow

STEP-BY-STEP 10.5

1. While still viewing the fourth page in the publication, change to the **Fit in Window** viewing size.

2. Use the menu to expand tracking for text in the second column by clicking on the **Text** tool, then clicking an insertion point anywhere in that column of text and choosing **Select All** from the **Edit** menu. Next, choose **Expert Tracking** from the **Type** menu, and finally choose **Very Loose** from the submenu.

3. Use the Control palette to decrease tracking for text in the third column by clicking the **Text** tool, then clicking an insertion point anywhere in that column of text and choosing **Select All** from the **Edit** menu. Next, click the **Tracking** drop-down arrow in the Control palette and choose **Very Tight** from the submenu. Notice how the text in the third column is now several lines shorter because of the very tight tracking.

4. Click once anywhere in the publication to deselect the text. Keep this publication on-screen for use in the next Step-by-Step.

Changing Character Width

Whereas kerning and tracking adjust the space between characters, the character width feature adjusts the actual width of the characters. You can use this technique to make all characters wider or thinner. The height of each character, however, will remain unchanged.

The character width is adjusted by a percentage. Normally, characters appear at 100 percent of their normal width. Changing the character width to a smaller percentage, such as 70 percent, makes those characters less wide. Selecting a larger percentage, such as 130 percent, produces wider characters. Figure 10-15 shows examples of the same text using different character width settings.

FIGURE 10-15
Different character widths

Enjoy a relaxing Caribbean holiday vacation this year.	70%
Enjoy a relaxing Caribbean holiday vacation this year.	80%
Enjoy a relaxing Caribbean holiday vacation this year.	90%
Enjoy a relaxing Caribbean holiday vacation this year.	Normal
Enjoy a relaxing Caribbean holiday vacation this year.	110%
Enjoy a relaxing Caribbean holiday vacation this year.	120%
Enjoy a relaxing Caribbean holiday vacation this year.	130%

To adjust character width, select the text you want adjusted. Then use the menus or the Control palette to adjust the tracking. To use the menus, choose Horizontal Scale from the Type menu to reveal a submenu of widths ranging from 70 to 130 percent.

To adjust character width using the Control palette, select the text you want to adjust. Then, use the Width drop-down arrow shown in Figure 10-16 to display the list of percentages. You can then select a percentage from this list.

FIGURE 10-16
Control palette width features

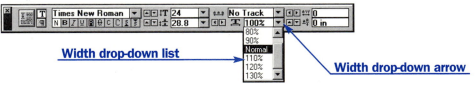

Width drop-down list   **Width drop-down arrow**

STEP-BY-STEP 10.6

1. Turn to page five in the on-screen publication and then enlarge the area around the text to **Actual Size**. Notice how this page contains numerous entries, and how each entry contains the same text.

2. Using the **Text** tool, select all the text in the third entry.

3. Using the menu, change the character width of the selected text to 70% by first choosing **Horizontal Scale** from the **Type** menu and then choosing **70%** from the submenu that appears.

4. Using the **Text** tool, select all the text in the second entry.

STEP-BY-STEP 10.6 Continued

5. Using the Control palette, change the character width of the selected text to 90 percent by clicking the **Width** drop-down arrow in the Control palette and then choosing **90%** from the submenu that appears.

6. Following instructions similar to those above, change the width of the fourth, fifth, and sixth entries to 110 percent, 120 percent and 130 percent, respectively. When finished, examine the differences created by the various character width settings.

7. Using the Save As command, save this publication under the new name **Align-track Revised**. Then, close the publication.

SUMMARY

In this lesson you learned how to:

■ Describe the different types of text alignment that are possible in PageMaker.

■ Change text alignment using the Control panel or menu bar.

■ Describe the terms leading, kerning and tracking.

■ Adjust the leading, kerning and tracking of certain text.

■ Automatically indent and also adjust the space between paragraphs.

VOCABULARY *Review*

Define the following terms:

Em space	Leading	Right alignment
Justify alignment	Left alignment	Tracking
Kerning	Ragged right alignment	

REVIEW *Questions*

TRUE/FALSE

Circle T if the statement is true or F if the statement is false.

T   F   **1.** When using a proportional font, it's a good idea to use two spaces at the end of each sentence.

T   F   **2.** By default, PageMaker creates leading that is twenty percent larger than the font size.

T F 3. Reducing the leading is a good way to improve the appearance of short lines of text, such as text found in columns.

T F 4. A type specification of 13/15 (13 on 15) means 13 points of leading and a 15-point font size.

T F 5. PageMaker cannot automatically indent the first line of each paragraph.

T F 6. Kerning is a technique for reducing the point size of two consecutive characters.

T F 7. Tracking adjusts the space between both the characters and words within selected text.

T F 8. One tracking option is called Very Loose.

T F 9. Kerning is normally used only with text of 12 points or less.

T F 10. Unlike most other spacing adjustments, you do not see the effect of kerning on the screen. It is only noticeable on a printout.

FILL IN THE BLANK

Complete the following sentences by writing the correct word or words in the blanks provided.

1. The space that is automatically inserted between two lines of text is called _____.

2. Two letter combinations that often appear to have too much space between the characters are _____ and _____.

3. To display the dialog box in which you can specify a first line indent, choose _____ from the Type menu.

4. The width of the letter m in the current font is called the _____ space.

5. In typography, a good rule of thumb is to separate paragraphs with between one-half and _____ line of space.

PROJECTS

SCANS PROJECT 10-1A

1. Begin a new publication. When the Document Setup dialog box appears, specify a **single-sided** publication. Also, change the right margin setting to **4** inches and change the left, top and bottom margin settings each to **1** inch.

2. Start the story editor and then key the text shown in Figure 10-17. Wherever the ¶ symbol appears to indicate the end of a paragraph, press **Enter** once. As you key, remember to separate one sentence from the next with only one space. Also, make certain to spell check and proof your work before proceeding to step 3.

FIGURE 10-17
Text for video publication – Project 10-1A

> VIDEO¶
> PLANNING¶
> Caribbean Sun Travel Tours is pleased to announce the opening of its video travel-planning service. This new service, the first of its kind in the country, lets customers view information about their planned destination.¶
>
> The video travel-planning service works this way. A customer sits at a personal computer and enters information about a specific travel destination. Then he or she selects information about that destination from a list of topics. Although these topics vary by destination, they usually include lists of resorts, hotels, shops, and local points of interest. Based on the selection, the computer then plays a 5-15 minute video segment.¶
>
> The video programs are made by the staff of Caribbean Sun Travel Tours and are updated every six months. The staff visits each of the destination cities on a regular basis to ensure that the video information is accurate and up-to-date. During these visits, they prepare their programs on-site using state-of-the-art television cameras. For video programs about hotels and resorts, the program is shown immediately to the owners of the facility to make certain the information is accurate.¶
>
> This new service was developed by Caribbean Sun Travel Tours late last year and is already receiving interest from other travel agencies worldwide. As the result of an article in a national travel magazine, inquiries about purchasing the service have been received from agencies in California, Alaska, Mexico, Canada, and Australia.¶

3. Choose **Edit Layout** from the **Edit** menu and when the Text Placement icon appears, place the icon slightly below the top margin guide and just to the right of the left margin guide. Finally, click to insert the text from the story editor into the publication.

4. Center (align) the first two lines of text (the words **VIDEO** and **PLANNING**).

5. Select all of the remaining text in the story. Specify a first line paragraph indent of **0.15** inches and adjust the paragraph spacing so that one-half line of space appears after each paragraph.

6. Print the publication and handwrite on the printout **Printed Result of Project 10-1A**.

7. Save this publication under the name **Video 1**. Keep the publication on-screen for use in the next project.

PROJECT 10-1B

1. Select all of the text in the on-screen publication, except the title. Then, specify a first line paragraph indent of **0.25** inches, one full line of space after each paragraph, and change the leading to **13** points.

2. Print the publication and handwrite on the printout **Printed Result of Project 10-1B**.

3. Compare the printouts from Project 10-1A and 10-1B, and examine the differences in leading, indents, and paragraph spacing.

4. Using the Save As command, save this publication under the name **Video 2**. Then, close the publication.

SCANS PROJECT 10-2

In this project, you will use various alignment methods to create the announcement shown in Figure 10-18. Take a moment to examine the figure now.

FIGURE 10-18
Solution to Invitation Publication—Project 10-2

Invitation

Caribbean Sun Travel Tours
cordially invites you to attend
their Holiday Open House
Saturday, December 14th
between 5:00 - 9:00 PM
6600 Duval Street
Key West, FL

RSVP by December 6
(303) 555-1234

1. Begin a new publication. When the Document Setup dialog box appears, specify a **single-sided** publication. Also, change the top and bottom margin settings to **1.5** inches and change the left and right margin settings to **1** inch.

2. Click the **Text** tool, and then click an insertion point slightly below the top margin guide and just to the right of the left margin guide.

3. Select an **18-point** font size and change to **right alignment**. Then, key **Invitation** and press **Enter** seven times.

4. Change to **center alignment** and turn on the **italic** type style. Then, key the following lines of text, and press **Enter** at the end of each line:

   Caribbean Sun Travel Tours
   cordially invites you to attend
   their Holiday Open House
   Saturday, December 14th
   between 5:00 - 9:00 PM
   6600 Duval Street
   Key West, FL

5. Press **Enter** seven times.

6. Change to **left alignment** and turn off italic. Next, key **RSVP by December 6** and press **Enter**. Then, key **(303) 555-1234**.

7. Compare your entire publication to Figure 10-18 and make any corrections needed.

8. Using the **Text** tool, select the seven lines of centered text in the publication. Then, while that text is selected, change the character width to **120%** and change the leading to **27** points.

9. Using the **Pointer** tool, drag all the text in the publication up or down as needed until the text is centered vertically between the top and bottom margin guides.

10. Print the publication. Save the publication under the name **Invitation** and close it.

PROJECT 10-3

1. Begin a new publication. When the Document Setup dialog box appears, click **OK**.

2. Key the word **LOOK** anywhere on the page in a serif font, in **bold**, and in a **72-point** font size. Then place the insertion point between the letters OO and use kerning to reduce the space between those characters by 30/100s of an em space. When finished, your text should look similar to the sample solution shown in Figure 10-19.

3. Print the publication and then close the publication without saving it.

FIGURE 10-19
The word LOOK after kerning 30/100s of an em space

SCANS 🤝 TEAMWORK PROJECT

Form a desktop publishing team by selecting a partner. Choose one partner who will work as the designer and the other partner who will work as the desktop publisher. As the designer, select a small 150-250 word article from a national newspaper or magazine and have your desktop publishing partner begin keying the text from that article into a new PageMaker publication. While your partner is keying the text, examine the article closely and create type specifications that you feel would allow your partner to duplicate the article as closely as possible. For example, you will need to determine the approximate width of the column in which the article appears. Also, you will need to select a typeface that is the same or similar to the one used in the article as well as a font size, leading size and alignment method. When your partner finishes keying the text, work with him or her to apply the type specifications you created. Then, as needed, try changing different specifications to see how close the layout of your publication can match the national newspaper or magazine article.

CRITICAL*Thinking*

SCANS ACTIVITY 10-1

In this lesson you learned various ways to adjust the amount of space that text of the same font size uses on a page such as leading, paragraph spacing, tracking and others. Take some time now to review each of these methods and think of several examples in which you might use each one. Can you also think of certain situations in which you might use two or more of these methods for adjusting text?

USING HYPHENATION AND PUNCTUATION

Introduction

This lesson explains various typographic techniques that you can use when creating various types of publications. In this lesson you will learn how to control hyphenation, produce different types of hyphens and dashes, insert various types of spaces and slashes between words, and produce true quotation marks in PageMaker. People are used to seeing these techniques in professionally produced publications, and the absence of these techniques is often quickly noticed.

Automatic Hyphenation

PageMaker provides several ways to control what happens when a long word extends beyond the right edge of a text block. By default, the program will try to hyphenate any such word. There are times, however, when this automatic hyphenation is not appropriate. For example, words in titles or headlines should rarely be hyphenated. Likewise, too many hyphens in a paragraph look strange and can make reading the paragraph more difficult.

PageMaker offers a number of hyphenation options. For example, you can turn hyphenation completely off or on, hyphenate only certain words, and control the number of words in a paragraph that are hyphenated.

Turning Hyphenation On/Off

To change the hyphenation settings for existing text, select the text. To change the default hyphenation settings for text that you will eventually place or key into a publication, click the Pointer tool. Next, choose Hyphenation from the Type menu to reveal the Hyphenation dialog box shown in Figure 11-1. To turn hyphenation off, select Off. Or, if you previously turned hyphenation off and now want to turn it back on, select On. Then click OK.

FIGURE 11-1
Hyphenation dialog box

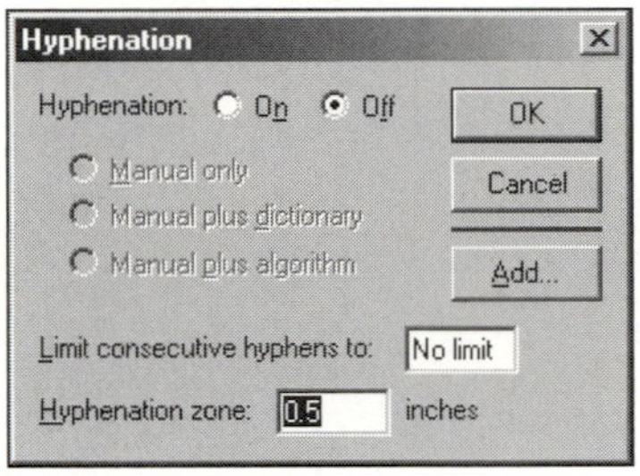

Controlling the Type of Hyphenation

When hyphenation is turned on, you can select from three hyphenation options: Manual only, Manual plus dictionary, and Manual plus algorithm. Each option produces different amounts of hyphenation.

Manual only: If you choose this option, PageMaker will hyphenate only those words in which a hyphen was keyed, such as mother-in-law, and only when such words extend beyond the right edge of the text block.

Manual plus dictionary: If you choose this option, PageMaker will hyphenate any word that overlaps the right edge of a text block in which a hyphen was keyed or any word that is found in the PageMaker spelling dictionary. Any other words are not hyphenated.

Manual plus algorithm: This option produces the greatest amount of hyphenation possible. With this option, when a word extends beyond the right edge of a text block, hyphenation will occur if the word contains a hyphen character, appears in the spelling dictionary, or if the word can be hyphenated based on certain rules for hyphenation. These rules are called an *algorithm* and they identify situations when a word can be hyphenated, such as if it ends in *ing* or *ed*.

Additional Hyphenation Options

The Hyphenation dialog box also contains a Limit consecutive hyphens to option, which lets you control the maximum number of consecutive hyphens that can appear in a paragraph. You can vary the number between 1 and 255. The default setting for this option is *No limit*. The No limit setting means that a paragraph can have an unlimited number of consecutive lines ending with a hyphen. Having too many consecutive hyphens can make text difficult to read and unattractive to look at. Generally it's a good idea to limit the number of consecutive hyphens to one or two. To do so, key the maximum number of consecutive hyphens you want into the Limit consecutive hyphens to text box.

The Hyphenation zone lets you control the amount of white space at the end of a line. As a result, this option does not apply to justify or force justify aligned text. By default, the hyphenation zone is set at 0.5 inches, which means that PageMaker will not hyphenate a word unless it falls within 0.5 inches of the right edge of the text block. If you enter a smaller value, such as 0.25 inches, there will be less white space at the end of the lines but more hyphenated words. On the other hand, entering a larger value produces more white space but less hyphenation.

> **Hot Tip** ◎
>
> Because editing often changes where lines of text end and where hyphenation might occur, wait until a publication is nearly complete before spending time trying to control hyphenation.

STEP-BY-STEP 11.1

1. Begin a new publication. When the Document Setup dialog box appears, specify a **single-sided** publication and change both the left and right margins to **2.75** inches.

2. Choose **Place** from the **File** menu. Then, from the data files that are provided with this book, select the file named **Hyphenation.rtf**. When the Text Placement icon appears, position the icon slightly below the top margin guide and just to the right of the left margin guide, and then click.

3. Enlarge the area around the text to **Actual Size** and notice if any lines of text end in hyphenated words.

4. Select all the text in this story. Then choose **Hyphenation** from the **Type** menu and select **On**, if it is not already selected. Now, select the **Manual plus dictionary option**. Next, using the mouse, select the words **No limit** in the Limit consecutive hyphens to text box, key **2** and then click **OK**. Now, notice how many lines of text end with hyphenated words.

5. If it is not already selected, select all the text in the story. Then choose **Hyphenation** from the **Type** menu. Now, use the mouse to select the entry **0.5** that appears in the Hyphenation zone text box. Key **0.7** and then click **OK**. Now, notice how many lines of text end with hyphenated words. Keep this publication on-screen for use in the next Step-by-Step.

Adding Manual Hyphens and Dashes

Some words or phrases naturally contain a short line (-) called a hyphen that is used to join the parts of a compound word, for example, Smith-Gomez. Hyphens can also be used to indicate a compound number such as 127-42-1000 or to separate a prefix from its root word, such as re-elected. As you've just learned, PageMaker can automatically hyphenate a long word that extends beyond the right edge of the text block. For words that include a hyphen character, PageMaker offers three types of hyphens—required, hard hyphen, and discretionary.

Required Hyphen

Pressing the minus (-) key creates a required hyphen character. Although this is the most common way people create a hyphen, it is usually not the best way in PageMaker. Using a required hyphen inserts a hyphen character into the word or phrase. Problems can arise, however, if an entry that contains a required hyphen character overlaps the right edge of the text block. In those instances, PageMaker splits the entry at the hyphen, moving the remainder to the next line. For example, if a number like the ZIP code 34630-1009 or telephone number 323-1009 extends beyond the right edge of the text block, the characters after the hyphen would move to the next line. As you will learn in a moment, such compound numbers are never split onto two lines.

Hard Hyphen

When you are working with a compound word or number in a professional publication, you should never split the compound word or number between two separate lines of text. Doing so can often lead to confusion and misunderstanding, and can make the entry difficult to read. A *hard hyphen* (also known as a nonbreaking hyphen) glues the parts of a compound word or compound number together. If part of the compound word or number extends beyond the right edge of the text block, the entire word or number moves to the next line.

To create a hard hyphen press Ctrl+Alt+- (hold down the Ctrl and Alt keys and then press the minus key). For example, in the name Smith-Gomez you would key Smith, press Ctrl+Alt+- and then key Gomez. Now, if you edit the publication and any portion of the name overlaps the end of the line, the entire name will move to the next line.

Discretionary Hyphen

As you've learned, when hyphenation is turned on, PageMaker hyphenates any word that extends beyond the right edge of a text block if that word contains a hyphen, or if that word appears in its spelling dictionary. Often, publications contain peoples' last names or unique street or product names that do not appear in the spelling dictionary. And, if such a word overlaps the right edge of the text block, PageMaker moves the entire word to the next line. That can create a large gap at the end of the line from which the word was moved. To avoid this gap, you can use a *discretionary hyphen* to force the hyphenation of a word, keeping the first part of the word on one line and moving the remainder of the word to the next line. Then, as you edit the publication, if you add or delete text that causes the word to move away from the right edge of the text block, PageMaker will join the word together again and hide the discretionary hyphen.

To create a discretionary hyphen, press Ctrl+Shift+-. For example, to insert a discretionary hyphen between the letters l and a in the word *galaxy,* you would first key *gal,* press Ctrl+Shift+- and then key *axy.*

Preventing Hyphenation of One Word

You can also prevent a word from ever being hyphenated, no matter where it falls on the line by placing a discretionary hyphen at the beginning of the word. To do so, place the insertion point just to the left of the first character in the word and then press Ctrl+Shift+-.

Hot Tip

When two or more lines of consecutive text end in a hyphen, those lines are referred to as a ladder. This is because the hyphens appear one below the other, like steps on a ladder. Whenever possible, avoid ladders in your publications because they look visually disruptive and can slow down the reading rate. If ladders occur, use the techniques mentioned in this lesson to eliminate them.

S TEP-BY-STEP 11.2

1. Click the **Text** tool, and click an insertion point at least 1 inch below the last line of text and just to the right of the left margin guide. Then, enlarge the area around the insertion point to **Actual Size**.

2. Key **You can find us on the Internet at** and press the **Space bar** once.

3. Now key **Caribbeansun.com** and insert a discretionary hyphen between the letters *bb* by first keying **Carib** and then pressing **Ctrl+Shift+-** (hold down the **Ctrl** and **Shift** keys and then press the **minus** key). Next, key **beansun.com** and press the **Space bar** once. (*NOTE: The discretionary hyphen may not appear after completing this step, but it will appear later in this exercise.*)

4. Key **or receive more information by contacting Reginald** and then press the **spacebar** once.

5. Now, key the name **Smith-Ferguson** using a nonbreaking space by first keying **Smith** and then pressing **Ctrl+Alt+-** (hold down the **Ctrl** and **Alt** keys and then press the **minus** key). Then, key **Ferguson for more information.**

6. Move the insertion point just to the left of the f in the word find. Then, slowly press **Delete** several times to delete several characters of text. When you have removed enough characters, notice how PageMaker removes the hyphenation from the entry *Carribeansun.com*. Now rekey the characters you deleted. As you do, notice how PageMaker hyphenates the entry again. Keep this publication on-screen for use in the next Step-by-Step.

Dashes

A dash is used to indicate a series or a pause in a sentence. Unlike basic word processed documents where dashes are usually shown as two hyphens (- -), published documents use two kinds of dashes: an en and an em dash. Each is used for a different purpose, which is described in the following paragraphs.

An *en dash* is a short line (–) which is slightly longer than the hyphen character. It is called an en dash because it has the same width as a lowercase letter n. In published documents, an en dash is used in place of the word *to* or *through*, such as A–Z. To create an en dash, press Alt+- (hold down Alt and then press the minus key). Here are some other examples of entries that would require an en dash:

May–June

See pages 127–134

200–280 pounds

5:30–9:30 P.M.

An *em dash* is a long line (—) that is roughly twice the width of an en dash. An em dash is used to show a pause or a break in a sentence such as "I—I won the sweepstakes!" To create an em dash, press Alt+Shift+- (hold down the Alt and Shift key and then press the minus key.).

Here are some rules to consider when using en and em dashes.

■ Use an en dash when indicating time, or to indicate a series, such as April–July; 8–21 years old; or 9–11 A.M.

- Use an en dash in place of the word *to* such as "She boarded the Miami–New York train."

- Use an em dash before the name of an author at the end of a quotation, such as "Experience is one thing you can't get for nothing." —Oscar Wilde

- Use an em dash to show a sudden change or break in a sentence such as "The entire computer—monitor, keyboard, and CPU—needs cleaning."

STEP-BY-STEP 11.3

1. Click an insertion point at least 1 inch below the last line of text and just to the right of the left margin guide.

2. Key **March** and then press **Alt+-** to create an en dash. Key **April** and then press **Enter**.

3. Key **If** and then press **Alt+Shift+-** to create an em dash. Then, key **if I could just explain it to you** and press **Enter** twice. Keep this publication on-screen for use in the next Step-by-Step.

Nonbreaking (Fixed) Space

As you know, when two words are separated by a space and one of those words extends beyond the right edge of the text block, PageMaker moves that word to the next line. There are some instances, however, when a series of words that are separated by a space should never be broken between two lines. Examples of such entries include a person's name, such as Donna Lewis, or a date, such as May 15.

To make certain that two words always remain together on the same line, you can insert a nonbreaking space called a *fixed space* between those words. To create a fixed space, press Ctrl+Alt+Space bar.

STEP-BY-STEP 11.4

1. Make certain that the insertion point is at the beginning of a new line. Then, key the words **The meeting in Denver on May**.

2. Press **Ctrl+Alt+spacebar** to create a fixed space and key **15 will be coordinated by Tierney.** Then, press **Ctrl+Alt+spacebar** to create another fixed space, key **Coad,** and then press **Enter** twice. Keep this publication on-screen for use in the next Step-by-Step.

Ellipsis

An *ellipsis* is a series of three dots that indicates missing text. An ellipsis usually appears within a quotation, such as:

"It is not a question of timing ... or patience."

The best way to create an ellipsis is not by keying three periods (...) between the words. If you do so, several problems can arise. The first is legibility. When three periods appear one after the other, they can sometimes look like a single distorted dot, especially in small point sizes. To avoid this problem, some people insert spaces after each period. But, this can create another problem associated with word wrap. Because PageMaker will treat each period followed by a space as a separate word, if one of those three periods extends beyond the right edge of the text block, PageMaker will move it to the next line.

To avoid these potential problems, you can create a single ellipsis character containing three periods by using a special PageMaker command. This ellipsis character joins the words on both sides of the character together so that the words will not break at the end of a line. To create an ellipsis character, press Alt+0133 (hold down the Alt key and key 0133 using the keys on the numeric keypad).

Here are some additional rules to follow when using an ellipsis.

- When words are missing from the beginning of a quotation, place the ellipsis followed by a nonbreaking space at the beginning, such as "... to follow your heart."

- When words are missing from the middle of a quotation, place the ellipsis surrounded by nonbreaking spaces where the words are missing, such as "During the past twenty years ... much has happened."

- When words are missing from the end of a quotation, place a nonbreaking space and then the ellipsis at the end of the quote. Follow the ellipsis immediately with the appropriate end-punctuation mark, such as "What is the best way ... ?"

STEP-BY-STEP 11.5

1. Make certain the insertion point is at the beginning of a new line.

2. Key **It's not impossible** and then press **Alt+0133** to insert the ellipsis. Next, key **nor is it easy** and then press **Enter** twice. Keep this publication on-screen for use in the next Step-by-Step.

Nonbreaking Slashes

Word wrap can also cause problems with entries that contain a slash (/) character. Slashes are frequently used in dates, such as 8/15/03, or in place of one-or-the-other word combinations, such as and/or. If an entry containing a slash extends beyond the right edge of the text block, PageMaker splits the entry at the slash.

To make certain that an entry containing a slash always remains together on the same line, you can insert a nonbreaking slash within the entry. To create a nonbreaking slash, press Ctrl+Alt+/ (hold down the Ctrl and Alt keys and then press /).

STEP-BY-STEP 11.6

1. Make certain that the insertion point is at the beginning of a new line.

2. Key **Please respond by 11** and then press **Ctrl+Alt+/** to insert the nonbreaking slash. Next, key **15** and press **Ctrl+Alt+/** to insert another nonbreaking slash. Finally, key **03** and then press **Enter** twice. Keep this publication on-screen for use in the next Step-by-Step.

Quotation Marks

Quotation marks are placed before and after a quotation. Quotation marks are used to identify a person's spoken word or to emphasize certain text. People often surround quotations with inch (") and foot (') characters. In published documents, however, a quotation never uses these characters. Instead, true quotation marks—characters that curve toward the quoted material (that is, "Hello" and 'Hello') are used.

In published works, an open quotation mark is placed at the beginning and a close quotation mark is placed at the end of a quotation. By using various key combinations, PageMaker lets you select from two types of single and double quotation marks. The different characters and the keys used to create them are as follows:

Character	Description	Keystrokes
"	Open quotation mark	Alt+Shift+[
"	Close quotation mark	Alt+Shift+]
'	Single open quotation mark	Alt+[
'	Single close quotation mark	Ctrl+]

Open and closed quotation marks are normally used at the beginning and end of a quotation, whereas single quotation marks are used within a quotation when additional emphasis is required, like this:

"Often, the 'power' of the written word has changed the course of human events."

Here are some rules to consider when using quotation marks.

■ When keying a quotation, place all commas and periods within the quotation marks.

■ Place question marks and exclamation points inside the quotation marks only when they are part of the actual quotation.

■ If the original quotation contains an error, such as a misspelling that you wish to point out, key the word *sic* within brackets like this: "There are to [sic] ways to do this." The letters *sic* is used to point out that a quotation contains a misspelling or the unconventional spelling of a word.

■ If you are quoting long passages of several paragraphs or more, do not use quotation marks. Instead, indent the paragraphs. The indentation helps the reader identify the quoted material more easily.

> **Hot Tip**
>
> You can also insert copies of a hyphen, nonbreaking space or slash, quotation mark, or ellipsis at other points in a publication. While using the Text tool, select one of those characters that you've already inserted into a publication and choose Copy from the Edit menu. Then, place the insertion point where you want a copy to appear and choose Paste from the Edit command.

STEP-BY-STEP 11.7

1. Make certain the insertion point is at the beginning of a new line.

2. Press **Alt+Shift+[** to create an open quotation mark and then key **Don't find a fault. Find a remedy.** Next, press **Alt+Shift+]** (to create a close quotation mark) and finally press **Enter** twice.

3. Save this publication under the name **Techniques,** print, and then close the publication.

SUMMARY

In this lesson you learned how to:

■ Explain how to control the hyphenation of words in a publication.

■ Explain the difference between required, hard, and discretionary hyphens and how to use them in a publication.

■ Explain an en dash, em dash, nonbreaking space and nonbreaking slash, and be able to use them in a publication.

■ Create the special character called an ellipsis character.

■ Create true open and close quotation marks.

VOCABULARY *Review*

Define the following terms:

Algorithm	Em dash	Hard hyphen
Discretionary hyphen	En dash	Sic
Ellipsis	Fixed space	

REVIEW *Questions*

TRUE/FALSE

Circle T if the statement is true or F if the statement is false.

T   F   1. A hyphen is a short line used to join parts of a compound word or compound number and to separate a prefix from its root word.

T   F   2. By default, PageMaker will not hyphenate any words that extend beyond the right edge of the text block.

T   F   **3.** The hyphenation zone lets you control how much white space can appear at the end of a line.

T   F   **4.** An en dash is longer than an em dash.

T   F   **5.** An en dash is used in place of the words to or through, as in A–Z.

T   F   **6.** An em dash is used to show a pause or a break in a sentence such as "I—I won the sweepstakes!"

T   F   **7.** Quotation marks in a publication are characters that curve away from the quoted text.

T   F   **8.** Single quotation marks are used within a quotation when additional emphasis is required.

T   F   **9.** In PageMaker's hyphenation feature, an algorithm is a series of rules that identify instances when words can be hyphenated.

T   F   **10.** The hyphenation zone determines the maximum number of consecutive hyphens that can appear in a paragraph.

FILL IN THE BLANK

Complete the following sentences by writing the correct word or words in the blanks provided.

1. You press Ctrl+Alt+- to create a(n) _____ hyphen.

2. Write an example of the ellipsis character in the space provided: _____.

3. To make certain that a compound word or entry, such as the ZIP code 34630-1952, is never split between two lines, you can use a(n) _____ hyphen.

4. You use a(n) _____ dash before the name of an author at the end of a quotation.

5. To make certain that a date entry containing slashes, such as the date 8/15/05, is never split between two lines, you need to use a(n) _____ slash.

6. You press Ctrl+Alt+/ to create a(n) _____ slash.

7. You use a(n) _____ dash to show a sudden change or pause in a sentence.

8. To make certain that a date entry, such as May 15, is never split between two lines, you would use a(n) _____ space.

9. If a quotation that you are including in a publication contains a spelling error and you want to point out the error to the reader, you can key the characters _____ within brackets.

10. Generally, it's a good idea to limit the number of consecutive hyphens to _____.

PROJECTS

PROJECT 11-1

1. Begin a new publication. When the Document Setup dialog box appears, specify a **single-sided** publication. Also, change both the left and right margin settings to **2.5** inches. Keep the top and bottom margins at their default settings.

2. When the new publication appears, click the **Text** tool, and then click an insertion point slightly below the top margin guide and just to the right of the left margin guide. Then, enlarge the area around the insertion point to **Actual Size**.

3. Change to an **18-point** font size.

4. Using a hard hyphen, key the telephone number **555-1234** and then press **Enter** twice.

5. Using hard hyphens, key the Social Security number **111-11-1111** and then press **Enter** twice.

6. Using an en dash, key the range of dates **April–May** and then press **Enter** twice.

7. Using an en dash, key **See pages 14–22** and then press **Enter** twice.

8. Using an em dash, key the following sentence **Your work is—-fantastic!** and then press **Enter** twice.

9. Print the publication and examine the results.

10. Save this publication with the name **Hyphen-dash** and then close this publication.

SCANS PROJECT 11-2

1. Open the publication named **Sales Report 3 Columns** from the data files that accompany this book. Turn to the first page, if needed. As you may recall from Lesson 5, this publication contains two stories. The first story contains all the text in the first column of the first page. The second story contains the rest of the text in the publication.

2. This publication was created using the default hyphenation settings. Examine the text in the first column (the one containing the heading SUMMARY), and observe the number of hyphenated words, if any. If no words are hyphenated in the first column, go on to step 3. Otherwise, select all the words in the first column (story) and then turn off hyphenation.

3. For all the remaining text in the publication (all the text in the second story), turn hyphen on (if needed), change the number of consecutive hyphens to **2** and change the hyphenation zone to **0.15** inches. (*Note: Although the text in the second story spans two pages, you can select all the text on both of those pages by clicking once anywhere in the story and then choose Select All from the Edit menu.*)

4. Save this publication under the name **Sales Report 3 Columns Revised**, print, and then close the publication.

PROJECT 11-3

In this project, you will use various types of dashes, as well as quotation and ellipsis characters, to create the publication shown in Figure 11-2. Examine that publication carefully before you begin, and note where those special characters are required.

1. Start a new publication. When the Document Setup dialog box appears, specify a **single-sided** publication with **2** inch margins on the top, bottom, left and right.

2. Working carefully, key the text using a serif font such as Times New Roman, Times, or Times Roman. Make certain that the first line appears in **18-points**, in **bold** and with **center alignment**. Make certain that all remaining lines of text appear in **12-points** and with **left alignment**. Begin and end each quotation with open and close quotation marks, and include the ellipsis (...), en dash (–), and/or em dash (—) where required. When finished, use the Pointer tool to center the text vertically between the top and bottom margin guides.

3. Save this publication under the name **Customers Say It Best**, print, and then close the publication.

FIGURE 11-2
Customers Say It Best publication

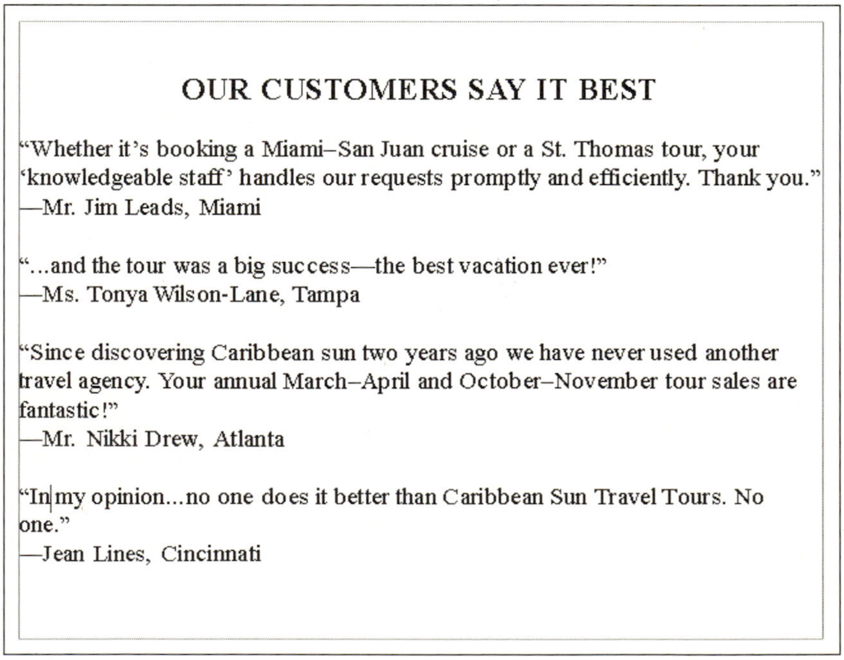

OUR CUSTOMERS SAY IT BEST

"Whether it's booking a Miami–San Juan cruise or a St. Thomas tour, your 'knowledgeable staff' handles our requests promptly and efficiently. Thank you."
—Mr. Jim Leads, Miami

"...and the tour was a big success—the best vacation ever!"
—Ms. Tonya Wilson-Lane, Tampa

"Since discovering Caribbean sun two years ago we have never used another travel agency. Your annual March–April and October–November tour sales are fantastic!"
—Mr. Nikki Drew, Atlanta

"In my opinion...no one does it better than Caribbean Sun Travel Tours. No one."
—Jean Lines, Cincinnati

SCANS **TEAMWORK PROJECT**

As you now know, you can use a hard hyphen to stop a compound number or word from hyphenating. There are many different examples of such compound numbers that could appear in a publication, such as a ZIP code or telephone number. With your instructor and classmates, see how many other different types of compound numbers you can list in five minutes.

CRITICAL*Thinking*

SCANS **ACTIVITY 11-1**

In this lesson, you learned about certain rules to follow when creating a publication. These and many other such rules have evolved over time to help make a publication easier to read, more visually pleasing, and more grammatically correct. There are two excellent sources for information about these rules: *The Chicago Manual of Style* and the *New York Times Manual of Style and Usage*. During the next week, visit the reference section of your school or public library and examine one or both of these books to become generally familiar with their content and layout. Also, browse through the material to discover two or three new rules or guidelines to follow when creating a publication or document that you were unaware of.

WORKING WITH GRAPHICS

OBJECTIVES

Upon completion of this lesson, you should be able to:

- Identify and change both the fill and stroke of a PageMaker-created graphic.

- Use the Shift key for drawing perfect squares and circles.

- Layer text or a graphic over another graphic.

- Describe programs that create graphics you can import into PageMaker.

- Describe different types of graphic file formats.

- Import or place a graphic into a publication.

- Resize, move, and rotate a graphic.

- Explain how to remove an unwanted portion of a graphic.

Estimated Time: 5 hours

VOCABULARY

Crop

Electronic clip art

File format

Fill

Graphic composition program

Import

Layering

Reverse type

Rotate

Scanner

Stroke

Introduction

Earlier in this book, you learned how to use PageMaker's drawing tools to create simple graphics such as lines, rectangles and circles. This lesson expands upon these concepts and explains additional graphics techniques, such as how to add shading to a graphic, draw lines of various widths, and layer one drawing over another. You'll also learn how to place graphics created in other programs or graphics purchased from various sources into a publication, as well as learn to resize, move, rotate, and even remove an unwanted portion of that graphic.

PageMaker-Created Graphics

As you learned in Lesson 3, the toolbox contains various tools for drawing graphics, such as a straight line or rectangle, within a publication. In this section, you will learn additional techniques for creating and using PageMaker-created graphics in your publications.

Review

PageMaker offers five standard tools for creating different types of graphics: the Line, Constrained-line, Rectangle, Ellipse, and Polygon tools. To create a graphic with one of these tools, click on the appropriate tool, position the crosshair pointer where you want the drawing to begin, and drag the pointer to where you want the graphic to end. To edit a graphic, use the Pointer tool to select it and display its sizing handles. Then, you can resize the graphic by dragging a sizing handle, move the graphic by dragging along its edge, or remove the graphic by deleting it.

Drawing Perfect Squares and Circles

As you may have discovered already, it can take considerable patience trying to use only the Ellipse or Rectangle tools to draw an exact square or an exact circle. However, you can draw a perfect square (one with exactly the same height and width) or a perfect circle (where all portions of its line are equal distance from the center) easily by holding down the Shift key as you create the drawing. For example, to draw a perfect square, first select the Rectangle tool, hold down the Shift key and then hold down the mouse button. Now, as you drag the crosshair, PageMaker will automatically create a perfect square with equal height and width. When you are finished creating the square, release the mouse button and then release the Shift key.

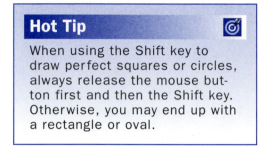

Hot Tip

When using the Shift key to draw perfect squares or circles, always release the mouse button first and then the Shift key. Otherwise, you may end up with a rectangle or oval.

S TEP-BY-STEP 12.1

1. Start a new publication and when the Document Setup dialog box appears, specify a **single-sided** publication and then click **OK**.

2. Click the **Oval** tool and then place the crosshair pointer that appears near the intersection of the top and left margin guides.

3. Read this instruction completely before beginning. First, hold down the **Shift** key; then hold down the mouse button. Next, drag the crosshair pointer downward and to the right until you have created a perfect circle roughly 3 to 4 inches across. Then release the mouse button, and finally release the **Shift** key.

4. Click the **Rectangle** tool and then place the crosshair pointer near the intersection of the bottom and the right margin guides.

5. Read this instruction completely before beginning. First, hold down the **Shift** key; then hold down the mouse button. Next, drag the pointer upward and to the left until you have created a perfect square roughly 3 to 4 inches across. Then, release the mouse button, and finally release the **Shift** key. Keep this publication on-screen for use in the next Step-by-Step.

Changing the Fill and Stroke

With PageMaker-created graphics, you can vary the width of the line that surrounds the graphic, referred to as the *stroke*, and add color or a pattern to the inside the graphic, called the *fill*.

To change the stroke or fill of an existing graphic, select the graphic first. To create a new graphic and specify a stroke or fill at the same time, first click the appropriate graphic tool in the toolbox, such as the Rectangle tool. Next, choose Stroke or Fill from the Element menu, and then make the appropriate stroke and/or fill selection from the submenus shown in Figure 12-1. The Stroke submenu lists the different line widths available measured in points as well as different line types, such as single, double, or dotted lines. Choosing the 12pt selection, for example, would produce a line roughly one-sixth of an inch wide. The Fill submenu lists the different colors or patterns available. For example, choosing Solid would completely shade the inside of the graphic, whereas choosing one of the bottom eight pattern selections would fill the inside of the graphic with a particular pattern of lines.

FIGURE 12-1
Stroke (left) and Fill (right) submenus

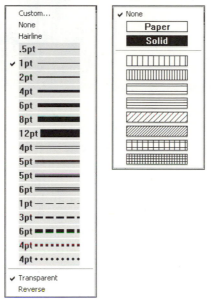

STEP-BY-STEP 12.2

1. Using the **Pointer** tool, click along the outside edge of the circle to select it.

2. Choose **Stroke** from the **Element** menu and then choose **4pt** from the submenu.

3. With the circle still selected, choose **Fill** from the **Element** menu and then choose the vertical line pattern (the one immediately below the Solid entry) from the submenu. Notice how the pattern fills the circle.

4. Using the **Pointer** tool, click along the outside edge of the square to select it.

5. Choose **Fill** from the **Element** menu and then choose **Solid** from the submenu. Notice how the solid color fills the square. Keep this publication on-screen for use in the next Step-by-Step.

Layering and Reverse Type

To create certain drawings, it is sometimes necessary to position one graphic over another, or to place text over a graphic. Placing one element on top of or underneath another element is called *layering*. A shadow box, such as the one shown in Figure 12-2, is actually two rectangles that have different fill colors or patterns and are layered one over the other. In this example, the rectangle on the top is filled using the Paper selection (the color White) while the one on the bottom is filled using the Solid selection. You can also use layering to produce *reverse type*—light type over a dark background—by positioning text with the Reverse type style over a PageMaker-created drawing, such as a rectangle, that has a dark background.

FIGURE 12-2
Example of a shadow box (left) and reverse type (right)

To layer objects, use the Pointer tool to drag one object so that it overlaps a different object. Then, while still using the Pointer tool, select either one of the objects you want to layer. To move the selected object behind the other object, choose Arrange from the Element menu and then choose Send to Back from the submenu that appears. To move the selected object on top of the other object, choose Arrange from the Element menu and then choose Bring to Front from the submenu that appears. (If you are layering several objects, you can choose Bring Forward or Send Backward to move the object forward/backward one layer at a time.)

S TEP-BY-STEP 12.3

1. Using the Pointer tool, drag the square so that it covers one-half of the circle

2. Select the square, if it is not already selected. Next, choose **Arrange** from the **Element** menu and then choose **Send to Back** from the submenu to move the selected square behind the circle.

3. With the square still selected, choose **Arrange** from the **Element** menu and then choose **Bring to Front** from the submenu to move the selected square in front of the circle.

4. Repeat step 2 to send the selected square behind the circle again.

5. Click the **Text** tool and then click an insertion point in an area of the Pasteboard somewhere near the top edge of the page. Key the word **Layering** in a 30-point font size.

6. Use the **Pointer** tool to select the text block containing the word Layering, and then drag that text block to the center of the circle. Finally, click in a blank area of the page to deselect the text block.

STEP-BY-STEP 12.3 Continued

7. To create reverse type, first use the **Text** tool to select the word **Layering**. Next, choose **Type Style** from the **Type** menu and then choose **Reverse** from the submenu. (*NOTE: Don't worry if the word seems to disappear—it has simply turned the same color as the inside of the circle.*) Next, use the **Pointer** tool to select the circle, then choose **Fill** from the **Element** menu, and finally choose **Solid** from the submenu. Notice how the word Layering is now readable.

8. Click in a blank area of the page to deselect the circle.

9. If you wish, print this publication. Then close the publication without saving it.

Using Graphic Images in Publications

A graphic image is an electronic picture or illustration that is stored in a computer file. You can add an almost unlimited number of graphic images into a PageMaker publication. These graphic images might come from a variety of places, such as disks or CD-ROMs purchased at a computer store, or from the Internet. The files could also have been created using certain types of computer programs, or with a scanner that converts photographs or paper illustrations into machine-readable images. They could have also come from a digital camera.

Graphic images that are added to a PageMaker publication can be placed anywhere on a numbered or a master page. Once placed into a publication, you can change the size of the image, move it to any position on the page, remove an unwanted portion of the image, and even control whether any text on the page flows over or around the image.

Sources for Graphic Files

In PageMaker, the term *import* means to electronically read and place work created using a different program into a publication. PageMaker can import graphic files from many of the leading computer programs in use today, such as a spreadsheet program, paint or draw program, or a graphic composition program.

Spreadsheet / Presentation Programs

Spreadsheet programs let you use the computer to record numeric information and perform different types of calculations on that information. Microsoft Excel and Lotus 1-2-3 are two popular examples of such programs. Most spreadsheet programs also let you create bar or pie graphs from numeric information.

Presentation programs let you use the computer to create professional-looking electronic slides or printouts for making presentations. PowerPoint is an example of a widely used presentation program. Figure 12-3 shows two examples of graphics created in a spreadsheet and a presentation program that could be imported into PageMaker.

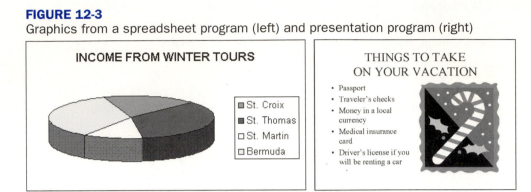

Paint and Draw Programs

Paint and draw programs let you use the computer to create freehand drawings. Two of the popular programs in this category include Microsoft Paint and PaintShop. With these programs, you can create drawings that go far beyond those available with only PageMaker's graphic tools. Besides line, rectangle and ellipsis tools, these programs also offer tools for painting with an electronic paintbrush, erasing with an electronic eraser, and performing freehand drawings. Figure 12-4 shows an example of a drawing created with such a program. After creating these drawings, you can save them as a graphic file that can be imported into PageMaker.

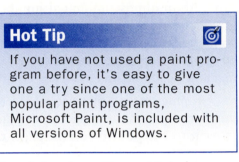

Hot Tip

If you have not used a paint program before, it's easy to give one a try since one of the most popular paint programs, Microsoft Paint, is included with all versions of Windows.

FIGURE 12-4
Image created with a paint program

Graphic Composition Programs

Although paint and draw programs are easy to use, it can take a considerable amount of time to create detailed, complex or elaborate drawings with such programs. *Graphic composition programs*, like Corel Draw, Adobe Illustrator, or Arts & Letters, are popular because of the drawing precision they offer and their wide range of drawing and painting tools. These programs let you create highly complex drawings and illustrations in full color, as well as create special effects like twisting or rotating portions of an image. Figure 12-5 shows an example of a drawing created with a graphic composition program.

FIGURE 12-5
Drawing created using a graphic composition program
(Courtesy of Computer Support Corporation, *Arts & Letters*)

Electronic Clip-Art Libraries

With some experience, most people who use PageMaker can master the skills needed to create reasonably good-looking text in their publications. Creating good-looking graphics, however, is often another story. By simply looking at magazines and newspapers, it's easy to see that the right graphic can make a publication look more interesting or help explain the material contained in the text. Many people lack the time or skills needed to create these graphics using the programs mentioned above. To add graphics quickly and easily to a publication, you can turn to *electronic clip art*—which are electronic drawings or illustrations that have already been created as a computer file that you can import into PageMaker.

Starting with version 7.0, PageMaker provides a limited number of electronic clip-art images that you can use in your publications, such as cartoons, pictures and illustrations. But most electronic clip art is available through other companies who specialize in digital art, such as Corel,

Image Club Graphics, and T/Maker. Individual graphics or even entire libraries containing hundreds of graphics can be purchased from these companies on CD-ROM, or downloaded from the Internet. Today you can also find thousands of free clip-art images available at various sites on the Internet. Examples of electronic clip art and digital photographs are shown in Figure 12-6.

FIGURE 12-6
Examples of digital art
(Used with express permission. Adobe® and Image Club GraphicsTM
are trademarks of Adobe Systems Incorporated.)

Scanned Images

A *scanner* is a photocopier-like device (see Figure 12-7) that is connected to a computer. You place a paper document, like a photograph, into the device and then start the machine. The scanner then creates a scanned image of the paper document and saves the image as a computer file. PageMaker can easily import graphic files created with most scanners. Two popular manufacturers of scanners are Hewlett-Packard and Microtek.

FIGURE 12-7
A flatbed scanner (left) and a scanned image (right)
(Scanned image © Copyright 2001 Susan Flick)

Two popular types of scanners are referred to as personal and flatbed. There are two kinds of personal scanners: hand-held and page scanners. A hand-held scanner looks like a large computer mouse or pen, while a page scanner is a small, desktop device that closely resembles a fax machine. Both devices connect to a computer with a small cable. These scanners are relatively inexpensive, with most costing a hundred dollars or less. Such scanners are ideal for low-volume scanning, or scanning where high quality is not important.

To use a hand scanner, you hold the device in your hand, place it over the paper document that you want to scan, and then move the scanner slowly over the document. To use a page scanner, you place the paper document into the scanner where it is automatically fed through the machine. The scanned image is then saved as a computer graphic file.

In comparison to personal scanners, a flatbed scanner looks like a small photocopier with a lift-up cover and a cable that's connected to your computer. To use this type of scanner, you open its cover, place the paper document inside, lower the cover and then press the start button on the machine. After a few seconds, the electronic image is scanned and can then be saved as a computer graphic file.

Digital Cameras

A digital camera, like the one shown in Figure 12-8, works much like a regular 35mm film camera. However, instead of recording a photo on film, it stores a digital photo as a computer file on a computer chip or disk inside the camera. This file can be transferred to a hard disk or network server and then placed into a PageMaker publication.

FIGURE 12-8
Digital camera (left) and digital photo (right)
(Photograph copyright Rick Braveheart)

Both 35mm and digital cameras contain a lens for focusing, an aperture that allows light to enter the camera, and a shutter for controlling how long the light remains inside the camera. Instead of film, digital cameras use an electronic sensor containing thousands or millions of light-sensitive squares called pixels. Each pixel records one small dot of a photograph. When a picture is taken, the presence or absence of light on each pixel is stored in a computer file. When they are viewed together, the pattern of these pixels produces a photograph.

After a digital photo is taken, the photo becomes a file, which can then be transferred to the computer. This is normally done by connecting the camera and computer together with a cable, or by removing a special disk from the camera and inserting it into the computer's floppy disk drive. Finally, a computer program transfers the files to the computer's hard disk or network server. Once the file is on the computer, it can be placed into a publication.

Today, there are three categories of digital cameras, with prices ranging from just a few hundred dollars to well over $10,000. The biggest reason for the difference in price is the number of pixels used for storing an image—the higher the number of pixels, the higher the cost of the camera, and the higher the quality of the photograph. These categories include:

- *Point-and-shoot camera*—These inexpensive, easy-to-carry cameras are fully automatic—you just point the camera at the subject and press the shutter to take a picture. Such cameras cost less because they have fewer pixels for recording a photograph. These cameras do produce good quality results when pictures are printed in a smaller size, such as 3 × 5 inches.

- *Megapixel camera* —These medium-priced cameras are somewhat larger than point-and-shoot cameras because they contain more circuitry that allows them to store over one million pixels per photograph. A megapixel camera can normally produce high quality printed photos as large as 8 × 10 inches.

- *Professional-level digital camera* —These large and more costly cameras can create photos with as many as six million pixels. Because of this, the photographs they produce rival those created with the most expensive film cameras. Such cameras can normally produce large high-quality photographs, such as poster-size photos.

Digital Stock Photography

Digital stock photographs, also referred to as Photo CDs, are electronic photographic images supplied on CD-ROM disks. Whereas clip-art images consist of drawings or illustrations, digital stock photography are high-quality scanned photographs or images created using a digital camera and then stored as a graphic file. Some of the leading digital stock photography suppliers include PhotoDisc, Comstock, and Corbis. Figure 12-9 shows some examples of digital stock photography.

FIGURE 12-9
Examples of digital stock photography
(Courtesy and © PhotoDisc, Inc.)

Graphic File Formats

The method in which a file is saved on a computer is called its *file format*. Every format has its own unique characteristics, advantages and disadvantages. When you create a graphic image using one of the programs discussed earlier, or after scanning the image and saving it on disk, you can normally select from several different file formats. Each file format has its own unique three-character file extension. This file extension helps other programs know how to read that particular file. Just as all PageMaker 7.0 publications have the file extension PMD, graphic files have extensions such as GIF, JPG or TIF. Some of the more popular file formats you can use with PageMaker include:

- *BMP (Bitmapped)*: Files in this format are normally created with paint or draw programs and have one of several file extensions such as BMP, PCX, or PIC. They contain dot-by-dot representations of the image and normally require a moderate amount of disk space. Graphics in this format can contain thousands of colors, but because of the method used to store these images, they can sometimes look jagged, especially when viewed or printed in large sizes.

- *GIF (Graphic Interchange Format)*: First made popular as a way of exchanging graphic files over the Internet, files in this format normally include those created with paint and draw or graphic composition programs. Graphics stored in this format are limited to 256 colors. Because of this, as well as the method used to store the file, these files use a relatively small amount of disk space, but can become distorted if somewhat enlarged.

- *TIF (Tagged Image Format)*: This format was created as a way to exchange files between different computers and different programs. Graphics in TIF file format can contain millions of colors and are stored on disk in a high-quality format. Because of these factors, such files usually require large amounts of disk space, but do not become distorted unless greatly enlarged.

- *EPS (Encapsulated PostScript)*: Files stored in this format produce the highest quality images available. EPS format images remain exceptionally sharp and crisp, even when greatly enlarged. Their disadvantage, however, is that you can only print EPS images in high quality on laser printers known as PostScript printers.

Importing or Placing a Graphic Image

To import a graphic file into PageMaker, first turn to the page in the publication on which you want the image to appear. Then, click the Place button on the toolbar or choose Place from the File menu. Either method reveals the File Place dialog box, which is the same dialog box used to place a text file into a publication. Next, select the graphic file that you want to import and choose Open.

Hot Tip

In addition to the toolbar button and menu method, you can also issue the Place command by using the Ctrl+D keyboard shortcut.

After a short pause, the mouse pointer changes into a graphic icon. As shown in Figure 12-10, a different icon will appear depending on the format of the file you are placing. Now, position the icon where you want the upper-left corner of the image to appear and then click. After a short pause, the graphic image appears on the screen. Later in this lesson, you will learn techniques to change the size of the image, move it to a different location on the page, and even hide unwanted parts of the image.

FIGURE 12-10
Icons indicate the type of graphic file

STEP-BY-STEP 12.4

1. Start a new publication and when the Document Setup dialog box appears, specify a **single-sided** publication and then click **OK**.

2. Click the **Pointer** tool. (Although the Pointer tool is automatically selected when you begin a new publication, it's a good idea to remember to click on this tool before placing a graphic file.)

3. Choose **Place** from the **File** menu and then select the graphic file named **Trees.tif** from the data files. Click **Open**. When the mouse pointer changes into a Graphic icon, place the icon slightly below the top margin guide and just to the right of the left margin guide and then click to insert the graphic. Keep this publication on-screen for use in the next Step-by-Step.

Resizing a Graphic Image

You can change the size of a graphic image anytime after placing it into a publication. To do so, you need to select the graphic image first by clicking on the Pointer tool and then clicking once anywhere on the graphic. As shown in Figure 12-11, when you select a graphic, PageMaker surrounds the image with eight sizing handles. Similar to the handles used to change the size of a selected text block, you can use the sizing handles around a selected graphic image to change its size. You can use the center handle found at the top or bottom to change its height or use the center handle on the left or right to change its width. You can also use any of the four corner handles to change both the height and width at the same time. *NOTE: Handles also appear around a graphic immediately after you place it into a publication.*

FIGURE 12-11
Handles appear around a selected graphic

Handle

To resize a selected graphic image, carefully place the mouse pointer in the center of any sizing handle and then hold down the mouse button. The mouse pointer will turn into a two-headed arrow indicating the directions in which you can change the size of the image. Now, drag the sizing handle to change the image's size. You could drag one of the top handles upward, for example, to increase the height. Click once anywhere outside the graphic image to deselect it and hide the handles.

If you're not careful when resizing a graphic image, it can become distorted. This could happen, for example, if you change the width but not the height. To help make resizing a graphic image easier, PageMaker offers a feature that lets you resize an image proportionally so that the height and width are resized by the same amount. To use this feature, select the image and then hold down the Shift key. Next, drag any corner handle of the selected image. As you do, PageMaker will automatically adjust both the height and width to keep the image proportional. When finished, make certain to release the mouse button first, and then release the Shift key. Otherwise, the image may become distorted.

S TEP-BY-STEP 12.5

1. If handles still appear around the graphic image of the palm trees that you placed into the publication in the previous exercise, go on to step 2. Otherwise, click once on the graphic to select it and display its handles.

2. Read this instruction completely before beginning. Press and hold down the **Shift** key. Then, carefully place the mouse pointer on the bottom right corner handle. Next, while holding down the mouse button, drag this handle downward and to the right on a 45-degree angle until it is positioned near the center of the page. Finally, release the mouse button and then release the **Shift** key. (*NOTE: If you release the Shift key first, the image may become distorted.*)

3. Click once in the publication window anywhere away from the image to deselect it. Keep this publication on-screen for use in the next Step-by-Step.

Moving a Graphic Image

You can easily move a graphic image anywhere on a page. To do so, first select the graphic image that you want to move. Then, place the mouse pointer in the center of the graphic and drag the image to its new location.

When you finish moving the graphic, remember to click once anywhere away from the graphic to deselect it, and then continue working with the publication.

STEP-BY-STEP 12.6

1. Using the **Pointer** tool, select the graphic image of the palm trees.

2. Place the mouse pointer in the center of the graphic. Then, drag the graphic until it is positioned roughly in the center of the page and release the mouse button.

3. Click once in the publication window anywhere away from the image to deselect it. Keep this publication on-screen for use in the next Step-by-Step.

Cropping a Graphic Image

Crop means to cut off or hide from view an unwanted portion of a graphic image. Cropping lets you hide or eliminate a portion of a graphic that is distracting, irrelevant, or of poor quality. To crop a graphic image, select the image first and then click the Cropping tool (see Figure 12-12). The mouse pointer then changes into the cropping icon.

FIGURE 12-12
The Cropping tool (left) and cropping icon (right)

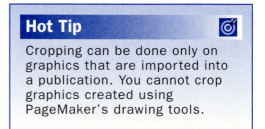

As shown in Figure 12-13, place the cropping icon directly over any sizing handle on any of the four sides of a graphic image that you want to remove or hide. Next, drag the cropping icon slowly inward toward the opposite side of the image. As you do, part of the image will begin to disappear. When you are finished removing the unwanted portion of the graphic, release the mouse button and then click anywhere away from the image to deselect it. If you later decide that you removed too much of the image, perform the same steps again, but this time drag the cropping icon outward to reveal the portion of the image you cropped earlier.

> **Hot Tip**
>
> Cropping can be done only on graphics that are imported into a publication. You cannot crop graphics created using PageMaker's drawing tools.

FIGURE 12-13
Cropping a graphic

FIGURE 12-13
Cropping a graphic

Place cropping icon on handle   **Drag icon in direction to crop**   **Click to remove handles**

STEP-BY-STEP 12.7

1. Click the **Cropping** tool to reveal the cropping icon. Then, click anywhere on the graphic to select it.

2. Place the cropping icon directly over the center handle on the left side of the graphic image. Then, slowly drag the cropping icon to the right, until you have removed roughly one-half of the image. Release the mouse button. Notice how part of the image is no longer visible.

3. Click once in the publication window anywhere away from the image to deselect it. Keep this publication on-screen for use in the next Step-by-Step.

Rotating a Graphic Image

With PageMaker, you can rotate a graphic image. *Rotate* means to turn a graphic image on its end. For example, you can rotate an image 45 degrees or even turn it completely upside down.

To rotate a graphic, use the Pointer tool to select the image first and then click on the Rotating tool (see Figure 12-14). The mouse pointer then changes to the rotating icon. Next, place the rotating icon on any corner sizing handle of the selected graphic (see Figure 12-15). Then, press and while holding down the mouse button move the rotating icon outward, slightly away from the graphic (a thin line will appear when you do this). Then, begin moving the icon in a clockwise or counter clockwise direction. As you do, the graphic image will begin to rotate as well. When finished, release the mouse button and then click anywhere outside the image to deselect it.

FIGURE 12-14
The Rotating tool (left)
and rotating icon (right)

FIGURE 12-15
Rotating a graphic

| Place rotating icon over a corner handle | Drag handle outward slightly | Rotate handle in clockwise/ counterclockwise direction |

STEP-BY-STEP 12.8

1. Click the **Rotating** tool to reveal the rotating icon. Then, click anywhere on the graphic to select it.

2. Read these instructions completely before beginning. Place the rotating icon over the upper right handle of the graphic image. Then, press and while holding down the mouse button, drag the rotating icon outward and to the right until a thin line appears. Now, while continuing to hold down the mouse button, move the rotating icon downward slightly. Notice how the image begins to rotate. Continue to rotate the image until it is turned on its side (rotated 90 degrees). Then release the mouse button.

3. Click once in the publication window anywhere away from the image to deselect it. Close this publication without saving it.

SUMMARY

In this lesson, you learned how to:

- Change the stroke and fill of a PageMaker-created graphic.

- Use the Shift key to draw perfect circles and squares.

- Identify different types of graphic file formats, and explain how each format tells PageMaker how to read the graphic.

- Import graphics images that were created in other programs into PageMaker.

- Move, crop, and rotate a graphic image using various tools found in the PageMaker toolbar.

VOCABULARY *Review*

Define the following terms:		
Crop	Graphic composition program	Rotate
Electronic clip art	Import	Scanner
File format	Layering	Stroke
Fill	Reverse type	

REVIEW *Questions*

TRUE/FALSE

Circle T if the statement is true or F if the statement is false.

T   F   1. In PageMaker, the Cropping tool removes an unwanted part of a graphic image.

T   F   2. The method a program uses to store its files on disk is called the file format.

T   F   3. Photo CDs is another name for digital stock photography.

T   F   4. Paint and draw programs let you use the computer to create freehand drawings.

T   F   5. An image in EPS file format will become greatly distorted if you enlarge the size of the image.

T   F   6. Choose Graphic from the File menu to import a graphic file into a PageMaker publication.

T   F   7. To keep both the height and width proportional when changing the size of a graphic image, hold down the Shift key.

T   F   8. Most graphic composition programs let you draw lines with great precision and also offer a wide range of drawing tools.

T   F   9. You cannot rotate a graphic image more than 45 degrees.

T   F   10. To select a graphic image, click once anywhere on the image with the Pointer tool.

FILL IN THE BLANK

Complete the following sentences by writing the correct word or words in the blanks provided.

1. The term _____ means to electronically read and place work created using a different program into a publication.

2. Electronic _____ _____ is the term used to describe electronic drawings or illustrations that have already been created that you can import into a publication.

3. A device that converts paper images, like photographs or drawings, into computer files is called a(n) _____.

4. The width of a line that surrounds a PageMaker-created graphic, such as a rectangle, is also referred to as the _____.

5. The term _____ means to cut off or remove an unwanted portion of a graphic image.

PROJECTS

SCANS PROJECT 12-1

In this project, you will create the publication shown in Figure 12-16 by keying text and importing a graphic image file. Take a moment to examine that figure now.

FIGURE 12-16
Minisolution to the announcement publication

WINTER TOUR
SALES

Sales figures for Caribbean Sun Travel Tours' winter season were the best ever reported during our entire history! Sales for all travel destinations were up 35 percent over last year. More importantly, sales of Caribbean tours rose 65 percent from last year. The chart below shows the total income by travel destination.

INCOME FROM WINTER TOURS

- St. Croix
- St. Thomas
- St. Martin
- Bermuda

1. Begin a new publication. When the Document Setup dialog box appears, specify a **single-sided** publication with top and bottom margin settings of **2** inches, and left and right margin settings of **1.5** inches.

2. Click the **Text** tool, and then click an insertion point slightly below the top margin guide and just to the right of the left margin guide. Then, turn on **center alignment**, turn on the **bold** type style, and select the **30-point** font size.

3. Key **WINTER TOUR** and press **Enter**. Then key **SALES** and press **Enter** twice.

4. Change to **left alignment**, turn off the **bold** type style, and select the **16-point** font size.

5. Key the following paragraph:

   Sales figures for Caribbean Sun Travel Tours' winter season were the best ever reported during our entire history! Sales for all travel destinations were up 35 percent over last year. More importantly, sales of Caribbean tours rose 65 percent from last year. The chart below shows the total income by travel destination.

6. Click the **Pointer** tool and then choose **Place** from the **File** menu. Then, from the data files, select the graphic file named **Income.tif** and click **Open**. Finally, when the graphic icon appears, place the icon slightly below the last line of text and just to the right of the left margin guide and then click.

7. Resize the graphic proportionally so that the left and right edges of the image fall near the left and right margin guides.

8. Drag the image up or down as needed so that the top of the graphic begins roughly one inch below the last line of text.

9. Print the publication and then save the publication under the name **Announcement**. Close the publication.

PROJECT 12-2

In this project, you will create the flyer shown in Figure 12-17. You will key several words into the publication. Then, you will import a graphic image of an arrow into the publication four separate times, and rotate three of those graphic images. Take a moment to review that figure now.

FIGURE 12-17
Minisolution to the big sale today publication

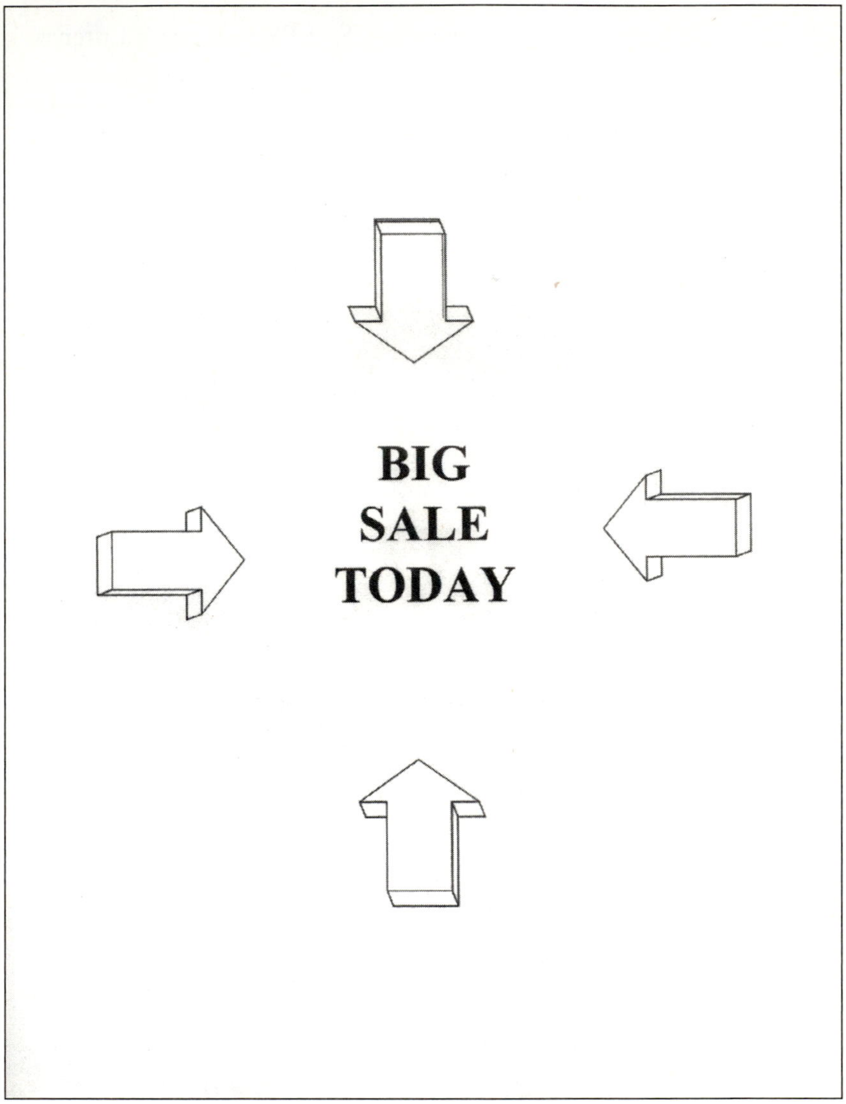

1. Begin a new publication. When the Document Setup dialog box appears, specify a **single-sided** publication with the top and bottom margin settings of **2** inches and left and right margin settings of **1** inch.

2. Click the **Text** tool, and then click an insertion point slightly below the top margin guide and just to the right of the left margin guide. Then, turn on **center alignment**, turn on the **bold** type style, and select the **36-point** font size. Key the following three lines of text and press **Enter** at the end of each line:

    BIG
    SALE
    TODAY

3. Using the **Pointer** tool, drag the text block containing the three lines of text that you just keyed straight downward on the page so that it is centered between the top and bottom margin guides.

4. Import the graphic file named **Arrow.tif** from the data files. Next, rotate the graphic 90 degrees (so that it points downward), and then drag the graphic so that it is centered along the top margin guide.

5. Once again, import the graphic file named **Arrow.tif**. Next, rotate the graphic 180 degrees (so that it points to the left), and then position the graphic so that it is centered along the right margin guide.

6. Import the graphic file **Arrow.tif** for a third time. Next, rotate the graphic 270 degrees (so that it points upward), and then position the graphic so that it is centered along the bottom margin guide.

7. Import the graphic file **Arrow.tif** for the final time. Then, position the graphic so that it is centered along the left margin guide.

8. Print the publication and then save the publication under the name **Big Sale Today**. Close the publication.

SCANS **PROJECT 12-3**

In this project you will create the flyer shown in Figure 12-18. Take a moment to review that figure now before continuing.

FIGURE 12-18
Minisolution to the winter escape publication

1. Begin a new publication. When the Document Setup dialog box appears, specify a **single-sided** publication with top and bottom margin settings of **1** inch and left and right margin settings of **1.75** inches.

2. Click the **Text** tool, and then click an insertion point slightly below the top margin guide and just to the right of the left margin guide. Then, turn on **center alignment**, turn on the **bold** type style, and select the **48-point** font size. Key the following two lines of text and press **Enter** at the end of each line:

CARIBBEAN

TOURS

3. Click the **Pointer** tool and then import the graphic file named **Island.tif** from the data files.

4. Resize the graphic proportionally so that the left and right edges of the image fall near the left and right margin guides.

5. Drag the graphic up or down as needed so that the top of the image begins roughly 0.5 to 0.75 inches from the last line of text.

6. Using the **Text** tool, click an insertion point roughly 0.5 to 0.75 inches below the bottom of the graphic image and just to the right of the left margin guide. Then, change to **center alignment** and select the **12-point** font size (if not already selected). Next, key the following lines of text, pressing **Enter** once after keying each line. Press **Enter** twice after keying the last line.

Come and experience how a real vacation was meant to be.
We have over one hundred resorts ready to serve you.
Let someone else make the beds and do dishes.
Rent a sports car, bike, sailboat, or surfboard.
You can tan by day and dance by night.
Best of all, it is only hours away.
For more information call us
at (800) 555-1212.

7. Press **Enter** twice, then turn on the **bold** type style and select the **24-point** font size. Next, key the following two lines of text, pressing **Enter** after keying each line:

Caribbean Sun
Travel Tours

8. Using the **Pointer** tool, drag the text block that you just created straight down so that the last line of text (Travel Tours) falls on the bottom margin guide.

9. Move the graphic image up or down as needed so that it is centered vertically in the space between the top and bottom text blocks.

10. Use the **Rectangle** tool to draw a rectangle having a **2-point line** (stroke) completely around the text and graphic (like the one shown in Figure 12-18). Keep the lines of this rectangle roughly one-half inch away from the text and the graphic.

11. Print the publication and then save the publication under the name **Winter Escape.** Close the publication.

SCANS PROJECT 12-4

In this exercise you will create the publication shown in Figure 12-19. Take a moment to review that figure now before continuing.

FIGURE 12-19
Minisolution to Project 12-4

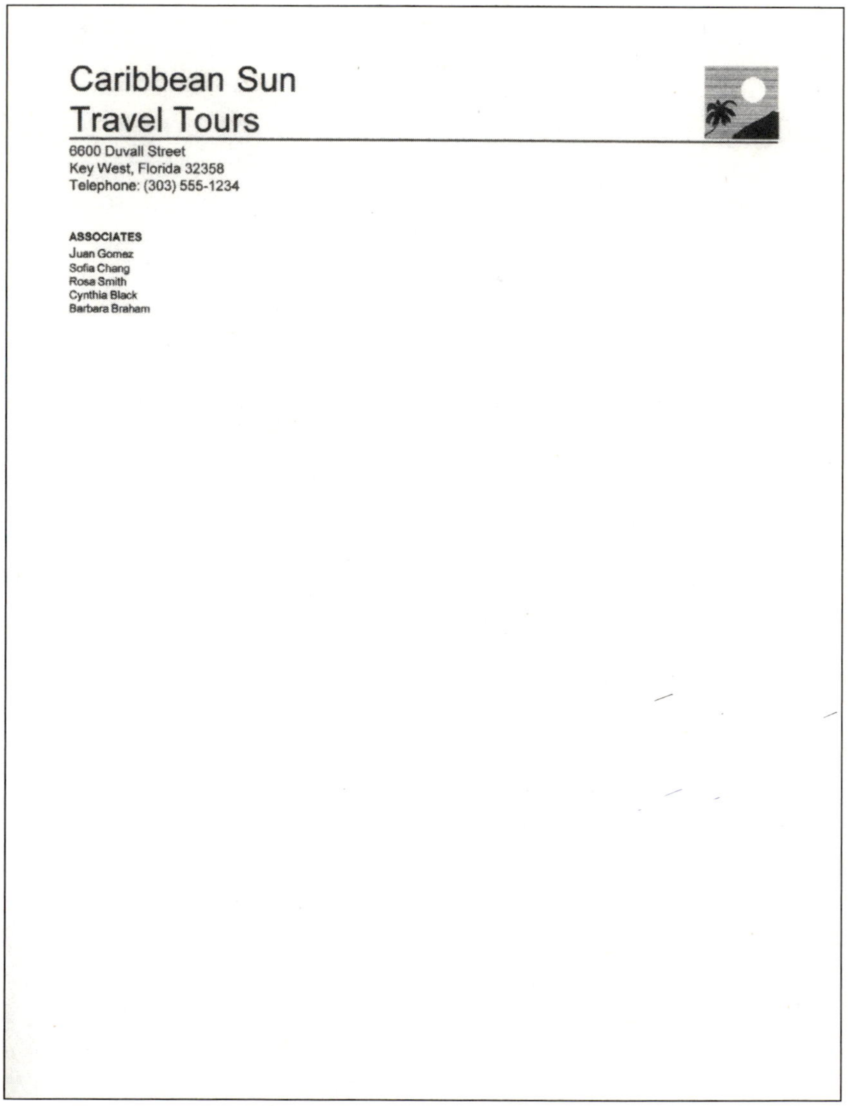
Caribbean Sun
Travel Tours
6600 Duvall Street
Key West, Florida 32358
Telephone: (303) 555-1234

ASSOCIATES
Juan Gomez
Sofia Chang
Rosa Smith
Cynthia Black
Barbara Braham

1. Open the publication named **Letterhead** that you created in Lesson 8.

2. Import the graphic named **Carsun.tif** from the data files and reduce the size of this graphic proportionally to roughly a 0.75 inch square. Use the on-screen rulers as a guide. Then, position the graphic along the top and right margin guides.

3. Print the publication. Then, using the **Save as** command, save this publication under the new name **Letterhead 2**. Finally, close the publication.

TEAMWORK PROJECT

Discuss with your classmates any graphic programs you currently use or that you have used, and how easy or difficult you feel each program is compared to others you have worked with. Also, if you have used a scanner or digital camera, discuss your experience with these as well.

CRITICAL *Thinking*

SCANS

Visit the Web sites of one or two electronic clip-art and digital stock photography firms to gain an understanding of the type of graphics they offer. Several of the firms mentioned in this lesson include Corel *(http://www.corel.com,)* Eyewire *(http://www.eyewire.com)*, Corbis *(http://www.corbis.com)* and PhotoDisc *(http://www.photodisc.com)*. Then, using a search engine, locate and visit several Web sites that offer free clip art to gain an understanding of the type of graphics they offer.

ADVANCED GRAPHIC FEATURES

OBJECTIVES

Upon completion of this lesson, you should be able to:

■ Explain the different methods for wrapping text around a graphic image.

■ Create a customized graphic boundary.

■ Define the term inline graphic and explain how to create an inline graphic.

■ Reflect (flip) and skew (slant) a graphic image.

■ Define and use masking with a graphic image.

■ Change screen resolution and explain the advantages/disadvantages of doing so.

Estimated Time: 4.5 hours

VOCABULARY

Anchored

Graphic boundary

Inline

Masking

Reflecting

Screen resolution

Skewing

Standoff

Text wrap

Introduction

This lesson introduces you to advanced graphic techniques that let you create more sophisticated graphic and text combinations. For example, you will learn how to flow text around a graphic image and how to include a graphic within a line of text. You'll also learn how to flip and slant a graphic image and use masking to create images with unusual designs. In addition, you'll learn how to control the display quality of your images by varying the screen resolution.

Understanding Text Wrap

PageMaker gives you many options for controlling how text and graphic images work together when they both appear on the same page. The term *text wrap* means positioning text around a graphic.

When you key or place text onto a page that already contains a graphic, that text, by default, will fall on top of the graphic (see the first column in Figure 13-1). By selecting different text wrap options, however, you can keep text away from a graphic image. For example, you could have text appear above and below the graphic or flow text completely around the graphic in a variety of shapes. It's also easy to change from one text wrap method to another.

FIGURE 13-1
Different types of text wrap

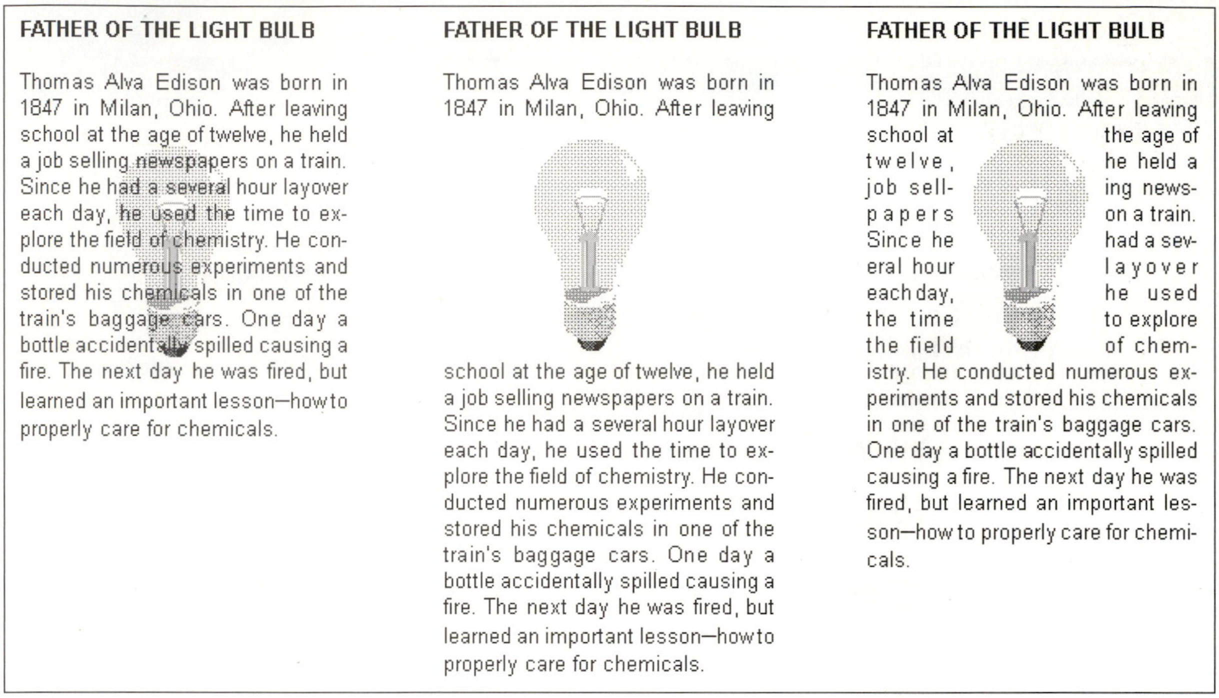

FATHER OF THE LIGHT BULB

Thomas Alva Edison was born in 1847 in Milan, Ohio. After leaving school at the age of twelve, he held a job selling newspapers on a train. Since he had a several hour layover each day, he used the time to explore the field of chemistry. He conducted numerous experiments and stored his chemicals in one of the train's baggage cars. One day a bottle accidentally spilled causing a fire. The next day he was fired, but learned an important lesson—how to properly care for chemicals.

FATHER OF THE LIGHT BULB

Thomas Alva Edison was born in 1847 in Milan, Ohio. After leaving

school at the age of twelve, he held a job selling newspapers on a train. Since he had a several hour layover each day, he used the time to explore the field of chemistry. He conducted numerous experiments and stored his chemicals in one of the train's baggage cars. One day a bottle accidentally spilled causing a fire. The next day he was fired, but learned an important lesson—how to properly care for chemicals.

FATHER OF THE LIGHT BULB

Thomas Alva Edison was born in 1847 in Milan, Ohio. After leaving school at　　　the age of twelve,　　he held a job sell-　　ing news-papers　　on a train. Since he　　had a several hour　　layover each day,　　he used the time　　to explore the field　　of chemistry. He conducted numerous experiments and stored his chemicals in one of the train's baggage cars. One day a bottle accidentally spilled causing a fire. The next day he was fired, but learned an important lesson—how to properly care for chemicals.

You can use text wrap with imported graphic files and with drawings you've created using PageMaker's drawing tools. The text wrap feature gives you an easy way to control how text flows around nearly any type of graphic, and, as you'll see later, provides ways to create interesting designs with your text.

Controlling Text Wrap

To control text wrap, use the Pointer tool to select the graphic image or PageMaker-created drawing that you want to control. Then choose Text Wrap from the Element menu to display the Text Wrap dialog box shown in Figure 13-2. The dialog box options are described in the following subsections.

FIGURE 13-2
Text Wrap dialog box

Wrap Options

As shown in Figure 13-3, the Wrap option section of the dialog box contains three icons that identify the different text wrap options. These options let you control whether text flows over a graphic, or the general shape in which text flows around that graphic.

FIGURE 13-3
Text wrap options

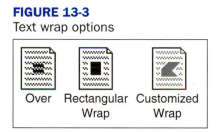

The text wrap options include:

- *Over*: This option is the standard default text wrap setting. With this option, text flows over any graphic that it encounters on the page. Because text that appears on top of anything other than a very lightly shaded graphic can be extremely difficult to read, this option is rarely used.

- *Rectangular Wrap*: All graphics, whether placed into a publication or created using PageMaker's drawing tools, are surrounded by an invisible, rectangular-shaped **graphic boundary** that controls how close text comes to the graphic. When a graphic is selected, this boundary is identified through a series of handles which can also be adjusted to vary the distance between the text and the graphic. Once you select the Rectangular Wrap option, you can then choose one of three text flow options (described below) to control how the text flows.

■   *Customized Wrap:* Although every graphic originally has a rectangular shape, you can create a customized graphic boundary of almost any other shape, such as a circle or triangle.
Then, text can wrap around the graphic in this customized shape. Although you can't select
the Customized Wrap icon by clicking it, PageMaker will automatically select this wrap
option for you when you create a customized graphic boundary. This will be described later
in this lesson.

Text Flow Options

By choosing the Rectangular wrap option, you can then select one of three Text flow icons
(see Figure 13-4) that let you control whether text will flow up to or around that graphic
boundary.

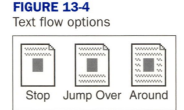

FIGURE 13-4
Text flow options

The text flow icons include:

■   *Stop:* By selecting this icon, text will flow until it reaches the top of the graphic and then
stop. If you have previously selected the Autoflow option (by choosing Autoflow from the
Layout menu), text will then automatically flow into the next page or column. If Autoflow
is not turned on, a continuation symbol will appear at the bottom of the text block which
you can click to continue placing the remaining text.

■   *Jump Over:* By selecting this icon, text will automatically flow, or jump, over the graphic.
Text, however, will not appear on either side of the graphic.

■   *Around:* By selecting this icon, text will flow completely around the graphic on all four sides.

Standoff Distance

If you specify that you want text to flow around a graphic, you can then indicate how much
distance you want to appear between the text and the graphic. This distance is referred to as the
standoff distance, or simply the ***standoff.*** By default, this standoff is 0.167 inches on the left,
right, top, and bottom of the graphic. To move the text closer to or farther away from the
graphic, you can key a new standoff in the Left, Right, Top, and/or Bottom text boxes of the Text
Wrap dialog box. For example, if you wanted to keep the text one-quarter inch away from each
side of the graphic, you would key 0.25 in each of these four text boxes.

You can also adjust the standoff manually by dragging one or more graphic boundary handles. These handles appear once you choose the Rectangular wrap option or begin customizing
the graphic boundary. Dragging a graphic boundary handle farther away from the graphic, for
example, automatically increases the standoff.

STEP-BY-STEP 13.1

1. Begin a new publication. When the Document Setup dialog box appears, specify a **single-sided** publication.

2. Choose **Place** from the **File** menu. Select the file named **Guidebk1.rtf** from the data files. When the Text Placement icon appears, position the icon slightly below the top margin guide and just to the right of the left margin guide, and then click.

3. Click the **Pointer** tool and then choose **Place** from the **File** menu. Next, select the graphic file named **Services.tif** from the data files. Finally, when the graphic icon appears, place the icon near the center of the on-screen page and then click. Notice how the text does not wrap around the graphic.

4. If the graphic image that you placed into the publication in step 3 is not selected, select the graphic image. Then, choose **Text Wrap** from the **Element** menu. In the Wrap option section of the dialog box, click the **Rectangular Wrap** icon. (Refer to Figure 13-3 if you forget what this icon looks like.) Next, in the Text flow section of the dialog box, click the **Around** icon. (Refer to Figure 13-4 if you forget what this icon looks like.) Finally, click **OK**. Notice how the text now wraps completely around the graphic. Keep this publication on-screen for use in the next Step-by-Step.

STEP-BY-STEP 13.2

1. If the graphic in the center of the page is not selected, select it.

2. Choose **Text Wrap** from the **Element** menu. Now, change the standoff on the left, right, top and bottom to 0.5 inches by keying **0.5** in the Left, Right, Top, and Bottom text boxes. Then click **OK**. Observe how the graphic boundary and text move farther away from the graphic.

3. Following instructions similar to step 2, change the standoff distance to **0.2** inches on all four sides of the graphic and observe how the text moves closer to the graphic. Keep this publication on-screen for use in the next Step-by-Step.

Customizing a Graphic Boundary

As mentioned earlier, PageMaker automatically creates an invisible rectangular-shaped boundary around a graphic, by default. Once you instruct PageMaker to wrap text around a graphic, the graphic boundary is visible whenever you select the graphic. As shown in Figure 13-5, when you select such a graphic, the standard eight square-shaped sizing handles appear around the graphic as usual. But now PageMaker has added graphic boundary handles, which are four diamond-shaped handles connected by a dotted line. (The dotted line represents the graphic boundary). You can use several techniques to change the shape of this boundary.

FIGURE 13-5
The graphic boundary is visible
when text wrap is activated

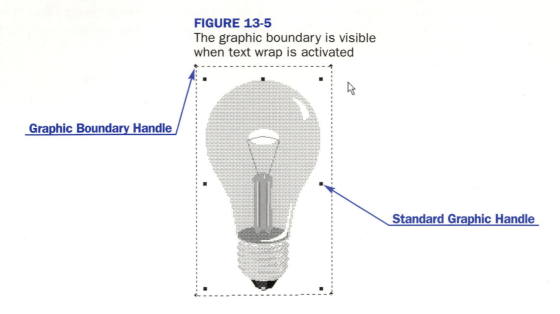

Graphic Boundary Handle

Standard Graphic Handle

Dragging the Graphic Boundary

An easy way to change the shape of the graphic boundary is to drag one of the graphic boundary handles. As shown in Figure 13-6, place the mouse pointer over the graphic boundary handle that you want to move, hold down the mouse button, and then drag that handle to a new position. As you do, the graphic boundary (shown by the dotted line) will move as well. When you release the mouse button, PageMaker will shift the text to fit around the new boundary. Dragging a graphic boundary handle closer to the graphic, for example, would move any text closer to the graphic.

FIGURE 13-6
Drag a graphic boundary diamond-shaped
handle to adjust the graphic boundary

Adding a Graphic Boundary Handle

With only the four default graphic boundary handles, it would be difficult to create graphic boundaries with unusual shapes, such as a circle or triangle. Because of this, PageMaker lets you add an unlimited number of graphic boundary handles in order to create almost any shape you need.

To add a new graphic boundary handle, place the mouse pointer over the graphic boundary where you want the new handle to appear and double-click. Then, if you move the mouse pointer away slightly, you'll see that PageMaker has added a new handle to the boundary that you can now drag into position as needed.

You can create unusually shaped boundaries, such as a circle, by adding and dragging additional handles until the desired shape is achieved. For example, a total of 20 handles were used to create the graphic boundary around the light bulb in Figure 13-7.

FIGURE 13-7
A graphic boundary containing 20 handles

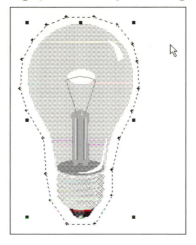

Although creating these additional handles might seem time-consuming, usually it's not. With only a little practice, you can add dozens of them in less than a minute. Also, because the graphic boundary (and its handles) forms a permanent part of the graphic, PageMaker will maintain the shape of the boundary even if you drag the graphic elsewhere in the publication.

Removing a Graphic Boundary Handle

You can also remove a graphic boundary handle that you no longer need, or that you added by mistake. To do so, drag the handle that you want to remove onto the nearest handle on the graphic boundary. When you release the mouse button, PageMaker will remove one of the handles.

Hot Tip

Each time you change the shape of a graphic boundary by adding, deleting or moving a graphic boundary handle, PageMaker reflows text around that graphic. While this process is helpful, it's time-consuming and can become distracting. To temporarily stop the program from reflowing text, hold down the Spacebar after selecting the graphic while you add, delete or move handles. When finished, release the Spacebar to reflow the text.

STEP-BY-STEP 13.3

1. If the graphic in the center of the page is not selected, select the graphic.

2. Enlarge the area around the graphic to **Actual Size**.

3. Place the mouse pointer in the center of the top graphic boundary (see Figure 13-8 for the correct position). Then, carefully, and without moving the mouse pointer, double-click. Now, move the mouse pointer away from the graphic boundary and view the new graphic handle you created.

4. Place the mouse pointer on the diamond-shaped graphic boundary handle located at the upper right corner of the graphic boundary. Then, carefully drag the handle straight downward until it is positioned over the graphic boundary handle located at the lower right corner of the graphic boundary. After you release the mouse button, observe how PageMaker removed the handle that you dragged, and also how the text adjusts to the new graphic boundary.

5. Place the mouse pointer on the graphic boundary handle located at the upper left corner of the graphic boundary. Then, carefully drag the handle straight downward until it is positioned over the graphic boundary handle located at the lower-left corner of the graphic boundary. After you release the mouse button, observe how the text now wraps around the new triangular-shaped graphic boundary. Keep this publication on-screen for use in the next Step-by-Step.

FIGURE 13-8
The mouse pointer positioned for adding a graphic boundary handle

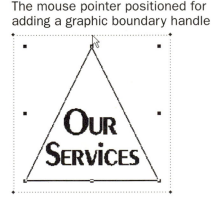

Creating Inline Graphics

When you place (import) a graphic file into a publication, that graphic can be placed as either an anchored or inline graphic. To anchor the graphic on the page, place the graphic file as you normally do by using the Pointer tool. Then, the only way the *anchored*, or locked, graphic will move is if you drag it elsewhere on the page. An anchored graphic is ideal for those times when you never or rarely want the graphic to move.

Instead of anchoring a graphic , you can place the graphic within a line of text by using the Text tool. This type of graphic is called an *inline* graphic. Unlike an anchored graphic, an inline graphic will automatically move along with the text in which it was placed. The portion of the publication shown in Figure 13-9, for example, contains two inline graphics. The first graphic (a picture of a car) was placed in the text just before the word PARKING. The other graphic (a picture of a swimmer) was placed in the text before the word POOL. If you positioned the insertion point in the blank line between the Parking and Pool entries and then pressed the Enter key, not only would the word POOL and the paragraph below it move downward, but the graphic image of the swimmer would move downward as well.

FIGURE 13-9
Examples of two inline graphics

PARKING

We provide free parking for registered guests. Please make certain to attach your parking pass to the mirror on your windshield. Valet parking is also available at the Main Entrance. **Dial 420**

POOL

You will find the outdoor pool located next to the Bay Café on the lobby level. Pool hours are from 7 AM until 9 PM. Towels are available from the attendant. **Dial 125**

As stated above, to create an inline graphic, you use the Text tool instead of the Pointer tool. While using the Text tool, place the insertion point where you want the graphic image to appear in the text. Then, choose Place from the File menu and select the graphic file as you normally would. The graphic will then appear within the text on the page.

> **Note** ☑
>
> Inline graphics also let you create unusual bulleted entries, because you can use small graphic images as the bullet character. And, since an inline graphic becomes part of the text, the bullet character will move along with the text as the text is edited.

STEP-BY-STEP 13.4

1. Use the **Hand** tool or scroll bar to move the last two entries (PARKING and POOL) from the on-screen page into view.

2. Click the **Text** tool. Then, place the insertion point just to the right of the G in the word PARKING.

3. Choose **Place** from the **File** menu. Then, select the graphic named **Auto.tif** from the data files that are provided with this book, and click **Open**. Observe how the graphic of the automobile appears just after the word PARKING in the text.

4. Press the arrow keys on the keyboard to position the insertion point in the blank line, just above the entry titled MESSAGES. Then, press the **Enter** key to insert a blank line. Observe how the inline graphic moved downward along with the entry labeled PARKING.

5. Press **Backspace** to remove the blank line that you inserted in step 4. Keep this publication on-screen for use in the next Step-by-Step.

Additional Ways to Adjust a Graphic

In the previous lesson, you learned how to resize and rotate a graphic. PageMaker also provides ways to flip, twist, and stretch a graphic to create just the effect you need.

Reflecting a Graphic

Reflecting is a technique used to flip a graphic either horizontally or vertically. The result is similar to viewing an object in a mirror. Figure 13-10 shows a graphic before and after reflecting was used. It's important to note that reflecting is not the same as rotating a graphic. Rotating simply moves a graphic in a circular direction, whereas reflecting completely flips the graphic left to right or top to bottom.

FIGURE 13-10
A graphic before (left) and after (right) reflecting

Reflecting is especially useful when working with graphics of people or animals. Generally, a page looks best when pictures of people or animals face into the page, not away from it. For example, if you placed the original graphic in Figure 13-10 onto the left side of a page, the graphic would face away from the text. By using reflecting, however, you could flip the picture toward the text.

To reflect a graphic image, select the graphic using the Pointer tool. Next, click the Horizontal or Vertical Reflecting button on the Control palette (shown in Figure 13-11). Use the Horizontal Reflecting button to flip a graphic image from left to right. Use the Vertical Reflecting button to flip a graphic image from top to bottom.

FIGURE 13-11
Reflecting buttons and skewing option

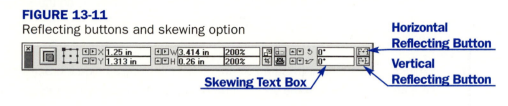

Horizontal
Reflecting Button

Vertical
Reflecting Button

Skewing Text Box

STEP-BY-STEP 13.5

1. Click the **Pointer** tool. Then, select the inline graphic of the automobile by clicking anywhere on that graphic.

2. If the Control palette is not on-screen, display it. Then, click the **Horizontal Reflecting** button in the Control palette. Observe how the graphic now faces in the opposite direction. Keep this publication on-screen for use in the next Step-by-Step.

Skewing a Graphic

Skewing is a technique used to slant a graphic by as much as 85 degrees to the left or to the right. Figure 13-12 shows a graphic before and after skewing. Skewing is normally used to create special effects with graphic images.

To skew a graphic image, select the graphic image while using the Pointer tool. Then, key the number of degrees that you want the image skewed (between –85 and 85) in the Skew text box identified in Figure 13-11, and finally press Enter. Keying a positive number into the text box, such as 25, slants the graphic to the right, whereas keying a negative number, such as –45, slants the graphic to the left.

FIGURE 13-12
A graphic before (left) and after (right) skewing (–20 degrees)

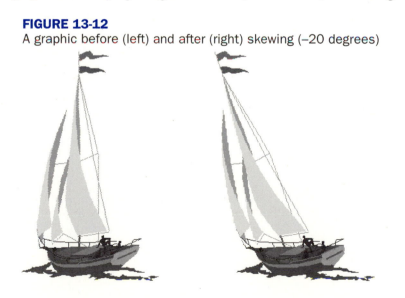

S TEP-BY-STEP 13.6

1. If the inline graphic of the automobile is not selected, select it.

2. On the Control panel, double-click on the current entry (0) found inside the **Skewing** text box (refer to Figure 13-11, if needed). Then, key **20** and press **Enter**. Observe how the graphic now slants slightly to the right.

3. Using instructions similar to Step 2 above, change the entry inside the **Skewing** text box to **–15** and press **Enter**. Observe how the graphic now slants slightly to the left. Keep this publication on-screen for use in the next Step-by-Step.

Removing Settings from a Graphic

Y ou've learned to work with many graphic settings in this and in previous lessons. What you haven't learned yet is that you can use any combination of graphic settings with any graphic image. For example, on the same graphic, you can wrap text around it, customize its graphic boundary, and also apply reflection and even skewing to it. If you want to restore the graphic to its original state, you do not have to undo each of the graphic settings you applied. Instead, while using the Pointer tool, select the graphic image and then choose Remove Transformation from the Element menu.

S TEP-BY-STEP 13.7

1. If the inline graphic of the automobile is not selected, select it.

2. Choose **Remove Transformation** from the **Element** menu to remove reflecting and skewing from this graphic. Observe how the graphic returns to its original form. Keep this publication on-screen for use in the next Step-by-Step.

Masking a Graphic

A s you learned in Lesson 12, cropping lets you remove part of a graphic, but only in a horizontal or vertical direction. *Masking*, on the other hand, lets you crop a graphic into any shape or design that you can create using PageMaker's drawing tools. Figure 13-13, for example, shows an original graphic (left) and then the same graphic after masking with a polygon (center) and with an oval (right).

FIGURE 13-13
A graphic before and after masking
(Image Copyright © 2002 Paige Tinker)

Masking a graphic is performed in three steps. First, place the graphic image into the publication. Second, use one of PageMaker's drawing tools, like the Ellipse or Rectangle tool, to draw a masking shape—a shape within which you want the final graphic image to appear. Finally, use the Pointer tool to select both the graphic image and the masking shape, and then choose Mask from the Element menu. Figure 13-14 shows the same graphic before (left) and after (right) masking with an oval shape.

FIGURE 13-14
A graphic immediately before (left) and after (right) masking
(Image Copyright © Tammy Davis)

After masking, you may want to adjust or reposition the masking shape. To do so, simply select the masking shape with the Pointer tool and then drag the shape as needed. If you want to remove a mask from a graphic, select the masking shape and then choose Unmask from the Element menu. The graphic will then return to its original state.

STEP-BY-STEP 13.8

1. Insert one new page into the on-screen publication. Then, choose **Place** from the **File** menu and select the graphic file named **Kids.tif** from the data files. When the graphic icon appears, place the icon near the center of the page and click.

2. Enlarge the area around the graphic to **Actual Size**.

3. Click the **Rectangle** tool in the toolbox and then draw a small rectangle over the portion of the graphic that includes only the two children.

4. Click the **Pointer** tool and then hold down the **Shift** key. Now, carefully click the rectangle and then click the graphic image. Finally, release the **Shift** key. (Handles will appear around both objects when they are selected.)

5. Choose **Mask** from the **Element** menu.

6. Click anywhere in the publication away from the selected graphic image to deselect the masked graphic. Observe how only the masked portion of the graphic remains. Keep this publication on-screen for use in the next Step-by-Step.

Hot Tip ◎

A mask is created by positioning one graphic over another. So, if you want to move the graphic elsewhere on the page, you need to move both graphics together to maintain the mask. An easy way to do this is to join the two graphics together into one element. While using the Pointer tool, hold down the shift key and click both graphics, one after the other. Then, choose Group from the Element menu. Now, when you drag the image, both graphics will move together.

Changing Screen Resolution

Two problems can arise when you work with graphics: (1) the images can sometimes be difficult to see on-screen, and (2) PageMaker may seem to work more slowly.

To solve these problems, PageMaker lets you control the screen resolution of all on-screen graphic images. *Screen resolution* controls the quality of the on-screen graphics. By default, graphic images appear on-screen with a medium resolution setting. By varying this setting, you can increase the resolution so that any graphic image appears in the highest quality possible, or you can hide the graphic images temporarily so they do not appear on-screen.

To change the screen resolution, choose Preferences from the File menu and then choose General from the submenu that appears. This reveals the Preferences dialog box shown in Figure 13-15.

FIGURE 13-15
The Preferences dialog box

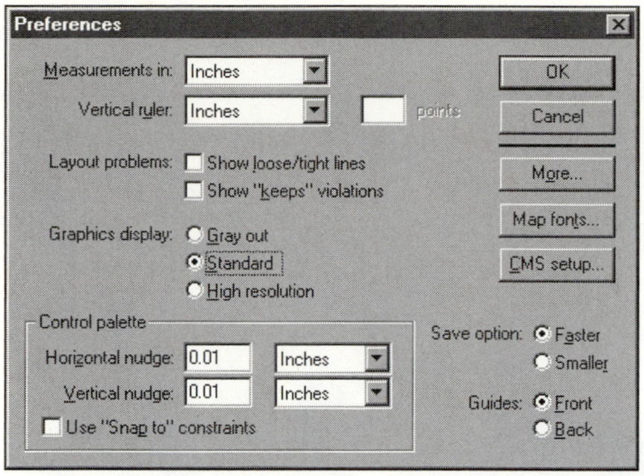

The Graphics display section of the dialog box offers three options: *Gray out, Standard* (the default), and *High* resolution. If you choose *Gray out*, any graphic image in your publication appears as a lightly shaded gray box. Creating publications that contain graphic images when using a slower computer can often mean waiting long periods of time for the computer to display those graphics. On such computers, choosing *Gray out* lets the computer work faster because the graphic images do not appear. The Standard setting allows graphic images to appear with reasonably good quality and speed on the screen. The High resolution setting allows images to appear in the highest quality your monitor can produce, but they will take the longest time to display on the screen. When finished selecting the screen resolution, choose OK to close the dialog box. Figure 13-16 shows that the difference in the on-screen quality of a graphic image is often dramatically different between the Standard and High resolution settings, but it has no effect on print quality.

FIGURE 13-16
A graphic image shown in standard (top) and high (bottom) resolution

Which resolution setting to choose depends on the situation. The following are some suggestions to use: Use *Gray out* if you are working on a publication that contains graphic images and your computer appears to work more slowly than usual. Use the High resolution setting when you need to see all the details within a graphic, such as when cropping or masking. Use the Standard resolution setting in all other instances.

STEP-BY-STEP 13.9

1. Display the Preferences dialog box by choosing **Preferences** from the **File** menu and then choose **General** from the submenu that appears. Next, select **Gray out** from the Graphics display options and then click **OK**. Observe how the graphic has been replaced with a lightly shaded rectangle.

2. Following instructions similar to those in step 1, display the Preferences dialog box again. Next, select the **Standard** Graphics display option and then click **OK**. Observe the quality of the graphic in Standard resolution.

3. Following instructions similar to those in step 1, display the Preferences dialog box again. Next, select the **High resolution** Graphics display option and then choose **OK**. Observe the quality of the graphic in High resolution.

4. Save this publication under the name **New Services**. Then, close the publication.

SUMMARY

In this lesson, you learned how to:

- Control whether or not text flows around a graphic, and if so, the way in which it appears around that graphic.

- Create both anchored graphics that remain locked in position on a page, as well as inline graphics that move with text.

- Reflect or flip a graphic, as well as skew or slant a graphic.

- Mask a graphic in order to hide unwanted or distracting portions of that graphic.

- Control the screen resolution or quality with which graphics appear on your monitor.

VOCABULARY *Review*

Define the following terms:

Anchored	Masking	Skewing
Graphic boundary	Reflecting	Standoff
Inline	Screen resolution	Text wrap

REVIEW *Questions*

TRUE/FALSE

Circle T if the statement is true or F if the statement is false.

T   F   **1.** When you first import a graphic file and place it onto a page that already contains text, the text automatically wraps around the graphic.

T   F   **2.** If you select the Jump Over text wrap option, text will automatically flow over the graphic and then continue beneath the graphic. Text will not appear on either side of the graphic.

T   F   **3.** Normally, the standoff distance for a graphic image is 0.5 inch.

T   F   **4.** Masking a graphic lets you crop a graphic image into any shape or design that you can create using PageMaker's drawing tools.

T   F   **5.** When customizing a graphic boundary, you can add a maximum of ten graphic boundary handles to the boundary.

T   F   **6.** To remove a graphic boundary handle, click on the handle and then press the Delete key.

T   F   **7.** You must use the Text tool to import an inline graphic into a publication.

T   F   **8.** Reflecting is a technique used to flip a graphic either horizontally or vertically.

T   F   **9.** Generally, a page containing a picture of a person or an animal looks better if the person or animal is facing into the page.

T   F   **10.** You can use text wrap with imported graphic files and with graphics created using PageMaker's drawing tools, such as the Rectangle tool.

FILL IN THE BLANK

Complete the following sentences by writing the correct word or words in the blanks provided.

1. When you place a graphic image into a publication while using the Text tool, that image is referred to as a(n) _____ graphic.

2. The term _____ _____ means controlling how text falls on a page when the area in which that text would normally appear is occupied by a graphic.

3. The distance between text and a graphic image is called the _____.

4. The technique used to slant a graphic image to the left or right is called _____.

5. The name of the resolution setting in which a gray box appears on-screen in place of a graphic image is _____.

PROJECTS

SCANS PROJECT 13-1

1. Begin a new publication. When the Document Setup dialog box appears, specify a **single-sided** publication. Also, change the top and bottom margin settings to **1** inch and change the left and right margin settings to **1.5** inches.

2. Click the **Text** tool, and then click an insertion point slightly below the top margin guide and just to the right of the left margin guide. Then, enlarge the area around the insertion point to **Actual Size**.

3. Turn on **center alignment,** select the **36-point** font size, and select a sans serif font such as Arial, Helvetica or Univers. Next, key **Fly and Drive** and press **Enter.** Then, key **Vacation Packages.**

4. Click the **Pointer** tool. Then, from the data files, place the graphic file named **Palmtree.tif** into a blank area of the on-screen page.

5. **Flip** the graphic horizontally and then skew the graphic **10 degrees** to the left.

6. Drag the graphic image so that the top of the palm tree begins roughly one-half inch below the last line of text and is centered beneath the word Vacation.

7. Following instructions similar to those given in steps 4–6, place **Palmtree.tif** again into another blank area of the page. This time, however, when the graphic appears, skew the graphic **10 degrees** to the right. Next, drag the graphic so that the top of it begins roughly one-half inch below the last line of text and is centered beneath the word Packages.

8. From the data files, place the graphic file named **Auto.tif** into a blank area of the page. Then, drag the graphic so that it is positioned between the base of the two palm trees.

9. Click the **Text** tool and then click an insertion point roughly one-half inch below the bottom of the automobile graphic and just to the right of the left margin guide.

10. Turn on **center alignment,** select the **14-point** font size, and select a sans serif font such as Arial, Helvetica or Univers. Then key the following lines of text, pressing **Enter** at the end of each line:

    We have over 30 fly and drive vacation packages.
    Select the type of car you want, tell us where
    you want to stay and we'll do the rest.
    Enjoy a Caribbean vacation and
    experience the islands up close.

11. Press **Enter** three times. Then key the following lines of text, pressing **Enter** at the end of each line:

    Caribbean Sun Travel Tours
    6600 Duval Street, Key West, FL 32358
    Telephone: (305) 555-1234

12. Select the words **Caribbean Sun Travel Tours** and change the selected text to the **24-point** font size.

13. Compare your publication to the sample solution in Figure 13-17 and make any needed adjustments or corrections.

14. Print the publication. Save the publication with the name **Flydrive** and then close the publication.

FIGURE 13-17
Minisolution to Flydrive publication from Project 13-1

**Fly and Drive
Vacation Packages**

We have over 30 fly and drive vacation packages.
Select the type of car you want, tell us where
you want to stay and we'll do the rest.
Enjoy a Caribbean vacation and
experience the islands up close.

Caribbean Sun Travel Tours
6600 Duvall Street, Key West, FL 32358
Telephone: (305) 555-1234

SCANS PROJECT 13-2

1. Begin a new publication. When the Document Setup dialog box appears, specify a **single-sided** publication and change all of the margins to **0.75** inches.

2. While using the **Pointer** tool, import the graphic file named **Starfish.tif** from the data files. Then, drag the graphic so that it appears in the center of the page. With the graphic still selected, display the Text Wrap dialog box and then select the second Text wrap option (Rectangular Wrap) and the second Text flow option (Jump Over).

3. While still using the Pointer tool, import the graphic file named **Turtle.tif**. from the data files.
    Then, drag the image of the turtle to any blank area of the page. Next, use the **Cropping** tool to
    remove or hide the left half of this graphic image (see Figure 13-18 to see how much you need to
    crop) and then drag this graphic so that it is positioned along the bottom and left margin guides.

4. Using the **Pointer** tool, select the graphic image of the turtle. Then display the Text Wrap
    dialog box and select the second Text wrap option (Rectangular Wrap) and the third Text
    flow option (Around). Next, customize the graphic boundary around the turtle so that it
    follows the shape of the turtle. To do so, add a number of graphic boundary handles and
    then drag those handles into position. Use Figure 13-18 as a general guideline.

FIGURE 13-18
Import the graphic; crop the left half of the graphic; customize the boundary

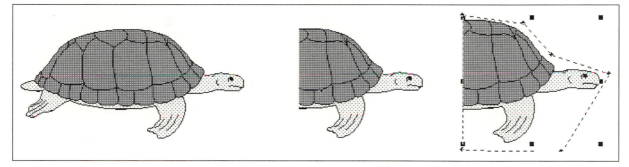

5. While using the **Pointer** tool, import the text file named **Island.rtf** from the data files into
    the publication. When the Text Placement icon appears, position the icon just below the top
    margin guide and slightly to the right of the left margin guide. Then click once to place the
    text onto the page.

6. Drag the image of the starfish upward so that the top of the image falls just below the first
    paragraph.

7. Compare your publication to the sample solution shown in Figure 13-19 and make any adjustments or corrections needed.

8. Print the publication. Save the publication with the name **Cayman Flyer** and then close the publication.

FIGURE 13-19
Minisolution to Cayman Flyer publication from Project 13-2

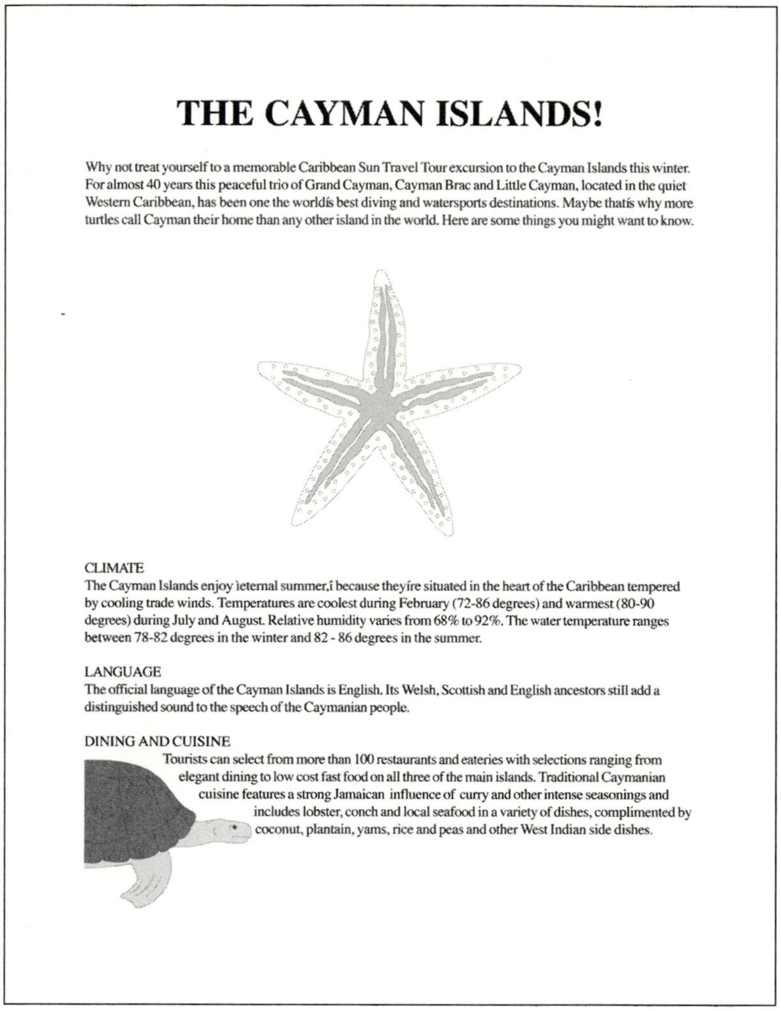

THE CAYMAN ISLANDS!

Why not treat yourself to a memorable Caribbean Sun Travel Tour excursion to the Cayman Islands this winter. For almost 40 years this peaceful trio of Grand Cayman, Cayman Brac and Little Cayman, located in the quiet Western Caribbean, has been one the worldís best diving and watersports destinations. Maybe thatís why more turtles call Cayman their home than any other island in the world. Here are some things you might want to know.

CLIMATE
The Cayman Islands enjoy ìeternal summer,î because theyíre situated in the heart of the Caribbean tempered by cooling trade winds. Temperatures are coolest during February (72-86 degrees) and warmest (80-90 degrees) during July and August. Relative humidity varies from 68% to 92%. The water temperature ranges between 78-82 degrees in the winter and 82 - 86 degrees in the summer.

LANGUAGE
The official language of the Cayman Islands is English. Its Welsh, Scottish and English ancestors still add a distinguished sound to the speech of the Caymanian people.

DINING AND CUISINE
Tourists can select from more than 100 restaurants and eateries with selections ranging from elegant dining to low cost fast food on all three of the main islands. Traditional Caymanian cuisine features a strong Jamaican influence of curry and other intense seasonings and includes lobster, conch and local seafood in a variety of dishes, complimented by coconut, plantain, yams, rice and peas and other West Indian side dishes.

TEAMWORK PROJECT

Form a team consisting of 5-10 students each, and appoint a team leader. Then, during the next week, have each team member collect a number of different examples of publications in which text was wrapped around a graphic. When finding your examples, try to find ones in which text wraps around the graphics in different ways, and with different designs and shapes. Next, have each team member present to the group all the examples they found and explain how those examples might be created using PageMaker. Finally, as a team, vote on the three most interesting examples of text wrap presented by your group and then have the team leader present and explain those examples to the class.

CRITICAL *Thinking*

ACTIVITY 13-1

In this lesson, you learned how inline graphics can be placed within a line of text, and how such a graphic will move if the text surrounding it moves. During the next week, look closely at the documents you encounter on a daily basis, such as flyers, menus, catalogs, and directories. Challenge yourself to see how many different examples you can find where inline graphics could have been used. Think about how you might create one or more of those same documents in a PageMaker publication using inline graphics.

WORKING WITH STYLES

Introduction

This lesson describes how to create and use styles. Styles are valuable ways to reduce the time it takes to create many types of publications and to ensure consistency between publications.

Introduction to Styles

Most professional publications, such as books and magazines, use a technique called styles to ensure consistency. Think for a moment about any national magazine that you have seen recently. Although there are different articles in each issue, the layout or design of the pages usually stays the same from one page to the next and from one issue to the next. The titles of every story, for example, might appear in bold with a specific font and point size. The text for every story, on the other hand, will usually appear in a smaller point size and often in a different font. The reason that each type of entry looks the same within the magazine is because of styles.

A *style* is the formatting specification needed for a particular type of entry in a publication, like a title, subheading, or body text. A *style sheet* lists all of the styles used in a publication. PageMaker comes with a style sheet containing a handful of styles that you can use right away. It's also easy to create your own styles. To create a style, you first need to determine what kind of entry it will be used for, such as a title or bulleted text. Then, assign a name to the style, and specify any font, tab, or paragraph specifications that you want to use with that particular type of entry. To use a style that you just created, simply identify the text that you want to apply a particular style to, and then you select its the style name from the list of available styles. Almost immediately, the text changes to the specifications that you defined earlier for the style.

Styles can save you much time, especially when creating medium to lengthy publications, and they can help provide a consistent look from one page to the next, and even between similar publications.

To gain a better understanding of styles, imagine the process of formatting a simple report that you've already placed or keyed into a publication. Suppose that this report is divided into ten sections, with each section having its own title. To format the title for each section of this report without the use of a style, you would first select the text, then select a variety of type specifications, such as the Arial font in a 24-point size, with the bold type style and center alignment. You'd apply all of the same type specifications to each section title. Although not complicated to do, selecting all of these type specifications for just the titles alone could prove time-consuming and tedious.

Instead, you could create a style for the section titles and assign the style a name, such as *Section title.* This style would contain all of the specifications needed for a section title such as the Arial font in a 24-point size, in bold, and with center alignment. Then, to format any section title in the report, you would simply place the insertion point anywhere in the title and then select the style's name (Section title) from an on-screen list of available styles. Immediately, the section title would be formatted with all of the correct type specifications.

Although styles can save time when you are formatting the text in a publication, they can save even more time when you need to change the layout of the publication. Imagine that you've just completed a 20-page newsletter. Mixed throughout the newsletter are the titles for 40 articles that appear in 24-point size and with the Times New Roman font. Suppose you then decide to change the format for all of the titles to Arial in an 18-point font size. Doing so without the use of styles might easily take five to ten minutes, even for a highly skilled PageMaker user. However, if you had used styles when creating this newsletter, you could accomplish the same task in only seconds simply by changing the specifications for one style. Styles let you change the format of a publication quickly, see the results, and then change it again if needed.

Because a publication normally has many different types of entries, such as titles and subtitles, PageMaker lets you create as many styles as needed in a publication. Each style has its own specifications. The publication in Figure 14-1, for example, uses three separate—styles, one for the Report title, Section title, and the Body. In Figure 14-1, the style named Report Title uses the Arial font in an 18-point font size, in bold, with center alignment. The style named Section title uses the Arial font in a 14-point font size, in bold with small caps and left alignment. Finally, the style named Body uses the Times New Roman font in a 12-point size with left alignment and a 0.25-inch first line indent.

FIGURE 14-1
Styles used in a sample publication

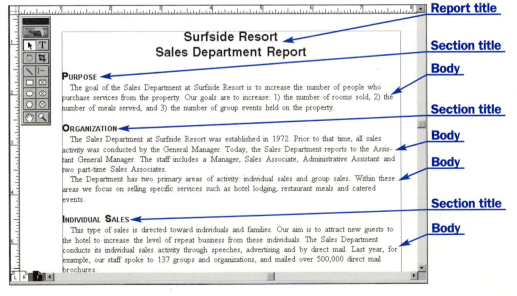

Understanding the Styles Palette

While working in PageMaker, you can display a Styles palette. The Styles palette, like the one in Figure 14-2, lists the names of all the styles in the current publication. To display (or hide) the Styles palette, choose Show Styles from the Window menu. *NOTE: Normally, the Styles and the Color palettes both appear together on-screen. Each palette is identified with a tab. Click on the Tab labeled Styles to bring the names of all available styles into view.*

FIGURE 14-2
Styles palette

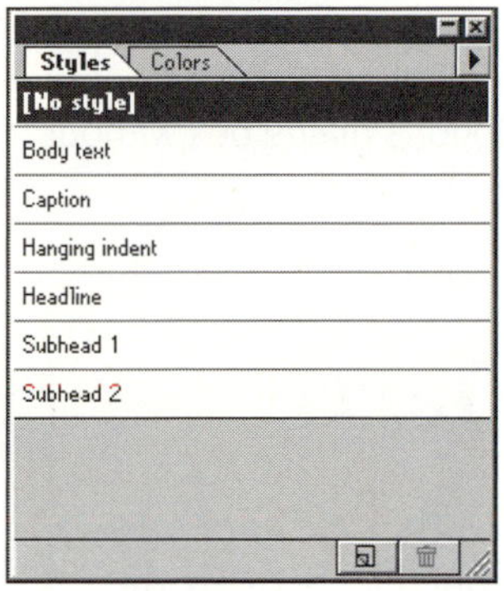

PageMaker includes several default styles, with names such as Body text, Caption, and Headline, in each new publication. These are standard, default styles that you can use right away to format different types of entries. Each style has its own name and specifications.

To see the specifications for a certain style, hold down the Ctrl key and then click on the style name in the Styles palette. This command displays a Style Options dialog box like the one in Figure 14-3. The specifications for the style appear in the bottom half of the dialog box. Although abbreviated because of space limitations, the specifications are fairly easy to understand. In Figure 14-3, for example, the highlighted style named Body text uses the Times New Roman font in a 12-point size with automatic leading. It also includes left alignment, a 0.333-inch first line indent, and automatic hyphenation. To close the dialog box, click Cancel.

FIGURE 14-3
Style Options dialog box

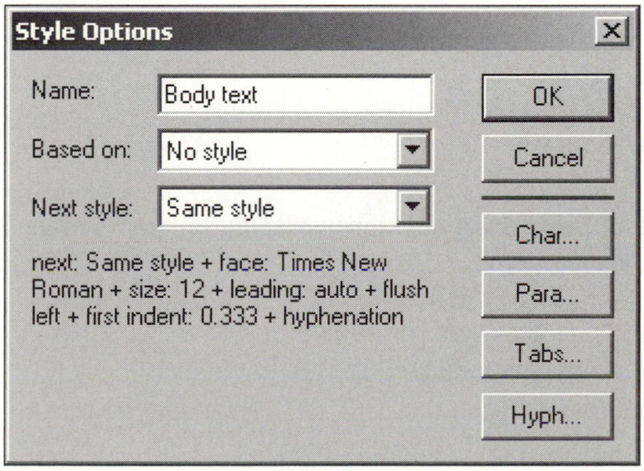

STEP-BY-STEP 14.1

1. Begin a new publication. When the Document Setup dialog box appears, specify a **single-sided** publication, then click **OK**.

2. If the Styles palette is not on-screen, choose **Show Styles** from the **Window** menu to display the palette.

3. While holding down the **Ctrl** key, click **Headline** on the Styles palette and then release the **Ctrl** key. (*NOTE: If Headline does not appear in the Styles palette, use the scroll arrows in the Styles palette to bring that style name into view.*) When the Style Options dialog box appears, examine the specifications for the Headline style that appear at the bottom of the dialog box.

4. Click **Cancel** to close the Style Options dialog box without making any changes. Keep this publication on-screen for use in the next Step-by-Step.

Applying a Style to Text

You can apply a style to text when that text appears in the publication window (in the layout view) or in the story editor. To apply a style to existing text while using the Text tool, select the paragraph(s) that you want to style. (If you want to style only one paragraph, you can also simply place the insertion point anywhere within that paragraph.) Then, click the name of the style in the Styles palette (or choose Style from the Type menu and then click on the style to use from the submenu). After a brief pause, the text will change to the specifications for that style.

> ### Hot Tip
>
> You can also apply a style to text by using the Control palette instead of the Styles palette. First, select the paragraph(s) to style. Then, click the Paragraph (¶) button on the Control palette and select a style from the Styles drop-down list located in the upper-left portion of the Control palette.

STEP-BY-STEP 14.2

1. Click the **Text** tool, and then click an insertion point slightly below the top margin guide and just to the right of the left margin guide.

2. Enlarge the area around the insertion point to **Actual Size**.

3. Key the following text. Press **Enter** at the end of each line.
   INTRODUCTION TO
   PageMaker 7.0
   PageMaker is one of the leading desktop-publishing programs available for use on the personal computer and the Macintosh.

4. Place the insertion point anywhere in the line of text that reads INTRODUCTION TO. Then, click **Headline** on the Styles palette to apply that style to the text.

5. Place the insertion point anywhere in the line of text that reads PageMaker 7.0.Then, click **Subhead 2** in the Styles palette**.**

STEP-BY-STEP 14.2 Continued

6. Place the insertion point anywhere in the paragraph beginning PageMaker is one ..... Then, click **Body text** on the Styles palette.

7. Place the insertion point anywhere in the line of text that reads PageMaker 7.0. Then, click **Subhead 1** on the Styles palette and observe how easy it is to change text from one style to another style. Keep this publication on-screen for use in the next Step-by-Step.

Creating a Style

As mentioned earlier in this lesson, you can create as many additional styles as you need in a publication. To create a new style, choose Define Styles from the Type menu to display the Define Styles dialog box like the one in Figure 14-4.

FIGURE 14-4
Define Styles dialog box

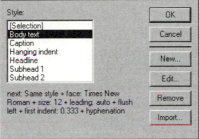

Next, choose New to display the Style Options dialog box shown earlier in Figure 14-3. To create a style, you need to complete three steps. You need to assign the style a name, decide if you want the new style to be based on specifications that are already used in a different style, and then tell PageMaker what specifications you want for the new style. The steps for creating a style are described in more detail in the following sections.

Enter a Style Name

To create a new style, key a name for that style in the Name text box of the Style Options dialog box. Although a style name can contain up to 255 characters (including spaces), it's best to use shorter names of 15 characters or less. When naming a style, try to use a name that helps you remember the purpose of the style, such as Section Title, Bibliography Entry, and Footnote. If you accidentally key a name for a style that already exists in the publication, PageMaker displays an alert box asking if you want to replace the existing style. If so, choose Yes to replace the existing style with the one you will be creating, otherwise, choose No to key a different name for the style.

Use the Based On Option to Select a Style

The *Based on* option lets you use all the specifications from one style to create a different style. When you change specifications for the original style, any styles that are based on the original style will change as well. For instance, if you change the font on the original style from Arial to Times New Roman, the font of any based on style will also change to Times New Roman.

Using the *Based on* option also helps ensure consistency. For example, suppose you want all titles in a publication to appear in the Arial font, in bold, and with a 24-point size. You also want all the subtitles to appear in the Arial font and in bold, but in an18-point size. In this instance, you could create a style called Titles that uses the Arial font in a 24-point size. Then, you could create a different style called Subtitles that is based on the Titles style but has only an 18-point font size. To use this option, select the name of an existing style from the *Based on* drop-down list. (Based on styles are discussed in depth in the next lesson.)

Select Using the Next Style Option

The Next style option lets you select the name of a different style that will be applied to the paragraph that follows the one to which the style is being applied. In certain publications, one style is always followed by a different style. For example, a title might always be followed by paragraphs of body text. By default, if you select a certain style, and then begin keying text (either in the layout view or in the story editor) PageMaker continues to apply the current style to all future paragraphs. Use the Next style option to select the name of a different style that will automatically be selected whenever you press Enter to end the current paragraph. *NOTE: The Next style option is only useful when you are keying text directly into PageMaker and not applying styles to text that you are placing into a publication.*

Select the Style's Specifications

When selecting a style's specifications, use the buttons labeled Char, Para, Tabs, and Hyph that are located on the Style Options dialog box. Char is used for type specifications, Para for paragraph specifications, Tabs is for tab settings , and Hyph is for hyphenation settings. Clicking the Char button, for example, displays the Type Specifications dialog box in which you can select the font, point size, type styles, and so on.

When you've finished creating the style, click OK to close the Style Options dialog box, and then click OK again to close the Define Styles dialog box.

> ### Hot Tip ◎
> Style names can contain as many as 255 characters. PageMaker's Control palette and story editor, however, display only the first 14–20 characters of a style name, depending upon your computer. Thus, keeping style names to 15 characters or less can avoid confusion.

STEP-BY-STEP 14.3

1. Click the **Pointer** tool to make certain that the new style you are about to create is not applied accidentally to any text in which the insertion point is located.

2. Choose **Define Styles** from the **Type** menu. When the Define Styles dialog box appears, choose **New**.

3. When the Style Options dialog box appears, key **Titles** in the Name text box.

STEP-BY-STEP 14.3 Continued

4. Click the **Char** button. When the Character Specifications dialog box appears, choose a sans serif font, such as Arial, Helvetica or Univers, from the Font drop-down list. Also, choose **24** from the Size drop-down list and select **Bold** in the Type style section of the dialog box. Finally, click **OK**.

5. Click on the **Para** button. Then, choose **Center** from the Alignment drop-down list and click **OK**.

6. Click **OK** to close the Style Options dialog box.

7. Click **OK** to close the Define Styles dialog box.

8. Click the **Text** tool and then click anywhere in the line of text that reads INTRODUCTION TO. Next, click **Titles** in the Styles palette and observe how the specifications for the Titles style are applied to the text. Keep this publication on-screen for use in the next Step-by-Step.

Editing a Style

PageMaker makes it easy to edit or change the specifications for any style in your current publication. To change a style, choose Define Styles from the Type menu to display the Define Styles dialog box. Then, click on the name of the style that you want to change and finally click Edit. When the Style Options dialog box appears, you can follow the same steps that you used to create the style, and use the Char, Para, Tabs, and Hyph buttons to select different specifications for the style.

To end your style editing session, click OK to close the Style Options dialog box, then click OK to close the Define Styles dialog box. If you have already applied the edited style to existing entries within your publication, those editing changes will immediately be made to each of the entries. For example, suppose you had already applied a style named Section to five different paragraphs in a publication. If you edit the Section style and select a different font, each of the five entries to which that style was already applied would change.

STEP-BY-STEP 14.4

1. Choose **Define Styles** from the Type menu to display the Define Styles dialog box.

2. Click **Titles** in the Style list box and then click the **Edit** button to display the Style Options dialog box.

3. Click the **Char** button to display the Character Specifications dialog box. Choose **36** from the Size drop-down list.

4. Click **OK** to close the Character Specifications dialog box.

5. Click **OK** to close the Style Options dialog box.

6. Click **OK** to close the Define Styles dialog box.

7. Observe how the INTRODUCTION TO entry automatically changes from 24 to 36 points. Remember, you applied the Titles style to this text in the last Step-by-Step. Keep this publication on-screen for use in the next Step-by-Step.

Removing a Style

If you create a style but then decide not to use it, or if you create a style in error, you can delete it. This can cut down on the confusion of having lots of styles on the style sheet. You can also delete any or all of PageMaker's default styles if you are not going to use them. To delete an unneeded style from your publication, choose Define Styles from the Type menu to display the Define Styles dialog box, and then click on the name of the style to delete. Finally, click on the Remove button and then click OK to close the dialog box.

Removing a style only removes the name of that style from the Styles palette. PageMaker does not remove the actual style specifications from any entries to which that style was applied, so the text will continue to look the same as it did before you removed the style.

Although there's little problem in removing an unused style or a style that you created in error, be careful about removing any style that you have already used in a publication. When you remove a style, PageMaker removes the name of the style from all the paragraphs to which it was applied. As a result, if you remove a style and later decide to add that same style back into the publication, you will need to apply the style one entry at a time to any entries that previously used the style.

S TEP-BY-STEP 14.5

1. Choose **Define Styles** from the Type menu.

2. Click **Hanging indent** in the Style list box and then click **Remove** to delete that style from the publication. Observe how this style name no longer appears in the Styles palette.

3. Following instructions similar to step 2, remove the style named Caption.

4. Click **OK** to close the Define Styles dialog box.

5. Save this publication under the name **Styles Introduction** and then close this publication.

Saving Styles

Styles are automatically saved with your publication. Thus, whenever you open a publication, the styles that you created are still included in the Styles palette. In the next lesson, you will see how you can copy styles from one publication to another.

SUMMARY

In this lesson, you learned how to:

■ Explain how styles help ensure consistency for similar types of text entries throughout a publication and how a style sheet contains all the styles used in a specific publication.

■ Use the Styles palette to apply PageMaker's standard, default styles to text within a publication.

■ Create, apply, edit, and remove styles within a publication.

VOCABULARY *Review*

Define the following terms:
Style   Style sheet

REVIEW *Questions*

TRUE/FALSE

Circle T if the statement is true or F if the statement is false.

T   F   **1.** Styles can help provide a consistent look to similar entries in a publication.

T   F   **2.** You can create a maximum of ten new styles in a publication.

T   F   **3.** When you create a new publication, PageMaker automatically adds several standard, default styles to the publication.

T   F   **4.** All the styles used in a publication are called a style sheet.

T   F   **5.** A style's name cannot exceed eight characters in length.

T   F   **6.** If you have applied a style named Body text to 20 paragraphs in a publication, and then change the type specifications for that style from 12- to 14-points, all 20 paragraphs will change immediately to 14-points.

T   F   **7.** After adding a style to the Styles palette, you must apply the style to at least one paragraph in the publication.

T   F   **8.** When you delete a style from a publication, PageMaker keeps the name of the style in the Styles palette.

T   F   **9.** If you delete a style from a publication, any text to which that style has been applied is also removed from the publication.

T   F   **10.** Any styles that you create or edit are automatically saved with the publication.

FILL IN THE BLANK

Complete the following sentences by writing the correct word or words in the blanks provided.

1. A collection of all the styles used in a publication is called a(n) _____ _____.

2. All the styles available in a publication are listed in and selected from the _____ _____.

3. The name of a style can be up to _____ characters long.

4. When creating a new style, the _____ _____ option lets you use all the specifica-
    tions from one style to create a style that has only a few differences.

5. When creating a new style, click the _____ button in the Define Styles dialog box to
    select the font that you wish to use with the new style.

PROJECTS

SCANS PROJECT 14-1A

1. Begin a new publication. When the Document Setup dialog box appears, specify a **single-sided**
    publication and then click **OK**.

2. If the Styles palette is not on-screen, display it.

3. Choose **Define Styles** from the Type menu. When the Define Styles dialog box appears,
    click **New** to display the Style Options dialog box.

4. Key **Report Entry** as the name of a new style.

5. Click the **Char** button. Select the appropriate specifications so that any text you apply this
    style to will appear in italic and in a 14-point font size. Then, click **OK** to close the
    Character Specifications dialog box.

6. Click the **Para** button. Select the appropriate specifications so that any text with the Report
    Entry style will be indented on the left 0.5 inches, indented on the right 2 inches, have a
    first line indent of 0.15 inches and also Justify alignment. Then, click **OK** to close the
    Paragraph Specifications dialog box.

7. Click **OK** to close the Style Options dialog box. Then, click **OK** to close the Define Styles
    dialog box. Keep this publication on-screen for use in Project 14-1B.

PROJECT 14-1B

1. Open the story editor. *(NOTE: Remember that you can select Edit Story from the Edit
    menu to open the story editor.)*

2. Key **Cruise Ship Tours** and then press **Enter**.

3. Key the following two paragraphs. Whenever the ¶ symbol appears to indicate the end of a
    paragraph, press the **Enter** key once.

    Sales of cruise ship tours are up 130 percent over last year. During the first six months
    alone, we booked 1,435 people on Caribbean cruises.¶
    There are several reasons for this increase. The first reason is our newspaper and television
    advertising. The second reason is the increase in national advertising by the Caribbean
    Travel Commission. ¶

4. Close the story editor (by choosing **Edit Layout** from the **Edit** menu). When the Text Placement icon appears, position it slightly below the top margin guide, and just to the right of the left margin guide, and then click.

5. Enlarge the area around the text to the **Actual Size**.

6. Apply the style named **Headline** to the title Cruise Ship Tours.

7. Apply the style named **Report Entry** to the two paragraphs in the publication.

8. Print the publication. Save the publication with the name **Cruise Sales** and then close the publication.

SCANS PROJECT 14-2A

1. Begin a new publication. When the Document Setup dialog box appears, specify a **single-sided** publication and then click **OK**.

2. If the Styles palette is not on-screen, display it.

3. Create a new style named **First Paragraph**. Using instructions you now know, specify a sans serif typeface, such as Arial, Helvetica or Univers, in a **14-point** font size. Also, insert **0.15** inches of space before each paragraph to which that style is applied.

4. Create a new style named **Benefits**. Using instructions you now know, specify a serif typeface, such as Times New Roman, Times, or Times Roman in a **12-point** font size and **Italic** type style. In addition, select the appropriate specifications so that any paragraph with the Benefits style will be indented on the left **0.5** inches, have a first line indent of **-.5** inches, and have **0.15** inches of space before the paragraph.

5. Close both the **Style Options** and the **Define Styles** dialog boxes. Keep this publication on-screen for use in Project 14-2B.

PROJECT 14-2B

1. Open the story editor. Then, key the following four paragraphs. Whenever the ¶ symbol appears to indicate the end of a paragraph, press the **Enter** key once.

At Caribbean Sun Travel Tours, our many years of experience will help you enjoy your vacation more. Our firm has over twenty years of travel and tour experience. More importantly, we listen to what you have to say. Because of this, we offer these benefits:¶
We provide frequent-travel awards to our customers. For each 100 dollars worth of travel you book (and complete), you receive 1 credit point. You can exchange 20 credit points for a weekend vacation at a local resort.¶
Unless requested, we will quote the most economical fares available and tell you any travel restrictions that might apply.¶
We make travel easier and more enjoyable by keeping a detailed personal profile about you. It helps us remember the type of airline seats and cruise accommodations you prefer and any diet or health restrictions you may have.¶

2. Close the story editor (by choosing **Edit Layout** from the **Edit** menu). When the Text Placement icon appears, position the icon slightly below the top margin guide, and just to the right of the left margin guide, and then click.

3. Apply the style named **First Paragraph** to the first paragraph in the publication.

4. Apply the style named **Benefits** to the last three paragraphs in the publication. Keep this publication on-screen for use in Project 14-2C.

PROJECT 14-2C

1. Edit the style named **First Paragraph** as follows:
    A. Change the type specifications for this style to a serif font such as Times New Roman, Times, or Times Roman.
    B. Change the paragraph specifications for this style so that the first line indent is **0.5** inch.

2. Edit the style named **Benefits** as follows:
    A. Change the type specifications for this style to a **10-point** font size.
    B. Change the paragraph specifications for this style so that there is **0.10** inch of space before each paragraph.

3. Print the publication. Save the publication with the name **Benefits** and then close the publication.

SCANS TEAMWORK PROJECT

Collect two different issues of the same national magazine or national newspaper. Then, with a partner, visually compare the various types of entries such as titles, subtitles, body copy and captions in both issues of that magazine or newspaper. In most cases, you will find that each of the entries looks the same because the same styles were used to create both issues. Then with your partner, imagine that your job was to create that same magazine or newspaper using PageMaker. Make a list of the different styles you feel would be needed to create that publication. In your list, provide a descriptive name for each style that clearly identifies the type of entry for which it would be used, such as Title of Article, Picture Caption, Body Copy and so on. See how many different styles you can identify in 10 minutes.

CRITICAL *Thinking*

SCANS ACTIVITY 14-1

In this lesson, you learned that a style name can consist of as many as 255 characters. Yet, it was advised to use shorter style names of 15 characters or less, when possible. Now that you've had some experience working with styles, list several reasons why using shorter style names is better.

ADVANCED STYLE TECHNIQUES

Introduction

This lesson describes advanced style features that can save you time as you create your publications. First, you will learn how to create a new style from existing text and from settings used in an existing style. You then practice applying styles while using the story editor and adding styles to a new publication that you already created in a different publication. You will also find out how to override or customize text that you have already styled.

Creating a Style From Existing Text

Normally when creating a style, you select all the specifications for the style, such as the type and paragraph specifications one at a time. However, instead of having to select the specifications individually, you can create a new style by using text that you've already formatted in the publication. To do so, you first select the text containing the formatting that you want included in the new style, and then you issue the commands to create the style as you normally would. PageMaker then copies any formatting specifications found within the selected text into the contents of the new style.

As an example, suppose you have already formatted a title in a publication with a sans serif font such as Arial, in italic type style, and in 14-point font size. To create a new style that contains all the formatting information from this title, you would select the text in the title first. Then you would choose Define Styles from the Type menu, and then click New. Next, you would key a name for the new style in the Name text box. If you then examined the lower-left corner of the dialog box you would see how PageMaker copied the formatting specifications from the selected text into the style's contents. You can also edit or add other specifications to the style as you normally would. When finished, click OK to close the Style Options dialog box and then click OK to close the Define Styles dialog box.

S TEP-BY-STEP 15.1

1. Begin a new publication. When the Document Setup dialog box appears, specify a **single-sided** publication.

2. If the Styles palette is not on-screen, display the Styles palette.

3. Click the **Text** tool and then click an insertion point slightly below the top margin guide and just to the right of the left margin guide.

4. Enlarge the area around the insertion point to **Actual Size**.

5. Key **Visiting the** and then press **Enter**. Then key **Caribbean** and press **Enter**. Finally, key **Things to Know** (but *do not* press Enter).

6. Select the words **Visiting the**. Then, apply the following changes:
   a. Change the selected text to a sans serif typeface such as Arial, Helvetica, or Univers.
   b. Change the selected text to the 36-point size.
   c. Change the selected text to italic and bold.
   d. Change the selected text to center alignment.

7. If the words *Visiting the* are not still selected, select that text. Next, choose **Define Styles** from the **Type** menu and then click **New**. When the Style Options dialog box appears, key **Heading** in the Name text box. Observe how PageMaker copied all the formatting from the selected text into this new style. Finally, click **OK** to close the Style Options dialog box and then click **OK** to close the Define Styles dialog box.

8. Select the word **Caribbean** and apply the new Heading style you created in step 7. Keep this publication on-screen for use in the next Step-by-Step.

Creating "Based On" Styles

A t times, you will find yourself creating several similar styles within the same publication. Styles used for formatting titles and subtitles are often similar. For example, suppose you create a style called Titles to format all the main titles in the publication in a sans serif typeface, bold and italics, and in a 36-point size. You might then create a style called Subtitles for formatting subtitles that also uses the same sans serif typeface in bold and italic, but in a smaller 24-point size. When creating similar styles, you can use a feature called *Based on* to save time by creating one style that is based on all the specifications from a different style.

While creating a new style, you can choose to have the new style based on the formatting from a different, existing style. To create a based-on style, choose Define Styles from the Type menu and then click New. Next, key a name for the new style. Now choose the name of the existing style that contains the specifications on which you want this new style based. To do this, click on the Based-on drop-down arrow to display a list of all the styles in the publication, then choose the style on which the new style will be based.

PageMaker will then display all of the formatting specifications for the existing style in the lower-left corner of the dialog box. You can now edit or add other specifications to the new style as you normally would. When finished, click OK to close the Style Options dialog box, and then click OK to close the Define Styles dialog box.

STEP-BY-STEP 15.2

1. If it is not still selected, select the word **Caribbean**.

2. Choose **Define Styles** from the **Type** menu and then click **New**. When the Style Options dialog box appears, key **Subheading** in the Name text box.

3. If *Heading* does not already appear in the Based on text box, click the **Based on** drop-down arrow and then choose **Heading** from the list.

4. If *Same style* does not already appear in the Next style text box, click the **Next style** drop-down arrow and then choose **Same style** from the list.

5. In the Style Options dialog box, click the **Char** button and then choose **24** from the Size drop-down list. Finally click **OK** to close the Character Specifications dialog box.

6. Click **OK** to close the Style Options dialog box, and then click **OK** to close the Define Styles dialog box.

7. On your own, apply the style named **Subheading** to the Things to Know entry. Keep this publication on-screen for use in the next Step-by-Step.

Using Styles in the Story Editor

As mentioned in the previous lesson, you can apply a style to text while using the story editor. And, unlike the layout view, the story editor shows the style names, if any, that have already been applied to each paragraph in the story. In addition, you can use the story editor to replace one style with a different style in part or all of a publication.

Viewing and Applying Style Names

While using the story editor, the names of any styles that have been applied to paragraphs appear to the left of those paragraphs. To display or hide the style names, choose Display Style Names in the Story menu. Figure 15-1 shows an example of the story editor with the style names displayed. A small dot appears in place of a style name when no styles have been applied to a certain paragraph.

FIGURE 15-1
Story editor with style names displayed

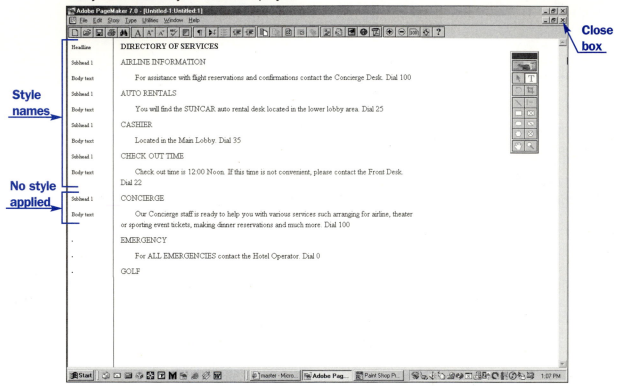

To apply a style while using the story editor, select the paragraph(s) that you want to style and then click on the style name in the Styles palette. To apply a style quickly to just one paragraph, place the insertion point anywhere in the paragraph and then click on the style name in the Styles palette. While using the story editor, you can also select an entire paragraph quickly by clicking on the style name for that paragraph.

Using Find/Change with Styles

You can use the story editor's Find feature to find out where (or if) a certain style was used in a story. You can also automatically replace one style with a different style. Here's how.

Finding Where a Style Was Used in a Story

While using the story editor, choose Find from the Utilities menu. Next click on the Para attributes button to display the Find Paragraph Attributes dialog box, and then choose the style to find from the Paragraph style drop-down list. Figure 15-2 shows an example of this dialog box with the list of styles displayed. Then click OK. Finally, choose Find to highlight the first occurrence of the style and then choose Find Next to locate any additional occurrences. To close the dialog box when finished using it, click on its Close box.

FIGURE 15-2
Find Paragraph Attributes dialog box with
Paragraphs styles list displayed

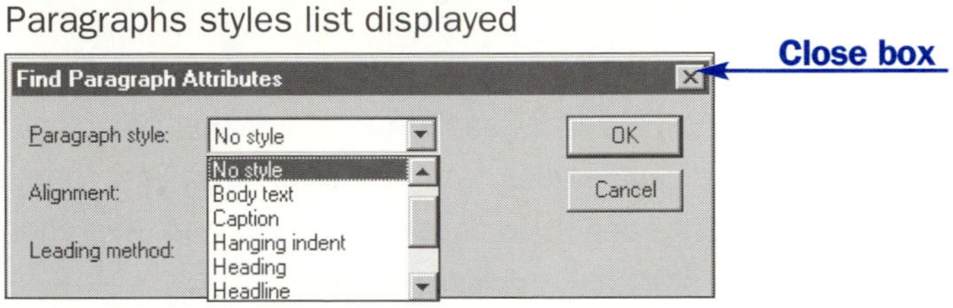

Automatically Replace One Style with a Different Style

While using the story editor, choose Change from the Utilities menu. Next click the Para attributes button to display a dialog box like the one shown in Figure 15-3. Now, in the Find what section of the dialog box, choose the style to find from the Paragraph style drop-down list. Then, in the Change to section of the dialog box, choose the style that you want to replace it with from the Paragraph style drop-down list. Then click OK. Now choose Change all to replace the styles automatically throughout the entire story, or choose Find and then Change to replace styles one at a time. To close the dialog box when finished using it, click on its Close box.

FIGURE 15-3
Change Paragraph Attributes dialog box

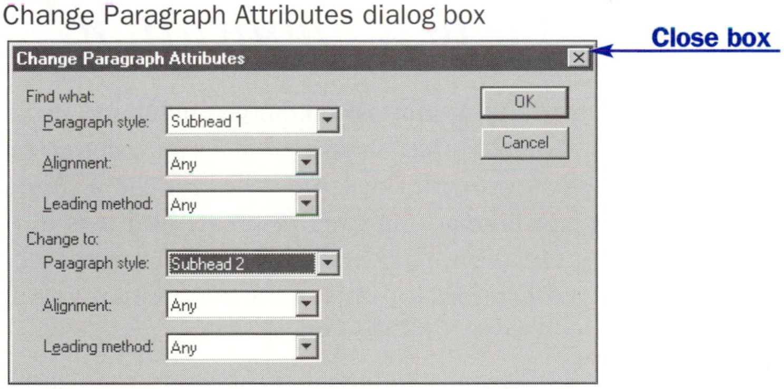

S TEP-BY-STEP 15.3

1. Make certain the insertion point is located anywhere in the on-screen text, and then choose **Edit Story** from the **Edit** menu to display the story editor.

2. If the style names do not appear along the left side of the story editor window, choose **Display Style Names** from the **Story** menu. (*NOTE: No style name will appear next to the first line of text since it was used to create the Headline style.*)

3. Use the mouse or arrow keys on the keyboard to position the insertion point at the beginning of the story, if necessary.

STEP-BY-STEP 15.3 Continued

4. Choose **Find** from the **Utilities** menu. Then, when the Find dialog box appears, click on the **Para attributes** button. When the Find Paragraph Attributes dialog box appears, choose **Subheading** from the Paragraph style drop-down list and then click **OK.** Finally, choose **Find** and observe how PageMaker highlights the *Things to Know* entry.

5. Click the **Close** box in the Find dialog box.

6. Move the insertion point back to the beginning of the story.

7. Choose **Change** from the **Utilities** menu. When the Change dialog box appears, click on the **Para attributes** button. In the Find what section of the dialog box, click the **Paragraph style** drop-down arrow, and then choose **Subheading** from the drop-down list. Then, in the Change to section of the dialog box, click the **Paragraph style** drop-down arrow and then choose **Heading** from the drop-down list. Finally, click **OK** to start the change process.

8. Click the **Change all** button to change all occurrences of the Subheading style to the Heading style. Observe how all paragraphs in the story now use the Heading style. Then, click on the **Close** box in the Find dialog box.

9. Choose **Edit Layout** from the **Edit** menu to close the Story Editor window to display the publication window.

10. Save this publication with the name **Visiting** and then close the publication.

Importing Styles into a Publication

When working with styles, you may often find yourself creating and using the same styles with different publications. For example, if you create a newsletter each month, you might find yourself creating a new publication with the same styles for the headline, body text, captions, and so on. Because some styles can take a long time to create and it is important to create consistent styles in the same type of publication, PageMaker lets you import or copy all the styles from one publication into a different publication. It's important to note that you cannot select which styles to import. PageMaker will simply import all the styles.

As you learned in the last lesson, PageMaker saves any styles along with the publication. Instead of creating new styles in a publication that are similar to ones you have already used in a different publication, you can simply import them from the existing publication into the new one.

To import styles, start the new publication or open the publication into which you want the existing styles imported. Next choose Define Styles from the Type menu, and then click the Import button. PageMaker then displays an Import Styles dialog box that's similar in content to the Open dialog box. Here, select the name of the existing publication that contains the styles you want imported, and finally click Open.

PageMaker adds the imported styles to those styles already in the current publication. In some instances, both publications may contain a style with the same name. This is especially true of publications that contain PageMaker's default styles such as Headline or Subhead 1. If both publications contain the same style name, an alert box containing the message Copy over existing styles? appears. Click OK to import the new, duplicate style(s), or choose Cancel to cancel the importing.

> **Hot Tip** 🎯
>
> If you find that you use various styles regularly in your PageMaker work, you can create all of those styles in a separate publication and save it with an easily remembered name such as My Styles. Then, whenever one or more of those styles is needed, you can simply import it from the My Styles publication.

S TEP-BY-STEP 15.4

1. Begin a new publication. When the Document Setup dialog box appears, specify a **single-sided** publication.

2. Display the Styles palette, if necessary.

3. Choose **Define Styles** from the **Type** menu and observe how the Styles list box contains only PageMaker's standard default styles.

4. Click the **Import** button. When the Import styles dialog box appears, select the publication named **Visiting** that you created in Step-by-Step 15.3, and then click **Open**. (*NOTE: If an alert box containing the message Copy over existing styles? appears, click **OK**.*) By using the scroll box next to the Style list, observe how the list now contains the imported styles named Heading and Subheading.

5. Click **OK** to close the Define Styles dialog box.

6. Close this publication without saving it.

Overriding a Style

When you apply a style to a paragraph, all of the style's specifications are applied to all of the text in the paragraph. In some instances, however, you may want to override a style by choosing a different format for one or more words in a styled paragraph. For example, you may want to italicize a single word in a paragraph to which you have already applied a style. Changing the format for certain text within a styled paragraph is called *overriding a style*, also known as local formatting.

PageMaker provides two types of overrides: temporary and permanent. You create a temporary override whenever you apply any type specification, except a type style change (bold, underline, or italic) to a styled paragraph. For example, changing the font for one word within a styled paragraph will create a temporary override. If a paragraph contains an override, the formatting from that override disappears if you apply the same or a different style to the paragraph. In other words, any overriding style changes that you make to a styled paragraph, such as indents, alignment, typeface, or point size changes, are removed if you apply a different style to the paragraph.

A permanent override stays with the paragraph when you change its style. A permanent override is created whenever you apply any type style change such as bold, underline, or italic. For example, if you apply a style to a paragraph and then italicize one word within the paragraph, the word remains italicized if you apply a different style to the same paragraph.

Monitoring Overridden Styles

Whenever the insertion point is located within text, the name of the style applied to the text appears highlighted in the Styles palette. When a paragraph contains a temporary override, such as if you change the alignment from left to right, a plus sign (+) appears after the style name in the Styles palette (see Figure 15-4). When a paragraph contains a permanent override, such as if you underline one word, the plus sign (+) will appear after the style name, but only when the insertion point is located within the text that is creating the override or when that text is selected.

FIGURE 15-4
A plus sign follows overridden styles names

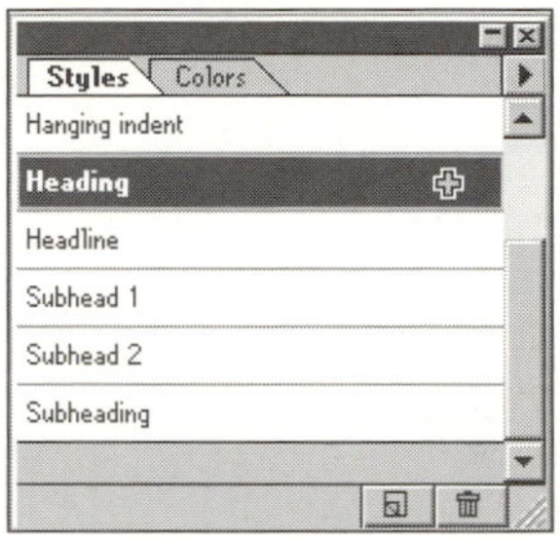

S TEP-BY-STEP 15.5

1. Begin a new publication. When the Document Setup dialog box appears, specify a **single-sided** publication containing a total of **two** pages.

2. Display the Styles palette, if necessary.

3. Click the **Text** tool and then click an insertion point slightly below the top margin guide and just to the right of the left margin guide.

4. Enlarge the area around the insertion point to **Actual Size**.

5. Key **Travel the Caribbean** and press **Enter.** Then, key **For Less Cost With** and press **Enter**. Finally, key **Caribbean Sun Travel Tours** (but *do not* press Enter).

6. Apply the style named **Headline** to the words **Travel the Caribbean**.

7. Apply the style named **Headline** to the words **For Less Cost With**.

8. Apply the style named **Subhead 1** to the words **Caribbean Sun Travel Tours**.

9. Place the insertion point anywhere in the entry that reads **For Less Cost With**. Notice in the Styles palette how the style name of the current paragraph (Headline) is highlighted.

10. Select the words **Less Cost** and then apply the underline type style to those selected words. Notice in the Styles palette how a plus sign (+) appears after the style name. *(NOTE: If a plus sign (+) does not appear in the Styles palette this feature may have been turned off by a previous user. To turn this feature on click on the right arrow button ▶ located in the upper-right corner of the Styles palette. Then if the Display Overridden Icons option is not preceded by a check mark, choose Display Overridden Icons.)*

11. Select the word **Caribbean** in the line of text that reads Travel the Caribbean and then change the size of the selected word to **36** points. Notice in the Styles palette how a plus sign (+) appears after the style name.

12. Select **For Less Cost With**. Then apply the style named **Subhead 1** to the entry. Notice how the words Less Cost remain underlined because of the permanent override.

13. Select **Travel the Caribbean**. Then apply the style named **Subhead 1** to the entry. Notice how all the words change to the same point size because of the prior temporary override.

14. Keep this publication on-screen for use in the next Step-by-Step.

Importing Text Files that Contain Styles

Although not difficult to do, applying styles to lengthy text files that you have imported can be a detailed and time-consuming process. To make your work easier, you can include style names in the original text files. Then, as you import the text file, PageMaker will automatically apply the correct styles to the appropriate text.

Importing Word Processing Styles

Like PageMaker, many popular word processing programs, such as Word and WordPerfect, have a built-in style feature. If you use such a word processing program, you can create and apply styles to your text like you can within PageMaker. Then, when you import the word-processing file into a publication, PageMaker will automatically style the text and add the styles from the text file into the Styles palette.

Importing Styles from Tags

If you don't know how to use the styles feature in your word processing program, or if you use a program that does not have such a feature, you can still tell PageMaker what styles you want applied to specific entries by adding tags to your word processing file. A *tag* is the name of a style from a PageMaker Styles palette that is surrounded with angled brackets (<>) and placed at the beginning of a paragraph. When you import a text file with tags into a publication, PageMaker will automatically apply the style whose name appears within the brackets to the paragraph that follows it. When consecutive paragraphs use the same style name, you need only to place the tag at the beginning of the first paragraph because PageMaker will continue to apply the style to all text until it locates the next style tag.

Figure 15-5 shows an example of how a tagged file would look in a word processing program. It contains three tagged paragraphs. When imported into a publication, PageMaker would apply the style named Title to the first paragraph, Subtitle to the second paragraph, and Body text to the third paragraph.

FIGURE 15-5
Tags in a word processing file

<Title>Sales Report
<Subtitle>Purpose
<Body text>The goal of the Sales Department at Caribbean Sun Travel
Tours is to increase the number of people who purchase services from
our firm. Our goals are to increase both the number of corporate and
individual customers who purchase our services.

Besides matching on upper- and lowercase, it's important to know that the style name appearing in the tag must be exactly the same as the one in PageMaker's Styles palette. For example, the tag <Subhead1> in a word processing file will not work correctly if the style name was actually Subhead 1 (with a space) in PageMaker's Styles palette.

Importing Styles with Your Text Files

You use a different procedure to import a text file that contains styles or tags than you do to simply import a text file. First, choose Place from the File menu, and then select the name of the text file that you want to import as you normally would. Then, deselect the Retain format option, and select the Read tags option before clicking on the Open button.

STEP-BY-STEP 15.6

1. Turn to the second page of the on-screen publication.

2. Enlarge the area around the top and left margin guides to **Actual Size**.

3. In a moment you will place a tagged text file into this publication. The tags in this file contain the default style names found in PageMaker's Styles palette. Figure 15-6 shows the complete text from this file. Review that figure now before going on to step 4.

4. Click the **Pointer** tool and then choose **Place** from the **File** menu.

STEP-BY-STEP 15.6 Continued

5. From the data files supplied with this book:

   a. Select the file named **Tagged.rtf**.

   b. If the Retain format option located near the bottom of the dialog box is already selected, deselect the **Retain format** option.

   c. Select the **Read tags** option.

   d. Click **Open**.

6. When the Text Placement icon appears, position the icon just below the top margin guide and slightly to the right of the left margin guide. Then click once to place this file into the publication. Observe how PageMaker has automatically applied various styles to the text.

7. Click the **Text** tool. Then, click an insertion point anywhere in the main title ENJOY THE CAYMAN ISLANDS and observe in the Styles palette how the Headline style is used for that entry.

8. Click an insertion point anywhere in the first paragraph located below the main title and observe in the Styles palette how the Body text style is used for that entry.

9. Save this publication under the name **Styled Report** and then close this publication.

FIGURE 15-6
Contents of the tagged file named Tagged.rtf

<Headline>ENJOY THE CAYMAN ISLANDS!
<Body text>Why not treat yourself to a memorable Caribbean Sun Travel Tour excursion to the Cayman Islands this winter. For almost 40 years this peaceful trio of Grand Cayman, Cayman Brac and Little Cayman, located in the quiet Western Caribbean, have been one the world's best diving and watersports destinations. Maybe that's why more turtles call Cayman their home than any other island in the world. Here are some things you might want to know.
<Subhead 1>Climate
<Body text>The Cayman Islands enjoy "eternal summer," because they're situated in the heart of the Caribbean tempered by cooling trade winds. Temperatures are coolest during February (72-86 degrees) and warmest (80-90 degrees) during July and August. Relative humidity varies from 68% to 92%. The water temperature ranges between 78-82 degrees in the winter and 82-86 degrees in the summer.
<Subhead 1>Language
<Body text>The official language of the Cayman Islands is English. Its Welsh, Scottish and English ancestors still add a distinguished sound to the speech of the Caymanian people.

SUMMARY

In this lesson, you learned how to:

■ Create new styles by specifying their individual settings.

■ Create a new style by using all the settings from an already formatted entry in a publication.

■ Import styles from one publication into a different publication.

■ Key style names or tags into a document that is created in a word-processing program and then import that document and its style tags.

■ Apply styles while using the story editor and override any style with a specific change for one or more entries.

VOCABULARY *Review*

Define the following terms:

Based on   Overriding a style   Tags

REVIEW *Questions*

TRUE / FALSE

Circle T if the statement is true or F if the statement is false.

T   F   **1.** You can apply a style to text while using the story editor.

T   F   **2.** A based-on style is a style based on a similar style in the publication.

T   F   **3.** You can use the story editor to find all paragraphs to which a certain style has been applied.

T   F   **4.** You can use the story editor to find all paragraphs to which a certain style has been applied and then replace that style with a different style.

T   F   **5.** While creating a based-on style, you can edit or add other specifications to the new style as you normally would for any other style.

T   F   **6.** PageMaker provides two types of overrides: temporary and permanent.

T   F   **7.** While using the story editor, the names of any styles applied to paragraphs can appear to the right of the paragraphs.

T   F   **8.** When a style has been overridden, a plus sign (+) appears after the name of the style in the Styles palette.

T   F   **9.** When importing styles into a publication from a different publication, you can select which styles to import.

T   F   **10.** A permanent override stays with the paragraph when you change its style.

FILL IN THE BLANK

Complete the following sentences by writing the correct word or words in the blanks provided.

1. A _____ is the name of a PageMaker style surrounded by angle brackets (< >) that is keyed at the beginning of a paragraph in a word-processing document and which will eventually be imported into a publication.

2. When creating similar styles, you can use a feature called _____ _____ to save time by creating one style that is based on all the specifications from a different style.

3. When viewing style names along the left side of the story editor window, the symbol _____ appears in place of a style name when no style has been applied to a certain paragraph.

4. Changing the format for certain text such as a word or phrase within a styled paragraph is called _____ a style.

5. You can use the story editor's _____ command to find out where (or if) a certain style was used in a story.

PROJECTS

SCANS **PROJECT 15-1**

1. Begin a new publication. When the Document Setup dialog box appears, specify a **single-sided** publication.

2. Click the **Text** tool, and then click an insertion point slightly below the top margin guide and just to the right of the left margin guide.

3. Enlarge the area around the insertion point to **Actual Size**.

4. Key **OUR SERVICES INCLUDE** in uppercase and then press **Enter** twice.

5. Key **Free travel insurance** and then press **Enter**.

6. Key **Discount airport parking** and then press **Enter**.

7. Key **Tickets delivered the next business day** and then press **Enter**.

8. Select the words **OUR SERVICES INCLUDE** and then change the selected text to **bold** in a 30-point size with **center alignment**.

9. Select the words **Tickets delivered the next business day** and then change the selected text to **italic** in an **18**-point size with **center alignment**.

10. Select the words **OUR SERVICES INCLUDE** and then create a new style called **Title** that uses all of the specifications used in the selected text.

11. Select the words **Tickets delivered the next business day** and then create a new style called **Benefits** that uses all of the specifications used in the selected text.

12. Apply the style named **Benefits** to the entry **Free travel insurance**.

13. Apply the style named **Benefits** to the entry **Discount airport parking**.

14. Save the publication with the name **Our services** and then close the publication.

SCANS PROJECT 15-2A

1. Begin a new publication. When the Document Setup dialog box appears, specify a **single-sided** publication.

2. Click the **Text** tool, and then click an insertion point slightly below the top margin guide and just to the right of the left margin guide.

3. Enlarge the area around the insertion point to **Actual Size**.

4. Key **CARIBBEAN SUN** and then press **Enter**.

5. Key **TRAVEL TOURS** and then press **Enter** twice.

6. Key the following lines of text and press **Enter** at the end of each line:
   Experienced staff
   Low priced fares
   Toll-free hotline number
   Caribbean specialists

7. Import all the styles from the publication named **Our services** into the current publication. (NOTE: *If an alert box containing the message Copy over existing styles? appears, click OK.*)

8. Apply the style named **Title** to the first two lines of text.

9. Apply the style named **Benefits** to all other lines of text in this publication.

10. Keep this publication on-screen and go on to Project 15-2B.

PROJECT 15-2B

1. In the publication from Project 15-2A, create a new style called **Lead-in**. As you do this, specify that this new style be based on the existing style named Benefits. Also, use the **Char** button to specify a **14**-point font size for the new style.

2. Close both the Style Options and Define Styles dialog boxes.

3. Keep this publication on-screen and go on to Project 15-2C.

PROJECT 15-2C

1. In the publication from Project 15-2B, click an insertion point anywhere in the existing text and then open the story editor.

2. Position the insertion point in the blank line located below the last line of text in the on-screen story and then press **Enter** to insert a new blank line.

3. Key the following paragraph:
   > **In the past twenty years of service to travelers around the world, Caribbean Sun Travel Tours has earned some of the highest travel awards. These include the Golden Travel Award from the National Travels Association and the Silver Award from the American Travelers Association.**

4. Select all of the text in the paragraph that you just keyed in step 3 and then apply the style named **Lead-in** to the selected text.

5. In the paragraph that you keyed in step 3, bold the words **Golden Travel Award**. Also bold the words **Silver Award**.

6. Close the story editor and then examine the publication to see the changes that were made by applying the different styles.

7. Print the publication. Save the publication under the name **About Us** and then close the publication.

SCANS 🤝 TEAMWORK PROJECT

Form a desktop publishing team by selecting a partner. Choose one partner who will work as the desktop publishing specialist and the other partner who will work as the word processing specialist. As the desktop publishing specialist, select a short 150-250 word article from a national newspaper or magazine containing a minimum of three different types of entries, such as a title, subheading and body text. Then, have your word processing partner begin keying the text from that article into a word processing document. While the word processing partner is keying the text, have the desktop publishing specialist create various style specifications for each of the different types of entries in the article. For each one, select a style name and then list the style specifications such as the typeface, point size, alignment and so on. When you finish, provide the word processing partner with the names of the styles to use for each entry in the article, and have that partner insert the appropriate style tags into the document. Then, as the desktop publishing specialist, create a new PageMaker publication containing the styles that you defined earlier and import the tagged word processing file into that publication. Do the results look like you expected? If not, figure out why.

CRITICAL *Thinking*

ACTIVITY 15-1

In this lesson you learned that you can easily import styles from one publication into another publication. Importing styles in this way saves time and is also an excellent way to ensure consistency between similar types of publications, such as publications that are produced on a daily or monthly basis. Take a few moments and list between five and ten publications that are produced on a regular basis, such as your local newspaper or a national magazine, and which, if you were producing them using PageMaker, you could do so by importing styles from previous versions of those publications.

ENHANCING PAGEMAKER DOCUMENTS

COMMAND SUMMARY

Note: Buttons marked with an asterisk (*) are found on the Control palette.

FEATURE	MENU COMMAND	KEYSTROKE	TOOLBAR BUTTON	LESSON
Indents/Tabs, Set or change	Type, Indents/Tabs	Ctrl+I	▸↓	9
Paragraph, Indent	Type, Indents/Tabs	Ctrl+I	▸↓	9
Bullet Entries	Utilities, Plug-ins, Bullets and numbering		▤	9
Align Text, Left	Type, Alignment, Align Left	Shift+Ctrl+L	* ▤	10
Align Text, Right	Type, Alignment, Align Right	Shift+Ctrl+R	* ▤	10
Align Text, Center	Type, Alignment, Align Center	Shift+Ctrl+C	* ▤	10
Align Text, Justify	Type, Alignment, Justify	Shift+Ctrl+J	* ▤	10
Align Text, Force Justify	Type, Alignment, Force Justify	Shift+Ctrl+F	* ▤	10
Leading, Specify	Type, Leading			10
Paragraph Spacing	Type, Paragraph	Ctrl+M	¶	10
Paragraph Indenting, Automatic	Type, Paragraph	Ctrl+M	¶	10
Kern Up 1/100th em		Alt+→	* ▣	10
Kern Down 1/100th em		Alt+←	* ▣	10
Kern Up 1/25th em		Ctrl+Alt+→	*Shift+ ▣	10
Kern Down 1/25th em		Ctrl+Alt+←	*Shift+ ▣	10
Tracking, Adjust	Type, Expert Tracking		No Track ▾	10
Character Width, Adjust	Type, Horizontal Scale		100% ▾	10
Hyphenation, Change	Type, Hyphenation			11
Hyphen, Insert Nonbreaking		Ctrl+Alt+-		11
En dash		Alt+-		11
En dash		Alt+Shift+-		11
Space, Nonbreaking		Ctrl+Alt+Spacebar		11

FEATURE	MENU COMMAND	KEYSTROKE	TOOLBAR BUTTON	LESSON
Ellipsis		Alt+0133		11
Slash, Nonbreaking		Ctrl+Alt+/		11
Quote, Open		Alt+Shift+[		11
Quote, Close		Alt+Shift+]		11
Quote, Open Double		Alt+[		11
Quote, Open Double		Alt+]		11
Send Object to Back	Element, Arrange, Send to Back	Shift+Ctrl+[		11
Send Object to Front	Element, Arrange, Bring to Front	Shift+Ctrl+]		12
Graphic, Import	File, Place	Ctrl+D	🖻	12
Graphic, Crop			🛱	
Graphic, Rotate			↻	12
Text Wrap, Control	Element, Text Wrap	Alt+Ctrl+E		13
Reflect Graphic, Horizontal			* ⊩⊣	13
Reflect Graphic, Vertical			* ⊩⊥	13
Skew Graphic			* ⟋ 0°	13
Mask Selected Graphics	Element, Mask	Ctrl+6		13
Resolution, Change Screen	File, Preferences, General	Ctrl+K		13
Styles palette, Show/Hide	Window, Show Styles	Ctrl+B		14
Styles, Create or Edit	Type, Define Styles	Ctrl+3		14
Styles, Import	Type, Define Styles, Import			15

REVIEW *Questions*

TRUE/FALSE

Circle T if the statement is true or F if the statement is false.

T   F   **1.** A Based-on style is a style based on a similar style in the publication.

T   F   **2.** A minus sign (−) appears after a style name in the Styles palette when that style has been overridden.

T   F   **3.** You cannot remove PageMaker's standard, default styles from a publication, such as the style named Headline or Subhead 1.

T   F   **4.** All the styles used in a publication are called a style sheet.

T   F   **5.** If you delete a style from a publication, any text to which that style has been applied is also removed from the publication.

T   F   **6.** You can create a maximum of 10 new styles in a publication.

T   F   **7.** A mask lets you crop a graphic image into any shape or design that you can create using PageMaker's drawing tools.

T   F   **8.** When customizing a graphic boundary, you can add a maximum of 10 diamond-shaped handles to the boundary.

T   F   **9.** Reflecting is a technique used to flip a graphic either horizontally or vertically.

T   F   **10.** In general, a picture of a person or an animal looks better if the person or animal is facing into the page.

T   F   **11.** The method a program uses to store its files on disk is called the file format.

T   F   **12.** You cannot rotate a graphic image more than 45 degrees.

T   F   **13.** To keep both the height and width proportional when changing the size of a graphic image, hold down the Shift key.

T   F   **14.** An em dash is used to show a pause or a break in a sentence.

T   F   **15.** Kerning is normally used only with text of 12 points or less.

FILL IN THE BLANKS

Complete the following sentences by writing the correct word or words in the blanks provided.

1. A _____ is the name of a PageMaker style surrounded by angle brackets (<>) that is keyed at the beginning of a paragraph in a word-processing document and which will eventually be imported into a publication.

2. When viewing style names along the left side of the story editor window, the symbol _____ appears in place of a style name when no style has been applied to a paragraph.

3. A collection of all the styles used in a publication is called a(n) _____ _____.

4. The name of a style can be up to _____ characters long.

5. All the styles available in a publication are listed in and selected from the _____ _____.

6. The distance that text is kept away from a graphic image is called the _____.

7. The technique used to slant a graphic image to the left or right is called _____.

8. A device that converts paper images, like photographs or drawings, into computer files is called a(n) _____.

9. The width of a line that surrounds a PageMaker created graphic, such as a rectangle, is referred to as the _____.

10. The term _____ means to cut off or remove an unwanted portion of a graphic image.

11. You use a(n) _____ dash before the name of an author at the end of a quotation.

12. _____ is the ellipsis character symbol.

13. The width of the letter *m* in the current font is called the _____ space.

14. In typography, a good rule of thumb is to separate paragraphs with between one-half and _____ line of space.

15. The indent method where each line of the paragraph including the first moves inward away from the left and right edges of the text block is called _____ .

SIMULATION

INTRODUCTION

In the past several lessons, you have learned many new ways to improve the appearance of your publications. In this simulation, you will create a brochure for Caribbean Sun Travel Tours. The purpose of this simulation is to help you practice your new skills. As you work on this assignment remember that the fonts you have available will vary based on the computer you are using. If your computer does not have a particular font called for in this simulation, select a similar font. Because of these font differences, your final publication might not look exactly the same as the examples shown throughout this simulation, but it should look similar.

Before doing any work on the computer, review the entire assignment first. Read all the pages and study their contents before you begin. Then, as you start to create the publication, work smart by saving your work regularly (every 10 to 20 minutes). When you save this publication on disk, name it **Travel Brochure**.

BACKGROUND

Caribbean Sun Travel Tours conducts over 100 tours to Caribbean destinations annually. In the past, they have used word-processing programs to prepare one-page information sheets describing each upcoming tour. Although these information sheets offer potential customers the essential information about each tour, their keyed appearance often makes them look boring and unprofessional.

To solve this problem, the company has decided to use PageMaker to produce a number of similar brochures describing tours to some of its more popular destinations. These brochures will be produced on standard, letter-size paper and, for visual interest, they will contain a variety of font sizes and graphics.

The following information contains the specifications for the first of these brochures, describing an upcoming tour to St. Thomas. Your job is to create this brochure.

GENERAL INSTRUCTIONS

You are acting as the PageMaker designer of Caribbean Sun Travel Tours. The brochure you will be creating will be two pages long and printed on letter-size (8.5 by 11 inch) paper using wide (landscape) orientation. These two printed pages will be sent to a commercial printer where the final brochure will be printed on both sides of a single sheet of paper and then folded into thirds.

Remember, begin by reading over the entire project. Study the full page sample of each completed page of the brochure that appears on the opposite page of the instructions for that page. Refer to these samples if you have any question on the layout or the content.

THUMBNAILS

To give you a general idea of how the final project will look, Figure UR-1 shows thumbnails of both pages in the completed brochure. These thumbnails are provided to give you an idea of what the project is all about. Don't worry about having difficulty reading the words. A full page figure from which you will be keying accompanies each page.

FIGURE UR-1
Thumbnails of the completed travel brochure

Page one

Page two

INSTRUCTIONS

The remaining pages of this simulation provide specific instructions on the overall project and the individual pages of the brochure. Review this material carefully for information on the exact layout required for each page.

Publication Setup

As you complete the Document Setup dialog box when creating this publication, specify a single-sided publication that uses standard, letter-size paper with Wide (landscape) orientation and that contains a total of 2 pages. Also specify the following margin settings:

Left: 0.35 inches
Right: 0.35 inches
Top: 0.75 inches
Bottom: 0.75 inches

Collecting the Resources Needed for this Project

The text files and graphic images needed for this brochure have been created for you and can be found on the data disk that accompanies this book. The complete listing of the files you will use in this project and information on where those files are used in the publication are detailed in Table UR-1.

TABLE UR-1
Files used in simulation

FILE NAME	TYPE	WHERE USED	DESCRIPTION
Thomas.tif	Graphic	Page 1, right panel	Beach picture
Carsun-logo.tif	Graphic	Page 1, middle panel	Caribbean Sun Travel Tours logo
Thomas-1.rtf	Text	Page 1, left panel	Contains all text that appears in this panel
Carsun.tif	Graphic	Page 2, middle/right panel	Illustration of sun and palm tree
Thomas-2.rtf	Text	Page 2, left panel	Contains all text that appears in this panel

The Text

Notice that all the text in this brochure uses a serif font. For this publication, select a serif font such as Times New Roman or Times Roman. Notice also that all titles and headings appear in bold and in a larger point size than the rest of the text. Except for keying the text that appears on the cover of the brochure (the panel that contains the words An Island You ...) all the other text needed for this brochure will come from text files that you will place into this publication.

Assembling the Brochure

When you finish printing both pages of this publication, you will assemble a mock-up of the final brochure. To do so, glue or tape the two pages back to back with the text and graphics facing outward. Then fold the paper into three, equal-size panels as shown in Figure UR-2.

FIGURE UR-2
How to fold the completed travel brochure

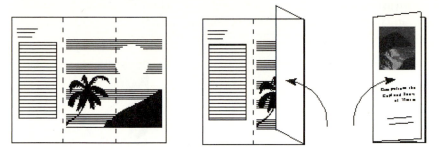

Description—Master Page

You use the master page as shown in Figure UR-3 to add columns to this publication. Because this brochure contains three panels on each page, you can then use those columns to hold the text and/or graphics needed for each panel.

Specifications

1. While viewing the master page, use the Column Guides dialog box to add three columns to all pages in the publication, and specify that there be 0.3 inches of space between each column.

2. Turn to page 1 in the publication to begin creating the brochure.

FIGURE UR-3
The Master page

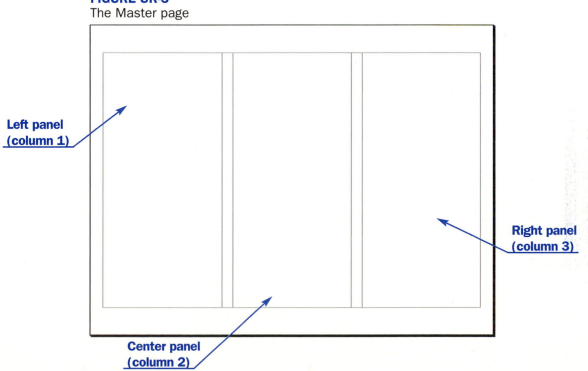

Left panel (column 1)

Right panel (column 3)

Center panel (column 2)

Description—Page 1

As shown in Figure UR-4, the first page contains three elements: the brochure cover (in the right panel), the company logo (in the center panel), and text containing general information about the company (in the left panel). For the right-hand panel, you will import a graphic file and then add several lines of text. For the center panel, you will import a graphic file. For the left-hand panel you place a text file containing the company description.

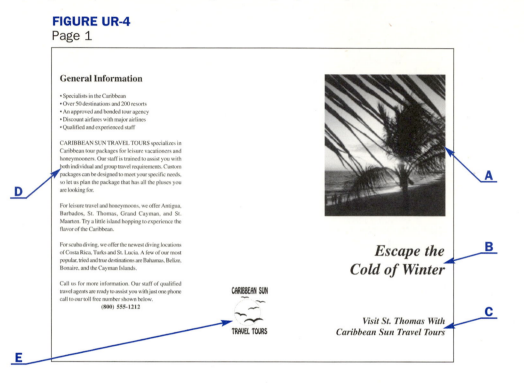

FIGURE UR-4
Page 1

Specifications

Directions for the right panel (column 3)

1. Begin by placing the graphic image (A) named **Thomas.tif** into a blank area of the upper right panel. Then resize the graphic proportionally so that it fits within the column guides for the right column. Finally, drag the picture so that the top of the picture falls on the top margin guide.

2. In the pasteboard or a blank area of the page, key the words **Escape the**. Then key the words **Cold of Winter** to create the title (B). Next select this text and change it to right alignment and a serif font in a 30-point size with both the bold and italic type styles. Finally, drag the text into the right-hand column so that it begins roughly 0.75 inches below the picture and aligns at the right margin guide.

3. In the pasteboard or a blank area of the page, key the words **Visit St. Thomas With** and press **Enter**. Then key the words **Caribbean Sun Travel Tours** to create the subtitle (C). Next, select this text and change it to right alignment and a serif font in an 18-point size with both the bold and italic type styles. Finally, drag the text into the right-hand column so that the last line of text aligns on both the bottom and right margin guides.

Directions for the center panel (column 2)

1. While using the **Pointer** tool, place the graphic image named **Carsun-logo.tif** (E) anywhere in the center panel.

2. Resize the graphic proportionally so that it is roughly one inch wide (use the on-screen rulers for reference). Then drag the graphic so that it is centered within the column and the bottom of the graphic aligns on the bottom margin guide.

Directions for the left panel (column 1)

1. Place the text file named **Thomas-1.rtf** (D) into the left panel.

2. Now change the type specifications for this text. The title *General Information* should appear in a serif font, an 18-point font size, and bold. All other text should appear in a serif font in an 11.5-point size with 15 points of leading. Also, the telephone number at the bottom should appear in bold with center alignment.

3. Turn to page 2 in the publication to continue creating the brochure.

Description—Page 2

As shown in Figure UR-5, the second page contains two elements: a large illustration, which fills both the center and the right-hand panels, and text containing information about the tour to St. Thomas, in the left-hand panel. For the illustration, you will import a graphic file and enlarge its size so that it spans both the right and center panel. For the left-hand panel, you will place a text file containing the tour description.

FIGURE UR-5
Page 2

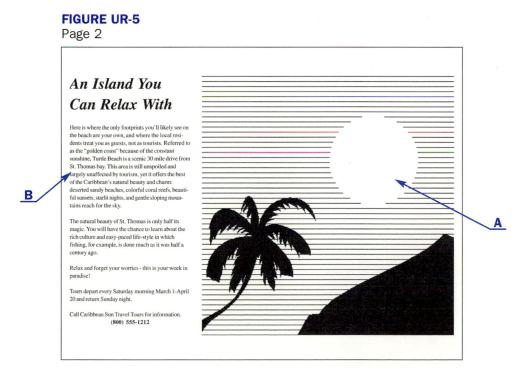

Specifications

Directions for the right and center panels (columns 3 and 2):

1. Begin by placing the graphic image named **Carsun.tif** (A) into a blank area of the page.

2. Resize the graphic proportionally so that it spans both the center and right panels, and then drag the graphic into position.

Directions for the left panel (column 1):

1. Place the text file named **Thomas-2.rtf** (B) into the left panel.

2. Now change the type specifications for this text. The two-line title *An Island You ...* should appear in a serif font, a 30-point font size with 40 points of leading, and bold. All other text should appear in a serif font, an 11.5-point size with 15 points of leading, except for the telephone number at the bottom of the column. This text should be centered in the column and bold.

COMMENTS/TIPS

When you finish this brochure save it with the name **Travel Brochure** and then print both pages. Your solution should look similar to those shown in Figures UR-6 and UR-7. Next, tape or glue the pages back to back and with the print facing outward. Finally, fold the brochure as described earlier.

FIGURE UR-6
Travel Brochure—Page 1 (shown reduced 40%)

Escape the Cold of Winter

Visit St. Thomas With Caribbean Sun Travel Tours

CARIBBEAN SUN

TRAVEL TOURS

General Information

- Specialists in the Caribbean
- Over 50 destinations and 200 resorts
- An approved and bonded tour agency
- Discount airfares with major airlines
- Qualified and experienced staff

CARIBBEAN SUN TRAVEL TOURS specializes in Caribbean tour packages for leisure vacationers and honeymooners. Our staff is trained to assist you with both individual and group travel requirements. Custom packages can be designed to meet your specific needs, so let us plan the package that has all the pluses you are looking for.

For leisure travel and honeymoons, we offer Antigua, Barbados, St. Thomas, Grand Cayman, and St. Maarten. Try a little island hopping to experience the flavor of the Caribbean.

For scuba diving, we offer the newest diving locations of Costa Rica, Turks and St. Lucia. A few of our most popular, tried and true destinations are Bahamas, Belize, Bonaire, and the Cayman Islands.

Call us for more information. Our staff of qualified travel agents are ready to assist you with just one phone call to our toll free number shown below.

(800) 555-1212

FIGURE UR-7
Travel Brochure—Page 2 (shown reduced 40%)

An Island You Can Relax With

Here is where the only footprints you'll likely see on the beach are your own, and where the local residents treat you as guests, not as tourists. Referred to as the "golden coast" because of the constant sunshine, Turtle Beach is a scenic 30 mile drive from St. Thomas bay. This area is still unspoiled and largely unaffected by tourism, yet it offers the best of the Caribbean's natural beauty and charm: deserted sandy beaches, colorful coral reefs, beautiful sunsets, starlit nights, and gentle sloping mountains reach for the sky.

The natural beauty of St. Thomas is only half its magic. You will have the chance to learn about the rich culture and easy-paced life-style in which fishing, for example, is done much as it was half a century ago.

Relax and forget your worries - this is your week in paradise!

Tours depart every Saturday morning March 1-April 20 and return Sunday night.

Call Caribbean Sun Travel Tours for information.
(800) 555-1212

ADVANCED FEATURES

Unit 3

🕐 **Estimated Time for Unit: 19 hours**

WORKING WITH LARGE PUBLICATIONS

OBJECTIVES

Upon completion of this lesson, you should be able to:

- Define an index and explain various types of index entries.

- Mark and unmark index entries and generate an index.

- Define a table of contents.

- Mark and unmark table of contents entries and generate a table of contents.

- Use PageMaker's book feature to create a large publication from smaller publications.

Estimated Time: 4.5 hours

VOCABULARY

Book

Book list

Cross-reference

Index

Index entry

Index subentry

Marking an index entry

Phrase

Table of contents

Introduction

With PageMaker it's easy to create indexes and tables of contents for your publications. To do so, you simply identify which words you want included and the program creates an alphabetical index or a table of contents in page-number order. You can also create large publications by linking two or more smaller publications together. Temporarily joining publications offers the same advantages of a large publication, such as consecutive page numbering and automatic indexing, with the speed and ease of use that you experience when working with smaller publications.

Understanding Indexes

In multi-page publications, such as reports, booklets, proposals, and books, indexes are valuable ways to help the reader find information quickly. An *index* is an alphabetical listing of key words, phrases, or topics within a publication that includes the page numbers on which those items are found.

In a document produced with a word-processing program that lacks an indexing feature, creating an index is difficult because it must be done manually. First, you must search through each page of the text for the words you want to index, making a written note of each word and the page on which it is found. Next, you alphabetize the list of words and then key the entire list of words and the page numbers on which they are found. Later, if you make major editing changes to the document, you need to review and possibly update the index with any page number changes.

PageMaker makes it easy to create and maintain various types of indexes, such as the one shown in Figure 16-1. You simply identify in the publication those words that you want included in the index. When you finish, the program automatically creates an alphabetical list of those words and the page number(s) on which they are found in the publication. More importantly, if you later edit the text in the publication, you can quickly create a new index that reflects the latest updated page numbers.

FIGURE 16-1
Example of an index

INDEX

A
Accessories, 27–29
Adjusting text, 117, 119–121
Autoflow, 150

B
Baseline
  aligning, 323–341
  measuring, 361

To create an index within a publication, you first read through the on-screen pages looking for those words that you want included in the index. When you find an entry to index, first select the entry and then issue the command that identifies it as an index entry.

With PageMaker's index feature, you can create two-level indexes, that is, an index containing both index entries and subentries. An *index entry* is a major subject or topic in an index. An *index subentry* is an entry that is part of a major subject or topic. The following index contains only index entries and the page numbers on which those entries are found.

C
Computers 1–3, 10

D
Data 2, 7
Disks 12, 18–21

By comparison, the following index contains both index entries, such as the entry for *Computer* or *Disks;* and subentries, such as *mainframe* or *floppy.*

C
Computers
      mainframe 1
      mini 2–3
      personal 10

D
Data 2, 7
Disks
      floppy 12
      hard 18–21

Assume for a moment that these two indexes just shown were from information in the same book. Both indexes tell you that information on a topic such as data is found on pages 2 and 7. Likewise, both indexes show that information about computers is found on pages 1–3 and 10. An index that contains subentries can be more useful to the reader, however, when a particular topic can be broken into various subtopics. For example, the second index example shows that information on minicomputers is found on pages 2–3, personal computers on page 10, and so on. If a topic is self-contained, it is appropriate to create it simply as an index entry. Otherwise, it is better to divide the entry into subentries, one for each topic that's discussed in depth. Indexes containing subentries usually take longer to create, but this type of index is generally more useful to readers because it helps them find the information they seek faster.

When you finish identifying all the index entries that you want included in the index, place the insertion point where you want the index to appear—usually at the end of the publication— and then issue the command to create the index.

Marking the Entry

Any index entry can consist of a single word or a *phrase*. A phrase is two or more consecutive words, such as the words *personal computers*. Identifying a word or phrase that you want included in the index is called **marking an index entry**. You can mark your index entries while using the story editor or while in the layout view. To mark a word or phrase, select the entry as you normally would with the Text tool and then choose Index Entry from the Utilities menu. This command displays a dialog box similar to the one shown in Figure 16-2.

FIGURE 16-2
Example of an Add Index Entry dialog box

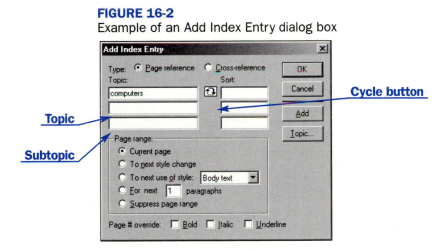

When the dialog box first appears, the word or phrase that you marked is shown in the Topic text box. Because indexing is case sensitive, the program displays the word in the Topic text box exactly as it is spelled in the publication. For example, if you index the word *computers* on one page and then the word *Computers* on a different page, the resulting index would contain two different entries; one labeled *Computers* and the other labeled *computers*. You can reword an index entry by rekeying it in the Topic text box. For example, you could change the word *computers* to *Computers* by rekeying the first character. Or, if you had originally selected the phrase *personal computers*, you could change the entry to *computers, personal*. Changing the entry in the Topic text box does not change how it appears in the publication, only how it will appear in the index.

You can use the Subtopic text box to identify an entry as a subtopic of a different index entry. For example, if the word *Computer* appears in the Topic text box, you could further identify that entry for the reader by keying a subtopic, such as *personal computers,* in the Subtopic text box. You can also move the entry that appears in the Topic text box to the Subtopic text by clicking the Cycle button (see Figure 16-2).

To finish marking an index entry, click OK. If you are using the story editor, an index marker like the one shown in Figure 16-3 will appear just in front of the word or phrase that you just marked. If you are using the layout view, the word or phrase will appear as it normally does. Then, continue marking all index entries and subentries in the publication that you want indexed.

FIGURE 16-3
An Index Marker

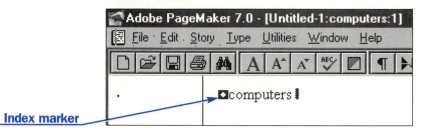

Index marker

STEP-BY-STEP 16.1

1. Begin a new publication. When the Document Setup dialog box appears, specify a **single-sided** publication.

2. Start the story editor. Then, key the following three lines of text and press **Enter** at the end of each line.
   Using Tables of Contents
   Introduction
   An index is a listing of key words, phrases, or topics within a publication.

3. In the last line of text that you just keyed, select the word **index**. Next, choose **Index Entry** from the **Utilities** menu. Notice how the word *index* appears in the Topic text box. Finally, choose **OK** to close the dialog box.

4. Click anywhere in the story editor window to deselect the word *index* and then notice how an index marker appears in front of the word *index*.

5. Select the word **publication**. Next, choose **Index Entry** from the **Utilities** menu and then choose **OK**.

6. Select the word **phrases**, and then choose **Index Entry** from the **Utilities** menu. Again, notice how the word *phrases* appears in the Topic text box. To identify *phrases* as a subtopic of the word *index*, first click the **Cycle** button (as shown in Figure 16-2). Next, inside the first (top) Topic text box, key **index** and then click **OK**. Finally, click anywhere in the story editor window to deselect the word *phrases*.

STEP-BY-STEP 16.1 Continued

7. Place the text from the story editor into the publication. When the Text Placement icon appears, position it just below the top margin guide and slightly to the right of the left margin guide, and then click. Then, click the **Pointer** tool to remove the windowshades from the text block.

8. Keep this publication on-screen for use in the next Step-by-Step.

Unmarking an Index Entry

As mentioned earlier, when you mark an index entry, PageMaker inserts an index marker. To unmark (remove) an index entry, locate the index marker in the story editor, and then delete it as you would any other character.

Creating the Index

After you have marked all the key words and phrases to index, you are almost ready to create the index. But first you need to decide where the index will appear in the publication. Normally indexes appear at the end of a publication, although they sometimes fall on the last page of text, if space permits. After deciding, turn to the page in the publication where you want the index to appear.

Next, choose Create Index from the Utilities menu to display the Create Index dialog box shown in Figure 16-4. The text box labeled Title shows the title PageMaker will display at the top of the index. Although the word *Index* appears by default, you can replace this word with any other word or phrase.

FIGURE 16-4
Create Index dialog box

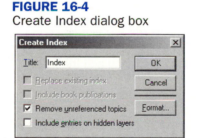

The Create Index dialog box contains four options. The Replace existing index option is available only after you have created an index in a publication, and when you want to update the index with new entries. The Include book publications option is available only if you are creating an index for a group of publications (discussed later in this lesson). The Remove unreferenced topics option removes any topics from the index that are not referenced with a page number. The Include entries on hidden layers option is an advanced feature used only in publications that contain layers (not discussed in this book). To create the index, select one of these options, if appropriate, and then click OK. After a short pause, a Text Placement icon appears. Place the icon where you want the index to appear and then click.

> **Hot Tip**
>
> If you are creating an index for a large publication, turn on the Autoflow feature before you issue the Create Index command. This way, as PageMaker creates the index, it will automatically insert as many new pages into the publication as needed to hold all the index entries.

STEP-BY-STEP 16.2

1. Insert one new page into the publication that will be used to hold the index.

2. Choose **Create Index** from the **Utilities** menu and then click **OK**. When the Text Placement icon appears, place the icon just below the top margin guide and slightly to the right of the left margin guide on the new page you just inserted, and then click.

3. Using the Actual Size, examine the topic and subtopic index. Keep this publication on-screen for use in the next Step-by-Step.

Editing Documents with Indexes

PageMaker does not automatically update page numbers in an indexed publication. If you edit a publication that also contains an index, it is important to update the index when you finish editing to make certain that the page numbers in the index are correct.

To update an index, turn to the page containing the index. Next, choose Create Index from the Utilities menu. When the Create Index dialog box appears, make certain that the Replace existing index option is selected, and then choose OK. After a short pause, the newly updated index will appear.

STEP-BY-STEP 16.3

1. Turn to the first page in this publication and enlarge the area around the text to **Actual Size**.

2. In the third line of text, select the words **key words**.

3. Choose **Index Entry** from the **Utilities** menu and then click **OK**.

4. Turn to the second page in this publication.

5. Choose **Create Index** from the **Utilities** menu. Next, make certain the Replace existing index option is selected, and then click **OK**.

6. Change to Actual Size if needed and notice how the new entry *key words* appears in the index. Keep this publication on-screen for use in the next Step-by-Step.

Creating a Cross Reference

A *cross-reference* is an index entry that refers the reader to a different and related index entry instead of to a specific page number. For example, suppose that a publication contained numerous entries regarding personal computers. Suppose that you indexed dozens of entries in a publication containing the phrase *Personal Computers*. Although many readers would look for that information in the index under Personal Computers, others might look instead under *Computers*. In a situation like this, you could create a cross-reference index entry, such as *Computers, see Personal Computers*.

You create a cross-reference entry in much the same way as you do an index entry. Because cross-reference entries do not reference a page number, however, it is not always necessary to select an entry in the publication to include it as a cross-reference entry in the index.

If the word or phrase that you want to cross-reference is in the publication, select the entry and then choose Index Entry from the Utilities menu. If the word or phrase to cross-reference is not in the publication, make certain that no word/phrase is selected and then choose Index Entry from the Utilities menu. When the Add Index Entry dialog box appears, select Cross-reference to reveal various Denoted by section options (see Figure 16-5).

FIGURE 16-5
Add Index Entry dialog box – cross-reference options

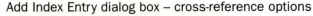

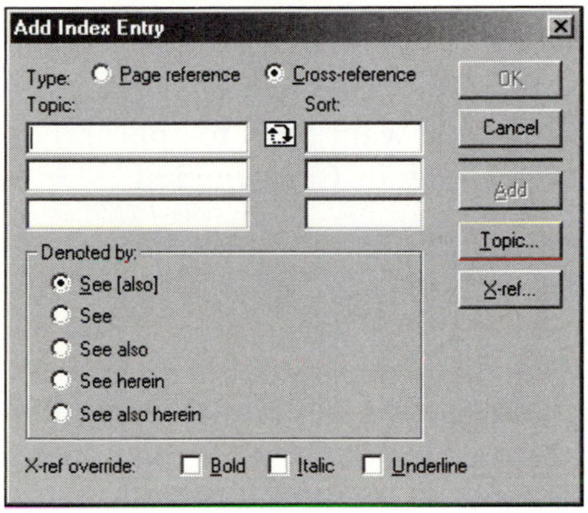

The Denoted by section of the dialog box lists the different types of cross-reference formats available, such as *See* or *See also*. In this section, select the format that you want to use. Next, identify the topic that you want to cross-reference for the reader. If you previously selected a word from the text, this word will appear in the Topic text box. Otherwise, key the word (or phrase). Then click the X-ref button to display the Select Cross-Reference Topic dialog box. Now key the topic name to which the reader will be referred, or select the topic from a list of topics that you have already added to the index. Finally, click OK to close the Select Cross-Reference Topic dialog box, and then click OK again to close the Add Index Entry dialog box.

STEP-BY-STEP 16.4

1. Turn to page 1 in this publication and then enlarge the text to the **Actual Size**, if needed.

2. Select the words *key words*.

3. Choose **Index Entry** from the **Utilities** menu. Then, select the **Cross-reference** option and click on the **X-ref** button. Now, key **phrases** and as you key, observe how the word appears in the first Topic text box. When finished, click **OK** to close the Select Cross-Reference Topic dialog box, and then click **OK** to close the Add Index Entry dialog box.

STEP-BY-STEP 16.4 Continued

4. Turn to page 2 in the publication. Then, choose **Create Index** from the **Utilities** menu. Next, make certain the **Replace existing index** option is selected and then click **OK**.

5. Using the Actual Size, notice how the new cross-reference entry appears in the index. Keep this publication on-screen for use in the next Step-by-Step.

Tips on Indexing

Although it is not difficult to create an index, producing a useful index takes some planning and thought. Here are some suggestions to help.

■ Index consistently. Keep a written list of the words you are indexing, not only to remember them but also to remember how you want them to appear. For example, decide if you want the topic in the index to be *Computer* or *Computers*.

■ Consider breaking long index entries into subtopics whenever possible. Look at the following index entry:

> Personal computers, 12–42

If you were trying to locate information on personal computer keyboards, for example, you would have no way of knowing which of those 30 pages, if any, contained the material you want. Using subtopics in an index can make information easier to locate and is a courtesy to the reader. Now look at the same entry broken into subtopics:

> Personal computers
>
> > caring for, 21
> >
> > keyboards, 18
> >
> > floppy disks, 24
> >
> > programs, 36–39

■ If it will help the reader, index the word or phrase in various ways. To find information about personal computers in an index, for example, some people might look under *personal computers* while others might look under *computers, personal,* and a third group might look under *PC*. You can index the same word or phrase several times, or use cross-references to create different index entries.

Understanding a Table of Contents

Like an index, a table of contents is used in publications to help the reader locate information. As shown in Figure 16-6, a *table of contents* is a listing of the major entries in a publication. A table of contents contains the title of sections and/or subsections of the publication and the page numbers on which each of these sections begins.

FIGURE 16-6
Example of a table of contents

Contents

Introduction to Desktop Publishing 1
Desktop Publishing versus Typesetting 1
Traditional Methods 3
Desktop Publishing Methods 6

Understanding Typography 8
Measuring Type 9
Understanding Fonts 12
Measuring Type 17

PageMaker makes it easy to create a table of contents. In fact, in many ways, it's even easier to create a table of contents than it is to create an index. You simply apply a style (such as one of PageMaker's default styles or a style that you create) to each entry that you want included in the table of contents. Then, when you issue a specific command, PageMaker automatically creates the table of contents from the entries you indicated and identifies the page number on which those entries are found. And, like indexes, if you edit the text in a publication, you can quickly create a new table of contents that reflects any changes to the publication.

Understanding Levels in a Table of Contents

Titles or sections within a publication are normally arranged in levels. In a book, for example, each lesson has a main title, and the sections within the lesson are identified with subtitles. With PageMaker, a table of contents can have many levels: a first level for major entries, such as the names of lessons; a second level for subsections; and so on. Look again at Figure 16-6. The section titled Introduction to Desktop Publishing is an example of a first-level entry, while the next three entries, Desktop Publishing versus Typesetting, Traditional Methods, and Desktop-Publishing Methods are each examples of second-level entries.

Creating a Table of Contents

To create a table of contents, first identify each of the entries in the publication that you want included. Next, determine where in the publication you want the table of contents to appear. And finally, issue the command to create the table of contents.

Identify the Contents Entry

Unlike indexing, you apply a style to each entry that you want included in the table of contents. First, identify the styles that you want to use for each level within the table of contents. PageMaker comes with three default styles that you can use for identifying table of contents entries. These include the styles named Headline for a publication title; Subhead 1 for a section title; and Subhead 2 for a subtitle. *NOTE: You can also create one or more styles to use for identifying table of contents entries. When creating these styles, however, identify them as table of contents styles by clicking the Para button and then selecting Include in table of contents.*

After identifying the style(s) that you want to use, apply the appropriate style to each table of contents entry in the publication. For example, to identify a title as a first-level entry by using the Headline style, click anywhere in the title and then choose Headline from the Styles palette. Remember that a major heading or title is a level-one entry, an entry within that is a level-two entry, and so on.

Continue applying styles to all table of contents entries in the publication. Remember to use the same style for the same level number of entry, such as the Subhead 1 style for each level-two entry.

Creating the Table of Contents

After you have applied a style to each table of contents entry, you are ready to create the table of contents. First, decide where the table of contents will appear. Normally, a table of contents appears on its own page and at the beginning of a publication, although it can fall on the first page of text, if space permits. To follow this format, turn to the page (or insert the page) where you want the contents to appear.

Next, choose Create TOC from the Utilities menu to display the Create Table of Contents dialog box shown in Figure 16-7. The Title text box contains the entry that will appear as the heading for the table of contents. Although the title *Contents* appears as the default, you can replace this word with any other text, if you wish.

FIGURE 16-7
Create Table of Contents dialog box

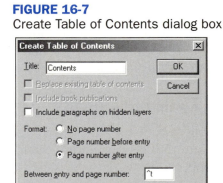

The Table of Contents dialog box also contains various options. The Replace existing table of contents option is available only after you have created a table of contents in the publication. By selecting this option, PageMaker will automatically update an existing table of contents with your latest changes. The Include book publications option is available only if you are creating a table of contents for a group of publications (discussed later in this lesson). The Include paragraphs on hidden layers option is an advanced feature used only in publications that contain layers (not discussed in this book). You can also select one of the three Format options (see Figure 16-7) to indicate where or if you want page numbers. When you finish, click OK. After a short pause, a Text Placement icon appears. Place the icon where you want the table of contents to begin, and then click to insert the table of contents. Also, you can select the text in a table of contents and change its font specifications to better fit the publication, if needed.

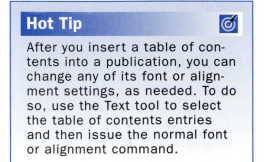

Hot Tip

After you insert a table of contents into a publication, you can change any of its font or alignment settings, as needed. To do so, use the Text tool to select the table of contents entries and then issue the normal font or alignment command.

S TEP-BY-STEP 16.5

1. Display the Styles palette, if necessary.

2. Turn to the first page in the publication.

3. Using the Text tool, click once anywhere in the line of text that reads *Using Tables of Contents*, and then click **Subhead 1** in the Styles palette.

4. Using the Text tool, click once anywhere in the word *Introduction*, and then click **Subhead 2** in the Styles palette.

5. Insert **one page** before the current page in this publication.

6. When the newly inserted page appears, choose **Create TOC** from the **Utilities** menu.

7. Observe how the default title *Contents* appears in the dialog box. Then, key **Table of Contents** to create a different title and click **OK**.

8. When the Text Placement icon appears, place the icon just below the top margin guide and slightly to the right of the left margin guide, and then click.

9. Using the Actual Size, examine the newly created table of contents.

10. Print all pages in the publication.

11. Save the publication under the name **Index-contents** and then close the publication.

Creating Books from Multiple Publications

At times, you may need to create large publications, such as a 100-page report or a 400-page book. Although such a large document could be created within one publication, it is often easier to break the material into several smaller, more easily managed publications. Unfortunately, creating a large publication from several smaller ones can pose many problems, such as numbering the pages correctly on the printouts, creating a table of contents or index, and so on.

PageMaker's book feature lets you create a large publication from many smaller publications. A *book* is a method for associating or identifying two or more publications as part of a single, larger publication. With this feature, you can continue to work with each small publication like normal, but you can ask PageMaker to treat all of the smaller publications as if they were one large publication for such tasks as printing, preparing a table of contents or an index.

Working with Books

A *book list* is an ordered list of the names of publications that make up the book. The order in which the publications appear in the book list determines the order in which they appear in the larger publication and, as a result, also determines the page number order. Thus, it is important to list publications in a book list in proper sequence, so that the page numbers and index entries are correct.

Creating a Book List

You create a book list in one of the publications that will be included in the book. Generally, it's easiest to create this list in the first publication that you want included in the book, such as the one containing the first lesson or the first section. If you consistently follow this procedure, it's easy to remember in which publication your book list appears.

After opening the publication in which you want to create the book list, choose Book from the Utilities menu. This command reveals a Book Publication List dialog box, such as the one in Figure 16-8.

FIGURE 16-8
Book Publication List dialog box

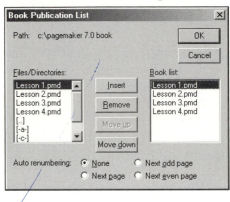

Next, use the Files/Directories list box to select, in order, those publication files that you want included in the book list. To add a file, click its name and then choose Insert. (Use the list box also to select a different disk drive or folder, if needed.) As you select the files to include, they will appear in the Book list text box. To remove a file that you added by mistake, click the file name in the Book list and then choose Remove. To move a file to a different position in the book list, click its name and then choose Move up or Move down.

Next, select an Auto renumbering option to specify how you want the pages numbered in the book. Choose Next page if you want all the pages numbered consecutively. For example, if the first publication ends on page 14, the second publication will begin on page 15. Choose Next odd page or Next even page to have the first page of each publication always begin on an odd or even page number. (PageMaker will insert a blank page at the end of the previous publication, if needed, to make certain that the next publication in the book starts on an odd or even page number.) Or, choose None if you want each publication to retain its own page numbering. *NOTE: Selecting an Auto Renumbering option does not add numbers to any publications that do not already have their own page-number markers.*

When you finish selecting all the files to include in the book, click OK. If you selected one of the Auto renumbering options, choose Yes when an alert box containing the message *Auto renumbering is selected* appears.

When the publication window reappears, your on-screen publication will still contain the same number of pages that it did before you added the book list. All the pages from each publication that appears in the book list, however, will be used whenever you create an index or table of contents, or when you print the entire publication.

Printing a Book

To print a book, open the publication containing the book list and then choose Print from the File menu. Next, select the Print all publications in book option, and then click Print.

STEP-BY-STEP 16.6

1. From the data files that accompany this book, open the publication named **Travel Guide**. Observe how this book contains only one numbered page.

2. Choose **Book** from the **Utilities** menu.

3. Using the Folders/Directories list box, navigate to the disk/folder in which the data files that are provided with this book are stored. Then, click on the publication named **Page 1** and click **Insert**. Then, following the same instructions, insert the file named **Page 2**, and finally, insert the file named **Page 3**.

4. Select **Next page** to request that all the pages from each publication be numbered sequentially, and then click **OK**.

5. When the alert box containing the message *Auto renumbering is selected* appears, click **Yes**. (*NOTE: When the publication reappears, it will still contain only one numbered page.*)

6. Choose **Print** from the **File** menu, select the **Print all publications in book** option, and then click **Print**. When finished printing, the book should contain the four numbered pages shown in Figure 16-9.

7. Use the Save as command to save this publication under the name **Cayman Travel Guide** and then close the publication.

FIGURE 16-9
Sample solution to the Cayman Travel Guide publication

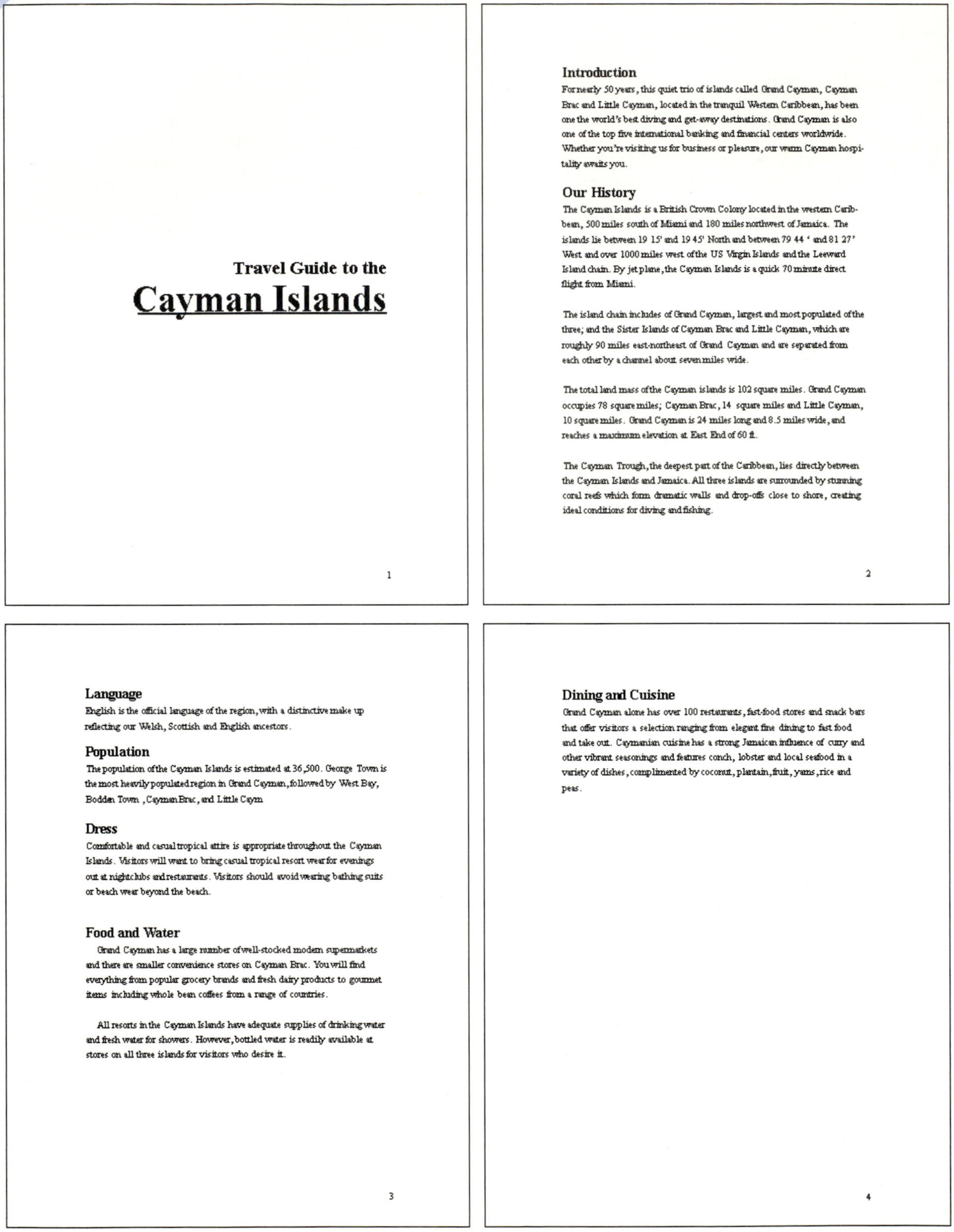

Travel Guide to the
Cayman Islands

1

Introduction

For nearly 50 years, this quiet trio of islands called Grand Cayman, Cayman Brac and Little Cayman, located in the tranquil Western Caribbean, has been one the world's best diving and get-away destinations. Grand Cayman is also one of the top five international banking and financial centers worldwide. Whether you're visiting us for business or pleasure, our warm Cayman hospitality awaits you.

Our History

The Cayman Islands is a British Crown Colony located in the western Caribbean, 500 miles south of Miami and 180 miles northwest of Jamaica. The islands lie between 19 15' and 19 45' North and between 79 44 ' and 81 27' West and over 1000 miles west of the US Virgin Islands and the Leeward Island chain. By jet plane, the Cayman Islands is a quick 70 minute direct flight from Miami.

The island chain includes of Grand Cayman, largest and most populated of the three; and the Sister Islands of Cayman Brac and Little Cayman, which are roughly 90 miles east-northeast of Grand Cayman and are separated from each other by a channel about seven miles wide.

The total land mass of the Cayman islands is 102 square miles. Grand Cayman occupies 78 square miles; Cayman Brac, 14 square miles and Little Cayman, 10 square miles. Grand Cayman is 24 miles long and 8.5 miles wide, and reaches a maximum elevation at East End of 60 ft.

The Cayman Trough, the deepest part of the Caribbean, lies directly between the Cayman Islands and Jamaica. All three islands are surrounded by stunning coral reefs which form dramatic walls and drop-offs close to shore, creating ideal conditions for diving and fishing.

2

Language
English is the official language of the region, with a distinctive make up reflecting our Welsh, Scottish and English ancestors.

Population
The population of the Cayman Islands is estimated at 36,500. George Town is the most heavily populated region in Grand Cayman, followed by West Bay, Bodden Town , Cayman Brac, and Little Caym

Dress
Comfortable and casual tropical attire is appropriate throughout the Cayman Islands. Visitors will want to bring casual tropical resort wear for evenings out at nightclubs and restaurants. Visitors should avoid wearing bathing suits or beach wear beyond the beach.

Food and Water
Grand Cayman has a large number of well-stocked modern supermarkets and there are smaller convenience stores on Cayman Brac. You will find everything from popular grocery brands and fresh dairy products to gourmet items including whole bean coffees from a range of countries.

All resorts in the Cayman Islands have adequate supplies of drinking water and fresh water for showers. However, bottled water is readily available at stores on all three islands for visitors who desire it.

3

Dining and Cuisine
Grand Cayman alone has over 100 restaurants, fast-food stores and snack bars that offer visitors a selection ranging from elegant fine dining to fast food and take out. Caymanian cuisine has a strong Jamaican influence of curry and other vibrant seasonings and features conch, lobster and local seafood in a variety of dishes, complimented by coconut, plantain, fruit, yams, rice and peas.

4

SUMMARY

In this lesson, you learned how to:

■ Explain how an index is an alphabetical listing of key words, phrases, or topics within a publication.

■ Mark index entries and add cross-reference index entries to a publication.

■ Create an index and update an index whenever a publication is edited.

■ Explain how a table of contents helps the reader locate major entries in a publication.

■ Apply PageMaker styles to entries that you want included in a table of contents.

■ Create a table of contents and update a table of contents index whenever a publication is edited.

■ Create a PageMaker *book* from multiple publications.

VOCABULARY *Review*

Define the following terms:		
Book	Index	Marking an index entry
Book list	Index entry	Phrase
Cross-reference	Index subentry	Table of contents

REVIEW *Questions*

TRUE / FALSE

Circle T if the statement is true or F if the statement is false.

T   F   **1.** In an index, all index entries appear in numerical order by page number.

T   F   **2.** In an index, a word or phrase that is part of a major subject or topic is called a subentry.

T   F   **3.** Any index entry can also have a subentry.

T   F   **4.** When indexing, the word *phrase* means two or more consecutive words.

T   F   **5.** You cannot identify a word or phrase to use in the index while using the story editor.

T   F   **6.** Indexing is case sensitive.

T   F   **7.** After creating an index in a publication, you will have to update the index if you later edit that publication.

T   F   **8.** If you edit a publication containing an index, you must issue the Create Index command again after editing to be certain the page numbers are correct.

T   F   **9.** A table of contents normally appears at the front of a publication.

T   F   **10.** A cross-reference is an index entry that identifies a different, related topic instead of a specific page number.

FILL IN THE BLANK

Complete the following sentences by writing the correct word or words in the blanks provided.

1. A word or phrase that is part of a major subject or topic in an index is called a(n) _____.

2. Identifying a word or phrase that you want included in an index is called _____ an index entry.

3. Normally, indexes appear on their own page(s) in a publication, and usually at the _____ of the publication.

4. A list of PageMaker publications that are electronically linked together as one large publication is called a(n) _____ list.

5. To include an entry in a table of contents, apply a PageMaker _____ to that entry.

PROJECTS

SCANS **PROJECT 16-1A**

1. From the data files that accompany this book, open the publication named **Package**. This publication contains four pages; the first three pages each contain a one-paragraph entry. The last page, which is now blank, will be used to hold the index.

2. Below is a list of words or phrases found in the publication and the associated page numbers on which they appear. Mark each of these entries as an index topic or subtopic as indicated in the list. Note that in some instances the topics need to be reworded in the Topic text box.

Page	Entry in the Text	Entry in the Index	Subtopic Entry
1	packaged tours	tours, packaged	
1	vacation	vacation	
2	Travel Council	Travel Council	
2	discounts	tours, packaged	discounts
2	hotels	hotels	
3	upgrades	tours, packaged	upgrades
3	hotels	hotels	

For example, to mark the first entry, *packaged tours,* that is found on page 1 of the publi-cation, select the words **packaged tours**. Then mark the selected phrase as an index entry by clicking **Index Entry** from the **Utilities** menu. Next, to reword the phrase from *packaged tours* to *tours, packaged,* key **tours, packaged** in the Topic text box and then click **OK**. HINT: *For entries that are listed as subtopics, remember to click the **Cycle** button before keying the name of the topic in the Topic text box.*

3. Turn to page 4 in the publication.

4. Create the index. When the Text Placement icon appears, place the icon just below the top margin guide and slightly to the right of the left margin guide, and then click.

5. Keep this publication on-screen for Project 16-1B

PROJECT 16-1B

1. With page 4 still on-screen, choose **Index Entry** from the **Utilities** menu.

2. Create a cross-reference entry in which the Topic is *resorts*, and the Level 1 entry is *hotels.* Then, close the Select Cross-Reference Topic and the Add Index Entry dialog boxes.

3. Create an updated index.

4. Use the Actual Size to examine the index entries.

5. Keep this publication on-screen for Project 16-1C

PROJECT 16-1C

1. Display the Styles Palette, if necessary.

2. Below is a list of section titles from the on-screen publication and the page numbers on which they appear. Apply the style named **Subhead 1** to each section title to identify that entry as a title entry in a table of contents that you will create in a moment.

Page	Section Title
1	Introduction
2	Advantages
3	Upgrades
4	Index

3. Turn to page 1 in the publication and then insert one **new page** before the current page.

4. When the new page appears, create a table of contents. Change the title from Contents to Table of Contents. Then, when the Text Placement icon appears, place the icon just below the top margin guide and slightly to the right of the left margin guide on the newly inserted page, and click.

5. Print all the pages in the publication.

6. Save the publication under the name **Package Revised** and then close the publication.

SCANS   **TEAMWORK PROJECT**

As you learned in this lesson, PageMaker's book feature is frequently used for creating lengthy works. In creating a textbook, for example, each chapter or lesson might be created as a separate publication, sometimes even by different individuals, and when finished, the book feature is used to link all those publications for indexing and printing. In situations such as these, it is extremely important that each individual publication look the same, by having a similar layout, format, and using the same type specifications. Discuss with your instructor and your classmates different procedures and techniques that you could use to ensure that these separate publications would all be created using the same layout, format and specifications.

CRITICAL *Thinking*

SCANS **ACTIVITY 16-1**

In this lesson, you learned how PageMaker's book feature lets you link two or more smaller publications into a larger publication for the purposes of printing, consecutive page numbering, indexing, and for creating a comprehensive table of contents. In a textbook, for example, each chapter or lesson can be created as a separate PageMaker publication, and the book feature can then link the publications together. Now, think about a national newspaper such as *USA Today*, a national magazine such as *Time* or *Newsweek*, and a printed version of an encyclopedia. Imagine that it were your job to create each of these three different printed works using PageMaker. How many different PageMaker publications might you create for each? What information for each of those works would you place into each publication?

WORKING WITH TABLES

OBJECTIVES

Upon completion of this lesson, you should be able to:

■ Define the terms table, column, row and cell.

■ Start the Adobe Table program and specify a size for a new table.

■ Key and edit table entries.

■ Adjust column size and row height.

■ Transfer a table into a PageMaker publication.

■ Format cells and cell entries.

■ Group and ungroup cells in a table.

Estimated Time: 5 hours

VOCABULARY

Border weight

Cell

Columns

Gutters

Range

Rows

Table

Tint

Introduction

In this lesson you'll learn how to use the Adobe Table program that's included with PageMaker to create tables. Tables provide an easy way to create and edit forms, charts, lists, and other specialized types of publication entries. In many instances, a table lets you create, in only minutes, a tabular entry that might normally require hours to create.

Understanding Tables

A table is perhaps one of the most unique and flexible desktop-publishing tools available. A *table* allows you to organize related information both horizontally and vertically. You can use tables to create lists, forms, and charts within a publication. PageMaker includes a separate computer program called Adobe Table that you use to create or edit a table.

The Adobe Table program combines many of PageMaker's features, such as columns, rules, tab alignment, and type specifications, into one easy-to-use program. These features let you create tables to handle a wide range of publishing needs. The different tables shown in Figure 17-1 were created with the Adobe Table program. Each was created in only a few minutes and then placed into a PageMaker publication. As you can see from these examples, tables can contain any combination of text, numbers, and even graphic images.

Examples of three different tables

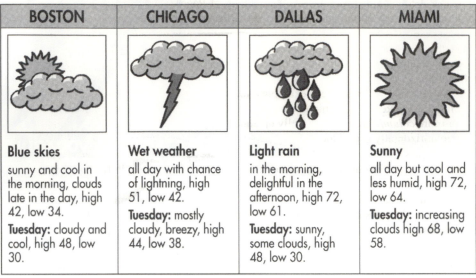

BOSTON	CHICAGO	DALLAS	MIAMI
Blue skies sunny and cool in the morning, clouds late in the day, high 42, low 34. **Tuesday:** cloudy and cool, high 48, low 30.	**Wet weather** all day with chance of lightning, high 51, low 42. **Tuesday:** mostly cloudy, breezy, high 44, low 38.	**Light rain** in the morning, delightful in the afternoon, high 72, low 61. **Tuesday:** sunny, some clouds, high 48, low 30.	**Sunny** all day but cool and less humid, high 72, low 64. **Tuesday:** increasing clouds high 68, low 58.

TODAY'S MONEY RATES

Lending rate at close of bus.	Thurs. rate	3 mos. ago	6 mos. ago	One yr. ago
Prime lending rate	8.5%	9.5%	9.9%	9.7%
Federal discount	3.7%	5.4%	6.9%	7.4%
Mortgage rates				
20-yr. fixed rate	8.9%	9.4%	9.8%	9.6%
20-yr. adjustable	7.9%	8.5%	9.1%	9.3%

MONDAY NIGHT TV

	7:30	8:00	8:30	9:00
4	**Family Time:** Mark learns Ann is dating.	**One Step:** The family fills in for the band.	**Baby Me:** Jan and John have a fight about the new job.	
6	**To You:** Tim teaches John to drive	**My House:** Learn how to paint your home. Part 1 of 2 in a series.		**Wildlife:** The search for the eagle.
8	**Molly:** The Smiths have a fight.	**Flight of the Hawk:** Two pilots hatch a plan to steal a high-tech plane. With Mark White and Dale Wash. (1 hr., 30 min.)		

As shown in Figure 17-2, a table contains one or more *columns* that run vertically up and down the table and one or more *rows* that run horizontally across the table. A *cell* is where a column and a row intersect. All entries within a table are stored within these cells. The table in Figure 17-2 contains three columns, five rows, and, as a result, fifteen cells. Tables created with the Adobe Table program are similar to spreadsheets created with programs like Microsoft Excel or Lotus. If you use one of those spreadsheet programs, you are probably already familiar with these terms.

FIGURE 17-2
Parts of a table

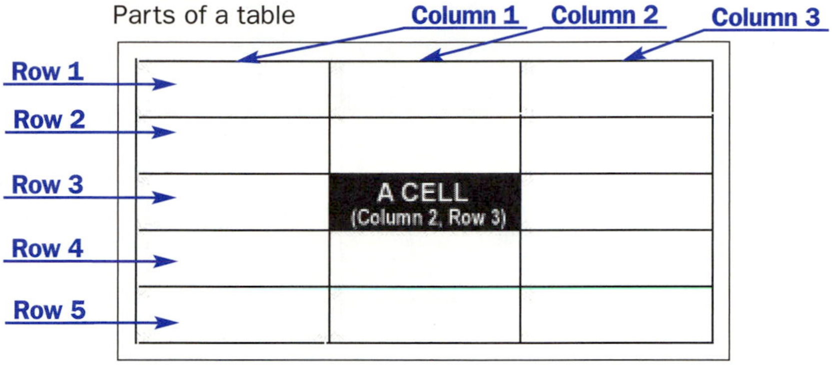

In a table, a number is used to identify the columns and rows. The first column in every table is known as column 1, the second as column 2, and so on. Rows are numbered beginning with row 1, then row 2, and so on. A cell is identified by the combination of the column number and row number in which it appears, such as column 2, row 3. Tables created with the Adobe Table program can have as many as 100 columns and 100 rows, and as many as 10,000 cells!

To create a table while working in a publication, start the Adobe Table program, specify the number of columns and rows you want, and then presto! A table appears. When you first create a table, the columns and rows are automatically separated with thin lines. You can remove any or all of these lines or change them to different line widths, if you desire. You can also select from numerous commands that let you decide how the table will look. For example, you can change the width of each column, the height of each row, shade the inside of a cell, or add or remove columns or rows at any time.

Creating a Table

To create a table while working on a publication, start the Adobe Table program by choosing Insert Object from the Edit menu. Doing so reveals the Insert Object dialog box, such as the one shown in Figure 17-3. Next, select Adobe Table 3.0 in the Object Type list box, and then select Create New, if not already selected. Finally click OK.

FIGURE 17-3
Insert Object dialog box

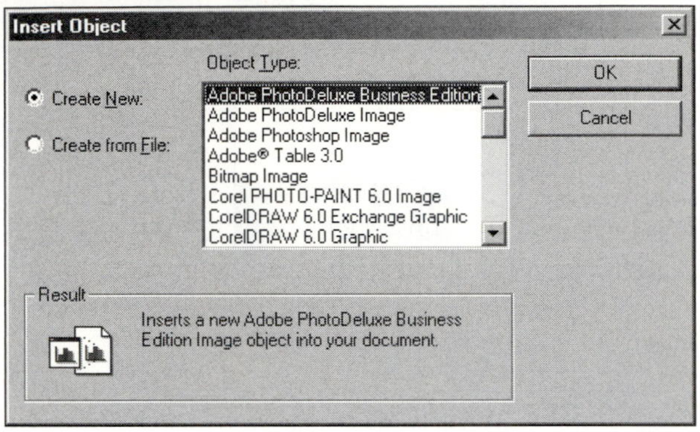

When the program begins, a New Table dialog box appears, like the one shown in Figure 17-4. You use this dialog box to specify the physical size of the table (such as 2 by 4 inches), as well as the number of columns and rows you want in the table. Although you can change the physical size of the table or the number of columns/rows later, it's generally easier if you make the table the size you need in the beginning.

FIGURE 17-4
New Table dialog box

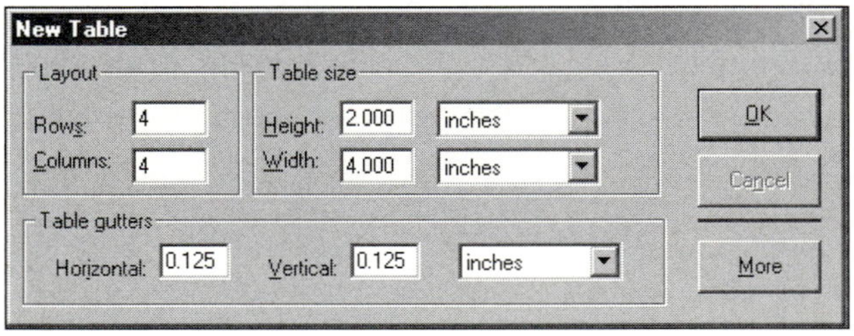

By default, the program assumes that you want to create a table 2 inches high and 4 inches wide and that the table will contain four columns and four rows. To create a table of a different physical size, such as 3 inches high by 5 inches wide, enter the new size in the Height and Width text boxes provided in the New Table dialog box. To specify a different number of columns and rows, key the number needed into the Rows and Columns text boxes. When finished specifying the table's size, click OK. After a short pause, the Table window, such as the one in Figure 17-5, appears containing a table of the size you requested. Depending on the previous user, a Table Attributes and/or a Text Attributes palette may appear. As you'll learn later in this lesson, you can display or hide these palettes, and each palette lets you quickly change the formatting of the table and its entries. Like any of PageMaker's palettes, you can drag these palettes out of the way if they hide any portion of the table.

FIGURE 17-5
The Table window

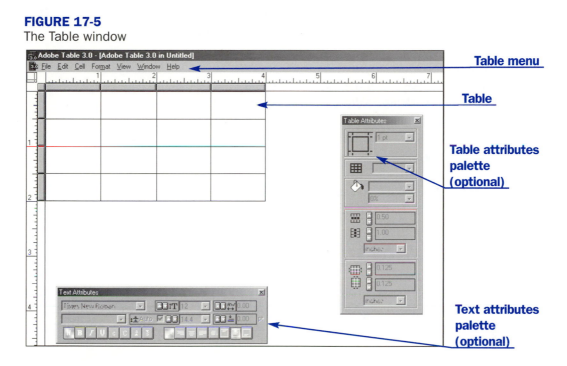

The table that first appears on-screen contains the number of columns and rows you requested, and the insertion point appears in the first cell of the table. The Adobe Table program determines the width of the columns by dividing the table width by the number of columns. The program determines the row height by dividing the height of the table by the number of rows. As you will see later in this lesson, you can manually adjust the width of any column or the height of any row, as needed.

S TEP-BY-STEP 17.1

1. Begin a new publication. When the Document Setup dialog box appears, specify a **single-sided** publication.

2. Choose **Insert Object** from the **Edit** menu.

3. When the Insert Object dialog box appears, select **Adobe Table 3.0** in the Insert Object list box and then select **Create New**, if not already selected. Finally, click **OK**. (IMPORTANT NOTE: On certain computer systems, Adobe Table 3.0 may not appear automatically in the Insert Object list box. If this occurs, click on the Start button. Next, from the Programs list, choose **Adobe**, then choose **Pagemaker 7.0**, and then choose **Adobe Table 3.0**. Finally, when the New Table dialog box appears, click **Cancel** button, switch back to the PageMaker publication and begin step #3 again.)

4. When the New Table dialog box appears, perform the following:
   a. Double-click inside the Rows text box (to select the entry) and then key **3**.
   b. Double-click inside the Columns text box and then key **3**.
   c. Double-click inside the Height text box and then key **1.5**.
   d. Double-click inside the Width text box and then key **5**.
   e. Click **OK** to complete the specifications and close the dialog box.

5. Keep this publication on-screen for use in the next Step-by-Step.

Entering Data into a Table

After creating a new table, you can immediately begin keying entries into its cells. Simply place the insertion point within the cell in which you want the entry to appear, and then begin keying. To enter data into other cells, move the insertion point to another cell and repeat the process.

Positioning the Insertion Point

To position the insertion point using the mouse, place the mouse pointer in the cell and click. You can also use the keyboard to position the insertion point. Press Tab (or Shift+Tab) to move the insertion point right (or left) one cell. (If the insertion point is already in the last cell of a row, pressing Tab moves it to the first cell on the next row.) Press ↑ (or ↓) to move the insertion point up (or down) one row. Press Home (or End) to move the insertion point to the first (or last) cell in the table.

S TEP-BY-STEP 17.2

1. Observe how the insertion point is located in the first cell of the table that you created in Step-by-Step 17.1.

2. Move the insertion point right one column by pressing **Tab**.

STEP-BY-STEP 17.2 Continued

3. Move the insertion point down one row by pressing the ↓ key.

4. Move the insertion point to the last cell in the table by pressing **End**.

5. Using the mouse, place the mouse pointer in the first cell of the first row and then click.

6. Keep this table on-screen for use in the next Step-by-Step.

Keying Entries

After you've positioned the insertion point in the proper cell, you can key the cell entry. If you key a long entry containing several lines of text, the program will automatically expand the height of the cell (and its row) to accommodate the text. The text will wrap (within the cell) to a new line.

When you finish keying a cell entry, you can use one of the techniques mentioned earlier to end the cell entry and reposition the insertion point in a different cell. For example, pressing the Tab key will end the entry in one cell and then move the insertion point to the next cell on the right.

STEP-BY-STEP 17.3

1. Make certain the insertion point is still located in the first cell of the table.

2. Key **First Name** and press **Tab**. Observe how the insertion point moves into the next cell.

3. Key **Initial** and press **Tab**, then key **Last Name** and press **Tab**. Observe how the insertion point jumps to the first cell in the next row.

4. With the insertion point now located in the first cell of the second row:
   a. Key **Chris** and press **Tab**.
   b. Key **F** and press **Tab**.
   c. Key **Chang** and press **Tab**.

5. With the insertion point now located in the first cell of the third row:
   a. Key your first name and press **Tab**.
   b. Key your middle initial and press **Tab**.

6. Key your last name but do not press Tab when finished.

7. Keep this table on-screen for use in the next Step-by-Step.

Selecting a Range of Cells

A *range* is a group of cells in a table that touch each other. Selecting a range of cells means to select or highlight one or more cells that you want to perform some type of action upon, such as changing the type specifications. Selecting a range of cells can save time while you edit a table. For example, to delete the entries in several cells, you could highlight those cells and then press the Delete key once rather than having to delete each cell entry individually.

To select a range of cells, simply drag the mouse over the cells you want to select. A selected range of cells appears highlighted, such as the six cells in Figure 17-6. If you select the wrong cells, just start again. To deselect a selected range of cells, click in any cell of the table.

FIGURE 17-6
A selected range of cells

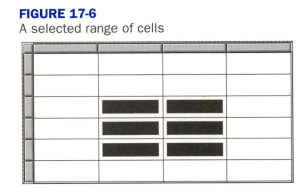

STEP-BY-STEP 17.4

1. Place the mouse pointer anywhere in the first cell of the first row. Then press, and while holding down the mouse button, drag the mouse to the right into the second cell of the first row to select both cells. When both cells are selected, release the mouse button. If you select the wrong cells, just start over.

2. Click once in any cell of the table to deselect the selected cells.

3. Following instructions similar to those in step 1, select the first two cells of the second row.

4. Press **Delete** to remove the entries in those cells. Then, click once in any cell of the table to deselect the cells.

5. Position the insertion point in the first cell of the second row.

7. Key **Sarah** and press **Tab**. Then, key **B** but do not press Tab.

8. Keep this table on-screen for use in the next Step-by-Step.

Special Selection Techniques

In some instances, using the mouse pointer to select a range of cells can be difficult, such as when you're trying to select all the cells in a long column or row. To make this task easier, Adobe Table offers various ways to select all the cells in a column, row, or in the entire table. You can even select several ranges of cells.

To select all the cells in the table, click the table select button. To select all the cells in a column, click on the column select button. To select all the cells in a row, click on the row select button. These select buttons are found in the gray, shaded area across the top of each column and to the left of each row and are shown in Figure 17-7.

FIGURE 17-7
Buttons for selecting a table, column, or row

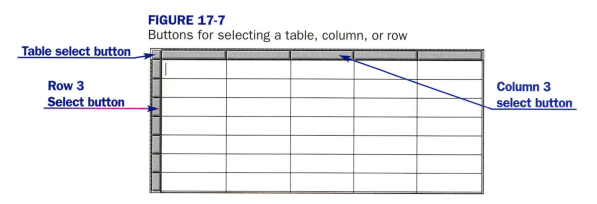

As shown in Figure 17-8, you can even select several ranges of cells at the same time. To do so, select the first range as you normally would. Then, hold down the Ctrl key and use the mouse to continue selecting the other ranges of cells. Once you've selected all the cells you want, release the Ctrl key.

FIGURE 17-8
Select multiple cell ranges

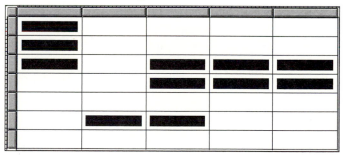

STEP-BY-STEP 17.5

1. Click the column select button at the top of the second column, to select that column. (In your on-screen table, this button is the gray, shaded area located just above the word *Initial.*)

2. Click the row select button at the left side of the third row to select that row. (In your on-screen table, this button is the gray, shaded area located just to the left of the cell containing your first name.)

3. Click the **table select** button, to select all cells in the table.

4. Click once in any cell of the table to deselect all the cells.

5. Keep this table on-screen for use in the next Step-by-Step.

Adjusting Column Width and Row Height

When you first create a table, each column has the same width and each row has the same height. Often, you will frequently need to adjust column width or row height. For example, you might want to reduce the width of a wide column that is used to hold two-character state abbreviations, such as NY or FL. Or, you might want increase the height of all rows in a table to improve readability.

You can change column width (or row height) by using either the menu found at the top of the table window or by using the mouse. To use the menu, first select the column (or row) you want to change by clicking on its column (or row) select button. Then choose Row/Column Size from the Cell menu to display the Row/Column Size dialog box shown in Figure 17-9. Now, in the Column width (or Row height) text box, key a new width (or height) that is measured in inches or fractions of an inch, such as 1.5, and then click OK.

FIGURE 17-9
Row/Column Size dialog box

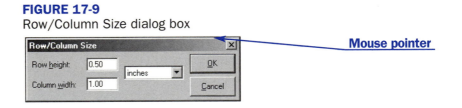

Mouse pointer

You can also use the mouse to change the column width (or row height). Carefully place the mouse pointer along the right edge of the column select button (or bottom edge of the row select button). When positioned correctly, the mouse pointer will turn into a double-headed arrow as shown in Figure 17-10. Then, drag the mouse in the direction needed to change the size. For example, to increase the width of a column, drag the mouse to the right, or, to increase the height of a row, drag the mouse downward.

FIGURE 17-10
Mouse pointer positioned for changing column width

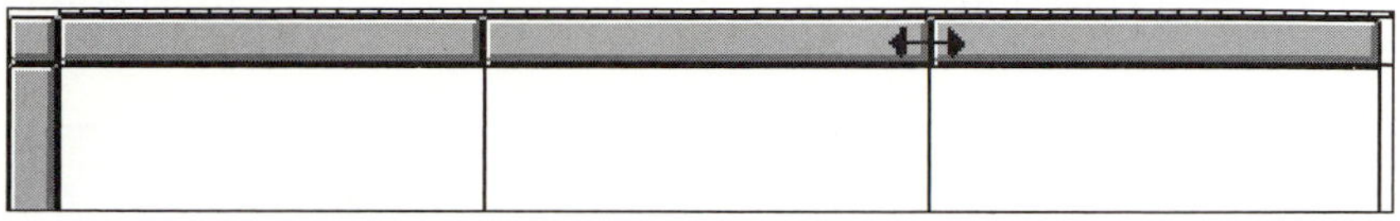

S TEP-BY-STEP 17.6

1. Click once on the **column select** button at the top of the first column to select that column.

2. Choose **Row/Column Size** from the **Cell** menu.

3. Key **1.25** in the Column width text box and then click **OK**.

4. Click once in any cell of the table to deselect all the cells.

5. Place the mouse pointer between the column select buttons of the second and third column. When positioned correctly, the mouse pointer will change into a double-headed arrow. Then, reduce the width of the second column by dragging the two-headed arrow to the left until it is located near the center of the column select button of the second column.

6. Click the **row select** button at the left side of the first row.

7. Choose **Row/Column Size** from the **Cell** menu.

8. Key **0.35** and then click **OK**. Observe how the height of the row is smaller.

9. Click once in any cell of the table to deselect all the cells.

10. Keep this table on-screen for use in the next Step-by-Step.

Changing the Number of Columns and Rows

At times, you will need to add or delete columns or rows from a table. The method you use varies slightly depending on whether you are inserting or removing columns or rows.

Inserting Columns and Rows

To insert a column, click the column select button where you want the new column inserted. Next, specify whether you want the new column inserted to the left or the right of the selected column. Choose Insert Column Before (or Insert Column After) from the Cell menu to insert the new column to the left (or right) of the selected column.

To insert a row, click on the row select button where you want the new row to appear. Next, specify whether you want the new row inserted above or below the selected row. Choose Insert Row Above (or Insert Row Below) from the Cell menu to insert the new row above (or below) the selected row.

While keying or editing cell entries, you can also insert a new row automatically at the end of the table. When the insertion point is located in the last cell of the table, you can press Tab to insert a new row at the bottom of the table.

Removing Columns and Rows

You can remove any column or row from a table. Think carefully before doing so, however, because PageMaker does not provide any warning messages asking you to confirm your action. To delete a column (or row), click the column (or row) select button. Then choose Delete Column (or Delete Row) from the Cell menu.

> **Hot Tip**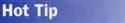
>
> If you delete a column (or a row) accidentally, you may be able to restore the entry by immediately choosing **Undo Delete Column** (or **Undo Delete Row**) from the **Edit** menu.

S TEP-BY-STEP 17.7

1. Click the **column select** button at the top of the second column.

2. Choose **Delete Column** from the **Cell** menu to remove the column.

3. Click the **row select** button at the left side of the last row.

4. Choose **Insert Row Above** from the **Cell** menu to insert a new row.

5. Click the **row select** button at the left side of the last row.

6. Choose **Insert Row Below** from the **Cell** menu to insert one row.

7. Click once in any cell of the table to deselect all the cells.

8. Keep this table on-screen for use in the next Step-by-Step.

Transferring a Table into a Publication

When you finish adding the cell entries to the table, you're ready to transfer the table into the PageMaker publication. To do so, choose Exit & Return to x (where x is the name of your publication) from the File menu. When the table appears in the publication, use the Pointer tool to drag the table to the desired location on the page, if needed.

S TEP-BY-STEP 17.8

1. Choose **Exit & Return to Untitled** from the **File** menu.

2. When the table appears, use the Pointer tool to drag the table so that both the top and left edges of the table fall along the top and left margin guides.

3. Enlarge the area around the table to **Actual Size** and then examine the table.

4. Keep this publication on-screen for use in the next Step-by-Step.

Editing a Table

After you have transferred a table into a publication, you may want or need to make changes to the table. Because PageMaker treats all tables as if they were graphic images, you cannot make changes to a table within PageMaker. Instead, you need to transfer the table into the Adobe Table program, make the necessary edits, and then transfer the table back into the publication.

To transfer a table from a publication into the Adobe Table program, simply double-click anywhere in the table. After a few moments, the table will appear in the Table window and you can then make any necessary changes. After you've finished editing the table, you transfer the table back into the publication by choosing Exit & Return to x from the File menu.

S TEP-BY-STEP 17.9

1. Double-click anywhere in the on-screen table. After a few moments, the table will appear in the Table window.

2. In the third row of the table, key the first name **Amanda** in the first cell, and then key **Foster** in the second cell of that row.

3. In the last row of the table, key the first name **Marcia** in the first cell, and then key **Gomez** in the second cell of that row.

4. Choose **Exit & Return to Untitled** from the **File** menu.

5. Enlarge the area around the table to **Actual Size**, if needed, and observe the editing change.

6. Save this publication under the name **Importing**. Then, close this publication.

Formatting Text Entries within Cells

As you have seen, you can quickly create and key entries into a table by using the Adobe Table program's standard default settings. But, in many instances, you will need to change those default settings to create the exact table that you need. For example, although cell entries are left aligned by default, you may want to center certain entries, such as a title, at the top of a column. Likewise, while a thin line automatically surrounds each cell, you may not want any lines, or you may need lines of a different style.

To format cell entries, first select the cells you want to format. Then, you can use the Adobe Table menu or Text Attributes palette discussed later in this lesson to format the selected entries.

Selecting What Entries to Format

You can format cell entries as you key them, or after they appear in the table. For example, if you select a range of cells that already contain entries and then issue a formatting command, such as selecting a different font, that formatting change will affect all the entries in the selected cells. You can even format cells before they contain cell entries. If you do, any entry you key into such a cell will automatically appear in the correct format as you key it.

Before you can issue the formatting commands you need to identify what cells in the table you want to format. Here are some guidelines.

To format one cell: To format a cell before it contains an entry, place the insertion point into the cell to format. To format a cell that already contains an entry, select all the characters in the cell.

To format all cells in a column: Click the column select button at the top of the column.

To format all cells in a row: Click the row select button at the beginning of the row.

To format all cells in a table: Click the table select button.

To format a range of cells: Select the range of cells to format.

Formatting Text Entries Using Menus

After selecting the cells to format, choose Format Text from the Format menu to display the Format Text dialog box shown in Figure 17-11. Use the drop-down lists in the Text area of the dialog box to change type specifications. For example, you could use the Font or Size drop-down list to choose a different font or point size. Use the check boxes in the Style area of the dialog box to select a different font style, such as bold or italic.

FIGURE 17-11
The Format Text dialog box

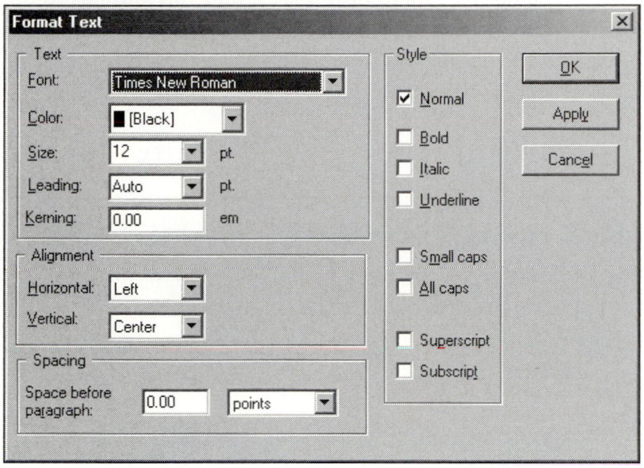

The Alignment section of the dialog box lets you control how entries align either horizontally or vertically within a cell. Horizontal alignment lets you control whether a cell entry aligns on the left or right edge of a cell, or whether an entry appears centered within a cell. You can also select Decimal alignment to align numeric entries in one or more cells on their decimal points. Vertical alignment lets you control whether a cell entry appears near the top or bottom edge of a cell, or whether a cell entry is centered between the top and bottom edge of the cell.

For cells that contain several paragraphs of text, the Spacing section of the dialog box lets you control how much space the program inserts between each paragraph. This setting inserts space before all paragraphs, except the first paragraph in a cell.

STEP-BY-STEP 17.10

1. Begin a new publication. When the Document Setup dialog box appears, specify a **single-sided** publication.

2. Using instructions you now know, begin creating a table by starting the Adobe Table program. When the New Table dialog box appears, create a new table containing three rows, three columns, a height of 1 inch, and a width of 5 inches. When finished, click **OK**.

3. Select the first row in the table by clicking its row select button.

4. Choose **Format Text** from the **Format** menu.

STEP-BY-STEP 17.10 Continued

5. In the Style section of the Format Text dialog box, select **Bold**.

6. In the Alignment section of the dialog box, choose **Center** from the Horizontal drop-down list.

7. Close the dialog box by clicking **OK**.

8. Click anywhere in the first cell of the table. Then, key **BUDGET**, press **Tab**, key **THIS YEAR**, press **Tab**, key **LAST YEAR**, and then press **Tab**. Observe how the entries you just keyed appear centered and in bold.

9. Keep this table on-screen for use in the next Step-by-Step.

Formatting Text Entries Using the Text Attributes Palette

You can also format text within cells by using the Text Attributes palette shown in Figure 17-12. To display the Text Attributes palette, choose Show Text Palette from the Window menu. (To hide the palette, if needed, choose Hide Text Palette from the Window menu.) If the palette hides your table entries, drag the palette to a different location on the screen.

FIGURE 17-12
The Text Attributes palette

Like PageMaker's Control palette, the Text Attributes palette contains text boxes and drop-down lists for changing the font, point size, and leading size. You can also use the buttons in the lower-left portion of the dialog box to select from different type styles, such as bold or italic. Unlike PageMaker's Control palette, however, the Text Attributes palette contains additional buttons that let you control both the horizontal and vertical alignment.

STEP-BY-STEP 17.11

1. With the insertion point now located in the first cell of the second row, key **Salary**, press **Tab**, key **$1,500,000**, press **Tab**, key **$1,750,000**, and then press **Tab**.

2. If the Text Attributes palette is not on-screen, display the Text Attributes palette by choosing **Show Text Palette** from the **Window** menu.

3. Select the second row in the table by clicking its row select button.

4. Click the **Bold** button on the Text Attributes palette.

STEP-BY-STEP 17.11 Continued

5. Click the **Italic** button on the Text Attributes palette.

6. Click the **Right** (alignment) button in the Text Attributes palette.

7. Click in any cell of the table to deselect the cells. Then, observe how all the entries in the second row appear in bold, italic, and right alignment.

8. Keep this table on-screen for use in the next Step-by-Step.

Formatting the Table's Appearance

Y ou can also issue various commands to change the size and appearance of certain cells, or of the entire table. For example, you can change or remove the lines around the table or around certain cells, shade the inside of one or more cells, and control how close text comes to the édge of a cell.

After selecting the cell(s) or the table that you want to change, choose Format Cell from the Format menu. The Format Cells dialog box shown in Figure 17-13 appears.

FIGURE 17-13
Format Cells dialog box

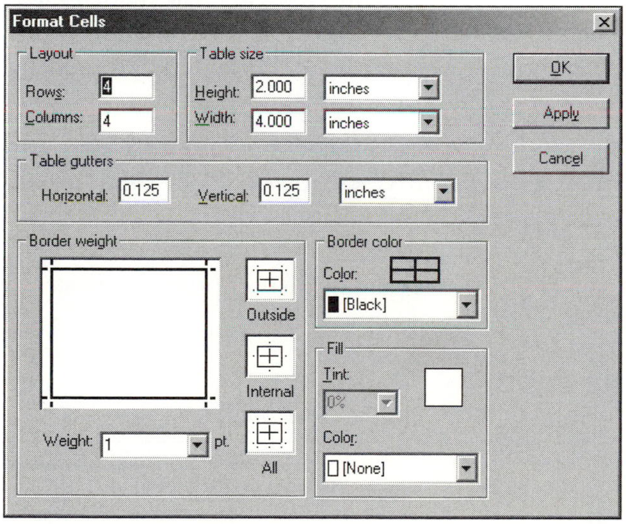

Changing the Table and Gutter Size

You can use the Rows and Columns text boxes to change the overall number of columns and rows in the table. Simply key the new number of columns (and/or rows) needed and those additional entries are added to the end of the table. You can also use the Table size text boxes to change the physical height and/or width of the table.

When working with a table, ***gutters*** control how close text in a cell comes to the edge of the cell. By default, an entry in a cell never comes closer than 0.125 inches to any edge. You can use the Horizontal and Vertical text boxes to increase or decrease this space. *NOTE: Changes to the gutter space affect all cells in the table, regardless of which cells were selected beforehand.*

Changing the Border Weight

You can quickly change the type of line (or border) that appears around one or more cells. As shown in Figure 17-14, every cell contains four lines that appear along the outside of the cell (at the top, bottom, left, and right edges). In a selected range of cells, the combined lines from all of the selected cells create lines both inside the range and along the outside edge of the range (at the top, bottom, left, and right edges).

FIGURE 17-14
Border terms for one cell and a range of cells

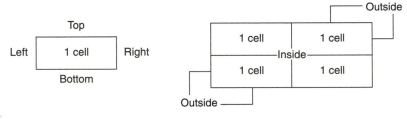

By default, a single thin line appears around each side of a cell. By using the Border weight section of the Format Cells dialog box, you can vary the width of these lines. The Outside, Internal, and All buttons let you choose which of the lines within the selected range you want to change. Click the Outside button, for example, to change the lines along the outside of a selected range of cells.

The term ***border weight*** refers to the thickness of the lines that surround a cell. Line thickness, like font size, is expressed in points. As you'll recall, there are 72 points to an inch. The Weight drop-down list lets you select from various border weights or line widths as expressed in point sizes. Figure 17-15 shows examples of the lines produced with each of the selections offered in the Weight drop-down list. You can also choose the first selection in the drop-down list, None, to completely remove a line from a cell.

FIGURE 17-15
Examples of different border (line) widths

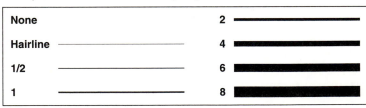

S TEP-BY-STEP 17.12

1. Click the **table select** button to select all the cells in the table.

2. Choose **Format Cells** from the **Format** menu.

3. In the Border weight section of the dialog box, click the **Outside** button. Then, choose **4** (points) from the Weight drop-down list.

4. Click **OK** to close the dialog box.

5. Click in any cell of the table to deselect the cells. Notice the thick line around the outside of the table.

6. Again, click the **table select** button to select all the cells in the table.

7. Choose **Format Cells** from the **Format** menu.

8. In the Border weight section of the dialog box, click the **Internal** button. Then choose **2** from the Weight drop-down list.

9. Click **OK** to close the dialog box.

10. Click in any cell of the table to deselect the cells. Notice how all the lines that surround the cells inside the table look thicker.

11. Keep this table on-screen for use in the next Step-by-Step.

Changing the Border Color

You can use the Color drop-down list in the Border color section of the Format Cells dialog box to change the line color for all lines in the table. Instead of the default color black, you can choose from other colors, such as blue, cyan, green, magenta, red, and yellow.

S TEP-BY-STEP 17.13

1. Click the **table select** button to select all the cells in the table.

2. Choose **Format Cells** from the **Format** menu.

3. In the Border color section of the dialog box, choose **Blue** from the top Color drop-down list.

4. Click **OK** to close the dialog box.

5. Click in any cell of the table to deselect the cells and then observe the new border color.

6. Keep this table on-screen for use in the next Step-by-Step.

Changing Fill Color and Tint

You can use the options in the Fill section of the Format Cells dialog box to add color and/or shading to a selected range of cells. Use the Color drop-down list to choose a solid color, such as red, blue, or black. Use the Tint drop-down list to select the tint. *Tint* is the strength or intensity of a color and is expressed as a percentage. Choosing 100% tint, for example, produces a solid color, whereas choosing a lower percentage, such as 20%, produces a lighter shade of the color. Figure 17-16 shows examples of different tint percentages.

FIGURE 17-16
Examples of different tint levels

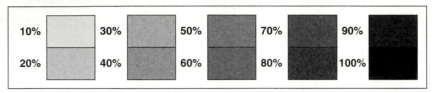

STEP-BY-STEP 17.14

1. Select all of the cells in the second row of the table.

2. Choose **Format Cells** from the **Format** menu.

3. In the Fill section of the dialog box choose **Magenta** from the Color drop-down list.

4. In the Fill section of the dialog box, choose **30%** from the Tint drop-down list. (*NOTE: If you cannot make a selection from the Tint drop-down list, perform step 3 again.*)

5. Click **OK** to close the dialog box.

6. Click in any cell of the table to deselect the cells and then observe the new colors and tints.

7. Keep this table on-screen for use in the next Step-by-Step.

Using the Table Palette

Another and often easier way to format a table is by using the Table Attributes palette (see Figure 17-17). To display the Table Attributes palette, choose Show Table Palette from the Window menu. To hide the palette, if needed, choose Hide Table Palette from the Window menu.

FIGURE 17-17
The Table Attributes palette

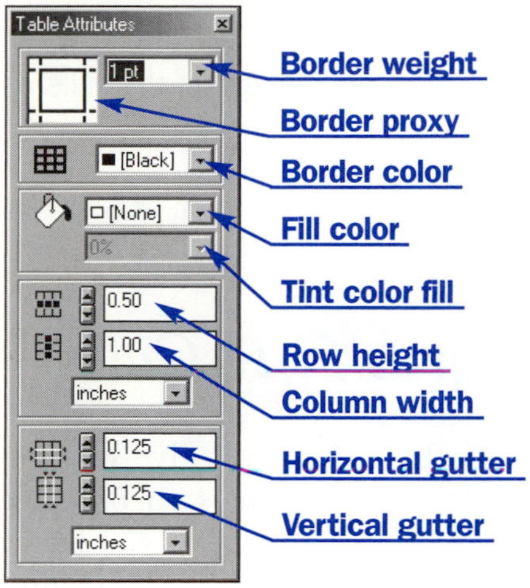

The Table Attributes palette includes text boxes and drop-down lists for changing border weight and color, fill color and tint, row and column height, and the gutter size. For example, to change the fill color for a range of cells, select those cells and then choose a different color from the Fill Color drop-down list in the Table Attributes palette. Or, to change the width of a column, select the column that you want to change and then specify a new width in the Column width text box.

When changing the border weight, you can use the Border Proxy tool to identify which lines within the selected range you want to change. The lines inside this Border Proxy identify which lines within the select range will change. Click on a line inside the Border Proxy to select or deselect a certain line. For example, to change the width of all lines except those at the top of a selected range, click in the center of the top line in the Border Proxy and then choose the new line width from the Border weight drop-down list.

STEP-BY-STEP 17.15

1. Choose **Show Table Palette** from the **Window** menu to display the Table Attributes palette, if necessary.

2. Select the first row of the table.

3. Make the following selections from the Table Attributes palette (consult Figure 17-17, if needed):
   a. Choose **Green** from the Fill Color drop-down list.
   b. Choose **20%** from the Tint drop-down list.

4. Click in any cell of the table to deselect the cells. Then, observe how all the cells in the first row of the table appear in a light green color.

5. Select the first column in the table.

6. On the Table Attributes palette, double-click inside the **Column width** text box. Then, key **1.25** and press **Enter**.

7. Click in any cell of the table to deselect the cells and then observe the new width of cells in the first column.

8. Keep this table on-screen for use in the next Step-by-Step.

Grouping/Ungrouping Cells

The Group and Ungroup commands give you great flexibility in customizing your tables. The Group command lets you combine two or more cells into one larger cell, whereas the Ungroup command lets you divide cells that you have already grouped. If you group all of the cells in the top row of a table, for example, you would create a single, large cell that would span the entire width of the table. In Figure 17-18, the single, large cell in which the table title appears was created by grouping the three cells in the top row of the table.

FIGURE 17-18
A table containing a grouped cell in the first row

SOUTH SEA TRADING COMPANY EMPLOYEE MASTER LISTING		
NAME	START DATE	SALARY
Ronald Blackfoot	November 2, 1996	$32,650.00
Elaine Fujimura	October 14, 1996	$29,750.00

First, select the range of cells that you want to group. Then choose Group from the Cell menu. After a moment, the lines between the selected cells will disappear, revealing the larger, grouped cell. To ungroup a cell, if needed, place the insertion point anywhere in that grouped cell and then choose Ungroup from the Cell menu.

Although you can group cells before or after they contain entries, it's easier to group cells that do not yet contain entries. If you must group cells that already contain entries, it's important to know that the entries from all those cells will be moved into the new, grouped cell.

This ability to group cells combined with other table commands, such as borders and shading, gives you tremendous flexibility in designing tables. The only limitation is your imagination.

STEP-BY-STEP 17.16

1. Select the third row of the table.

2. Choose **Group** from the **Cell** menu.

3. Click in any cell of the table to deselect the cells. Then observe how all of the cells in the third row have become one large cell.

4. Place the insertion point inside the large, newly grouped cell. Then, choose **Ungroup** from the **Cell** menu.

5. Click in any cell of the table to deselect the cells. Notice how the three cells in the third row reappear.

6. Select only the first and second cells in the third row. *Hint*: Remember, you can drag across cells that touch each other in order to select them.

7. Choose **Group** from the **Cell** menu.

8. Click in any cell of the table to deselect the cells and observe the newly grouped cell.

9. Choose **Exit & Return to Untitled** from the **File** menu to transfer the table into the PageMaker publication.

10. Save this publication with the name **Budget**.

11. Close the publication.

SUMMARY

In this lesson, you learned how to:

■ Define a table and table terms, including rows, columns and cells.

■ Explain how to start the Adobe Table program and describe how to create a Table with Adobe Table while using PageMaker.

■ Key and edit entries within a cell and also format cell entries.

■ Modify the size of a column or row and change the total number of columns or rows in a table.

■ Select one cell, a range of cells, or a series of non-touching cells.

■ Group two or more cells into one larger cell by using the Group command.

■ Use the Ungroup command to restore the original cells in a previously grouped cell.

VOCABULARY *Review*

Define the following terms:

Border weight	Gutters	Table
Cell	Range	Tint
Columns	Rows	

REVIEW *Questions*

TRUE / FALSE

Circle T if the statement is true or F if the statement is false.

T F **1.** When creating a table, you can specify the number of columns and rows that you want in the table, but you cannot specify the physical size of the table, such as 2 inches by 4 inches.

T F **2.** Columns run horizontally across a table.

T F **3.** If you format a cell before it contains an entry, any entry you later key into that cell will appear with that format.

T F **4.** A table in the Adobe Table program can contain up to 999 rows.

T F **5.** If you key a long entry of several lines of text into a single cell, the Adobe Table program will automatically expand the height of the cell to accommodate the additional text.

T F **6.** To format one cell that does not yet contain a cell entry, you can simply place the insertion point into the cell before changing its format.

T F **7.** After making an entry within a cell, you press Enter to move the insertion point to the next cell.

T F **8.** In a table, a range is a group of cells in a table that touch.

T F **9.** While working in a table, you can click the table select button to select all the cells in the table.

T F **10.** You cannot key more than one paragraph of text into a cell.

T F **11.** Before deleting a column or row from a table, PageMaker first issues a warning asking if you're certain you want to remove the column or row.

T F **12.** If you delete a column from a table by mistake, you may be able to restore your deleted entries by choosing Undo Delete Column from the Edit menu.

T   F   **13.** You cannot delete a row from a table if any cell in that row contains an entry.

T   F   **14.** The weight or width of a line in a table is expressed in points. An 18-point line would be roughly 1/4 inch wide.

T   F   **15.** If the insertion point is located in the last cell of a table, you can insert a new row automatically into the table by pressing Tab.

FILL IN THE BLANK

Complete the following questions by writing the correct word or words in the blanks provided.

1.   Where a column and row intersect in a table, they create a box that is called a(n) _____.

2.   A table can have as many as _____ columns.

3.   Suppose that the insertion point was located in the first cell of a table. Pressing the _____ key would move the insertion point to the last cell in the table.

4.   To move the insertion point one cell to the left you press _____.

5.   When changing the fill color of a cell, the term _____ means the strength or percentage of a color and is expressed as a percentage.

PROJECTS

PROJECT 17-1

1.   Begin a new publication. When the Document Setup dialog box appears, specify a **single-sided** publication and keep the margins at their default settings.

2.   Using the Text tool, click an insertion point slightly below the top margin guide and just to the right of the left margin guide. Then, enlarge the area around the insertion point to **Actual Size.**

3.   Key the words **PERSONNEL LISTING** using center alignment in a sans serif font and in a 36-point font size. Then press **Enter** twice.

4.   Start the Adobe Table program and create a table containing seven rows and four columns. Also, specify a 3.5-inch height and a 6-inch width.

5. Using Figure 17-19 as a guide, key the entries shown into the on-screen table.

FIRST NAME	LAST NAME	DEPT	EXTENSION
Linda	Allen	Personnel	510
Ronald	Blackfoot	Sales	565
Mark	Chang	Marketing	329
Elaine	Fujimura	Production	202
Joe	Santiago	Personnel	455
Sara	Thomas	Marketing	817

6. Insert a new row immediately below the row that contains information on Linda Allen.

7. Key the following entries into the new row.
   John   Abrahms   Sales   980

8. Transfer the new table into the PageMaker publication.

9. When the table appears in the publication, use the Pointer tool to drag the table so that it is centered between the left and right margin guides. Make sure that the top of the table appears roughly one inch below the title.

10. Save this publication under the name **Personnel**.

11. Close this publication.

PROJECT 17-2

In this project, you will create the table shown in Figure 17-20. Take a moment to examine that figure now.

1. Begin a new publication. When the Document Setup dialog box appears, specify a **single-sided** publication and keep the margins at their default settings.

2. Start the Adobe Table program.

3. Create a table containing 11 rows and 6 columns. Also, specify a table height of 5 inches and a width of 6 inches.

4. Group the six cells in the top row to create one large cell.

5. Format the cell that you just grouped in step 4 so that any entry keyed into the cell will appear in bold, centered (center horizontal alignment), and in an 18-point font size.

6. Select the first three cells in the second row and then group those selected cells. Format this newly grouped cell so that any entry keyed into it will appear in bold and with left horizontal alignment.

7. Select the last three cells in the second row and then group those selected cells. Format this newly grouped cell so that any entry keyed into it will appear in bold and with left horizontal alignment.

8. Add light gray tint to the two grouped cells in the second row (the ones you created in steps 6 and 7) by selecting the color Black with 20% tint.

9. Select all the cells in the third row of the table and format those cells so that any entry keyed into them will appear centered (center horizontal alignment) and bold.

10. Group the first three cells in the last row of the table. Then format this newly grouped cell so that any entry keyed into it will automatically appear centered (center horizontal alignment).

11. Group the last cells in the last row of the table. Then format this newly grouped cell so that any entry keyed into it will automatically appear centered (center horizontal alignment).

12. Using Figure 17-20 as a guide, key the text shown in that figure into the appropriate cells in your on-screen table. When finished, the entries in your table should look similar to those shown in Figure 17-20. Make any changes, as required.

13. Transfer the completed table into PageMaker.

14. When the table appears in the publication, use the Pointer tool to center the table on the page from top to bottom and left to right.

15. Save this publication under the name **Flights.**

16. Close this publication.

17. When the table appears, drag the table so that it is centered on the page both from top to bottom and left to right.

18. Print the publication and then save the publication

FIGURE 17-20
A sample solution for the Flights publication

Customer **Flight Itinerary**					
Customer:			Address:		
From	To	Flight #	Date	Time	Meals
Please reconfirm all flights at least 72 hours before departure			If you encounter any problems on your trip call us at (800) 555-1234		

SCANS TEAMWORK

Form a team consisting of 5-10 students, and appoint a team leader. Then, during the next week, have each team member collect as many different examples as possible of publications in which tables were used within the publication. Look closely as you examine these publications because the closer you look and the more you think about the ways in which you can customize a table's appearance, the more examples you usually find. Next, have each team member present to the group all the examples he or she found and explain how those examples might be created with Adobe Table. Finally, as a team, vote on the three most interesting table examples and then have the team leader present and explain those examples to the class.

CRITICAL*Thinking*

ACTIVITY 17-1

In this lesson, you learned how you can greatly change the appearance of a table by joining cells, changing border weight, adding tint and adjusting row height and column width. The television program guide shown in Figure 17-21 was created with the Adobe Table program. Now, imagine that it were your job to recreate that table. Think through how you would proceed. How many rows and columns would you need? What cells would you group? How would you key and format the various entries in the body of the table? And, how would you create the reverse type effect for the entry MONDAY NIGHT TV that appears in the first cell of the table?

FIGURE 17-21
A table example for the Critical Thinking activity

MONDAY NIGHT TV			
7:30	**8:00**	**8:30**	**9:00**
4	Family Time: Mark learns Ann is dating.	One Step: The family fills in for the band.	Baby Me: Jan and John have a fight about the new job.
6	To You: Tim teaches John to drive	My House: Learn how to paint your home. Part 1 of 2 in a series.	Wildlife: The search for the eagle.
8	Molly: The Smiths have a fight.	Flight of the Hawk: Two pilots hatch a plan to steal a high-tech plane. With Mark White and Dale Wash. (1 hr., 30 min.)	

WORKING WITH COLOR

OBJECTIVES

Upon completion of this lesson, you should be able to:

- Explain various guidelines for using color in a publication.

- Apply colors and tints to text and PageMaker-created graphics

- Explain the various methods for choosing appropriate colors.

- Add, remove and substitute colors from the Colors palette.

- Copy colors from one publication into a different publication.

- Explain the various methods for printing color publications.

- Print color separations and printer's marks.

Estimated Time: 5.5 hours

VOCABULARY

Applying a color

CMYK

Color-matching system

Color separation

Color specifier

Color swatch

Color wheel

Crop mark

Density bars

Plate

Printer's marks

Process color

Registration marks

Spot color

Tints

Introduction

Color publications look interesting, and colors can even make certain publications easier to read than if they are in black and white. This lesson describes how to use color with text and PageMaker-created graphics. You will learn how to work with PageMaker's basic default colors, create other colors, and copy colors from one publication into another. You'll also learn how to choose colors, select pleasing color combinations and use various options when you are printing color publications.

Introduction to Color

There's no doubt about it. Colorful publications, such as the ones in Figure 18-1, look interesting and attract attention. Color can also be used in a publication to help a reader locate specific information, or guide his or her eye to important entries. Colors can also evoke a certain psychological response in the reader. Using certain colors, such as blue, can have a soothing effect, whereas stronger colors, like red, can add a feeling of importance or urgency.

FIGURE 18-1
Colors can add interest and attention to publications

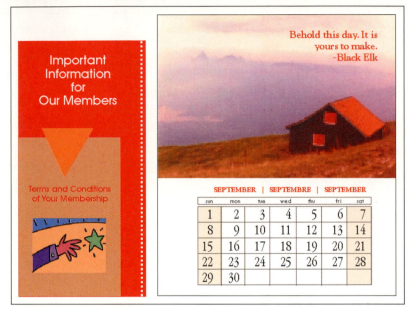

While using PageMaker, you can add color to any text or PageMaker-created graphics, such as rectangles or ovals. And there are thousands of colors from which you can select. If you have a color ink jet, bubble jet or laser printer attached to your computer, you can print your publication in color. If you do not have a color printer, you can still create color publications and then print them out on a different computer that's equipped with a color printer, or send your publication to a commercial printer for color printing.

Although there are many advantages, there are also some drawbacks to using color in a PageMaker publication. First, it takes longer to create a color publication because you need to determine what elements you want to appear in color, select the colors to use, and then match those elements, one at a time, with the proper color. Second, unless you know the certain techniques, selecting the colors is often frustrating because the colors you see on the screen rarely match the printed colors. Third, publications that use color require more disk space and, in some instances, can cause PageMaker to work more slowly on your computer.

Even with these disadvantages, creating color publications is almost always rewarding, satisfying, and fun. Desktop publishing has made color an affordable possibility for publications that were previously limited to black and white. It's important to know, however, that when not used carefully, color can produce disastrous, and often expensive, mistakes. In your own work, you may want to start by introducing color on a limited basis until you gain skill and an understanding of how to use color well in your publications.

Color Basics

Color publications are normally printed using one of two methods. These methods are called spot color and process color printing.

Spot Color

The least expensive way to add one, two, or three colors to a commercially printed publication is by using spot color. The term *spot color* refers to the process of selecting text or a graphic object, such as a circle, and then adding (a spot of) color to it.

Spot color uses premixed ink—one for each color in the publication. Although there are hundreds of spot color inks available, most printing presses can only work with one to four ink colors at a time. Likewise, with spot color, you can only use those specific colors that have been installed in the printing press, not a combination of them. So for example, if green and red spot color inks were installed in the printing press, only those two colors could be used when printing the publication (not yellow, for example, which can be created in process color by combining red and green ink).

Process Color

Publications that require many colors use *process color*. Most process color printing is created by combining different percentages of only four ink colors: cyan, magenta, yellow, and black. Because of the names of their colors, this method is also known as **CMYK**. Almost any color imaginable can be created by using different combinations of these four colors. Figure 18-2 shows examples of the different percentages of inks used to produce various colors.

FIGURE 18-2
Percentages of ink used for different colors (CMYK)

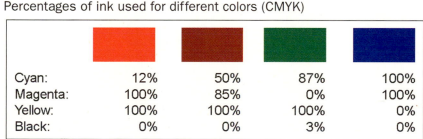

Cyan:	12%	50%	87%	100%
Magenta:	100%	85%	0%	100%
Yellow:	100%	100%	100%	0%
Black:	0%	0%	3%	0%

If you are using four or more colors in a commercially-printed publication, using process color is less expensive than using spot color. Process color is also necessary if you are including color photographs in your publications.

Guidelines for Choosing Spot or Process Color

Whether you use spot color, process color, or a combination of the two depends on several factors, such as the number of colors used in your publication, your budget, and so on. If all copies of the publication will be printed only on a personal ink jet or bubble jet printer, then the method used is not too important. For high-quality publications that are commercially printed, however, the method chosen is very important. Listed below are some general guidelines to consider for commercially printed publications.

When to Consider Spot Color

- When your project requires three or fewer colors.

- When you need to keep printing expenses low.

- When you need to match a specific color, such as a company logo color.

When to Consider Process Color

- When your project requires four or more colors.

- When the budget for printing is not limited.

- When your publication has full-color graphics such as photographs.

In addition, when you use a commercial printing company to print publications, it's also a good idea to talk to the printing company before creating the publication. They may be able to provide additional suggestions that can save you time or help reduce the printing costs.

Working with Colors in a Publication

Adding color to an object in PageMaker is called *applying a color*. To apply a color, you first select the element to color and then choose the color from the Colors palette.

Displaying the Colors Palette

The Colors palette, like the one shown in Figure 18-3, lists the names of the colors that are currently available in the publication. To display the Colors palette, choose Show Colors from the Window menu. *NOTE: PageMaker displays both the Colors and the Styles palette together in the same space on-screen, but shows the contents of only one palette at a time.* If the Styles palette is already displayed, click on the Colors tab to display the Colors palette. Also, if the palette appears with only a few colors showing, you can drag the bottom of the palette downward to reveal more colors.

FIGURE 18-3
Colors palette

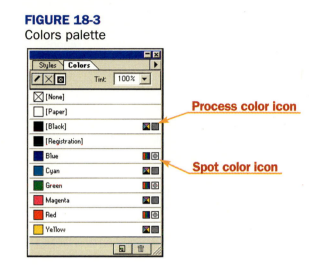

Initially, the Colors palette includes three spot colors—Blue, Green, and Red. It also includes the four process colors—Cyan, Magenta, Yellow, and Black. The symbols that appear at the far right of a color's name indicate whether it is a spot or process color.

The Colors palette also includes three other entries—Paper, Registration, and None. Paper represents the on-screen color of the simulated piece of paper on which you create your publication. Although this color, by default, is normally white, it can be changed to a different color. For example, if you are creating a publication that will be printed on green colored paper, changing the Paper color to green will let you see on the screen how the page will look when it is printed. Registration is the color used for special types of printouts called color separations or spot color overlays (discussed later in this chapter). The color selection labeled None is used to remove any color from the line that surrounds a PageMaker-created graphic and/or any fill (color or pattern) from inside that graphic.

Like other palettes, you can drag the Colors palette anywhere on the screen. If the palette is too small to show all of the available colors, a scroll bar will appear along the right side. Use this scroll bar to bring other color selections into view. To remove the Colors palette from the screen when it's no longer needed, choose Hide Colors from the Window menu.

STEP-BY-STEP 18.1

1. Begin a new publication. When the Document Setup dialog box appears, specify a **single-sided** publication.

2. If the Colors palette is not visible on the screen, choose **Show Colors** from the **Window** menu.

3. Choose **Hide Colors** from the **Window** menu to practice hiding the Colors palette.

4. Perform step 2 again to display the Colors palette.

5. Examine the various colors available in the Colors palette. If the palette contains a scroll bar, use the scroll bar to view all of the available selections.

6. Keep this publication on-screen for use in the next Step-by-Step.

Applying Color

How you apply color to an element depends on whether the element is text or a PageMaker-created graphic. To apply color to existing text, select the text with the Text tool. Then, click on the name of the color you want to apply in the Colors palette. To key new text that appears in a color, use the Text tool to place the insertion point where you want the text to begin, click on the color desired in the Colors palette, and then key the text.

> ### Hot Tip
>
> You can also use the Color drop-down list in the Character Specifications dialog box (by choosing Character from the Type menu) to change text color. This option is especially helpful when you want to change several type specifications at the same time, such as the font, point size, text color, and so on.

To apply color to a PageMaker-created graphic, select the graphic with the Pointer tool. Then, use the Color palette's graphic buttons, identified in Figure 18-4, to specify which part of the graphic to change. Click the Stroke button to change the line color, the Fill button to change the interior color, or the Stroke and Fill button to change both. Finally, click on the color desired in the Colors palette. For example, to change the color of a line that surrounds a rectangle to blue, you would: (1) select the rectangle with the Pointer tool, (2) click on the Stroke button in the Colors palette and then (3) click on the color Blue.

FIGURE 18-4
The Colors palette graphic buttons

Stroke   Fill   Stroke and Fill

S TEP-BY-STEP 18.2

1. Click the **Text** tool and then click an insertion point slightly below the top margin guide and just to the right of the left margin guide.

2. Enlarge the area around the insertion point to **Actual Size**.

3. Key **INTRODUCTION** and press **Enter**. Then, key **TO PAGEMAKER** and press **Enter**.

4. Click **Blue** in the Colors palette. Then, key **PageMaker is the** and press the spacebar once.

5. Click **Red** in the Colors palette, and then key **leading desktop-publishing program**.

6. Select the word INTRODUCTION. Then, click **Cyan** in the Colors palette.

7. Select the words TO PAGEMAKER. Then, click **Magenta** in the Colors palette.

8. Click anywhere on the page to deselect the text, and then examine the different text colors.

9. Click the **Rectangle** tool in the toolbox. Next, click the **Stroke** button in the Colors palette and then click **Red** in the Colors palette. Finally, in a blank area of the page (away from the text), draw a small rectangle roughly 1 inch tall and 2 inches wide. Click the **Pointer** tool to deselect the rectangle and to observe its color.

10. Click the **Ellipsis** tool in the toolbox. Next, click on the **Stroke and Fill** button in the Colors palette and then click **Blue** in the Colors palette. Then, in another blank area of the page, draw a small oval roughly 1 to 2 inches in diameter. Click the **Pointer** tool to deselect the oval and to observe its color.

11. While still using the Pointer tool, select the oval that you created in Step 10. Next, click the **Fill** button in the Colors palette and then click on **Green** in the Colors palette.

12. Click on the **Pointer** tool to deselect the oval and observe how it is now surrounded with a blue line and filled with the color green.

13. Keep this publication on-screen for use in the next Step-by-Step.

Adding New Colors to the Colors Palette

You can add new colors to the Colors palette in a publication at any time. To do so, choose Define Colors from the Utilities menu to display the Define Colors dialog box shown in Figure 18-5. Then click New to display a Color Options dialog box like the one shown in Figure 18-6.

FIGURE 18-5
Define Colors dialog box

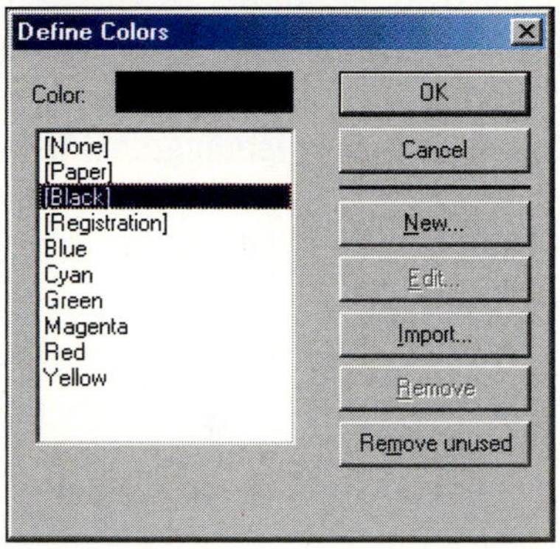

FIGURE 18-6
Color Options dialog box

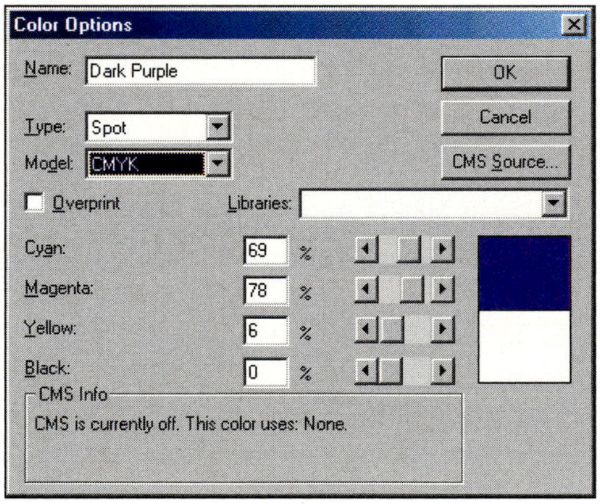

Next, specify the color to add. You can do so by selecting the color from a color-matching system or by defining the color yourself, as described in the following section.

Adding a Color From a Color-Matching System

In general, the easiest and most reliable way to add a color is to select it from a color-matching system. A *color-matching system* is a universally accepted standard or method for identifying specific colors. A color, such as blue, can mean different things to different people. But a specific color selected from a color-matching system means the same thing to everyone who understands that system. As a result, if you use a color matching system to define colors in a publication that will be printed commercially, the color will look exactly as you had intended it to look.

To avoid confusion or misunderstanding, many color-matching systems use code numbers instead of words to identify each color. The most reliable way to use a color-matching system is to purchase a book of color charts that shows samples of each color available with that color-matching system. Such a book is referred to as a *color specifier* or *color swatch* book and can be purchased from art stores, graphic supply houses, and many large bookstores. Figure 18-7 shows an example of the TRUMATCH® Colorfinder book and a sample color chart.

FIGURE 18-7
A color swatch book and sample page (courtesy of TRUMATCH®; TRUMATCH is a trademark of TRUMATCH, Inc.)

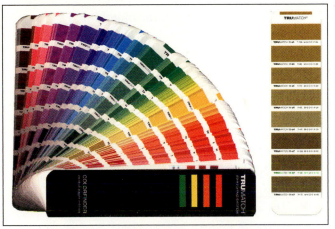

Companies who develop color matching systems, such as TRUMATCH® and Pantone®, license the systems to commercial printing companies. The printing companies, in return, agree to follow specific standards when printing jobs in which that matching system is used.

Table 18-1 lists the names of some popular color-matching systems and the type of color printing for which they are used. If your publication will be printed by a commercial printer, check with them beforehand to find out what color-matching systems they use and/or prefer. Then select your colors accordingly.

TABLE 18-1
Examples of color matching systems

SYSTEM	TYPE
DIC Color Guide	Spot
Focoltone	Process
Greys	Process/Spot
MUNSELL® Book of Colors	Process
MUNSELL® High Croma Colors	Process
PANTONE® Process CSG	Process
PANTONE® Uncoated	Spot
Toyo Color Finder	Spot
TRUMATCH 4-Color Selector	Process

To add a new color, select the name of the color-matching system, such as the TRUMATCH 4-Color Selector system, from the Libraries drop-down list in the Color Options dialog box. Doing so displays a Color Picker dialog box like the one in Figure 18-8. This dialog box lists each color (and its identifying code number or name) from that color-matching system. Use the horizontal scroll bar to bring different color selections into view and click the color you want to add. Then click OK three times to close the Color Picker, Color Options, and Define Colors dialog boxes.

FIGURE 18-8
Color Picker dialog box

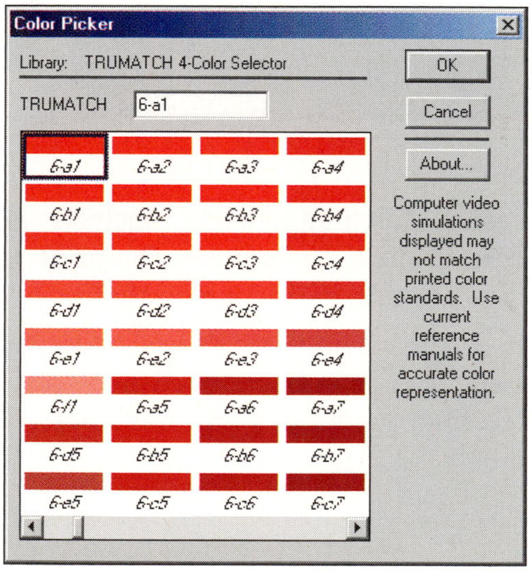

STEP-BY-STEP 18.3

1. Click the **Pointer** tool (to make certain that the new color you are about to add is not applied accidentally to anything on the page).

2. Choose **Define Colors** from the **Utilities** menu. Then, when the Define Colors dialog box appears, click **New**.

3. When the Color Options dialog box appears, choose **PANTONE® Coated** from the Libraries drop-down list. (*NOTE: If this color-matching system is not available on your computer, choose a different system from Pantone® or TRUMATCH®.*)

4. When the Color Picker dialog box appears, observe how each color is identified by a unique code number or name. Use the horizontal scroll bar at the bottom of the dialog box to display some of the other colors available.

5. Click any one color that you would like to add to the publication, and then click **OK** to close the Color Picker dialog box.

6. Click **OK** to close the Color Options dialog box.

7. Click **OK** to close the Define Colors dialog box.

8. Observe how the new color appears in the Colors palette. (*NOTE: If the new color does not appear, you may need to use the scroll bar in the Colors palette to bring the new color into view.*)

9. Keep this publication on-screen for use in the next Step-by-Step.

Adding a Color by Providing Specifications

Instead of selecting a new color by using a color-matching system, you can add a new color by identifying what percentages of different ink colors to use to create the new color. To do so, choose New in the Define Colors dialog box and, when the Colors Options dialog box appears, key a name for the new color, such as Violet or Orange, in the Name text box. Then choose Spot or Process from the Type drop-down list.

Next, select the color model that you will use to identify the new color. Although CMYK is the most popular model used for commercial printing, you can choose from two other color models: RGB (Red, Green, Blue) or HLS (Hue, Lightness, Saturation).

Finally, use the text boxes or scroll bars at the bottom of the Define Colors dialog box to identify the percentage of the different ink colors to use in this new color. If you selected the CMYK color model, for example, four text boxes and slider bars labeled Cyan, Magenta, Yellow, and Black will appear (see Figure 18-6). After specifying the different percentages, choose OK to close the Color Options dialog box, and then click OK to close the Define Colors dialog box.

STEP-BY-STEP 18.4

1. Click the **Pointer** tool (to make certain that the new color you are about to add is not applied accidentally to anything on the page).

2. Choose **Define Colors** from the **Utilities** menu. Then, when the Define Colors dialog box appears, click **New**.

3. Key **My Purple** in the Name text box.

4. Choose **Process** from the Type drop-down list, if not already selected. Then, choose **CMYK** from the Model drop-down list, if not already selected.

5. The color purple contains 79% Cyan, 100% Magenta, 31% Yellow, and 4% Black ink. To specify this new color:
   a. Double-click in the Cyan text box and then key **79**.
   b. Double-click in the Magenta text box and then key **100**.
   c. Double-click in the Yellow text box and then key **31**.
   d. Double-click in the Black text box and then key **4**.

6. Click **OK** to close the Color Options dialog box.

7. Click **OK** to close the Define Colors dialog box.

8. Observe the new color (My Purple) in the Colors palette.

9. Keep this publication on-screen for use in the next Step-by-Step.

Removing Colors from the Colors Palette

You can remove any color from the Colors palette, including any of PageMaker's default colors. You can also have PageMaker automatically remove all colors from the Colors palette that you have not yet used in the publication. Removing unneeded colors makes it easier to select from just those colors that you want to work with in the publication. Use care when removing colors, however, because mistakes can sometimes be time-consuming to correct.

To remove one or more colors, choose Define Colors from the Utilities menu to display the Define Colors dialog box. Then choose one of the following:

- To remove one color: Click its name in the Color list box and then click Remove.

- To remove all unused colors: Click Remove unused. A dialog box will appear showing the colors to be removed. Click Yes to all to remove all unused colors. Or, if you want to check each color that is being removed one at a time, click Yes to remove the color shown or click No to keep that color. PageMaker will then display additional dialog boxes for each additional unused color.

Finally, click OK to close the Define Colors dialog box. The color(s) you removed will no longer appear in the Colors palette.

S TEP-BY-STEP 18.5

1. Choose **Define Colors** from the **Utilities** menu.

2. When the Define Colors dialog box appears, click **Yellow** in the Color list box. Then, click **Remove**. Observe how the Yellow entry no longer appears in the Color list box.

3. Click **OK** to close the Define Colors dialog box.

4. Save this publication under the name **Color-it**. Then, close this publication.

Choosing Appropriate Colors

At this point you may be wondering which colors go well together. There is no easy answer because the colors used will depend on the type of publication, the message being communicated, the audience that it is directed toward, and so on. There are some methods, however, that you can use to help you select colors that, in general, will work well together. Three of the most popular techniques are built around a circle containing a spectrum of colors called the *color wheel*, shown in Figure 18-9. These methods are called complementary, split-complementary, and adjacent colors.

FIGURE 18-9
The color wheel

Complementary Colors

Complementary colors are located directly opposite one another on the color wheel. The color violet, for example, is the complementary color of yellow. Such color combinations attract attention and almost always work well together because of their striking contrast. Figure 18-10 shows an example of a publication created with complementary colors.

FIGURE 18-10
A publication using complementary colors

Split-Complementary Colors

Split-complementary colors consist of one color combined with the two other colors that are located on either side of its opposite (complementary) color. Green and orange are the split-complementary colors of violet. By using slightly less contrast, split-complementary colors draw less attention than complementary colors, yet tend to look more interesting. Figure 18-11 shows an example of a publication created with split-complementary colors.

FIGURE 18-11
A publication with split-complementary colors

Adjacent Colors

Adjacent colors are located next to one another on the color wheel. Violet, blue, and green are examples of adjacent colors. Adjacent colors create a harmonious color scheme and often blend well together to create a quiet, pleasing effect. Figure 18-12 shows an example of a publication created with adjacent colors.

FIGURE 18-12
A publication using adjacent colors

Adding Color Tints

Tints let you vary the intensity or shade of a particular color. In PageMaker, a tint is expressed as a percentage of a solid color. A 100% tint produces the strongest color, whereas a 30% tint produces a lighter shade of the same color.

As you know, spot-color publications are normally less expensive to print (when using a commercial printer) than process color publications. Tints can be used in a spot color publication to give the appearance of using additional colors without the added expense. For example, suppose you use a spot color such as blue in a publication. You can then add several colors to the Colors palette that are lighter tints (shades) of the same blue color. If you apply these different tints to various text or graphic elements, the printed publication will look as if it were printed using several types of blue inks.

If you expect to use a certain tint repeatedly in a publication, you can add the tint to the list of colors in the Colors palette. To add a tint for a color that already appears in the Colors palette (referred to as the base color), choose Define Colors from the Utilities menu. Next, click on the base color in the Color list box (such as the color Blue) and then choose New. When the Color Options dialog box appears, key a name for the new tint color that you wish to create in the Name text box. To help you remember the details of this tint, it's a good idea to include the name of the base color and the percentage of tint in this name, such as *Blue-20% Tint*.

Next, click on the Type drop-down arrow and choose Tint from the list that appears. Doing so will display various tint options in the dialog box like those shown in Figure 18-13. The base color that you selected appears in the Base color preview window. Use the Tint slider bar to specify the percentage of tint. Use the left and right arrows at the beginning and end of the slider bar, or drag the scroll box to change the percentage of tint. Clicking repeatedly on the left arrow on the slider bar, for example, reduces the percentage by 1% each time you click. As you change the percentage, the newly created color appears in the New color preview window. (You can also specify a certain percentage by keying the percentage in the Tint text box.) When finished, click OK to close the Color Options dialog box. Then, click OK to close the Define Colors dialog box. You can apply the new tint color to text or graphics as you normally would any other color in the Colors palette.

FIGURE 18-13
Adding a tint color

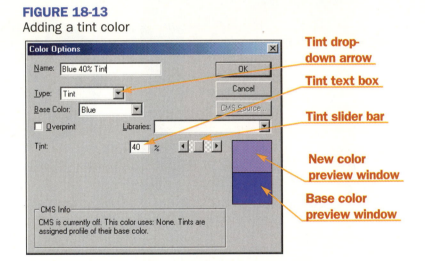

S TEP-BY-STEP 18.6

1. Open the publication named **Color-it** that you created in the previous Step-by-Step.

2. Choose **Define Colors** from the **Utilities** menu.

3. When the Define Colors dialog box appears, click **Cyan** in the Color list box and then click **New**.

4. When the Color Options dialog box appears:
   a. Key **Cyan-60% Tint** in the Name text box.
   b. Choose **Tint** from the Type drop-down list.
   c. Place the mouse pointer over the left arrow button at the beginning of the Tint slider bar. Then click or hold down the mouse button until the Tint text box indicates 60%. (*NOTE: If you hold down the button too long, click the right arrow button in the Tint slider bar to increase the percentage.*)

STEP-BY-STEP 18.6 Continued

   d. Observe how both the base color and the new tint color appear in the preview windows.
   e. Click **OK** to close the Color Options dialog box.

5. Click **OK** to close the Define Colors dialog box.

6. Observe the newly added tint color in the Colors palette.

7. Click the **Text** tool and then select the word INTRODUCTION at the top of the page.

8. Click **Cyan-60% Tint** in the Colors palette. Then, click the **Pointer** tool to deselect the text and observe how the word INTRODUCTION now appears in a lighter shade of Cyan.

9. Keep this publication on-screen for use in the next Step-by-Step.

Using As-Needed Tints

If you are only using a certain tint once or just a few times in a publication, you do not need to add it to the Colors palette. Instead you can simply select both the base color and tint each time from the Colors palette. To do so for text, select the text that you want to change and then click the base color in the Colors palette, such as Blue. Then choose the percentage of tint from the Tint drop-down list shown in Figure 18-14. The text will immediately appear in the new tint.

FIGURE 18-14
Selecting an as-needed tint

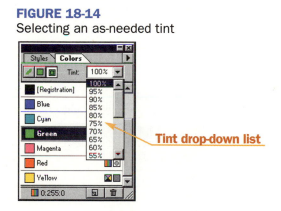

To apply an as-needed tint to a PageMaker-drawn graphic, select the graphic first. Then specify which part of the graphic you want the tint applied to by clicking on the Stroke, Fill, or Stroke and Fill button in the Colors palette. Finally, click the base color that you want to use in the Colors palette, and then choose the percentage of tint from the Tint drop-down list.

STEP-BY-STEP 18.7

1. Select the words **TO PAGEMAKER** located near the top of the page.

2. Click **Blue** in the Colors palette.

3. Choose **60%** from the Tint drop-down list in the Colors palette.

4. Click the **Pointer** tool to deselect the text and then observe how the words TO PAGEMAKER now appear in a lighter shade of blue.

5. Keep this publication on-screen for use in the next Step-by-Step.

Substituting Colors

As you know, choosing the proper colors to use in a publication is sometimes a trial-and-error process. To make this process easier, PageMaker lets you substitute one color with a different color. Suppose that you apply the blue color to twenty different entries in a publication. If you later decide to use green instead of blue for those entries, you can have PageMaker make the substitution automatically for you.

To substitute one color in the Colors palette with a different color, choose Define Colors from the Utilities menu. Next, in the Color list box, click on the color that you want to change, and then click Edit. When the Color Options dialog box appears, select the new color (that you want to substitute) as you normally would. As shown in Figure 18-15, when you return to the Color Options dialog box, the New color preview window will show the new (substituted) color, and the Base color preview window will show the old (original) color.

FIGURE 18-15
Substituting one color with another color

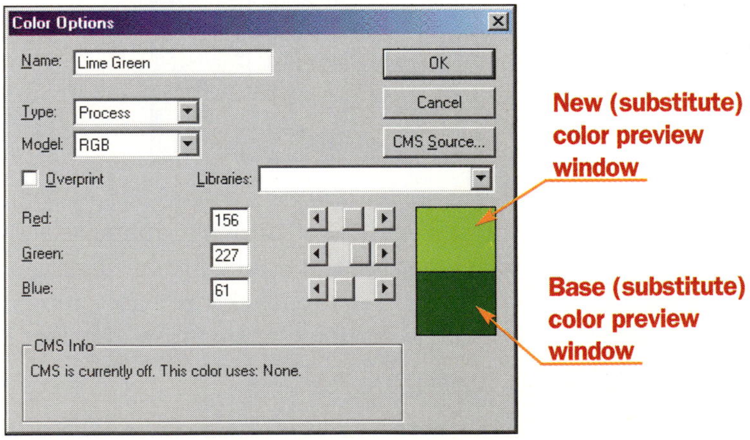

When finished, click OK to close the Color Options dialog box. Then, click OK to close the Define Colors dialog box. Within seconds, PageMaker will automatically apply the new, substituted color to all text and graphics that used the old, original color.

STEP-BY-STEP 18.8

1. Enlarge the area around the text to **Actual Size**, if necessary. Observe how the words *leading desktop-publishing program* and the line surrounding the rectangle appear in red.

2. Choose **Define Colors** from the **Utilities** menu.

3. When the Define Colors dialog box appears:
   a. Click on **Red** in the Color list box and then click **Edit**.
   b. When the Color Options dialog box appears, select any TRUMATCH or PANTONE® color-matching system you wish from the Libraries drop-down list. Then use the Color Picker dialog box to select any color (other than Red) that you want to substitute for Red. When finished, click **OK** to close the Color Picker dialog box.

4. Click **OK** to close the Color Options dialog box. Then, click **OK** to close the Define Colors dialog box.

5. Observe how the words *leading desktop-publishing program* and the line surrounding the rectangle immediately change from Red to the color you substituted. Also notice that the color red no longer appears in the Colors palette.

6. Keep this publication on-screen for use in the next Step-by-Step.

Printing Color Separations

If your color publication will be printed commercially, you can create color separations that the printing company might request in order to print your work. A *color separation* is a printed page containing only the elements from the page to which a certain color has been applied (see Figure 18-16).

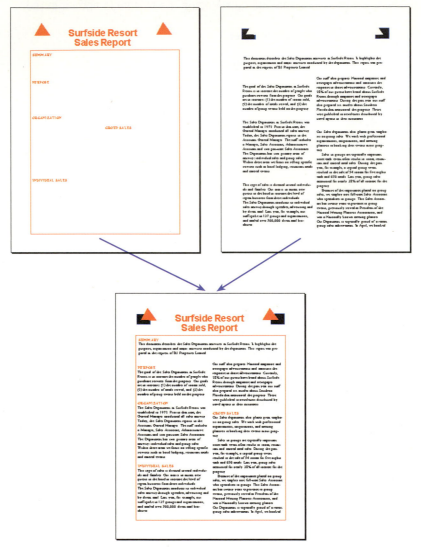

To print a page that contains two colors, such as red and black, a commercial printer makes two plates—one plate for each color. Printer *plates* are made of paper or metal and are similar to photographic negatives. Each plate contains only the items from the page that appear in a certain color, such as Red. The first plate is then inserted in the printing press and used to print everything for the first ink color. Then, the plate for the next color is inserted and the pages run through the printing press again to print all text and graphics that appear in the second color. This process is repeated until all the colors have been printed.

To print the color separations for a publication, choose Print from the File menu and then click Color to reveal the Print Color dialog box shown in Figure 18-17. Next, choose Separations by clicking the radio button preceding this option. A solid bullet (•) will appear inside the radio button when the option is selected.

FIGURE 18-17
Print Color dialog box for color separations

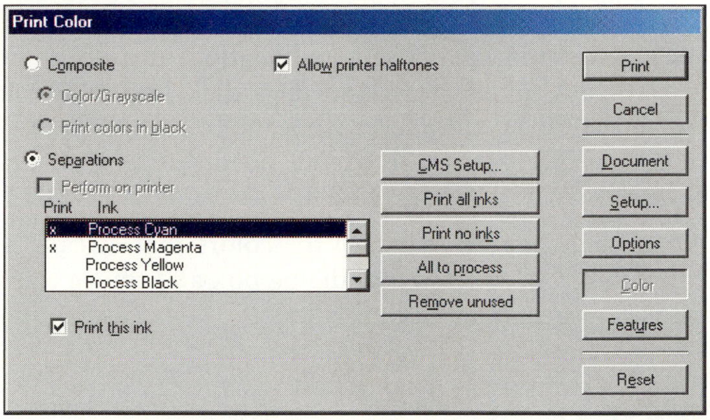

The Color list box displays the names of all colors that appear in the Colors palette. Within this list box, select only those colors for which you want separations printed. An "x" appears before the name of a color when it is selected. Click the *Print no inks* button to deselect any previously selected colors. Then, select only the colors that you want to print. To select a color, click its name, and then click inside the Print this ink check box, located just below the Color list box. If you used any tints in the publication, you must also select the original base color that was used in creating the tint. For example, if you used a color that is a 40% tint of the color Red, you need to select Red in order for the tint color to print. Continue selecting only those colors for which you want a color separation printed. When finished, click Print to begin the printing.

STEP-BY-STEP 18.9

1. Choose **Print** from the **File** menu.

2. Click the **Color** button and then select **Separations** by clicking the radio button preceding that option.

3. Click the **Print this ink** button to deselect all colors that are already selected for printing.

4. Select **Blue** in the Color list box, and then select the **Print this ink** check box.

5. Click **Print** to begin printing the color separation page for blue.

6. Using the Save As command, save this publication under the new name **Color-it Revised**. Then, close the publication.

Copying Colors from a Different Publication

You may often find yourself using the same colors repeatedly in similar kinds of publications. Adding many colors to a publication is time-consuming. Likewise, if you want to use the same colors in one publication as you did in a different publication, you need to be careful to select exactly the same colors. To make it easy to use the same colors in different publications, PageMaker lets you copy the Colors palette from one publication into a different publication.

To copy the Colors palette from a different publication into your on-screen publication, choose Define Colors from the Utilities menu and then click Import. An Import colors dialog box, which looks similar to the Open dialog box, appears. Inside this dialog box, select the publication containing the colors that you want copied (identify the disk drive and/or folder as needed), and then click Open.

The new, copied colors will then be added to the colors that already appear in the Define Colors dialog box. Finally, click OK to close that dialog box and return to your publication. The newly copied colors are now part of your Colors palette.

STEP-BY-STEP 18.10

1. Begin a new publication. When the Document Setup dialog box appears:
   a. Specify a **single-sided** publication.
   b. Key **5** in the first Dimension text box, then key **7** in the second Dimension text box.
   c. Click **OK**.

2. If the Colors palette is not on-screen, display the Colors palette.

3. Choose **Define Colors** from the Utilities menu and then click **Import**.

4. When the Import colors dialog box appears, select the publication named **Color-it Revised** that you worked on in the previous Step-by-Step exercise and then click **Open**.

5. When the Define Colors dialog box reappears, observe how several new colors, such as Cyan-60% Tint, have been added to the Color list box.

6. Click **OK** to close the Define Colors dialog box.

7. Click the **Text** tool and then click an insertion point slightly below the top margin guide and just to the right of the left margin guide.

8. Enlarge the area around the insertion point to **Actual Size**.

9. Click **Cyan-60% Tint** in the Colors palette. Then, key **Caribbean Sun Travel Tours**.

10. Keep this publication on-screen for use in the next Step-by-Step.

Including Printer's Marks in a Printout

Printer's marks are special entries that can appear on printed color separation pages to help a commercial printing company align those pages when printing. These printer's marks include a registration mark, crop mark, and density bar (see Figure 18-18). *Registration marks* are symbols used by a printer (the person) to help register or align the different color separations. These marks normally appear in the middle of the top, bottom, left, and right edge of each printed color separation page. *Crop marks*, also known as trim marks, are a series of lines that appear in each corner of a printed color separation page. Crop marks identify where each page is to be cut or trimmed after printing. For example, suppose you use PageMaker to create a 5- by 7-inch brochure. If this brochure is printed on 8.5 by 11 inch paper, the crop marks would indicate where to cut or trim the paper. *Density bars* are a series of small squares of decreasing tints (ranging from 100% to 0%) and colors. These density bars help the printer (the person) adjust his or her equipment so that it will more accurately reproduce any tints or colors you used in the publication.

FIGURE 18-18
Printer's marks

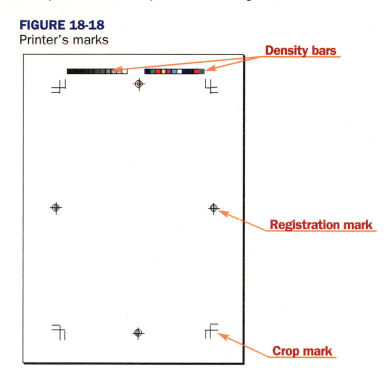

When printing a publication, you can add printer's marks whenever the page size of the publication is smaller than the size of the paper on which it will be printed (such as on your computer's printer). To include printer's marks in a printout, choose Print from the File menu and then specify the page number(s) to print, as you normally would. Next, click Options to display the Print Options dialog box shown in Figure 18-19. In the Options section of the dialog box, select Printer's marks to include registration marks, crop marks, and the density bar. If you want only crop marks printed, then select Crops only. Finally, choose Print to begin printing.

FIGURE 18-19
Print Options dialog box

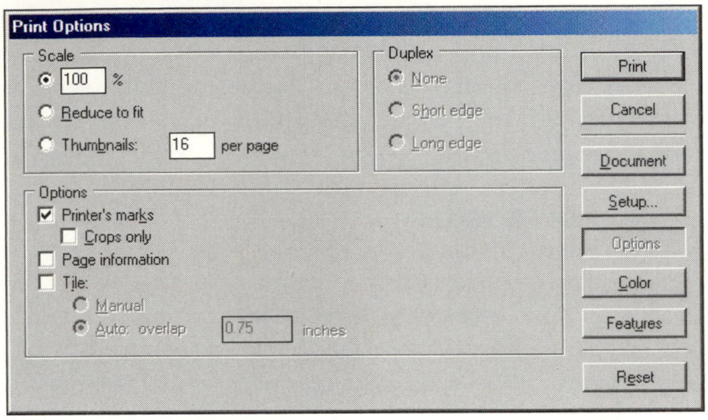

STEP-BY-STEP 18.11

1. Choose **Print** from the **File** menu.

2. Click **Options** and then select **Printer's marks**.

3. Click **Print** to start printing and when the printing finishes, examine the different printer's marks in the printout.

4. Using the Save as command, save this publication with the name **Printer's Marks**. Then, close this publication.

SUMMARY

In this lesson, you learned how to:

■ Apply colors from the Colors palette to text and to PageMaker-created graphics.

■ Add, remove and substitute colors from the Colors palette.

■ Identify various color printing methods and color-matching systems.

■ Explain the purpose of printer's marks and include printer's marks in printed publications.

■ Copy colors from one publication into a different publication.

■ Print color separation pages from a publication.

VOCABULARY *Review*

Define the following terms:

Applying a color	Color swatch	Printer's marks
CMYK	Color wheel	Process color
Color-matching system	Crop mark	Registration marks
Color separation	Density bars	Spot color
Color specifier	Plate	Tints

REVIEW *Questions*

TRUE / FALSE

Circle T if the statement is true or F if the statement is false.

T   F   **1.** In PageMaker, you cannot use more than three colors in a publication.

T   F   **2.** When you create a new publication, PageMaker automatically includes several standard, default colors in the Colors palette.

T   F   **3.** Spot color would be a good choice if a publication contained only two colors.

T   F   **4.** Color-matching systems are universally accepted libraries of predefined colors.

T   F   **5.** Colors that are located directly opposite one another on the color wheel are known as complementary colors.

T   F   **6.** In PageMaker, a tint is expressed as a percentage of a solid color.

T   F   **7.** You cannot create tints for any of PageMaker's default colors such as black, red, or blue.

T   F   **8.** Suppose that you had applied the color red to 10 different titles in a publication and now you want to substitute the color blue. To change the color, you could use the Define Colors dialog box to substitute the color blue for all entries that currently appear in the color red.

T   F   **9.** When printing color separation pages for a tint, you must select the color on which the tint was based.

T   F   **10.** Printer's marks are entries that can help a commercial printer (the person) align color separation pages.

FILL IN THE BLANK

Complete the following sentences by writing the correct word or words in the blanks provided.

1. To add color to a publication, you would first choose _____ from the Utilities menu.

2. The color upon which a tint color is based is called the _____ _____.

3. A(n) _____ _____ is a printed page containing only the elements from the page to which a certain color has been applied.

4. _____ _____ are a series of lines that appear in each corner of a printed color separation page.

5. Symbols used by a printer (the person) to help align different color separations is called a(n) _____ mark.

PROJECTS

SCANS **PROJECT 18-1**

1. Start a new publication. When the Document Setup dialog box appears:
   A. Change the paper size from 8.5 × 11 inches to 4.5 × 9 inches.
   B. Select **Tall** orientation if not already selected.
   C. Specify a **single-sided** publication.
   D. Change the top, bottom, left and right margin settings each to **0.25** inches.
   E. Click **OK**.

2. If the Colors palette is not on-screen, display the Colors palette.

3. Add the color named **9-a** from the TRUMATCH 4-Color Selector library to the Colors palette. (If that color-matching system is not available, choose **Orange Yellow** from the Crayon library or choose **2.5Y 8:13** from the MUNSELL® High Chroma Color library.)

4. Create a large rectangle that covers the entire page (within the margin guides) and shade the lines and inside of that rectangle with the color Cyan.

5. In the pasteboard, create a small rectangle 0.5 inches deep and 2.75 inches wide. Use the on-screen rulers or Control Palette to help determine the size. Also, shade the lines and inside of that rectangle with the color that you added in step 3. Finally, drag this new rectangle onto the page, and position the top of the rectangle on the top margin guide. Center the triangle horizontally between the left and right margin guides.

6. Create another rectangle of the same size and color as the one you created in step 5. Also, position the bottom of this new rectangle on the bottom margin guide, and center it horizontally between the left and right margin guides.

7. Click the **Text** tool and then click an insertion point roughly 2 inches from the top edge of the page and just to the right of the left margin guide. Next, turn on center alignment, select a sans serif font such as Arial, Helvetica or Univers in bold and in a 36-point font size.

8. Perform the following:
   A. Key **Caribbean Sun** and press **Enter** once.
   B. Key **Travel Tours** and press **Enter** three times.
   C. Key **Winter Travel** and press **Enter** once.
   D. Key **Guide**.

9. Apply the color named Paper (white) to the words Winter Travel Guide. Then, apply the color that you added to the Colors palette in step 3 to the words Caribbean Sun Travel Tours.

10. An example of how the elements of this publication should look appears in Figure 18-20. Make any changes or adjustments, as needed.

11. Print the publication. Then, save the publication with the name **Winter Tour**, and finally, close the publication.

FIGURE 18-20
Sample solution to the Winter Tour brochure

PROJECT 18-2A

1. Open the publication named **Sales Report 3 Columns.pmd** from the data files.

2. If the Colors palette is not on-screen, display it.

3. Define a new tint color, and when the Define Colors dialog box appears, click **Blue** in the Color list box. Then, as you continue to create this new color, assign it the name **Blue - 50% Tint** and use the tint slider bar or the Tint text box to specify a 50% tint.

4. After creating the new tint color, turn to the first page of the on-screen publication, if needed. Then, apply the color named Blue - 50% Tint to the words Caribbean Sun Travel Tours that appears at the top of that page.

5. On the first page of the on-screen publication, apply the color Magenta using a 60% as-needed tint to the word SUMMARY and to the paragraph immediately below it.

6. Click the **Pointer** tool to deselect any selected text and view the results.

7. Leave this publication on-screen for use in Project 18-2B.

PROJECT 18-2B

1. Add a new color to the Colors palette named **Royal Blue**. When defining this new color, select Process as the color type and CMYK as the color model. Then, define this new color with the following percentages: Cyan - 100%, Magenta - 80%, Yellow - 0%, Black - 0%.

2. One at a time, apply the color named Royal Blue to the following section headings that are located in the report:

    - PURPOSE
    - ORGANIZATION
    - INDIVIDUAL SALES
    - CORPORATE SALES
    - OTHER SERVICES
    - FUTURE PLANS

3. Copy into the on-screen publication all the colors from the Colors palette of the publication named Color-it that you created in Step-by-Step 18.5.

4. Apply the copied color named My Purple to the words **SALES DEPARTMENT ANNUAL REPORT** that appears at the top of the first page in the on-screen publication.

5. Apply the copied color named My Purple to **Sales Report (continued)** that appears at the top of the second page in the on-screen publication.

6. Print the publication. Then, using the Save as command, save this publication with the new name **Sales Report in Color**. Finally, close the publication.

SCANS   TEAMWORK PROJECT

Form a team consisting of five to ten students each, and appoint a team leader. Then, during the next week, have each team member collect two or three examples of professionally printed publications in which colors were used well, and bring those examples to class. Then, have each team member present to the group the examples they found and discuss how they feel the colors were used appropriately. Finally, as a team, vote on the three most interesting examples of publications that used colors well, and then have the team leader present and explain those examples to the class.

CRITICAL *Thinking*

ACTIVITY 18-1

As you may have already experienced when printing color publications with personal ink jet, bubble jet or certain color laser printers, the colors viewed on the screen often do not match to the colors seen in the printout. This is normally due to the printing and display limitations of these devices. While minor differences in color are sometimes acceptable, significant differences can often produce unattractive results.

Now, imagine that you have selected a page from a magazine containing a certain color you would like to use in a PageMaker publication. To specify that color in a publication, you could begin by holding the magazine page to the screen and displaying various Color Picker dialog boxes until you found a similar match. However, since printed colors rarely match the screen colors, this technique is normally just a starting point. After selecting a starting color, what additional techniques can you think of that would then help you match the color in your PageMaker printout more closely to the color from the magazine? Write a 50-100 word description of the process you might use.

Using Color in Publications

Y_{ou} can use color in an almost unlimited number of ways in any PageMaker publication. For example, you can use it with the drawing tools to add a simple, colorful line on a page, or you can use color with text to set off specific entries, such as all the titles in a publication. You can also use color as the main focal point of a publication, not only to guide the reader's eye, but also to help create a mood or convey a message.

It's often helpful when learning to use color to see examples of how it can be used effectively in real-life publications. Seeing how others use color in publications can help you better understand how you can use color in your own work.

The following pages contain examples of how color can be used in a publication. These pages are divided into two sections: Portfolio of Color Publications, and Drawing with Color.

Portfolio of Color Publications

T_{his} section presents many examples of color publications that were created by several of today's leading graphic design and production firms. These examples demonstrate both the wide range of publications that you can create with PageMaker, and the creativity of the graphic designer and desktop publishing professionals who created them.

It's important to understand that creating professional publications takes much time, patience, training, and practice. Some of the pieces that you'll see took weeks both to design and create with PageMaker.

Portfolio of Color Publications

Minelli Design, Boston, Massachusetts

1
Designer: Mark Minelli, Peter Minelli, Brad Rhodes, Lesley Kunikis
Client: Fidelity Institutional Retirement Services Company
Program(s): PageMaker, Illustrator, Photoshop

2
Designer: Mark Minelli, Peter Minelli, Brad Rhodes, Lesley Kunikis
Client: The Art Institute of Boston
Program(s): PageMaker, Illustrator, Photoshop

3
Designer: Mark Minelli, Peter Minelli,
Brad Rhodes, Lesley Kunikis
Client: Fidelity Investments
Program(s): PageMaker, Illustrator

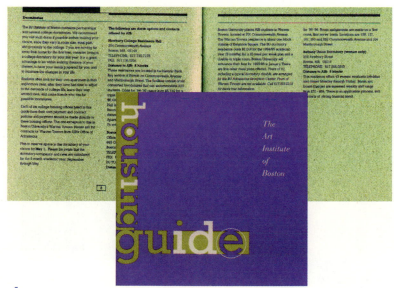

4
Designer: Mark Minelli, Peter
Minelli, Lesley Kunikis
Client: The Art Institute of Boston
Program(s): Unknown

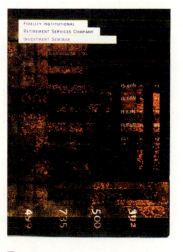

5
Designer: Lesley Kunikis
Client: Fidelity Investments
Program(s): PageMaker,
Photoshop

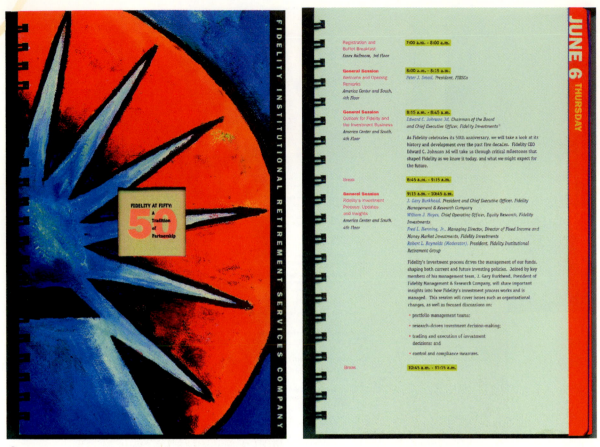

6
Designer: Mark Minelli, Peter Minelli, Brad Rhodes, Lesley Kunikis
Client: Fidelity Investments
Program(s): PageMaker, Illustrator, Photoshop

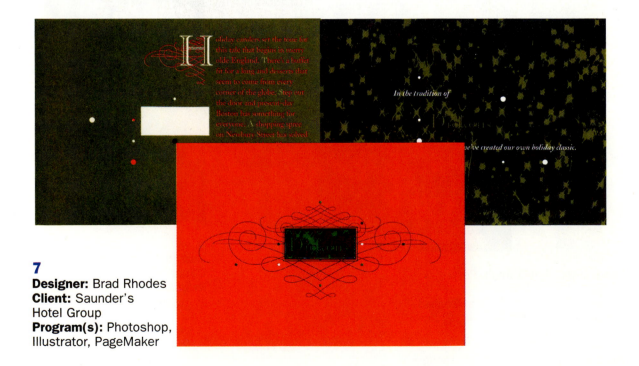

7
Designer: Brad Rhodes
Client: Saunder's
Hotel Group
Program(s): Photoshop,
Illustrator, PageMaker

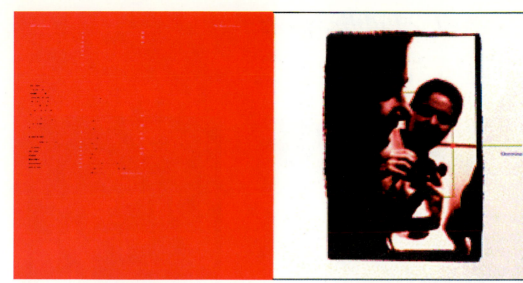

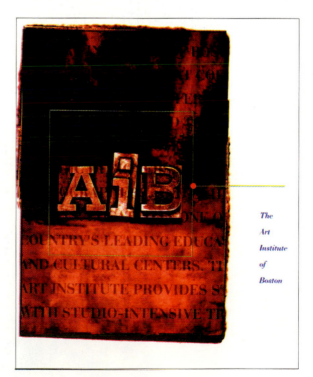

8
Designer: Lesley Kunikis
Client: The Art Institute of Boston
Program(s): PageMaker, Photoshop

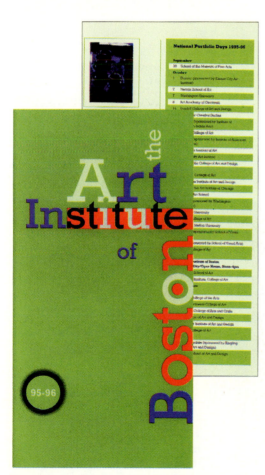

9
Designer: Mark Minelli, Peter Minelli,
Lesley Kunikis
Client: The Art Institute of Boston
Program(s): PageMaker, Photoshop

10
Designer: Mark Minelli, Peter Minelli,
Lesley Kunikis
Client: The Art Institute of Boston
Program(s): PageMaker, Photoshop

Portfolio of Color Publications

Strong Productions, Inc., Cedar Rapids, Iowa

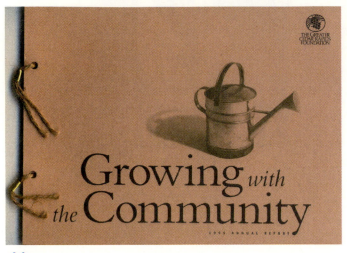

11
Designer: Todd Schatzberg, Matt Doty
Client: The Greater Cedar Rapids Foundation
Photographer: Barbara Doty
Program(s): PageMaker, Illustrator

12
Designer: Todd Schatzberg
Client: Brewed Awakenings
Program(s): PageMaker, Illustrator

13
Designer: Matt Doty, Barbara Doty
Client: Strong Productions, Inc.
Photographer: Barbara Doty
Program(s): PageMaker, Illustrator

14
Designer: Todd Schatzberg
Client: Iowa City Jazz Festival
Program(s): PageMaker, Illustrator

15
Designer: Matt Doty, Todd Schatzberg
Client: City of Cedar Rapids
Photographer: Matt Doty
Program(s): PageMaker, Illustrator

16
Designer: Matt Doty, Renee Kremer
Client: Nesper Sign Advertising
Program(s): PageMaker, Illustrator

17
Designer: Julie Kim, Matt Doty
Client: Strong Productions, Inc.
Photographer: Barbara Doty
Program(s): PageMaker, Illustrator

18
Designer: Todd Schatzberg
Client: Strong Productions, Inc.
Photographer: Barbara Doty, NASA
Program(s): PageMaker, Illustrator

19
Designer: Todd Schatzberg, Matt Doty
Client: Lueck Labels
Program(s): PageMaker, Illustrator

20
Designer: Todd Schatzberg
Client: The Greater Cedar Rapids Foundation
Program(s): PageMaker,Illustrator

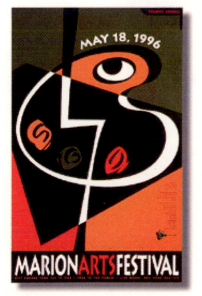

21
Designer: Todd Schatzberg
Client: City of Marion, Iowa
Program(s): PageMaker, Illustrator

22
Designer: Matt Doty, Victoria Quinn-Stephens
Client: Mercy Hospital
Photographer/Illustrator: Barbara Doty/ Erin Wells
Program(s): PageMaker, Illustrator

Portfolio of Color Publications

Marquand Books, Inc., Seattle, Washington

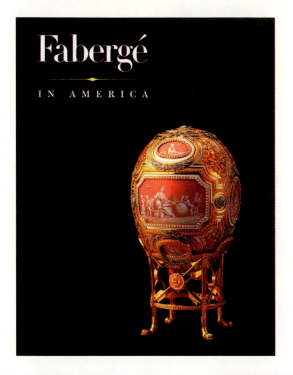

23
Title: *Fabergé in America* by Geza von Habsberg, The Fine Arts Museums of San Francisco and Thames & Hudson
Designer: Ed Marquand, Brian Ellis Martin and Noreen Ryan
Program(s): PageMaker

24
Title: *Shall We Dance?* by Manine Rosa Golden, Hyperion Books
Designer: Brian Ellis Martin and Noreen Ryan
Program(s): PageMaker, Freehand

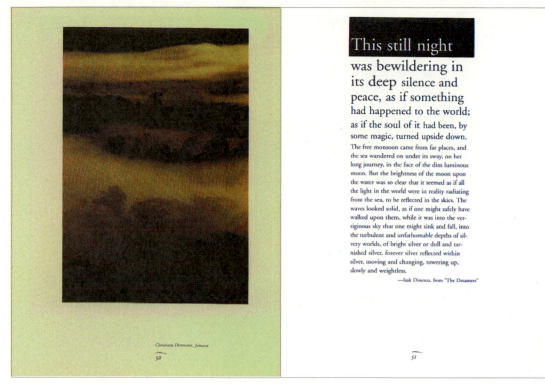

25
Title: *Nature Through Her Eyes,* edited and compiled by
Mary Bemis and Belinda Recio, The Nature Company
Designer: Ed Marquand and Bret Granato
Program(s): PageMaker

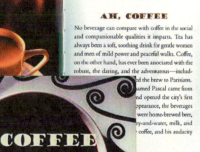

26
Title: *Coffee: Our Daily Cup* by Suzanne Kotz
and Ed Marquand, Warner Treasures
Designer: Ed Marquand
Program(s): PageMaker

27
Title: *Hot Drinks: Cocoas, Toddies, Punches &
Grogs* by Suzanne Kotz and Ed Marquand,
Warner Treasures
Designer: Ed Marquand
Program(s): PageMaker

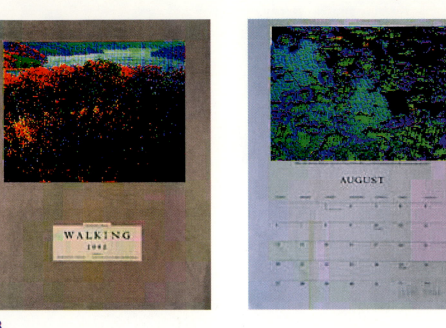

28
Title: *Walking Calendar,* The Nature Company
Designer: Bret Granato
Program(s): PageMaker

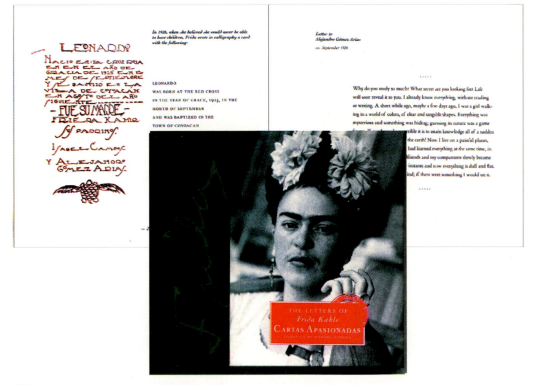

29
Title: *The Letters of Frida Kahlo: Cartas Apasiondas,* edited by Martha Zamora, Chronicle Books
Designer: Bret Granato
Program(s): PageMaker

30
Title: *Walking,* 1993, The Nature Company
Designer: Ed Marquand
Program(s): PageMaker

31
Title: *Home Spa: Recipes and Techniques to Restore and Refresh,*
by Manine Rosa Golden, 1997, Abbeville Press
Designer: Noreen Ryan
Program(s): PageMaker

Drawing with Color

This section shows examples of how to use PageMaker's drawing tools in place of clip art or digital stock photography to create interesting and colorful drawings within a publication. Although the program is not designed as a drawing program, you'll see examples of how you can use its basic drawing tools and color features to create interesting and attractive illustrations. The only limitations are your imagination and patience.

Take your time as you look through the following pages to see how you can use PageMaker in new and unusual ways.

Creating Simple Illustrations

After Drawing the Basic Shapes

After Adding Fill Color

With PageMaker's drawing tools, a few colors and some patience, it's possible to create a wide variety of colorful and good-looking graphics. The drawings above are created mostly with circles and an occasional rectangle or straight line and then filled with various colors. Because PageMaker gives you access to thousands of colors, you can make your drawings as colorful or as subdued as needed for your publication.

A Computer Disk

After Drawing the Basic Shapes

After Adding Fill Color

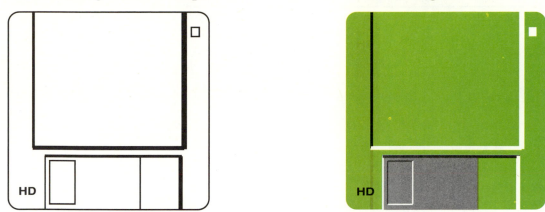

This computer disk is made entirely using the Rectangle and Constrained-line tools. The body of the disk is a square with rounded corners and green color fill, while the metal cover at the bottom is made from two rectangles; one containing green and the other containing gray color fill. The three-dimensional effect was created by drawing three lines with Paper (white) color fill along the right and along the lower-middle section.

Desktop and Desk Objects

After Drawing the Basic Shapes

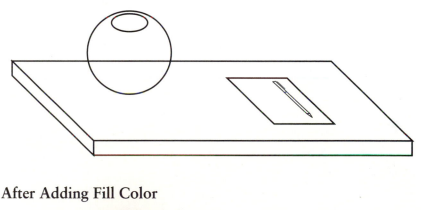

After Adding Fill Color

The illustration above is based on rectangles and ovals. The top of the desk and the paper are made by first drawing rectangles and then slanting those rectangles with PageMaker's skewing feature. Similarly, the front and left side of the desk are two rectangles (the one on the left side was rotated and skewed). One shade of brown fill is used for the table top, while a darker shade of brown fill is used on the side and the front rectangles to give the desk a three-dimensional look.

City at Night

After Drawing the Basic Shapes

After Adding Fill Color

This drawing is created with only the Rectangle and Ellipsis tools and two colors. The outline of the buildings and all the windows are made with rectangles (except the two "peaks" that were created with the Polygon tool). The rectangles are filled with either solid black (building) or black with 65% tint (windows). Each cloud is created from four ovals filled with 75% tint of the color black. The moon is made from a circle with Paper (white) fill color.

ADVANCED PUBLICATION TECHNIQUES

OBJECTIVES

Upon completion of this lesson, you should be able to:

- Define what a template is, and explain the advantages of using templates.

- Explain how to create a template from an existing publication.

- Explain how to replace text and graphics within a template.

- Describe how to edit a template file.

- Explain how to access and use PageMaker's built-in templates.

- Define what a PDF file is and explain how to create a PDF file of a publication.

- Explain how to create an HTML-format file from a publication.

Estimated Time: 4 hours

VOCABULARY

Exporting

HTML

PDF

Template

Introduction

In this lesson you will learn how to work with various advanced PageMaker techniques. First, you will learn how to save time and improve consistency through the use of templates. You'll see how to create a template, place text and graphics into a template, and save the newly created work as a regular PageMaker publication. You'll also see how to take advantage of PageMaker's professional templates for producing a variety of professionally designed publications quickly. Then you will learn how to create electronic versions of your publications known as PDF and HTML files, which can be distributed electronically or even placed onto the Internet.

Introduction to Templates

If you create many similar publications, you can save a great deal of time and ensure consistency by using templates. A **template** is a special publication from which other publications are created. A template contains the page layout, font specifications, and other elements needed for the master page(s) and for each numbered page that would normally appear in a certain type of publication, such as a flyer, newsletter, or brochure. After creating a template, you then use the template to create other publications for which it was designed.

The Process

You create a template in PageMaker in much the same way you create a publication—by specifying the page size, page orientation, and the number of pages needed. You also establish the overall layout of each page by adding columns, positioning ruler guides, and adding styles for each type of text entry. When you have finished creating the template, you save it on disk. If you have already created a publication for the type of template you want to develop, you can use that publication to quickly create a template.

To use a template to create a publication, first open the template as you would a standard PageMaker publication. Because the design work has already been done, you can then immediately add the actual text and graphics to this new publication. As you add text entries, for example, those entries will automatically appear in the correct location and with the proper type specifications. When you finish creating the publication, you save it with its own name, not with the name of the template. Doing so protects the original template so that you can use it again repeatedly in the future.

The Advantages

There are several important advantages of creating publications by using templates. The most important reason is saving time. When you create a publication from a template, all of the time-consuming decisions, such as the page layouts, type specifications, column settings, and styles have already been made. You simply add the necessary text and graphics for the particular version of the publication and you're finished.

Another advantage is that templates provide consistency among similar types of publications. Consistency means that publications have the same "overall look" in terms of the page size, number of pages in the publication, number of columns on a page, type specifications, and so on. Organizations that produce a monthly newsletter or magazine, for example, normally want those publications to look similar from one issue to the next. Likewise, readers come to expect that consistency. If you look at different issues of a national magazine or newspaper you will see this idea of consistency carried throughout each issue.

Creating Templates from Existing Publications

The easiest way to develop a template is to create it from an existing publication. To do so, you simply open the publication and then save it as a template. After opening the publication, choose Save As from the File menu to display the Save Publication dialog box. Next, key a name for the template in the File name text box, and then click the Save as type drop-down arrow to display the drop-down list shown in Figure 19-1. In this drop-down list, choose Template. Next, specify the location on the disk where you want the file stored as you normally would, and then click Save. Finally, close the newly created template publication by choosing Close from the File menu. You can now begin using the template to create new publications.

FIGURE 19-1
Save Publication dialog box – Template option

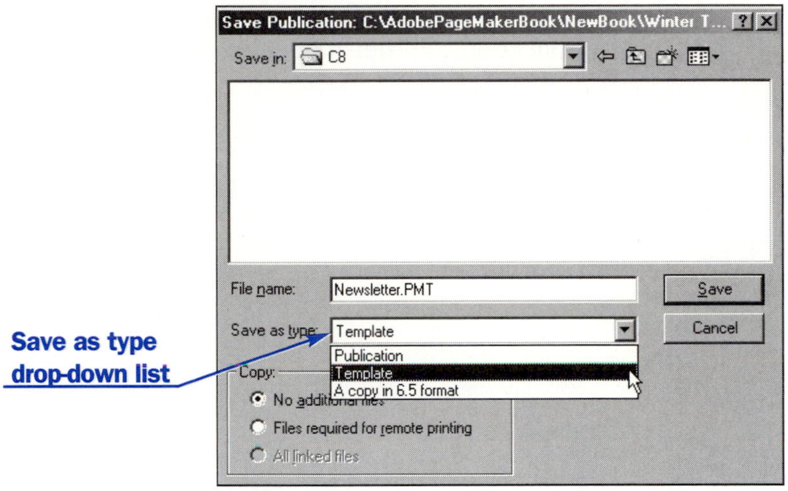

Save as type drop-down list

STEP-BY-STEP 19.1

1. Open the publication named **Winter Escape** that you created earlier in Lesson 12.

2. Save this publication as a template file by following these steps:
   a. Choose **Save as** from the **File** menu.
   b. Key **Flyer** in the File name text box.
   c. Choose **Template** from the Save as type drop-down list.
   d. Specify the location on the disk where you want the template stored. (This is normally the same location where you store your regular publications. Check with your instructor if you are uncertain.)
   e. Click the **Save** button.

3. Choose **Close** from the **File** menu to close the newly created template.

4. Keep PageMaker open and on-screen for use in the next Step-by-Step.

> **Important**
>
> Like PageMaker's PMD file extension, all template files are identified with the unique file extension PMT. You do not need to include that file extension when keying the template name because PageMaker adds the extension automatically.

Opening a Template

To create a publication from a template, you first open the template file. Choose Open from the File menu, and then select the name of the template in the Open publication dialog box, just as you would for a regular publication. When you click on the name of the template that you want to open, PageMaker automatically selects the Copy option in the dialog box (see Figure 19-2) so that a copy of the template's contents appears on the screen rather than the original template file. The original file then remains intact for creating other publications. To finish opening the template, click Open.

FIGURE 19-2
PageMaker normally opens copies of templates

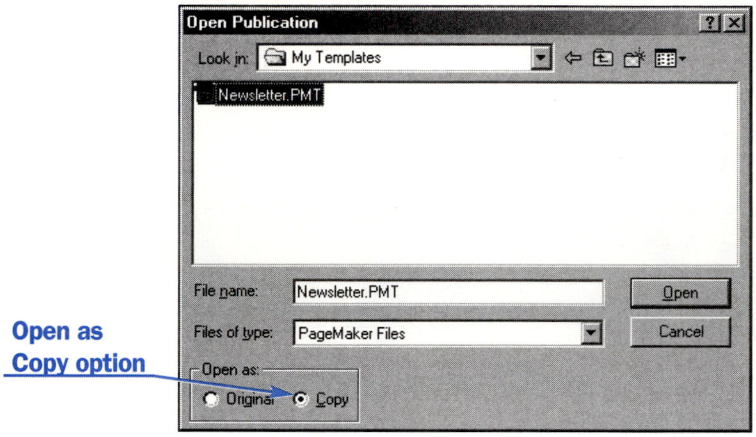

Open as
Copy option

STEP-BY-STEP 19.2

1. Open a template file by performing these steps:
   a. Choose **Open** from the **File** menu.
   b. In the Open Publication dialog box, click the template file named **Flyer**.
   c. Observe how PageMaker automatically selects the Copy option in the lower left portion of the dialog box.
   d. Click **Open**.

2. Keep this publication on-screen for use in the next Step-by-Step.

Replacing Text in a Template

Templates normally contain old or simulated text and graphics that you replace with the actual text and graphics for a new publication. You can key the replacement text within PageMaker, or import the replacement text from a word processing file. You can also replace a graphic in the template with a different graphic file by importing a replacement graphic.

Keying Replacement Text

To replace text, use the Text tool to select the text that you want replaced, and then key the replacement text. As you key, the new text will take on the characteristics of the text that you are replacing. For example, suppose a paragraph in the template appears in Arial typeface, in 14-point size and in italic. If you select the paragraph and then begin keying new text, the new text will appear in Arial, 14-point and italic.

Importing Replacement Text

You can also replace text from the template with text from a word-processing document. You can use this feature to replace any amount of text in the template, such as an entire story, or only a few paragraphs.

To replace an entire story, use the Text tool and click anywhere in the text that you want replaced. Next, choose Place from the File menu to display the Place dialog box, and then click the name of the word-processing file containing the replacement text. In the Place section of the dialog box, (see Figure 19-3) select *Replacing entire story* and make certain that the *Retain format* in the Options section is not selected. Finally, click Open. After a moment, the old text in the template file will be replaced with the new text from the word processing file.

FIGURE 19-3
Place dialog box – text replacement options

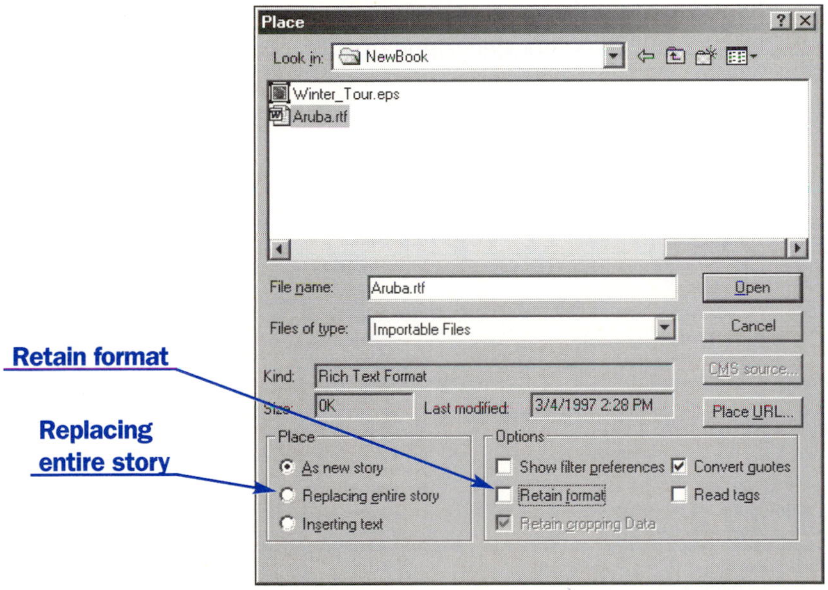

To replace several paragraphs, use the Text tool and select only the text that you want replaced. Next, choose Place from the File menu to display the Place dialog box, and then click the name of the word processing file containing the replacement text. In the Place section of the dialog box, select *Replacing selected text* and make certain that *Retain format* in the Options section is not selected. Finally, click Open. After a moment, the selected text will disappear and the text from the word-processing file will appear in its place.

STEP-BY-STEP 19.3

1. Click the **Text** tool and then select only the two-line title CARIBBEAN TOURS that appears at the top of the page.

2. Key **RELAX IN** and press **Enter**. Then, key **ARUBA**, but do not press Enter.

3. Enlarge the area of the page just below the graphic to **Actual Size**.

4. While still using the Text tool, select only the eight lines of text that appear immediately beneath the graphic. This text begins with the words *Come and experience* and ends just after the telephone number *(800) 555-1212. (NOTE: Make certain that you do not select any of the blank lines or the words Caribbean Sun Travel Tours).*

5. Import replacement text by performing these steps:
   a. Choose **Place** from the **File** menu.
   b. From the practice files that are provided with this book, click on the file named **Aruba.rtf**.
   c. In the Place section of the dialog box, select **Replacing selected text**.
   d. In the Options section of the dialog box, make certain that the Retain format option is not selected.
   e. Click **Open**.

6. Observe how the text from the template is replaced by the text from the word-processing file.

7. Keep this publication on-screen for use in the next Step-by-Step.

Replacing Graphics in a Template

To replace a graphic in the template with a different graphic, use the Pointer tool and select the graphic that you want replaced. Next, choose Place from the File menu to display the Place dialog box, and then click the name of the file containing the replacement graphic. Finally, in the Place section of the dialog box, select Replacing entire graphic, and then click Open.

STEP-BY-STEP 19.4

1. Click the **Pointer** tool and then, select the large graphic that appears in the center of the page.

2. Replace the graphic in the template by performing these steps:
   a. Choose **Place** from the **File** menu.
   b. From the data files that are provided with this book, select the file named **Beach.tif**.
   c. In the Place section of the dialog box, select **Replacing entire graphic**.
   d. Click **Open**.

3. Observe how the graphic from the template is replaced by the new graphic.

STEP-BY-STEP 19.4 Continued

4. Using the Save As command, save this publication under the name **Aruba**.

5. Close the publication and keep PageMaker on-screen for use in the next Step-by-Step.

Editing a Template

Occasionally, you may need to make editing changes to the original template file; perhaps to change the type specifications for a certain entry, or to resize or change the position of a graphic. To open an existing template for editing, choose Open from the File menu and then click the name of the template in the Open publication dialog box. Next, select the Original option found in the lower portion of the dialog box, and then click Open and make the editing changes required. When you are finished, save and close the template the same way you save and close any PageMaker publication.

STEP-BY-STEP 19.5

1. Open a template file for editing by performing the following steps:
   a. Choose **Open** from the **File** menu.
   b. In the Open Publication dialog box that appears, click the template file named **Flyer**.
   c. In the lower portion of the dialog box, select the **Original** option.
   d. Click **Open**.

2. Make an editing change to a template by performing the following steps:
   a. If the Colors palette is not on the screen, choose **Show Colors** from the **Window** menu.
   b. Click the **Text** tool. Then, select only the two-line title CARIBBEAN TOURS that appears at the top of the page.
   c. Click the color **Magenta** on the Colors palette.

3. Choose **Save** from the **File** menu to save the edited template with its existing name (Flyer).

4. Choose **Close** from the **File** menu.

5. Keep PageMaker open and on-screen for use in the next Step-by-Step.

Working With Professional Templates

NOTE: This section discusses optional program features that must be installed separately from PageMaker. Check with your instructor first to make certain this topic is covered in your course and that these features are available on your computer.

The PageMaker program includes over 300 professionally created templates. These templates were developed by professional graphic designers, and they make it easy to create a wide range of good-looking publications, such as advertisements, business cards, and brochures. Working with these professional templates makes it easy to create high-quality, good-looking publications even if you are relatively new to PageMaker. And, those same templates can provide you with a great way to study the techniques of graphic design professionals.

> ### Hot Tip
>
> Because the 300 professional templates use large amounts of disk space, or may not be needed in certain organizations, they are not automatically installed along with the PageMaker program. They can, however, be installed later if needed.

To select a professional template, choose Plug-in Palettes from the Window menu and then choose Show Template Palette from the submenu. Doing so reveals a Templates palette, like the one shown in Figure 19-4. Next, click on the Category drop-down arrow and select the category for the type of template that you need. For example, select the Brochures category to see a listing of the different brochure templates available. After selecting the category, thumbnails (small samples of the different templates that are available) appear in the Templates window.

FIGURE 19-4
Templates palette

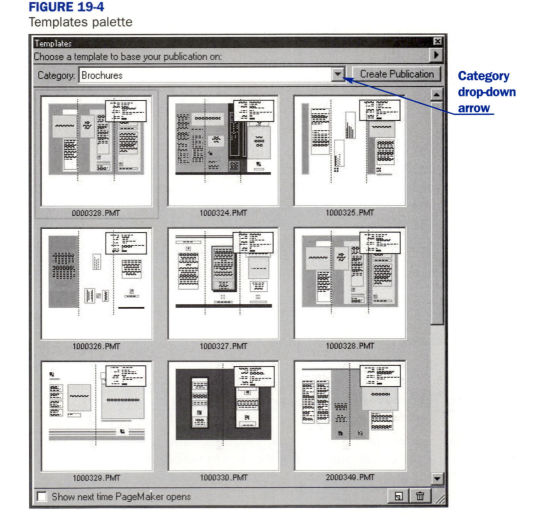

Category drop-down arrow

To open a professional template, double-click its thumbnail in the Templates palette. Then, use the instructions given earlier in this lesson to replace the template contents with your own contents. When finished, save the work as a PageMaker publication. *NOTE: When opening certain professional templates, the fonts used in the template may not be available on your computer. If this occurs, PageMaker will substitute the missing font with a different font that is available on your PC, and display both font names in a dialog box labeled PANOSE Font Matching Results. If this dialog box appears, click OK to accept the replacement fonts.*

STEP-BY-STEP 19.6

1. Choose **Plug-in Palettes** from the **Window** menu, then choose **Show Template Palette** from the sub-menu to display the Template palette.

2. Click the **Category drop-down arrow**, and then choose **Certificates** from the drop-down list that appears.

3. Examine the different thumbnails of the various certificate templates that are available. Then, double-click on a template that looks interesting to you. If a dialog box labeled PANOSE Font Matching Results appears, click **OK** to accept the font substitution(s).

4. Examine the template that appears in the Publication window and make whatever changes you feel necessary to the contents. For example, feel free to substitute any text in the template with different text. Many templates also contain informational boxes labeled Template Type that offer additional information on the template. After reading the information, delete the box using the Pointer tool or drag the box into the Pasteboard so it will not be included in the printout.

5. Print the on-screen publication.

6. Close the publication without saving it.

7. Keep PageMaker open and on-screen for use in the next Step-by-Step.

Creating PDF Files from Publications

NOTE: This section discusses optional features that must be installed separately from PageMaker. Check with your instructor first to make certain this topic is covered in your course and that these features are available on your computer.

PageMaker is an excellent program for producing printed publications that can be distributed by hand, mail, or express delivery methods. But in the fast-paced world in which we live, it is often necessary to share information with others, whether it is across the city or across the world, as soon as that information becomes available. Therefore, people often share files electronically either through the Internet or by attaching them to e-mails. But in order to share a PageMaker publication file with someone, the recipient would also need to have the PageMaker program installed on his or her own computer.

To more easily share PageMaker publications electronically with others, Adobe has created a method called *PDF* (Portable Document Format) for viewing files electronically. This method lets individuals view PageMaker publications even when PageMaker is not installed on the recipient's PC. Instead of printing a publication on paper, PageMaker can produce an electronic file in PDF format that contains images of each page in the publication. This process is done using a program that is included with PageMaker, called Acrobat Distiller. Once the PDF file is created it can be distributed electronically and viewed by anyone who has a copy of a free program called Acrobat Reader installed on their PC.

Creating a PDF file from a Publication

To begin, you first open the publication from which you want to create the PDF file. Next, click the Export Adobe PDF button in the toolbar. You can also choose Export from the File menu and then choose Adobe PDF from the submenu to reveal the PDF Options dialog box, shown in Figure 19-5. *NOTE: If the Adobe PDF option is not available in the submenu, this means that the Acrobat Distiller program was not installed on your PC or that it has become damaged and will need to be reinstalled. Notify your instructor if this occurs.*

FIGURE 19-5
PDF Options dialog box

PDF Options

PDF Style: [On Screen]

General | Doc. Info | Hyperlinks | Articles/Bookmarks | Security

Distiller Settings
  Job Name: Screen
  Edit Job Options...

Pages
  ○ All Pages in Book
  ● All Pages in Current Publication
  ○ Ranges 1-
  Enter page numbers and/or ranges separated by commas.
  For example: 1, 4, 6-11
  Page Size(s): Same as current publication

Printer
  Style: Acrobat
  ☑ Check for PageMaker printer style conflicts

☐ Embed Tags in PDF (for accessibility and reflow)

Export...
Cancel
Save Style...
Delete Style...
Add Style...

The PDF Options dialog box contains many options and settings as described in the following entries.

Choose the PDF Style

The PDF Style drop-down list lets you identify how the PDF file that you are about to create will be used by the recipient. The options include On Screen (for publications that will primarily be viewed on the screen) or Print (for publications that will normally be printed by the recipient). Either option will produce a PDF file that can be viewed on screen or printed. However, the selection you make will determine whether the resulting file will produce higher quality results when viewed on the screen or when printed. When you select either Print or On Screen from the PDF Style drop-down list, a similar entry will automatically appear in the Distiller Settings section of the text box.

Specify the Pages to Output

The Pages section of the dialog box lets you specify those pages of the publication that you want included in the PDF file. To include the entire publication, make certain the All Pages in

Current Publication option (the default setting) is selected. To include only certain pages, such as pages 3 through 6, key those page numbers in the Ranges text box. Use a hyphen (-) to separate a range of pages, such as 3-7. Use a comma (,) to separate individual pages, such as 2,6,8. You can also combine these methods. For example, keying 2,4-6 would print pages 2, 4, 5, and 6.

Specify the Paper Size

The Page Size(s) drop-down list lets you specify if the publication from which you are creating the PDF file is of a different size than the paper on which it will be printed by the recipient. Remember that in PageMaker, the size of the publication (as identified in the Page Setup dialog box) may sometimes be different than the size of the paper on which it is printed. Most often, publications are created in an 8.5 × 11 inch size and printed on paper of the same size. When the size of the publication and the size of the paper on which it will be printed are the same, choose *Same as current publication* (the default setting). Otherwise, choose *Same as printer style* from the Page Size(s) drop-down list.

Verify the Printer Settings

In the Printer section of the dialog box, the Style drop-down list lets you specify whether the file will be created so that it can be printed on most types of printers, or only with one specific model of printer. By choosing Acrobat (the default setting) the program will automatically adjust the printout to whatever printer the recipient is using. Similarly, if the option *Check for PageMaker printer style* is selected (the default) the program will warn you if certain features or layouts used in the publication may cause printing problems with certain printers.

Perform the Export

Exporting is a technique for transferring data from one program into a format that can be read by a different program. The Acrobat Distiller program lets you export a publication into a format that can be read by the Acrobat Reader program. When all the dialog box options are selected, click the Export button to begin creating the PDF file. An *Export PDF As* dialog box will appear, like the one in Figure 19-6. Here, select the disk/folder in which you want the PDF file stored and key a name for that file. Finally, click Save to begin the export process. After a short pause, the export will finish and the resulting PDF file will appear in an Acrobat Reader window (discussed in the next section of this lesson).

FIGURE 19-6
Export As dialog box

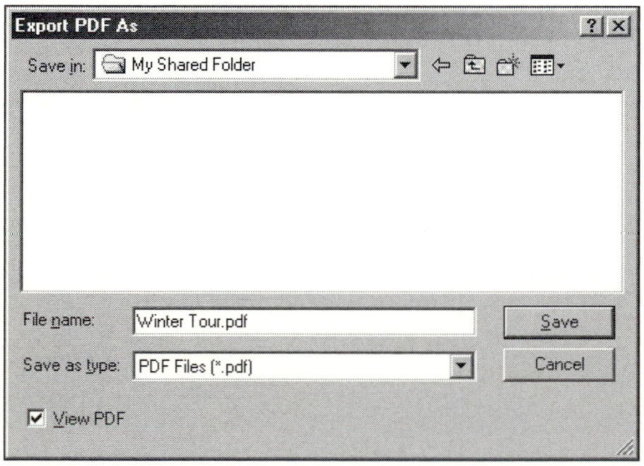

S TEP-BY-STEP 19.7

1. Open the publication named **Electronic File Example** from the data files that accompany this book.

2. Choose **Export** from the File menu and then choose **Adobe PDF** from the submenu that appears. (*NOTE: If the Adobe PDF option does not appear in the submenu, contact your instructor.*)

3. When the PDF Options dialog box appears, choose **On Screen** from the PDF Style drop-down list, if not already selected.

4. In the Pages section of the dialog box, do the following:
   a. Make certain that the *All Pages in Current Publication* option is selected.
   b. Choose **Same as current publication** from the Page Size(s) drop-down list, if not already selected.

5. In the Printer section of the dialog box, do the following:
   a. Choose **Acrobat** from the Style drop down list, if not already selected.
   b. Make certain that the *Check for PageMaker printer style conflicts* option is selected.

6. Click the **Export** button.

7. When the *Export PDF As* dialog box appears, key **Grand Cayman Information** in the File name text box. Then, specify the location on the disk where you want the PDF file stored. (Check with your instructor if you are uncertain.) Finally, click **Save**.

8. After a delay while the program starts, the publication will appear in an Acrobat Reader window. Keep that window on-screen for use in the next Step-by-Step.

Working with the Acrobat Reader

After exporting a PDF file, PageMaker starts the Acrobat Reader program and displays the resulting PDF file in a window (see Figure 19-7). Since Acrobat Reader is a separate program from PageMaker, an in-depth discussion of using that program is beyond the scope of this book. Since it is a fairly easy program to use, however, some basic techniques and commands are discussed in the paragraphs that follow.

FIGURE 19-7
Example of an Acrobat Reader window

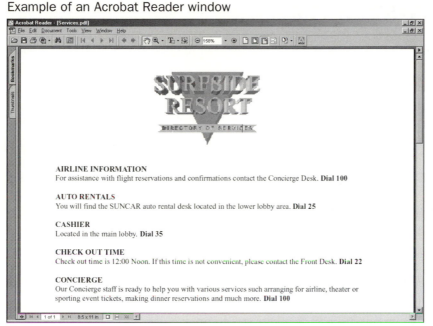

Like PageMaker, the Acrobat Reader window has a menu bar and a toolbar for issuing commands. Placing the mouse pointer on a toolbar button and pausing for a moment will reveal a tool tip describing the purpose of the button.

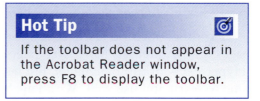

Hot Tip

If the toolbar does not appear in the Acrobat Reader window, press F8 to display the toolbar.

To Change the Viewing Area

Normally, only a portion of a page appears on screen. Choose Fit in Window from the View menu to display a full page from the publication. You can also choose Zoom In or Zoom Out from the View menu to enlarge (zoom in) or reduce (zoom out) the amount of the page you see on-screen. In addition, the vertical scroll bar, or the Page Up or Page Down keys, let you move different portions of the publication into view.

Viewing Different Pages

To view the next (or previous) page in the publication, choose Next Page (or Previous Page) from the Document menu. To view the first page (or the last page) in the publication, choose First Page (or Last Page) from the Document menu. Finally, to display a specific page in the publication, such as page 12, choose Go To Page from the Document menu, key the page number to view, and then click OK.

Other Useful Acrobat Reader Commands

To print the current publication, choose Print from the File menu. To print only part of the publication, use the Print Range section of the dialog box to specify the page(s) to print before clicking OK.

When you are finished viewing the publication in the Acrobat Reader window, choose Exit from the File menu to quit the program and return to PageMaker.

STEP-BY-STEP 19.8

1. Press **Page Down** on your keyboard to move a different part of the on-screen page into view.

2. Choose **Fit in Window** from the **View** menu to display a full page.

3. Choose **Next Page** from the **Document** menu to display the next page of the publication.

4. Choose **First Page** from the **Document** menu to display the first page of the publication.

5. Choose **Exit** from the **File** menu to close the PDF file, exit Acrobat Reader and return to PageMaker.

6. When PageMaker reappears, close the on-screen publication and keep PageMaker on-screen for use in the next Step-by-Step.

Creating HTML Files from Publications

NOTE: *This section discusses optional programs (a Web browser) that must be installed separately from PageMaker. Check with your instructor first to make certain this topic is covered in your course and that these features are available on your computer.*

Another method used today for distributing information electronically is through Web pages on the Internet. Most Web pages are created using a programming language called *HTML* (Hypertext Markup Language). But because it is a programming language, learning HTML takes time to learn and use well. With PageMaker 7.0, however, the program can automatically create HTML formatted Web pages from publications that can then be viewed in Web browsers and made available worldwide on the Internet.

Besides exporting publications in PDF format, you can also export a publication in HTML format. If you select this technique, PageMaker automatically scans your publication and then creates all the HTML programming language instructions needed to place that information into a Web page.

Formatting Publications for HTML

Compared to PageMaker, HTML has somewhat limited formatting capabilities. Here are a few simple, but important, differences to understand:

- While PageMaker can work with text sizes as large as 650 points, text in HTML is limited to only a few sizes.

- While you may be able to select from hundreds of typefaces in PageMaker, HTML has only a very limited set of typefaces.

■ While you can easily create squares, rectangles, ovals, circles and polygons in PageMaker, those shapes are not available in HTML.

Normally, PageMaker will automatically convert your publication into HTML format so that all text appears in only one typeface and point size. If you want to vary the size of text in the resulting HTML file, you need to apply PageMaker's built in styles to the text. As you learned earlier in this book, when you apply a built-in style, such as the Headline or Body text style, the text to which that style is applied automatically appears using specific font settings determined by PageMaker. For titles or headlines, applying the Headline style produces the largest point size possible, followed next by Subhead 1 and then Subhead 2. For the remaining body text on the page, applying the Body text style produces easily readable results in the final HTML file.

Creating an HTML Format File from a Publication

Start by opening the publication for which you want to create the HTML file. Next, click the Export HTML button in the toolbar, or choose Export from the File menu, and then choose HTML from the submenu to reveal the Export HTML dialog box, shown in Figure 19-8. *NOTE: If the Export option is not available in the submenu, this means that the Export feature is not installed on your PC or that it has become damaged and will need to be reinstalled. Notify your instructor if this occurs.*

FIGURE 19-8
Export HTML dialog box

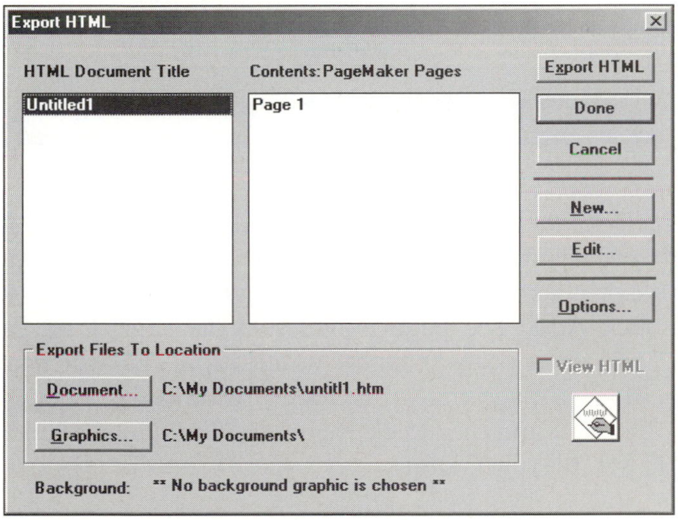

The Export HTML dialog box contains several buttons for controlling how the export occurs. These buttons, and the technique for creating the HTML file, are described in the following paragraphs.

Identify the Filename/Pages to Export

Begin by clicking the New button to reveal an Export HTML New Document dialog box, like the one shown in Figure 19-9. In HTML, the term Document Title refers to the name that appears at the top of the browser's window when you are viewing a Web page. In the Document Title window, key the words that you want to appear at the top of the HTML page. By default, PageMaker will automatically display a name, such as Untitled1, at the top of the browser window. To display a more meaningful name, such as Caribbean Sun Monthly Newsletter, key that name in the Document Title text box.

FIGURE 19-9
Export HTML New Document dialog box

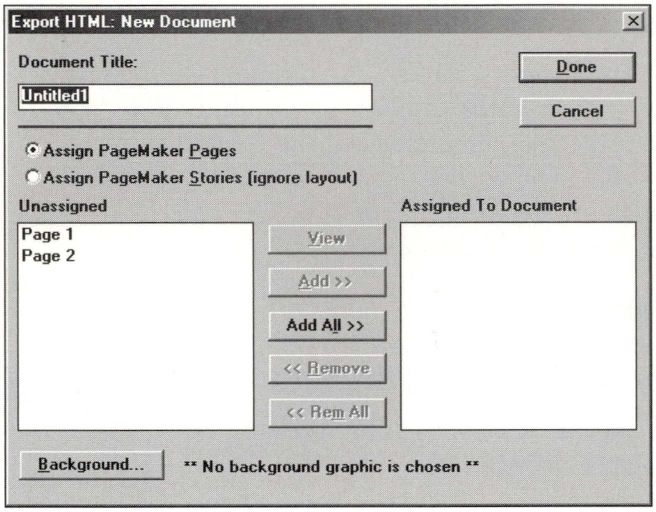

Next, select the page(s) from the publication that you want included in the HTML file, and also the order in which you want it to appear. To do so, first select Assign PageMaker Pages (if not already selected). Next, click on the name of the first page that you want included and the HTML file and then click Add. The page name, such as Page 1 or Page 2, appears in the Unassigned list box. To add other pages from the publication, click the page name and then click the Add button. To remove a page that you added by mistake, click the page name in the Assigned To Document list box and then click Remove. When finished identifying the pages you want included in the HTML file, click Done.

Identify Where the File Will Be Stored

Like other computer files, HTML files are stored on disk, and are assigned a standard file name. To identify where the HTML file will be stored, and to assign its name, click the Document button. This reveals the Document Save As dialog box, similar to the one shown in Figure 19-10.

FIGURE 19-10
Document Save As dialog box

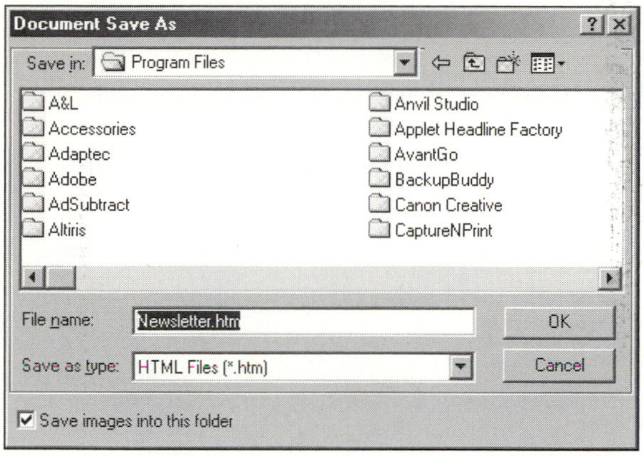

Next, select the disk/folder in which you want the HTML file stored and key a name for that file in the File name text box. Also, if your publication contains graphic files, select the *Save images into this folder* option to have your graphic files stored along with the HTML file. When finished, click OK.

Exporting the HTML File

When finished specifying the settings, click Export HTML to create the HTML file. When exporting is finished, the publication window will reappear. To view the HTML file, start your browser program, such as Microsoft Explorer or Netscape Navigator, and then use the program's Open command to view the HTML file. In Microsoft Explorer, for example, you choose Open from the File menu and click on the Browse button. Then, navigate to the disk/folder in which the HTML file is stored, select the HTML file, click Open, and finally click OK to view the file.

> **Hot Tip**
>
> Like PageMaker's PMD file extension, all HTML files are identified with the unique file extension HTM. You do not need to include that file extension when keying the filename, since PageMaker will add the extension automatically.

S TEP-BY-STEP 19.9

1. Again, open the publication named **Electronic File Example** that is supplied with the data files that accompany this book.

2. Choose **Export** from the **File** menu, and then choose **HTML** from the submenu that appears.

3. When the Export HTML dialog box appears, click **New**. Then, in the Document Title text box, key the new document name **Visit the Grand Cayman Islands**.

STEP-BY-STEP 19.9 Continued

4. Next, identify the pages to include in the HTML file by performing the following steps:

   a. If the Assign PageMaker Pages option is not selected, select that option.

   b. In the Unassigned list box, click **Page 1**, and then click the **Add** button.

   c. In the Unassigned list box, click **Page 2**, and then click the **Add** button.

5. Click **Done** to close the Export HTML: New Document dialog box.

6. When the Export HTML dialog box appears, click **Document**. When the Document Save As dialog box appears, perform the following steps:

   a. Select the disk/folder where you want the HTML file stored. (Check with your instructor if you are uncertain.)

   b. In the File name text box, replace the default filename by keying **Caymans**.

   c. Select the **Save images into this folder** option by clicking on the check box that precedes that option.

   d. Click **OK**.

7. When the Export HTML dialog box reappears, click **Export HTML**.

8. Close the publication without saving it.

9. OPTIONAL: If you wish to view the HTML file, exit PageMaker and then start your Web browser. Next, choose **Open** from the **File** menu and using instructions appropriate for your browser, navigate to the disk/folder in which the Caymans.htm file is stored (if you are uncertain, ask your instructor for details). Finally, open that file to view it. If you are using Microsoft Explorer, choose **Open** from the **File** menu and then click **Browse**. When the Microsoft Internet Explorer dialog box appears, you navigate to the appropriate disk/folder, click the file named **Caymans.htm**, click **Open** and then click **OK**.

SUMMARY

In this lesson, you learned how to:

- Explain the advantages of templates and the process of creating them from an existing publication.

- Open and edit a template file.

- Replace text and graphics within a template.

- Explain the advantages of creating PDF files from PageMaker publications.

- Create a PDF file from a publication and view that file in Acrobat Reader.

- Explain the advantages of creating HTML format files from PageMaker publications.

- Create an HTML file from a publication and describe the process necessary to view that file in a browser.

VOCABULARY *Review*

Define the following terms:

Exporting	PDF	Template
HTML		

REVIEW *Questions*

TRUE / FALSE

Circle T if the statement is true or F if the statement is false.

T   F   **1.** A template can contain both text and graphics.

T   F   **2.** When you open a template, PageMaker normally opens a copy of the file so that the original template file remains intact for creating other publications.

T   F   **3.** Once you create a template, you cannot edit it.

T   F   **4.** You cannot key replacement text within a template. You can only import replacement text.

T   F   **5.** Templates can be used to ensure consistency among similar types of publications.

FILL IN THE BLANK

Complete the following sentences by writing the correct word or words in the blanks provided.

1.   The abbreviation PDF stands for _____ _____ _____.

2.   The term _____ is a technique for transferring data from one program into a format that can be read by a different program.

3.   A publication from which other publications are created is referred to as a(n) _____ .

4.   A PDF file can be viewed by anyone who has a copy of a free program called _____ _____.

5.   The abbreviation HTML stands for _____ _____ _____.

PROJECTS

PROJECT 19-1

1. In this project, you will use an existing template to create the brochure shown in Figure 19-11 and Figure 19-12. Review those figures now before moving on to step 2.

FIGURE 19-11
Solution to Cayman Island publication – page 1

Summary

Capital: George Town

Official language: English

Population: 30,800

Currency: Cayman Islands (CI) dollar

Exchange rate: CI$ 1.00 = US$1.20

Time zone: EST

Area code: (809)

Driving: Driving is on the left side of the road.

Weather: The rainy season is between May and October.

Visas: No visas required for American and Canadian citizens. Proof of citizenship and a return plane ticket is required.

Climate: Average temperature is 78 degrees in the winter months and 84 degrees during the summer months. The Cayman Islands are positioned near the center of the northeast trade winds and a gentle breeze is extremely normal during even the hottest days.

Land area: Total land area of the Cayman Islands is 100 square miles: Grand Cayman, 76 sq. miles; Cayman Brac, 14 sq.miles and Little Cayman, 10 sq. miles.

Visiting the Cayman Islands

6600 Duvall Street
Key West, Florida 32358
Telephone: (303) 555-1234

2. From the data files that are provided with this book, open the template file named **Brochure**.

3. Turn to page number two in the on-screen publication.

FIGURE 19-12
Solution to Cayman Island publication – page 2

Why not treat yourself to a memorable Caribbean Sun Travel Tour excursion to the Cayman Islands this winter. For almost 40 years this peaceful trio of Grand Cayman, Cayman Brac and Little Cayman, located in the quiet Western Caribbean, has been one the world's best diving and water sports destinations. Maybe that's why more turtles call Cayman their home than any other island in the world. Here are some things you might want to know.

THE CLIMATE

The Cayman Islands enjoy ìeternal summer,î because they're situated in the heart of the Caribbean tempered by cooling trade winds. Temperatures are coolest during February (72-86 degrees) and warmest (80-90 degrees) during July and August. Relative humidity varies from 68% to 92%. The water temperature ranges between 78-82 degrees in the winter and 82 - 86 degrees in the summer.

THE LANGUAGE

The official language of the Cayman Islands is English. It's Welsh, Scottish and English ancestors still add a distinguished sound to the speech of the Island's people.

DINING AND CUISINE

Tourists can select from more than 100 restaurants and food shops with selections ranging from elegant dining to low cost fast food on all three of the main islands. Traditional Caymanian cuisine features a strong Jamaican influence of curry and other intense seasonings and includes lobster, conch and local seafood in a variety of dishes, complimented by coconut, plantain, yams, rice and peas and other West Indian side dishes.

SHOPPING

The island of Cayman is a duty-free port, offering visitors a wide selection of duty free items such as watches,

crystal, perfumes, china and fine jewelry. Visitors will find that our prices on imported perfume, watches and many luxury items may be as much as 40% cheaper here. In the town of George Town visitors will find both the duty-free shopping area and a large shopping center offering more than 60 shops and restaurants. All stores on the islands are closed on Sunday downtown.

LOCAL CURRENCY

Cayman Islands has its own dollar currency (CI). It was first issued in 1972 and has denominations issued in CI$100, 50, 25, 10, 5 and 1 as well as coins valued at 25 cents, 10, 5 and 1 cent. The CI dollar has a fixed exchange rate compared to the US dollar of US$1.25. In other words, the US dollar equals CI $.80. Also, there is no need for you to exchange US dollars into local currency. The US dollar is accepted throughout the islands at the fixed exchange rate. To avoid surprises, however, keep this exchange rate in mind. For example, a United States $20 bill becomes CI$16.

4. Select the three-line title *Key the Title in This Space* and replace the selected text with **Visiting the Cayman Islands**.

5. Select the word *Title* that is located at the top, left side of the page and replace it with the word **Summary**.

6. Select the three paragraphs of text that appear below the word *Summary* in the left-hand column. Then, replace the selected text with the text from the file named **Cayman-2.rtf** (this file is supplied with this book). While replacing this text using the Place command, make certain that the Replacing selected text option is selected and that the Retain format option is not selected.

7. Replace the rectangle that appears at the top of the left-hand column with the graphic file named **Starfish.tif** provided with the data files for this book. While replacing this graphic using the Place command, make certain that the *Replacing entire graphic* option is selected.

8. Turn to page number one in the on-screen publication.

9. All of the text in the left, middle, and right columns of this page in the template is a single story. Select and replace the text in this story with text from the word-processing data file named **Cayman-1.rtf**. While replacing this text using the Place command, make certain that the Replacing selected text option is selected and that the Retain format option is not selected.

10. Replace the graphic box at the bottom of the middle column with the graphic file named **Beach.tif** from the data files. While replacing this graphic using the Place command, make certain that the Replacing entire graphic option is selected.

11. Review your publication and make any corrections needed. Then, print both pages of the publication.

12. Using the Save As command, save this publication under the name **Cayman Island** and then close the publication.

PROJECT 19-2

1. Open the publication named **Services** from the data files.

2. Create a PDF format file of this one-page publication and name the PDF file **Services-PDF Format**.

3. Using Acrobat Reader, print the **Services-PDF Format** file.

4. Close Acrobat Reader. Then, save and close the publication.

SCANS 🌐 **WEB PROJECT**

Visit the Adobe Web site at *www.adobe.com* and navigate to the Acrobat product section of that site. See what information you can discover about the various ways organizations are using Acrobat to distribute information electronically.

CRITICAL *Thinking*

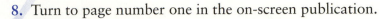

SCANS **ACTIVITY 19-1**

As you learned in this lesson, templates offer the great advantage of providing consistency between similar publications. When creating a magazine or a newspaper, for example, a template helps ensure that the same font specifications and page layouts are used from one issue of the magazine to the next. But some people avoid creating templates because they complain that a template takes too much time to create, and in some situations, they are correct. Take a few moments and think of three different kinds of publications in which creating a template with PageMaker could be helpful, and briefly list those on a piece of paper. Then, think of three different kinds of publications in which creating a template would not make sense, and list those on a piece of paper.

ADVANCED FEATURES

COMMAND SUMMARY

FEATURE	MENU COMMAND	KEYSTROKE	TOOLBAR BUTTON	LESSON
Index, Mark entry	Utilities, Index Entry	Ctrl+Y		16
Index, Create	Utilities, Create Index			16
Table of Contents, Identify	Apply the Headline, Subhead1, Subhead2 style or create new style and select Include in table of contents option.			16
Table of Contents, Create	Utilities, Create TOC			16
Book List, create	Utilities, Book, then list publications			16
Table, create	Edit, Insert Object, Adobe Table 3.0, Create New			17
Table, adjust column width	Select column, then Cell, Row/Column Size			17
Table, adjust column width	Select row, then Cell, Row/Column Size			17
Table, insert column(s)	Select column, then Cell, Insert Column Before (or After)			17
Table, insert row(s)	Select row, then Cell, Insert Row Above (or Below)			17
Table, remove column(s)	Select column(s), then Cell, Delete Column		Ctrl+K	17
Table, remove row(s)	Select row(s), then Cell, Delete Row		Ctrl+K	17
Table, format cell(s)	Select cell(s), then Format, Format Cell		Ctrl+F	17
Table Palette, hide	Window, Hide Table Palette	Ctrl+6		17
Table Palette, show	Window, Show Table Palette	Ctrl+6		17
Table, group cells	Select cells to group, then Cell, Group		Ctrl+G	17
Table, ungroup cell(s)	Select cell(s) to group, then Cell, Ungroup		Ctrl+U	17
Colors Palette, show	Window, Show Colors		Ctrl+J	18
Colors Palette, hide	Window, Hide Colors		Ctrl+J	18
Color, add or remove from palette	Utilities, Define Colors			18

FEATURE	MENU COMMAND	KEYSTROKE	TOOLBAR BUTTON	LESSON
Print color separations	File, Print, Color, Separations			18
Colors, import	Utilities, Define Colors, Import			18
Printer's Marks, include	File, Print, Options, Printer's marks			18
Template, create from publication	File, Save As, Template			19
Template, open built-in	Window, Plug-in Palettes, Show Template Palette			19
PDF, export	File, Export, Adobe PDF		🔳	19
HTML, export	File, Export, HTML		⬤	19

REVIEW *Questions*

TRUE/FALSE

Circle T if the statement is true or F if the statement is false.

T F **1.** A cross-reference is an index entry that identifies a different, related topic instead of a specific page number.

T F **2.** Indexing is case sensitive.

T F **3.** If you edit a publication containing an index, you must issue the Create Index command again after editing to be certain the page numbers are correct.

T F **4.** A table of contents normally appears at the front of a publication.

T F **5.** A table can contain up to 999 rows.

T F **6.** When creating a table, you can specify the number of columns and rows that you want in the table, but you cannot specify the physical size of the table, such as 2 inches by 4 inches.

T F **7.** In a table, a range is a group of cells in a table that touch.

T F **8.** Before deleting a column or row from a table, PageMaker first issues a warning asking if you're certain you want to remove the column or row.

T F **9.** You cannot delete a row from a table if any cell in that row contains an entry.

T F **10.** Color-matching systems are universally accepted libraries of predefined colors.

T F **11.** In PageMaker, a tint is expressed as a percentage of a solid color.

T F **12.** When printing color separation pages for a tint, you must select the color on which the tint was based.

T F **13.** Printer's marks are entries that can help a commercial printer (the person) align color separation pages.

T F **14.** Templates can be used to ensure consistency among similar types of publications.

T F **15.** Once you create a template, you cannot edit it.

FILL IN THE BLANK

Complete the following sentences by writing the correct word(s) in the space provided.

1. A word or phrase that is part of a major subject or topic in an index is called a(n) _____.

2. Identifying a word or phrase that you want included in an index is called _____ an index entry.

3. A list of PageMaker publications that are electronically linked together as one large publication is called a(n) _____ list.

4. Normally, indexes appear on their own page in a publication, and usually at the _____ of a publication.

5. When working in a table, the _____ controls how closely text comes to the edge of a cell.

6. To add color to a publication, you first choose Define Colors from the _____ menu.

7. The color upon which a tint color is based is called the _____ _____.

8. A(n) _____ mark is a series of lines that appear in each corner of a printed color separation page.

9. The abbreviation PDF stands for _____ _____ _____.

10. The abbreviation HTML stands for _____ _____ _____.

SIMULATION

INTRODUCTION

Throughout this book you have learned various techniques for creating professional-looking publications with PageMaker. In this simulation, you will combine many of these techniques to create a newsletter for Caribbean Sun Travel Tours. The purpose of this simulation is to help you integrate PageMaker features to produce a multi-page publication that contains both text and graphics and requires knowledge of fonts, tables, styles, and colors. As you work through this project, remember that the fonts you have available will vary based on the computer you are using. If your computer does not have a particular font called for, select a similar font. Because of these font differences, your final publication might not look exactly the same as the examples shown on the following pages, but it should look similar.

Before doing any work on the computer, review the entire assignment first. Read all the pages and study their contents before you begin. Then, as you start to create the publication, work "smart" by saving your work regularly (every 10 to 20 minutes). When you save this publication on disk, you will name it *The SunTimes*.

BACKGROUND

Caribbean Sun Travel Tours has decided to produce a quarterly, four-page newsletter that it will send to its current and previous customers. The newsletter will serve two purposes. First, it will provide a way to help educate customers about trends in the travel industry. Second, it will provide a way to notify customers about upcoming travel tours or special fare reductions.

In anticipation of this upcoming newsletter, other employees at Caribbean Sun Travel Tours have already created or selected the word-processing and graphic files needed for this project. Your job is to create the desktop-published newsletter.

GENERAL INSTRUCTIONS

As shown in Figure UR-1, the final newsletter publication will be four pages long and printed on letter size (8.5 × 11 inch) paper. Pages 1 and 4 will appear on the outside and pages 2 and 3 will appear on the inside. As you work on this project, remember it is an important advertising publication for the company, so take your time and work carefully. If you were working at Caribbean Sun Travel Tours, these four printed pages would be sent to a commercial printer where the newsletter would then be printed double-sided, in color on one sheet of tabloid size (11 × 17 inch) paper. The completed newsletter would then be folded in half and a name and address label attached to the back page for mailing.

FIGURE UR-1
The assembled newsletter

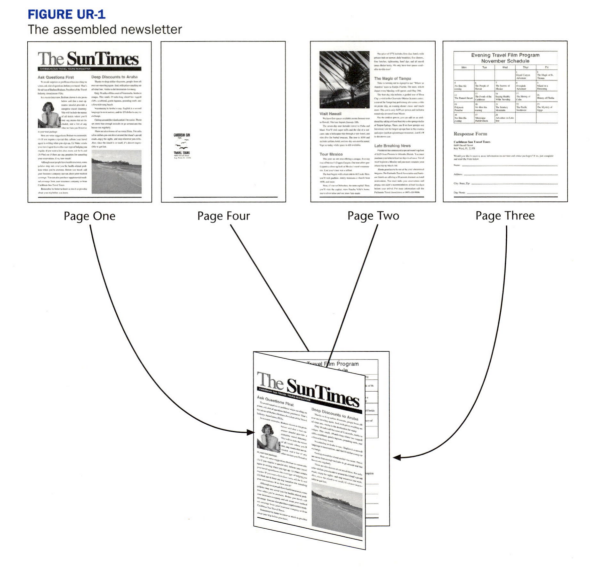

Page One   Page Four   Page Two   Page Three

THUMBNAILS

To give you a general idea of how the final project will look, Figure UR-2 shows thumbnails of each page from the newsletter. These thumbnails are provided to give you an idea of what the project is all about. Don't worry about reading the words. A full page figure from which you will be keying appears later.

FIGURE UR-2
Thumbnails of the complete newsletter

Page One

Page Two

Page Three

Page Four

INSTRUCTIONS

The remaining pages of this simulation provide specific instructions on the overall project and the individual pages of the newsletter. Review this material carefully for information on the exact layout required for each page.

Publication Setup

As you complete the Document Setup dialog box, specify it as a double-sided, facing-pages publication that uses standard, letter size paper with tall orientation and containing a total of four pages. Set the margins as follows:

Inside	1 inch
Outside	0.75 inches
Top	0.75 inches
Bottom	0.9 inches

When the new publication appears, make certain the on-screen Rulers are displayed at the top and left edge of the screen. You will need these rulers for positioning and measuring entries as you complete this project.

Collecting the Required Resources

The text and graphic files needed for this newsletter have been created for you and are included on the data disk that accompanies this book. Table UR-1 shows a complete listing of the files you will use in this project and information on where those files are used in the publication.

TABLE UR-1
Resources required for Sun Times publication

FILE NAME	TYPE	WHERE USED	DESCRIPTION
Ask-questions.rtf	Text	Page 1, column 1	Contains all the text for the article in the first column
Braham.tif	Graphic	Page 1, column 1	Scanned image of the person mentioned in the article
Deep-discount.rtf	Text	Page 1, column 2	Contains all the text for the article in the second column
Beach.tif	Graphic	Page 1, column 2	Beach picture
Sunset.tif	Graphic	Page 2, column 1	Sunset picture
Page-two.rtf	Text	Page 2, both columns	Contains the text for all of the four articles on this page
Carsun-logo.tif	Graphic	Page 4	Graphic image of the Caribbean Sun Travel Tours logo

DESCRIPTION: MASTER PAGES

You will use the master pages shown in Figure UR-3 to add columns (A) and lines (B) to all pages in the publication. You also create styles that will be used later in this project.

Specifications

1. While viewing the master pages, use the Column Guides dialog box to specify that this publication will have two columns on both the left- and right-hand pages with 0.3 inches of space between each column.

2. Using the Constrained-line tool, draw two horizontal lines; one on the left and the other on the right master page. Each line should be 4-points thick (stroke), in the color Cyan, and positioned 10.25 inches from the top edge of the page. Also, both lines should begin and end even with the left and right margin guides on the master pages.

3. Next, create two styles that will be used later in this publication. The style names, as well as the character and paragraph specifications to use in those styles, are identified in Table UR-2.

TABLE UR-2
Style specifications for SunTimes publication

STYLE NAME	SPECIFICATIONS
Title	**Character Specifications** Font: Depending on your computer, choose Arial, Helvetica, or Univers Size: 18 points with Auto leading Style: Bold Color: Cyan **Paragraph Specifications** Paragraph space before: 0.2 inches
Article	**Character Specifications** Font: Depending on your computer, choose Times New Roman, Times Roman, or Times Size: 11 points Leading: 18 points Style: Normal Color: Black **Paragraph Specifications** First line indent: 0.2 inches Paragraph space before: 0.0 inches Alignment: Justify

FIGURE UR-3
Master pages

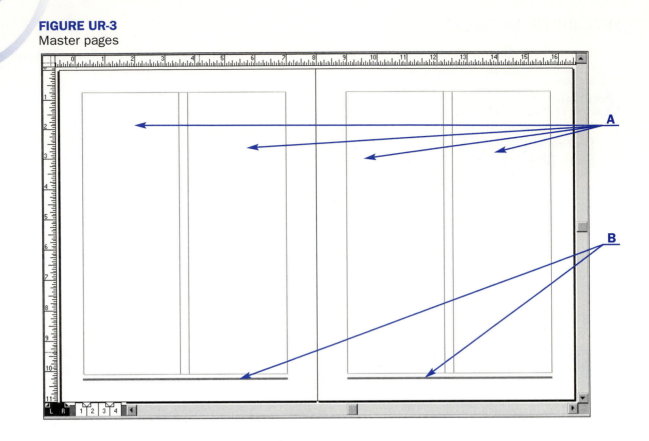

DESCRIPTION: PAGE 1

Create the title to identify the newsletter. Then add the text and graphics to the page.

Specifications

Create the Nameplate

1. As shown in Figure UR-4, begin the first page by creating the nameplate (A), or title, of the newsletter. The words *The SunTimes* should appear in a serif typeface such as Times New Roman, Times Roman, or Times and in a 90-point size. If the text is too big to fit onto one line, select both words and change the tracking to Tight or Very Tight, until the text fits on one line. Change the color of the word *The* to cyan. Finally, drag the text so that it aligns at the top margin guide and is centered horizontally.

2. Draw a rectangle (B) with solid (black) fill roughly 0.25 inches tall between the left and right margin guides on the page. Then drag the rectangle so that it is positioned about 0.125 inches (one-eighth inch) below the words *The SunTimes*.

3. In the pasteboard or in a blank area of the page, key the words CARIBBEAN SUN TRAVEL TOURS NEWSLETTER. Then select the text and change it to a sans serif font such as Arial, Helvetica, or Univers in a 10-point size, with bold and reverse type style. Finally, drag the text onto the rectangle (B) so that it is centered vertically and positioned as shown in Figure UR-4.

    WARNING: Carefully note the location of the text before you select the reverse type style because the text will turn white—the same color as the page—and you will need to select this text to drag it into position.

FIGURE UR-4
The top portion of page 1

ADD THE CONTENT TO PAGE 1

Next add the text and graphic files to create the completed page as shown in Figure UR-5.

Specifications

1.　Use the on-screen rulers to position a horizontal ruler guide 2.25 inches from the top edge of the page.

2.　Place the text file named **Ask-questions.rtf** into the first column. When the Text Placement icon appears, position the icon on the horizontal ruler guide and just to the right of the left margin guide before clicking. Apply the style named **Title** to the words *Ask Questions First*. Apply the style named **Article** to all remaining text in the story.

3.　Place the text file named **Deep-discount.rtf** into the second column. When the Text Placement icon appears, position the icon on the horizontal ruler guide and just to the right of the left column guide before clicking. Apply the style named **Title** to the words *Deep Discounts to Aruba*. Apply the style named **Article** to all remaining text in the story.

4.　Place the graphic file named **Braham.tif** into the pasteboard. Then resize the graphic proportionally so that its height is roughly 1.75 inches. Next, specify that the text wrap completely around the graphic and that it remain 0.05 inches away from the graphic. (When using the Text Wrap dialog box, use the second Wrap option, the third Text flow option, and change the Standoff in inches to 0.05 inch on all four sides.) Now drag the picture into the left column so that the left edge of the picture falls along the left margin guide and the top of the picture falls just below the first line of the second paragraph. Finally, reduce or enlarge the graphic proportionally if needed, so that the last line of text in the left column falls near the bottom margin guide.

5.　Place the graphic file named **Beach.tif** into the blank area at the bottom of the second column. Then resize the graphic proportionally so that it touches the left and right column guides. Finally, drag the picture so that the bottom of the picture falls on the bottom margin guide.

6.　Make certain that all the text from each story fits completely in its own column. If the text is too long for a column, slightly adjust or crop the graphic image in the column.

FIGURE UR-5
Page 1 (shown reduced 30%)

The SunTimes

CARIBBEAN SUN TRAVEL TOURS NEWSLETTER

Ask Questions First

To avoid surprises or problems when traveling on a tour, ask alot of questions before you travel. That's the advice of Barbara Braham, President of the Travel Industry Association (TIA).

In a recent interview, Braham shown in the photo below said that a tour op-  erator should provide a complete travel itinerary. This will include the names of all hotels where you'll stay, any means that are in- cluded, and a list of any other services you'll receive in your tour package.

Here are some suggestions Braham recommends: (1) If you require a special diet, inform your travel agent in writing when you sign up, (2) Make certain your travel agent knows the exact type of lodging you require. If you want a first class room, ask for it, and (3) Find out if there are any penalties for canceling your reservations. If so, how much?

Although most people have health insurance, some policies may not cover you for health related prob- lems when you're overseas. Before you travel, call your insurance company and ask about your medical coverage. You can also purchase supplemental medi- cal coverage from your insurance company or from Caribbean Sun Travel Tours.

Remember its better to know as much as possible about your trip before you leave.

Deep Discounts to Aruba

Thanks to deep airline discounts, people from all over are traveling again. And, with prices reaching an all-time low, Aruba is the destination for many.

Only 30 miles off the coast of Venezuela, Aruba is unique. This small, 19-mile-long island has rugged cliffs, scrubland, gentle lagoons, pounding surfs, and a five-mile-long beach.

Vacationing in Aruba is easy. English is a second language to most natives, and the US dollar is easy to exchange.

Getting around the island couldn't be easier. There are more than enough taxicabs to go around and the busses run regularly.

There are also dozens of car rental firms. For only a few dollars you can drive around the island's paved roads, enjoy the sights, and stop wherever you wish. Also, since the island is so small, it's almost impos- sible to get lost.

DESCRIPTION: PAGE 2

The second page, shown in Figure UR-6, contains a graphic image and four newsletter articles. All four of the articles are contained in a single text file.

Specifications

1. Place the graphic file named **Sunset.tif** into a blank area of the page. Then resize the graphic proportionally so that it touches the left and right column guides. Finally, drag the picture so that the top of the picture falls on the top margin guide.

2. Use the on-screen rulers to position a horizontal ruler guide 4.75 inches from the top edge of the page.

3. Turn on the Autoflow feature.

4. Place the text file named **Page-two.rtf** into the left column. When the Text Placement icon appears, position the icon on the horizontal ruler guide and just to the right of the left margin guide before clicking. Apply the style named **Title** to the following four text entries: *Visit Hawaii, Tour Mexico, The Magic of Tampa,* and *Late Breaking News.* Apply the style named **Article** to all other text on this page.

5. Make certain that all of the text from the text file fits completely on the second page. Adjust the windowshades and/or crop the top or bottom portion of the graphic image slightly, if needed. If the text still does not fit completely on the page reduce the leading in the style named Article by 1 or 2 points.

FIGURE UR-6
Page 2 (shown reduced 30%)

Visit Hawaii

We have five spaces available on our January tour to Hawaii. The tour departs January 10th.

The seven-day tour includes travel to Oahu and Maui. You'll visit sugar mills and the site of a volcano, take a helicopter ride through a rain forest, and skin dive for buried treasure. The tour is $599 and includes airfare, hotel, and one-day automobile rental. Sign up today while space is still available.

Tour Mexico

This year we are also offering a unique, five-day tour of Mexico's Copper Canyon. Our tour offers participants a close-up look at Mexico's rural communities. Last year's tour was a sellout.

The tour begins with a train ride to Al Creek. Here, you'll visit pueblos, stately mansions a church from 1650, and more.

Next, it's on to Chihuahua, the state capital. Here, you'll visit the capital, view Pancho Villa's home, tour a silver mine and see straw hats made.

The price of $775 includes first-class hotels with private bath or shower, daily breakfast, five dinners, four lunches, sightseeing, hotel tips, and all travel taxes. Better hurry. We only have four spaces available for this tour!

The Magic of Tampa

Time is running out to signup for our "Where in America" tours to Tampa, Florida. The tours, which depart every Monday, will operate until May 20th.

The four-day trip includes a guided tour of Ebor City, a visit to the Clearwater Marine Science center, a tour of the Tampa bay performing arts center, a ride on pirate ship, an evening dinner cruise, and much more. The cost is only $429 per person and includes round-trip air travel from Miami.

For the outdoor person, you can add on an additional day taking a 6-hour boat trip to the sponge docks at Tarpon Springs. There, you'll see how sponges are harvested, tour the largest sponge fleet in the country and enjoy lunch at a picturesque restaurant. Add $145 to the above cost.

Late Breaking News

FloridaAir has announced a special round-trip fare of $225 from Phoenix to Orlando, Florida. You must purchase your ticket at least ten days in advance. Travel must begin on a Monday and you must complete your return trip by March 3rd.

Alaska promises to be one of the year's best travel bargains. The Fairbanks Travel Association and Northern Hotels are offering a 30 percent discount on hotel reservations. You must make your reservations and prepay one night's accommodations at least ten days before your arrival. For more information call the Fairbanks Travel Association at (907) 450-9000.

DESCRIPTION: PAGE 3

Page 3 of the publication, shown in Figure UR-7, includes a table containing a schedule of upcoming travel films, and a form that the reader can send to Caribbean Sun Travel Tours to obtain more information on their services.

Specifications

Create the Table

1. Turn to page 3 in the publication, and create the table shown in Figure UR-7 on the top half of the page.

2. Use the Adobe Table program to create a table 6.75 inches wide and 5 inches tall that contains seven rows and five columns.

3. Join the five cells in the top row. In this newly joined cell, type **Evening Travel Film Program** and press **Enter**, then key **November Schedule**. Center the text that you just keyed and format the text so that it appears in a sans serif font, such as Arial, Helvetica, or Univers, in bold and in a 24-point size.

4. Reduce the height of the second row by roughly one half. Then key the column headings **Mon**, **Tue**, **Wed**, **Thur**, and **Fri** into their respective cells. Finally, center these five cell entries, and format them so that they appear in a sans serif font, such as Arial, Helvetica, or Univers, in bold and in a 12-point size.

5. Next, input the 20 daily entries by keying the day of the month, pressing **Enter**, then keying the text for the entry. For example, to create the entry for the first day key **1** and press **Enter**, then key **Grand Canyon Adventure**. Each daily entry should appear in a serif typeface, such as Times New Roman, Times Roman, or Times, and in a 12-point size.

6. When you finish, transfer the table into the publication and position the table so that it aligns along the top, left, and right margin guides on the third page.

Create the Response Form

Next create the Response Form, shown in Figure UR-7, on the bottom half of the page.

1. Key all the text required for this form in a serif font, such as Times New Roman, Times Roman, or Times. Make certain that the words *Response Form* begin 6 inches from the top edge of the page and appear in a 24-point size and in the color Cyan. The words *Caribbean Sun Travel Tours* should appear in bold and in a 14-point size. All the other text in the response form should be in a 12-point size. Use the Enter key to insert blank lines where needed.

2. Create the four, fill-in-the-blank lines either by drawing them with the Constrained-line tool or by using a tab setting with a line leader. In either case, make certain that each line ends at the right margin guide.

FIGURE UR-7
Page 3 (shown reduced 30%)

Evening Travel Film Program
November Schedule

Mon	Tue	Wed	Thur	Fri
			1 Grand Canyon Adventure	2 The Magic of St. Thomas
5 No films this evening	6 The People of Hawaii	7 The Secrets of Mexico	8 Everglade Adventure	9 Miami on a Shoestring
12 The Painted Desert	13 The Foods of the Caribbean	14 Staying Healthy While Traveling	15 The History of Cuba	16 History of Florida
19 Polynesia Paradise	20 No films this evening	21 The Smokey Mountains	22 The Pacific Northwest	23 The Mystery of Egypt
26 No films this evening	27 Mississippi Paddlewheels	28 Adventure on Lake Erie		

Response Form

Caribbean Sun Travel Tours
6600 Duvall Street
Key West, FL 32358

Would you like to receive more information on our tour and cruise packages? If so, just complete and mail the form below.

Name: _____

Address: _____

City, State, Zip: _____

Day Phone: _____

DESCRIPTION: PAGE 4

The fourth page, shown in Figure UR-8, contains the Caribbean Sun Travel Tours logo and the company's address.

Specifications

1. Use the on-screen rulers to position a horizontal ruler guide 6 inches from the top edge of the page.

2. Place the graphic file named **Carsun-logo.tif** into a blank area of the pasteboard or the page. Then resize the graphic proportionally so that its height is roughly 1.5 inches. Finally, drag the graphic so that the top of the graphic falls on the ruler guide and the left edge falls on the left margin guide.

3. Key the two-line address in a serif font in a 9-point size, and then position the address below the logo.

FIGURE UR-8
Page 4 (shown reduced 30%)

CARIBBEAN SUN

TRAVEL TOURS
6600 Duvall Street
Key West, FL 32358

WHEN YOU FINISH THIS PROJECT

Once you've completed all four pages, make certain to spell check the newsletter. If you wish, print each page of the publication and tape or glue the printed pages together (using Figure UR-1 as a guide) to see how the assembled newsletter will look.

Conclusion

This completes your PageMaker training. As you have seen, PageMaker is a powerful desktop-publishing program containing hundreds of features. Like any electronic tool, PageMaker requires practice and patience to learn and use comfortably. You will make mistakes as you try new features and commands—it's only natural. What is most important is to have the confidence to know you can do it. Having completed this course you already know that you can.

If you wish to learn more about desktop publishing, consider additional books and/or courses on PageMaker, graphic design, graphic layout, and typography. Each can help you to understand more about what goes into creating a good-looking publication and can help you work more easily with the program. The more you know, the better your work will look.

Best wishes on all your future endeavors.

GLOSSARY

A

Alert box A small dialog box containing a brief question or warning.

Algorithm (Hyphenation) Electronic rules that determine where a word can be hyphenated.

Alignment A method for controlling the placement of text between the left and right margin or column guides such as left, center, or right alignment.

Anchored (graphic) A graphic that remains in a fixed or locked position on a page. *See also* Inline.

Applying a color Adding color to an object such as a text or a PageMaker-created graphic.

Ascender The part of a lowercase letter that extends above the x-height as in the characters *b, d, f, h, k,* and *l. See also* X-height.

Auto leading A default PageMaker setting used to calculate leading that is based on 120 percent of the font size. For example, if the size of the font in use were 10 points, the auto leading would be 12 points. *See also* Leading.

Autoflow A method used when placing a text file into a publication in which the text flows continuously from one column or page to the next. *See also* Manual text flow, Semi-manual text flow.

B

Based on (style) A method used when creating similar styles that allows one style to use (be based on) the specifications of a different style, but which can also be customized.

Baseline An imaginary horizontal line on which the bottom of all uppercase characters and the base of all lowercase characters fall or rest.

Bitmapped (graphic file format) A method used for storing a computer graphic file that contains dot-by-dot representations of the original graphic image. *Compare to* EPS.

Boards A traditional typographic technique in which printed typeset pages and graphics are glued onto special pieces of paper (*boards*) which are then photographed onto plates and from which the publication is printed.

Body copy *See* Body text.

Body text Also called body copy, the text that makes up the body or major portion of a publication. *Compare to* Display text.

Bold Characters that appear darker than surrounding text, **like this example**.

Book A PageMaker technique used to identify two or more publications as part of a larger publication.

Book list The list of publication names, arranged in order, and from which a book publication is created.

Bounding box A rectangular area defined by dragging the I-beam and into which text can be keyed or placed. *See also* Drag-placing.

Bullet A character or symbol, such as a circle or diamond, that appears in front of each item in a list of items.

Button A rectangular- or oval-shaped area in a dialog box representing a specific command or feature.

C

Camera-ready Printed text, photographs, or drawings that can be photographed and from which plates can be used for printing.

Cell Within a table, a rectangular area where a column and row intersect.

Center aligned (Tab) A tab setting in which any entry aligned on that tab is centered at the setting.

Center alignment Lines of text that are centered between the left and right edge of a text block.

Character A single letter, such as a, b, or c; a symbol, such as &, #, or Ø; or number, such as 1, 2, or 3, in a typeface.

Check box A small square that appears in front of certain options in a dialog box and which is used to select (or deselect) the option.

Choose   To use the keyboard or mouse to select from a menu or dialog box.

Click   To press (click) the mouse button once.

Clip art   A ready-made drawing or illustration on paper.

CMYK   A color model used to identify a color as a percentage of the colors cyan, magenta, yellow, and black.

Color matching system   A universally accepted standard or method for identifying colors. *See also* Pantone and Trumatch.

Color model   A method used to identify a color. *See also* CMYK, RGB, and HLS.

Color separation   A method used to print only one color that is used in a publication.

Color specifier   A book containing color charts from a color-matching system that shows samples of printed colors and unique code numbers used to identify each color. Also referred to as a color swatch book. *See also* Color swatch.

Color swatch   *See* Color specifier.

Color wheel   A printed wheel or circle containing a spectrum of colors and arranged in a way to help in the selection of various colors that work well together.

Colors palette   An on-screen list showing the colors currently available for use in a publication.

Column (Table)   A series of cells that runs vertically across a table.

Column guides   Sets of nonprinting, vertical lines that appear on publication pages containing multiple columns of text. Column guides control where text begins and ends on each line when it is keyed or placed into a column.

Command   A program option for performing a specific task.

Command button   In a dialog box, tells the program to accept or forget all the selections that you have made.

Context-sensitive   A method in which the tools appearing inside a PageMaker palette will change based on the kind of Tool currently being used from the Toolbox.

Control palette   An on-screen window containing shortcuts for formatting text and modifying graphics.

Copywriter   A person who writes or refines text that will appear in a publication.

Crop   To remove or hide an unwanted portion of a graphic image.

Crop marks   A series of thin, intersecting lines that can appear around each corner on a printed page. Crop marks are used to trim the paper when the size of the publication page is less than the size of the paper on which the page is printed.

Cropping tool   A tool in PageMaker's toolbox that is used to hide part of a graphic.

Cross hair   A mouse pointer consisting of two intersecting lines that is used with drawing tools.

Cross-reference   An index entry that refers the reader to a different, yet related index entry instead of to a specific page number.

Cut   A technique used to remove text or a graphic element from the publication and place it into the computer's memory for possible use at a later time.

D

Decimal aligned (Tab)   A tab setting in which any numeric entry positioned on that tab setting aligns on its decimal point.

Default   A program setting that takes effect each time you start the program.

Density bar   A series of small squares containing decreasing levels of tints that appears at the top of printed pages and is used by a printer (the person) to accurately reproduce any tints or colors used in a publication.

Descender   The part of certain lowercase letters that fall below the baseline, as in the characters *g*, *j*, *p*, and *q*. *See also* baseline.

Deselect   To turn off a radio button or check box option, or to remove the selection from text or from a graphic.

Desktop publishing   Using a computer and software program to produce high-quality, printed documents that combine text and graphics.

Dialog box   A rectangular-shaped area that appears on-screen when further information is needed to perform a command.

Discretionary hyphen   A hyphen that only appears when the word or phrase in which it is inserted extends beyond the end of a line.

Display text   Text that appears larger than surrounding text, such as the headings and subheadings, in a publication. *Compare to* Body text.

Double-click   To place the mouse pointer on an item and then press the left mouse button twice, rapidly.

Double-sided   A publication in which printing will eventually appear on both sides of each page.

Drag   To place the mouse pointer over an on-screen object, press and hold down the mouse button, move the pointer to a different location, and then release the mouse button.

Drag and Drop   A method for copying or moving selected text that uses the mouse.

Drag placing   A rectangular area created while placing a text or a graphic file and into which the contents of the file will appear. *See also* Bounding box.

Drop-down list   Within a dialog box, a list of options that only appears when a drop-down arrow is clicked and from which you can select an option. *Compare to* List box.

E

Electronic Clip art   A ready-made electronic drawing or illustration that can be placed into a publication.

Ellipsis   A series of three dots (. . .) used to indicate missing text.

Em dash   A long line (—) that is used to show a pause or a break in a sentence such as "I—I won the sweepstakes!"

En dash   A line (–) that is slightly longer than a hyphen and is used in place of the word "to" or "through" such as A–Z.

EPS (Encapsulated PostScript)   A method used for storing a computer graphic file that contains the instructions needed to recreate the image in any size and with the highest quality possible, but only when printed on a PostScript laser printer. *Compare to* Bitmapped.

Export   A technique for transferring data from one program into a format that can be read by a different program.

F

Facing pages   A publication in which the printing on one page will face the printing on a different page as in a magazine or newspaper.

File   Related information stored on a computer disk as a single entry.

File format   A method used for storing a specific kind of computer file such as a PageMaker publication or a graphic file. *See also* Bitmapped and EPS.

Fill   A pattern, color, or tint applied to the inside of a PageMaker-created graphic.

Fixed space   A space also known as a nonbreaking space that is used to bond or glue two words together, so that if one of the words extends beyond the end of a line, both words are moved to the next line. *See also* Nonbreaking space.

Flush left   Text that aligns along the left margin or left column guide.

Flush right   Text that aligns along the right margin or right column guide.

Font   All alphanumeric characters in one typeface and in a specific point size.

Footer   Identifying text that appears at the bottom of pages in a publication, also called a running foot.

Force justify   An alignment method normally used with a short line of text, such as a title, that inserts equal amounts of space between each character so that all characters on the line begin/end at the left/right margin guide. *Compare to* Justify.

Format   Settings, such as font or paragraph, applied to text that change the appearance of the text.

G

Grabber hand   *See* Hand Icon.

Graphic artist   A person who produces the graphics used in a publication either by hand-drawing them or by selecting them from books of prepared pictures (clip art) or photographs (stock art).

Graphic boundary   A dotted line that surrounds a selected graphic in which text wrap has been activated and that determines how close text can come to the graphic. *See also* Standoff.

Graphic composition program   Software programs that offer a wide range of drawing and painting tools for creating highly complex drawings and illustrations in full color, as well as create special effects like twisting or rotating portions of an image.

Graphic designer   In desktop publishing, a person whose role is to understand what the client wants to accomplish, who also designs and develops detailed specifications for that work, and who oversees its development.

Gray scale A series of shades ranging from black to white.

Greeking A method used to speed up the display of pages containing text by substituting the text with simulated characters or lines.

Grid A series of ruler guides used to control the position of graphics and/or text on a page or within a publication.

Guides *See* Ruler guides.

Gutter In a publication the space or distance between two columns. In a table, the space or distance that controls how close an entry comes to the edge of a cell.

H

Hairline stroke or rule A thin line (rule or stroke) used in creating PageMaker-drawn objects such as a rectangle or horizontal rule.

Hand Icon A hand-shaped icon created by holding the Alt key and left mouse button that is used to move a different part of the on-screen page into view.

Hand tool A PageMaker tool for electronically grabbing hold of a page or pasteboard and moving it on-screen in any direction.

Handle A small square that appears around selected graphics or on the ends of windowshades for a selected text block. The handle is used to change the size or shape of the selected object.

Hanging Indent A form of paragraph indention in which the first line of the paragraph extends farther to the left than all other lines in the paragraph.

Hard hyphen Also known as a nonbreaking hyphen, used to hold all parts of a compound word or number together when the word or number extends beyond the end of the line.

Header Identifying text that appears at the top of pages in a publication, also called a running head.

Heading A title that identifies a story or article in a publication.

HLS A color model used to identify a color by its hue, lightness, and saturation.

HTML (Hypertext Markup Language) A programming language used for creating Web pages.

Hyphenation zone The area near the end of a line of text within which PageMaker will consider hyphenating a word.

I

I-beam A mouse pointer shaped like a capital letter I that appears when using the Text tool.

Import To read work created by one program into a different program. *See also* Place.

Index An alphabetical listing of key words, phrases, or topics within a publication that includes the page numbers on which those items are found.

Index entry An index entry identifying a major subject or topic. *See also* Index subentry.

Index subentry An index entry that is part of a major subject or topic, instead of a subject or topic in itself.

Inline (graphic) A graphic that is placed into a publication while using the Text tool and becomes anchored to the surrounding text. *See also* Anchored.

Insertion point A thin, blinking vertical bar showing where PageMaker is ready to insert new characters when using the Text tool.

Italic Text that slants slightly to the right, *like this example.*

J

Justify alignment An alignment method (also called justified) in which all lines of text in a paragraph, except the last line, begin and end at both the left and right edge of a text block. *Compare to* Force justify.

K

Kerning The process of manually adjusting the space between two characters.

Keyboard shortcut A command issued by using the keyboard instead of using a pull-down menu.

L

Landscape Text and/or graphics that prints sideways across the widest part of a page.

Layering The process of positioning one element, such as text or a graphic, over another element.

Layout view A method of working with text or graphics directly on an electronic page that simulates the final, printed page. *Compare to* Story Editor view.

Leaders A series of characters, such as dots or dashes, that can precede text aligned on a tab setting.

Leading (rhymes with wedding) The vertical space that appears between two lines of text, measured in points from the baseline of one line to the baseline of the next line. *See also* Auto leading.

Left aligned (Tab) A tab setting in which any entry aligned on that tab begins at the tab setting.

Left alignment Text that begins at the left edge of a text block and ends at different places near the right edge of the text block (also referred to as ragged right alignment).

Letterspacing The amount of space used by each character in a typeface. *See also* Monospacing and Proportional spacing.

List box Within a dialog box, a list of choices from which you can select an option. *Compare to* Drop-down list.

Local formatting *See* Overriding a style.

M

Manual text flow A method used when placing a text file into a publication in which the text flows down a column or page and then stops. To continue placing additional text, you click on the continuation (x) symbol, position the placement icon where the text will continue, and then click. *Compare to* Autoflow and Semi-manual text flow.

Margin An area between the edge of a page and the area of the page containing text and/or graphics.

Margin guide A nonprinting boundary that controls how close text comes to the edge of a page.

Marking an index entry The process of identifying a word or phrase within a publication that you want included in an index.

Masking The technique of combining a PageMaker graphic of a specific shape with a graphic file that causes the graphic file to take on the shape of the PageMaker graphic.

Master page A nonprinting page (identified by an L or R) that contains text and/or graphics that will appear on all numbered pages in a publication such as a header or footer. *Compare to* Numbered page.

Master page icon An icon that appears in the lower left corner of the publication window containing an L (for a left master page) or R (for a right master page). Clicking on a master page icon displays the master page. *Compare to* Numbered page icon.

Menu An on-screen list of commands or features from which you can make a selection.

Menu bar An on-screen list of words used to issue commands.

Mini-save The automatic saving of a publication to disk by PageMaker when certain actions are performed, for example, when pages are inserted or removed or when a different page is displayed.

Mnemonic An underlined letter found in a menu or dialog box representing a key that can be pressed to choose the item.

Monospaced Letterspacing in which all characters in a typeface have the same width. In typefaces with monospacing, thin letters, like the letter I, use the same amount of space as wider characters, like the letter X. *Compare to* Proportional spacing.

Mouse pointer A symbol used to select a tool or command or to position text or a graphic on the screen.

N

Nonbreaking hyphen A hard hyphen that is used to hold all parts of a compound word or number together. If one part of the word/number overlap the end of the line, the entire word/number is moved to the next line. *Compare to* Discretionary hyphen.

Nonbreaking space A space, also known as a fixed space, that is used to bond or glue two words together so that if one of the words extends beyond the end of a line, both words are moved to the next line.

Nudge button In the Control palette, buttons containing small arrows that, when clicked, adjust text or graphic settings by small amounts.

Numbered page A printable page (identified by a numbered page icon) within a publication. *Compare to* Master page.

Numbered page icon Icons containing numbers, such as 1, 2, 3, that appear in the lower left corner of the publication window and represent a specific numbered page in a publication. Clicking on a numbered page icon displays the numbered page. *Compare to* Master page icon.

O

Option A selection found within a dialog box or pull-down menu.

Orientation A term that specifies in which direction text and graphics print on a page. *See also* Portrait and Landscape.

Orphan A term applied to the last one or two lines of a paragraph when the text appears at the top of a column or page. *Compare to* Widow.

Overriding a style Applying additional formatting to certain text within a styled paragraph. Also referred to as local formatting.

P

Page number marker A symbol normally inserted into a master page that is used to produce page numbers on numbered pages in a publication.

Palette A group of related program tools or features, that can be displayed or hidden, that are used in creating or editing work.

Pantone A series of color-matching systems used in commercial printing that can be used for specifying colors.

Pasteboard The area outside the edge of the page in the publication window that can be used to temporarily store text or graphics. Anything stored in the pasteboard does not appear when the publication is printed.

Pasteup artist A person in traditional typesetting who aligns and glues or attaches typeset pages and graphics onto boards.

PDF (Portable Document Format) A method for electronically viewing the output of certain programs.

Phrase An index entry containing a series of two or more words.

Pitch The number of characters per inch (most commonly a typewriting or, occasionally, a word processing term).

Place A PageMaker command for importing text or graphics from a computer file into a publication.

Plate A special sheet of paper or a metal plate that is used to transfer ink directly to the printed page in a printing press.

Pointer tool A PageMaker tool used to move, remove, or resize a graphic or a text block within a publication.

Points The basic measurement system used to measure the size of type. There are 72 points to an inch.

Pop-up list A list of options that can appear in a dialog box.

Portrait Text and/or graphics that are printed upright across the narrowest part of a page.

PostScript A method developed by Adobe Systems that is used for producing high-quality printed output when using a PostScript laser printer or imagesetter.

Press To place the mouse pointer at a certain location on the screen and then hold down the left mouse button until the task is accomplished.

Printer's marks Special entries that can appear on printed color separation pages to help a commercial printing company align or trim those pages.

Process color A printing technique that uses cyan, magenta, yellow and black inks (CMYK) to create nearly any color possible. Normally used when printing publications containing four or more colors. *Compare to* Spot color.

Proportional spacing Letterspacing in which different characters in a typeface have different widths. In typefaces with proportional spacing, thin letters, like the letter I, use less space than wider characters, like the letter X. *Compare to* Monospaced.

Proxy In the Control palette (PageMaker) and Tables Attributes palette (Adobe Table), an icon that is used to select/deselect parts of an element, such as the lines within a selected range of cells in a table.

Publication A desktop-published document created using PageMaker.

Publication page The area in which all the text and graphics for one particular page appear.

Publication window While PageMaker is running, the area of the computer screen that contains the title and menu bar as well as one page (for single-sided publications) or two pages (for double-sided publications). All work on the publication is performed within the publication window.

Pull-down menu A vertical list of commands from which you can make a selection.

R

Radio button A small circle that appears in front of certain options in a dialog box and is used to select (or deselect) an option.

Ragged right   *See* Left alignment.

Range   Within a table, a group of cells that touch each other.

Reflecting   A technique used to electronically flip a graphic either horizontally or vertically. The result is similar to viewing an object in a mirror.

Registration marks   Symbols (normally a circle and cross hair) that appear around the edges of printed pages and are used by a printer (the person) to register or align color separations.

Repeating element   A single entry that appears on each page in a publication such as a header, footer, or page number.

Required hyphen   A hyphen inserted into a word or phrase by pressing the minus (–) key. When the word or phrase in which a required hyphen extends beyond the end of the line, the entry is divided at the hyphen character.

Reverse type   White or light-colored text that appears against a darker background.

RGB   A color model used to identify a color as a percentage of the colors red, green, and blue.

Right aligned (Tab)   A tab setting in which any entry aligned on that tab ends at the tab setting.

Right alignment   Lines of text that end at the right edge of a text block but begin at different places on the left edge.

Rotate (Graphic)   The process of turning or rotating a graphic image.

Row   A series of cells that runs horizontally across a table.

Ruler guides   Nonprinting horizontal and vertical lines that can be positioned on numbered and master pages to assist in aligning work.

Rules   In a publication, a line created by using any of the drawing tools.

Running foot   *See* Footer.

Running head   *See* Header.

S

Sans serif   A French term meaning without serif. Typefaces in which the characters lack serifs are referred to as sans serif typefaces. *Compare to* Serif.

Scanner   A photocopier-like device that converts a printed document into an electronic image.

Screen resolution   A term for varying and measuring the quality of how an image appears on-screen.

Script   A category of typeface in which the characters are designed to resemble handwritten characters.

Scroll   To move something on-screen using the mouse.

Scroll bar   An on-screen element used to move different parts of a publication or list into view.

Select   To highlight specific text or identify specific graphics to which an action will be performed, or to select a radio button or check box option in a dialog box.

Semi-manual text flow   A method used when placing a text file into a publication (by holding down the Shift key) in which the text flows down a column or page and then stops. The program then automatically displays the text placement icon for placing additional text. *Compare to* Autoflow and Semi-manual text flow.

Separation   *See* Color separation.

Serif   Small line or stroke that appears at the ends of characters in serif typefaces. *Compare to* sans serif.

Sic   Used to point out a spelling error within a quotation.

Sizing handles   Small squares that appear around a selected graphic or text block and that can be used to change the shape or size of that graphic or text block.

Skewing   To slant a graphic object.

Small caps   Uppercase letters that appear smaller than normal uppercase letters in the same font size.

Spot color   A printing technique that uses one pre-mixed color ink for each color used in a publication. Normally used when printing publications containing two or occasionally three colors. *Compare to* Process color.

Standoff   The distance, identified by a graphic boundary, within which text is kept away from a graphic. *See also* Text wrap.

Story   Within a publication, all text that is treated as a single unit such as a single article or a report. Any story can consist of one or more text blocks.

Story Editor   A word processing feature of PageMaker in which the text from one story can be keyed, edited, placed and checked for spelling errors. *Compare to* Layout view.

Stroke   The term used to specify the width of a line that surrounds a PageMaker-created graphic.

Style   A collection of font and paragraph settings that can be applied to text.

Style sheet   A listing of all the style names used in a publication.

Styles palette   An on-screen list showing the names of all styles currently available for use in a publication.

Subentry   *See* Index subentry.

T

Table   A method for organizing information both horizontally (in rows) and vertically (in columns).

Table of contents   A listing containing the title of sections and/or subsections in a publication and also the page numbers on which those entries begin.

Tabloid   A large paper size (11 inch × 17 inch) often used for printing newsletters.

Tags   A style name surrounded by brackets that is included within a word processing file. When a word processing file containing tags is placed into a publication, the specifications for the named styles are automatically applied to the text.

Tall orientation   *See* Portrait.

Template   A publication from which other publications are created.

Text block   A rectangular area within which text is stored and that, when selected, is surrounded at the top and bottom by windowshades.

Text box   A rectangular area within a dialog box in which information is keyed.

Text wrap   To flow text around a graphic object.

Tint   A specific shade or intensity of a certain color.

Title bar   An area at the top of a dialog box or a window that provides identifying information.

Toolbox   An on-screen window containing tools used for working with graphics and text.

ToolTip   An on-screen message that appears when the mouse pointer is placed over a toolbar button that identifies the purpose of that button.

Tracking   A technique for controlling the space between a series of characters and words. *Compare to* Kerning.

Trumatch   A color-matching system used in commercial printing that can be used for specifying colors.

Type specifications   All the settings that determine how certain text will appear on the screen and in a printout such as the typeface, point size, and type style.

Type style   A variety of methods used to change the look or the emphasis given to certain text (for example, bold, italic, underline, reverse).

Typeface   A family or a collection of alphanumeric characters of a specific design such as the Times or Helvetica typeface.

Typeset quality print   Print created with a laser, ink- or bubble-jet printer that resembles the quality of output produced with a traditional typesetting machine.

Typography   Using type to produce printed documents.

W

Wide orientation   *See* Landscape.

Widow   A term applied to the first one or two lines of a paragraph when the text appears at the bottom of a column or page. *Compare to* Orphan.

Windowshade   A thin line containing a hoop in the center and handles on both ends that appears at the top and bottom of a selected text block.

Word wrap   A technique in keying or placing text where a word that overlaps the right margin or right edge of the text block is moved to the next line.

X

X-height   The height of the body of all lowercase letters such as the letter x in a typeface. All lowercase characters in a typeface are designed to be no taller than the x-height.

Z

Zero point   The position on both the horizontal and vertical rulers where their zero position intersects.

Zero point marker   A small box containing intersecting dotted lines that is located at the far left of the horizontal ruler and at the top of the vertical ruler.

INDEX